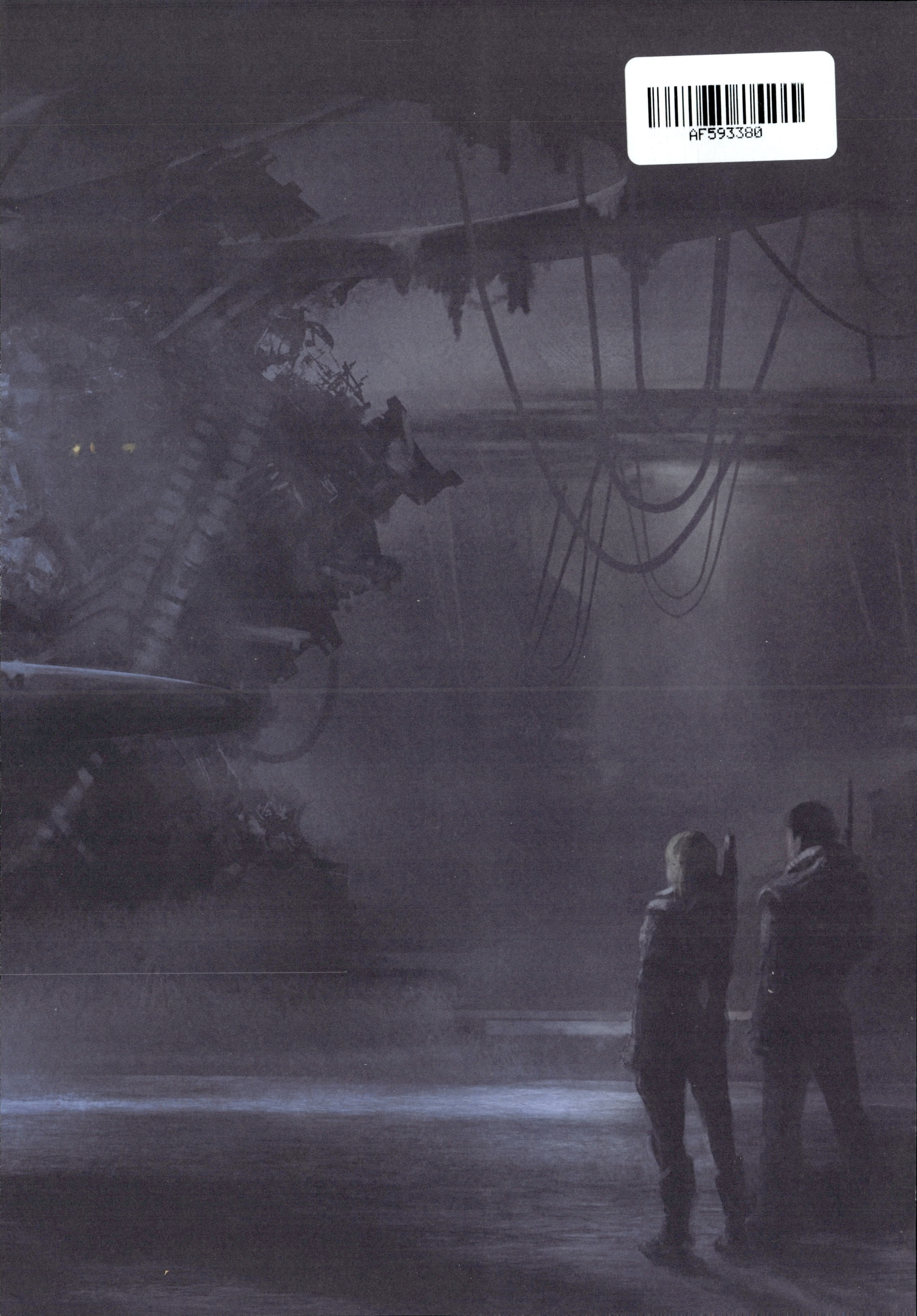

The Art of FRED GAMBINO

DARK SHEPHERD

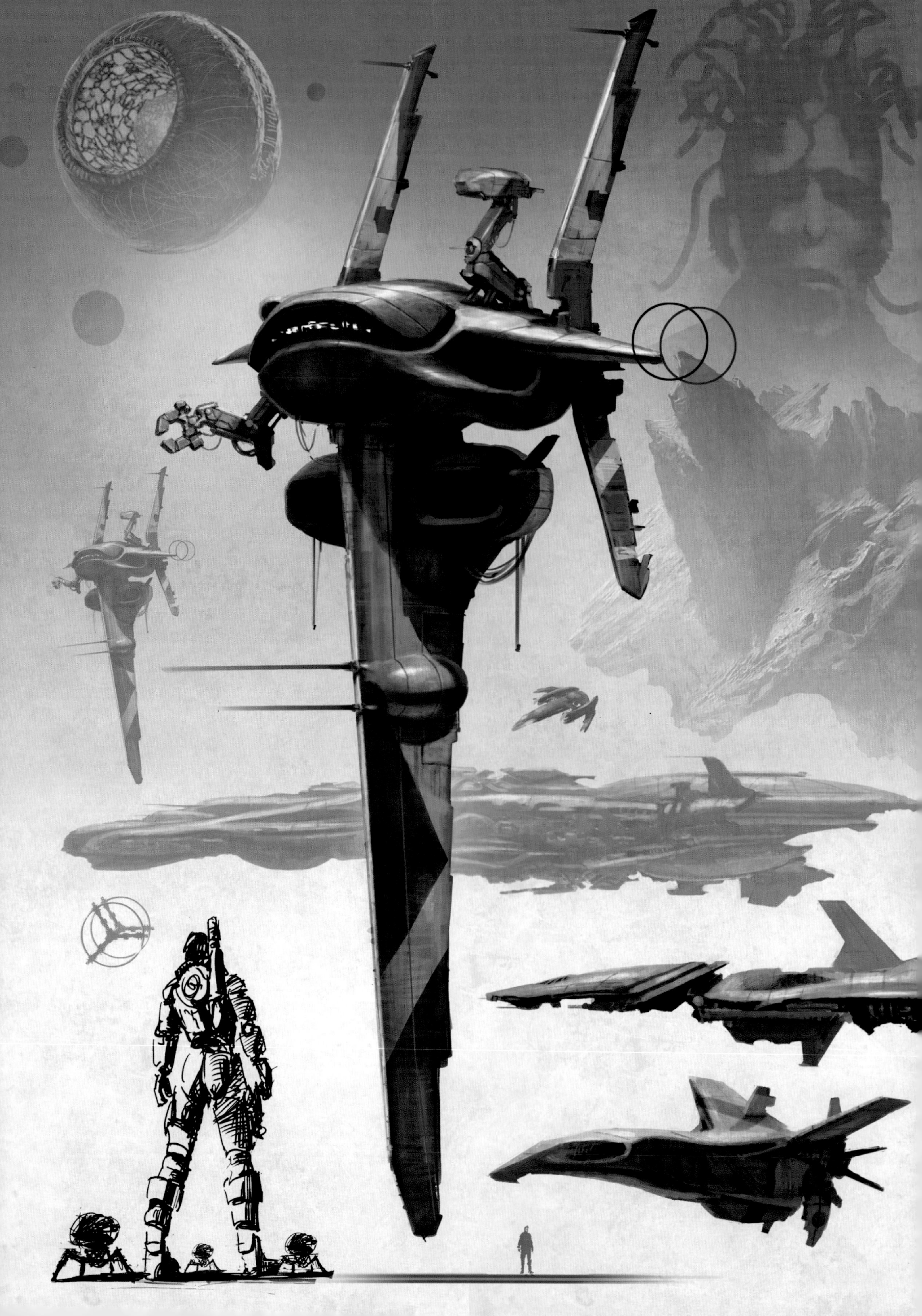

The Art of
FRED GAMBINO
DARK SHEPHERD

FOREWORD BY
JOHN A. DAVIS

COMMENTARY BY
FRED GAMBINO

TITANBOOKS

THE ART OF FRED GAMBINO – DARK SHEPHERD

ISBN: 9781781168431
Limited Edition ISBN: 9781783293162

Published by
TITAN BOOKS
A division of Titan Publishing Group Ltd.
144 Southwark Street
London
SE1 0UP

First edition: July 2014
10 9 8 7 6 5 4 3 2 1

Battletech and *Mechwarrior* images on pages 84–93 reprinted with permission of Roc, an imprint of New American Library, a division of Penguin Group (USA).

Guinness® advertisement on page 103 commissioned by IBBDO.

LEGO® development images for *Project X* on pages 110–115 courtesy of Dave Edwards Entertainment Media.

Escape From Planet Earth images and concepts on pages 116–127 reprinted with kind permission of The Weinstein Company and Rainmaker Entertainment, Inc.

Firebreather images and concepts on pages 128–137 copyright and courtesy of Cartoon Network. FIREBREATHER © 2010 Cartoon Network.

Robo Dragons images and concepts on pages 138–141 commissioned by Klutz Press.

Alienology images and concepts on pages 142–151 reprinted with permission from Templar Publishing.

Starbeast images and concepts on pages 152–159 reprinted with permission from John A. Davis.

A CIP catalogue record for this title is available from the British Library.

Printed and bound in China.

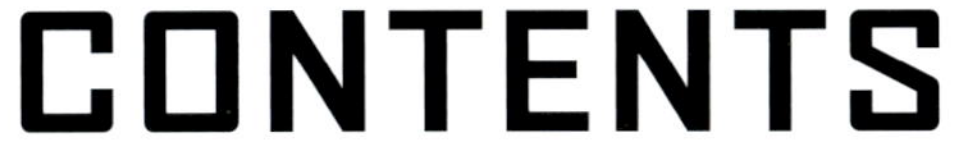

CONTENTS

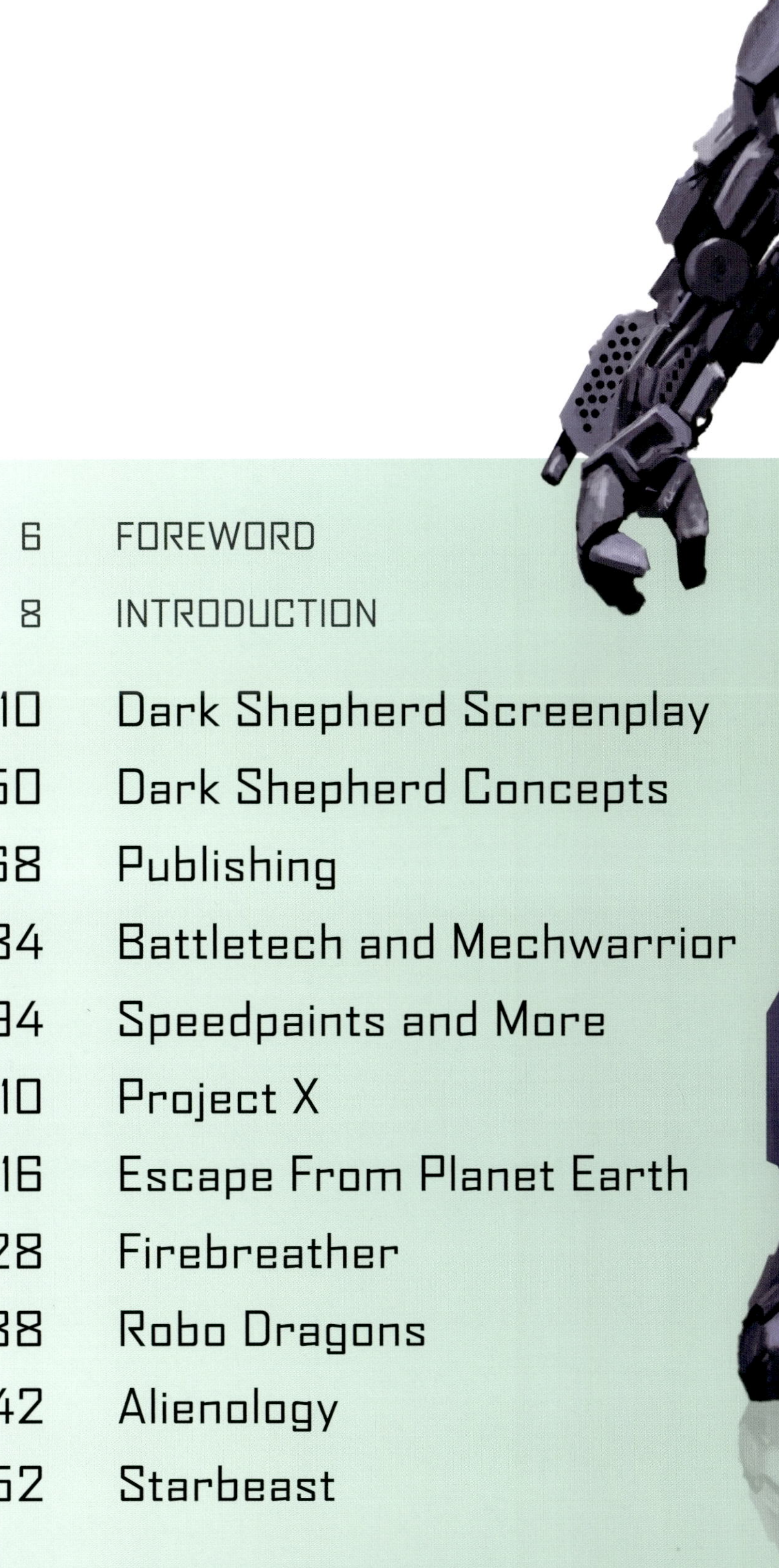

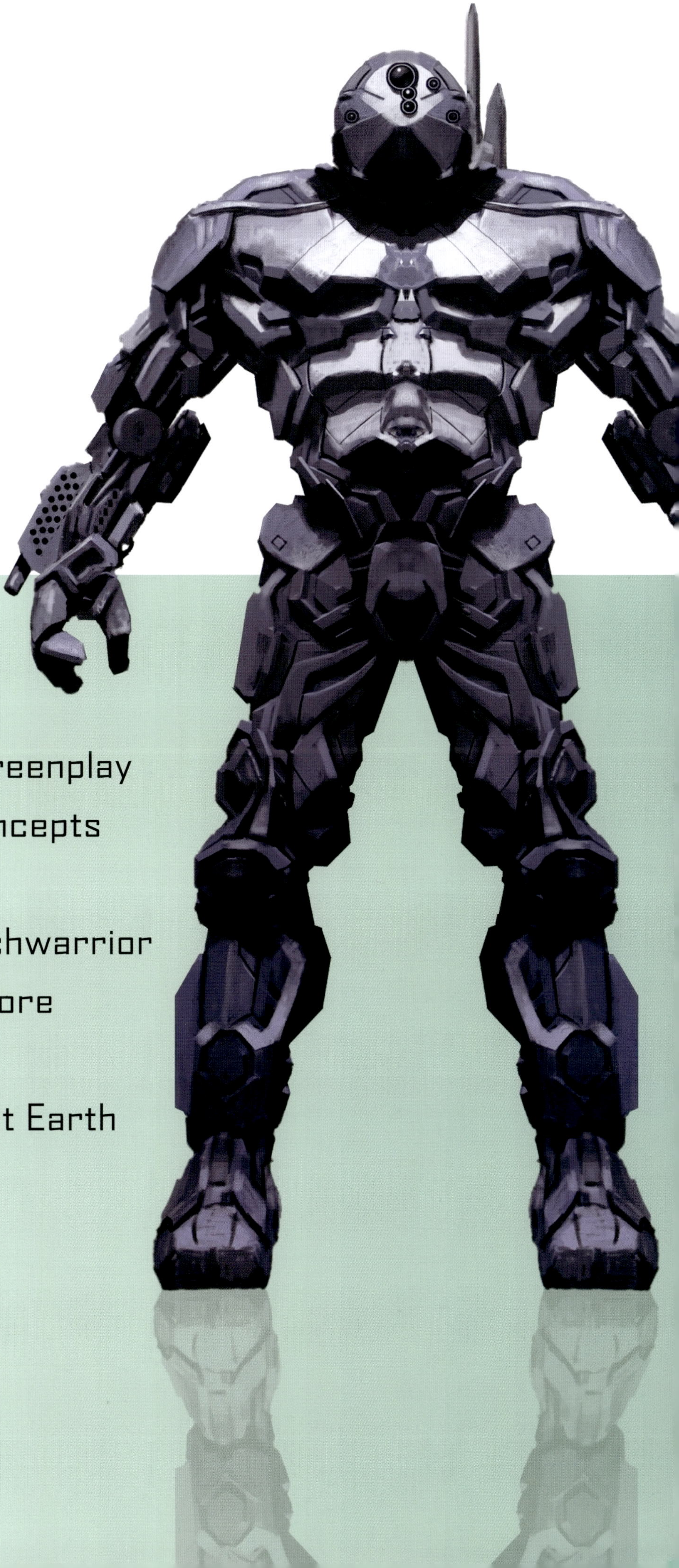

FOREWORD BY JOHN A. DAVIS

Concept art is all about ideas, specifically *visual* ideas. So when I found myself looking at concept artists for my first feature film, *Jimmy Neutron: Boy Genius*, back in 2000, I was looking for artists who not only had great technique but a great *imagination*.

I first encountered Fred's work while thumbing through an art book showcasing various artists and their techniques. I had never heard of Fred Gambino but his work immediately jumped out at me. His designs were bold and otherworldly, and what's more, his images had a strong sense of *cinema*. Fred's compositions often feel as though you're looking through a camera's lens, photographing a stylized drama that is playing out in his and our imaginations. Through Fred's 'camera lens', he carefully sets the stage and places the audience exactly where they should be to witness the events unfold. When the action is intense, the design and composition is dynamic and loud. When the scene is calm and intimate, one can hear a pin drop. His imagery is immersive – a prime ingredient for cinematic storytelling.

So, on our second feature film project together a couple of years later (*The Ant Bully*) there was good reason that Fred's initial three month contract became an *eighteen* month contract. During the conceptual art stages, Fred once again created exquisite 'alien' images, this time of the underground realm of the ants in our story. Several of Fred's images generated what I call the 'feedback loop', wherein these visual ideas spawn story ideas that get incorporated into the script and then spur further concepts – a wonderful and exciting synergy! It became clear that Fred had more to offer than wonderful design – he was really tuned-in to the storytelling. For the next year, Fred visualized exciting camera shots for our action scenes, created final production designs, and did beautiful matte paintings. Again, it is this double threat of visual ideas *and* story/cinema ideas that make Fred such a potent artist for film.

Of course, it was only a matter of time before Fred created his own story – *Dark Shepherd*. Here in these pages you can see Fred's talents as designer and storyteller on full display. The images excite the viewer to want to 'go there and see that', to witness the story unfold. It is immersive. So, what does it take to hold such sway over an audience? First and foremost, it takes a great imagination. Fred Gambino is one imaginative fellow!

John A. Davis
December 2013

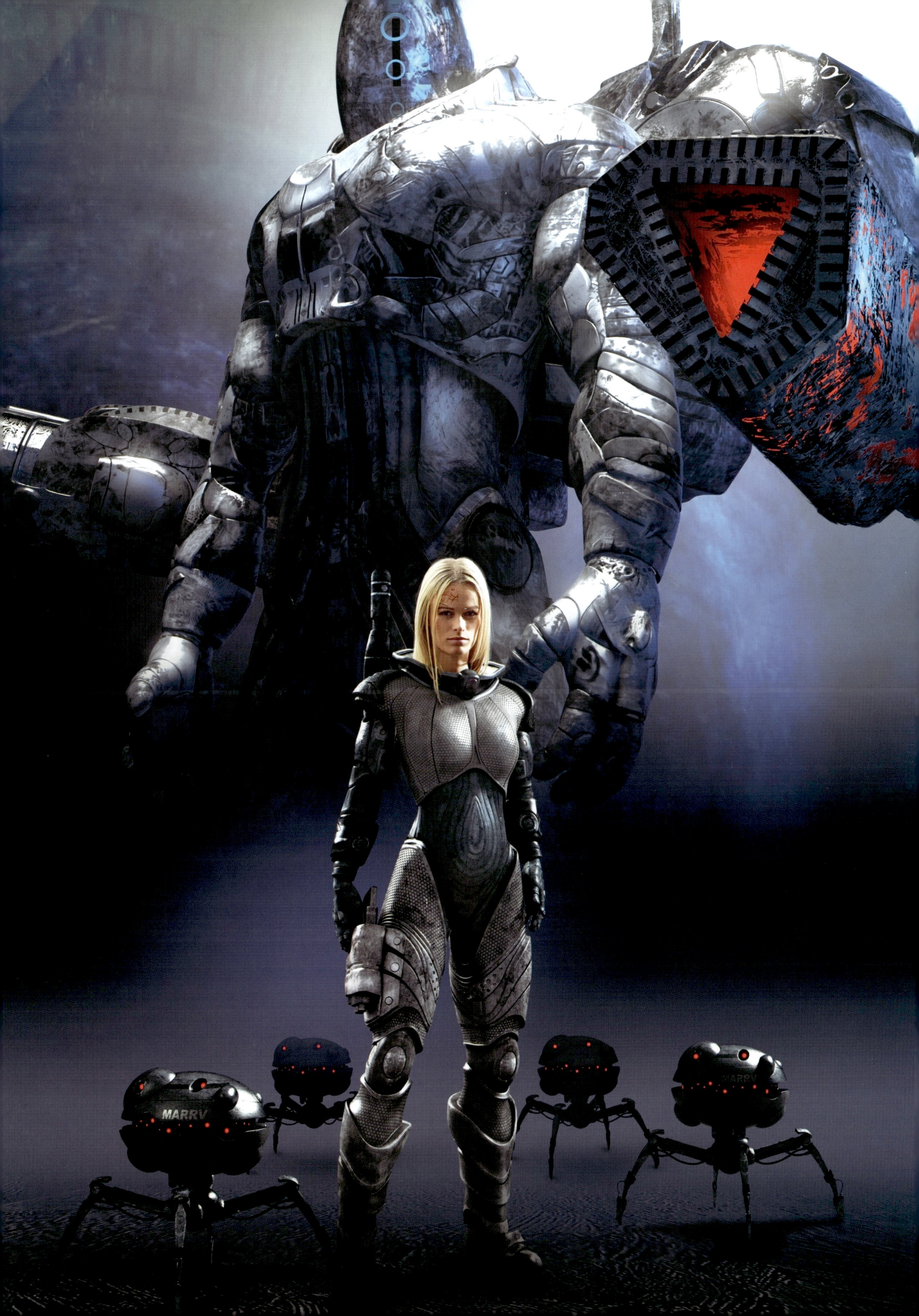
MARRV

INTRODUCTION BY FRED GAMBINO

So, here I am: it's 2014 and nearly fifteen years have passed since my last book, *Ground Zero*. A lot has happened in that decade and a half. I have gone from an illustrator working traditionally in acrylics and oils, mainly for publishing, to an illustrator and concept artist for the film and game industries, working mainly digitally. I have found myself working all over the world, from Dallas to Vancouver, and L.A. to Salamanca in Spain.

I've gone from the hermit-like existence that is the lot of most freelance illustrators to the hustle and bustle of busy film and game studios. I've worked with a lot of extremely talented people, something which has benefited my work immensely, and enjoyed the tension and even the occasional clash of egos around me.

Somewhere along the line I acquired a 'story'. Really, it began when I was working as a concept artist on Warner Bros.' *The Ant Bully* for DNA productions in Dallas. The concept team were all displaced from other parts of the US and the rest of the world, and as such, we became a fairly close knit group. Once a week we would have a film night, taking turns to host the evening at our various apartments. We would choose a film to watch and discuss it in-depth, and otherwise generally chew the fat. One evening one of the guys stood up and asked us all: 'What's your story?'

'What's my story?' I wondered. 'Is he asking me for a life history?' But no, I had forgotten I was with Hollywood folk. He meant the story that *we* were working on: our own story, script, book, whatever – because of course, everyone must have one. Annoyingly, I discovered that I was the only person in the room who didn't.

Several years later, I was out cycling – the place where I do my best creative thinking. All of a sudden, a story more or

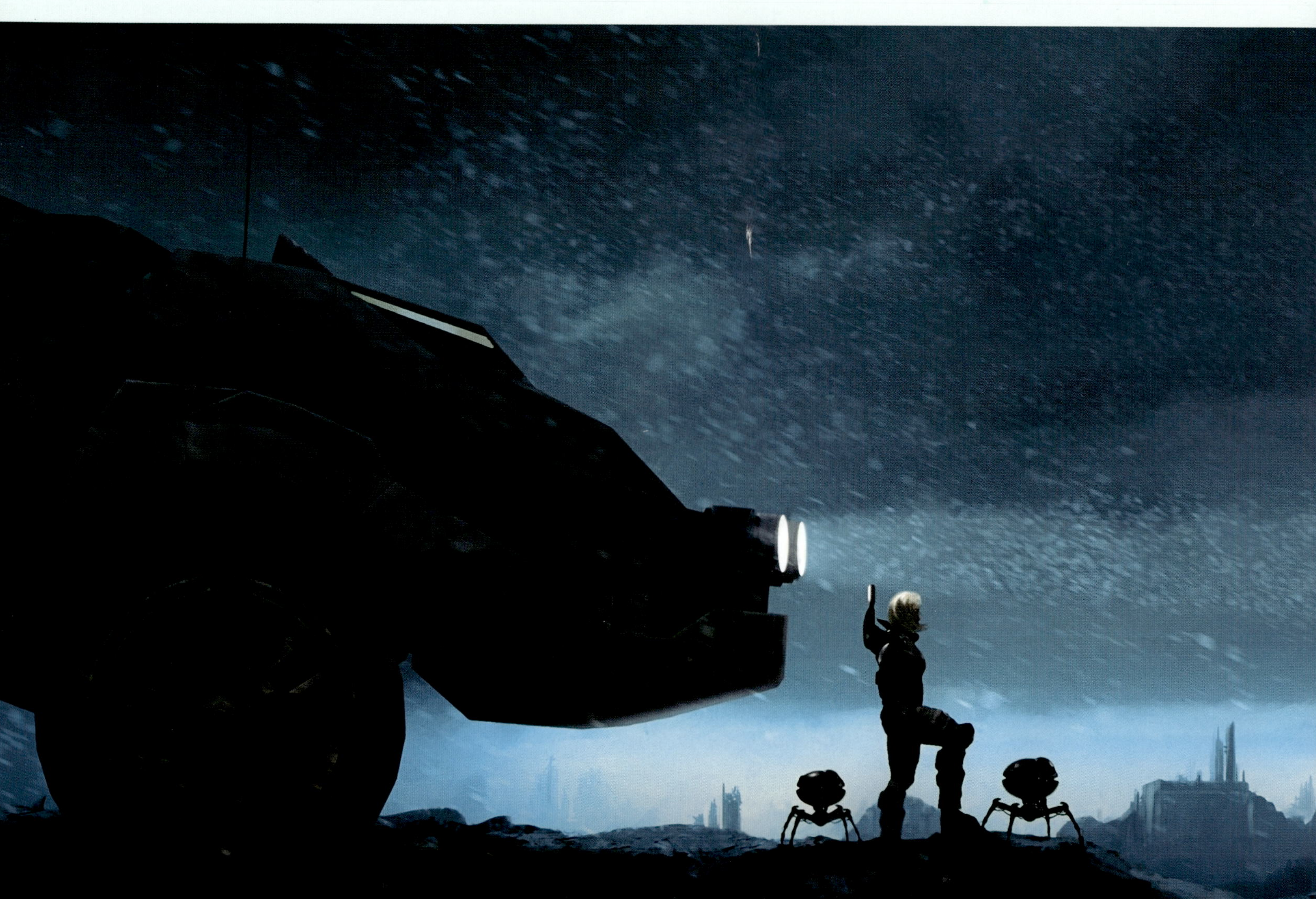

less popped into my head. That night in Dallas came back to me and I resolved to write this one up, to finally have my 'story'. I wasn't sure what to do with it next, so I sent it my agent, Alison Eldred, to see what she thought. Never lacking in enthusiasm or encouragement, Alison asked me if it was okay to send on to a literary agent. He came back saying, 'I love this, but what is it? A novel, a graphic novel, a screenplay – we need to turn it into something.' Encouraged, I decided to turn it into a script. That's what I have been doing, on and off, ever since.

The script languished over the next couple of years as I found myself working on other projects, until out of the blue, Titan Books came into the picture, interested in doing a collection of my art and illustrations. A retrospective of my work over the last fifteen years was great, but I suggested that we do something extra and include parts of the script, now called *Dark Shepherd*, with new illustrations created especially for it. It was a chance for it to see the light of day, albeit in an unexpected form.

So, dear reader (I always wanted to write that), you now hold in your hands the fruits of that labour. I hope you enjoy reading it as much as I have creating it, as well as the sampling of my other work. The last fifteen years have been a wild ride, and here's to the next fifteen.

Fred Gambino

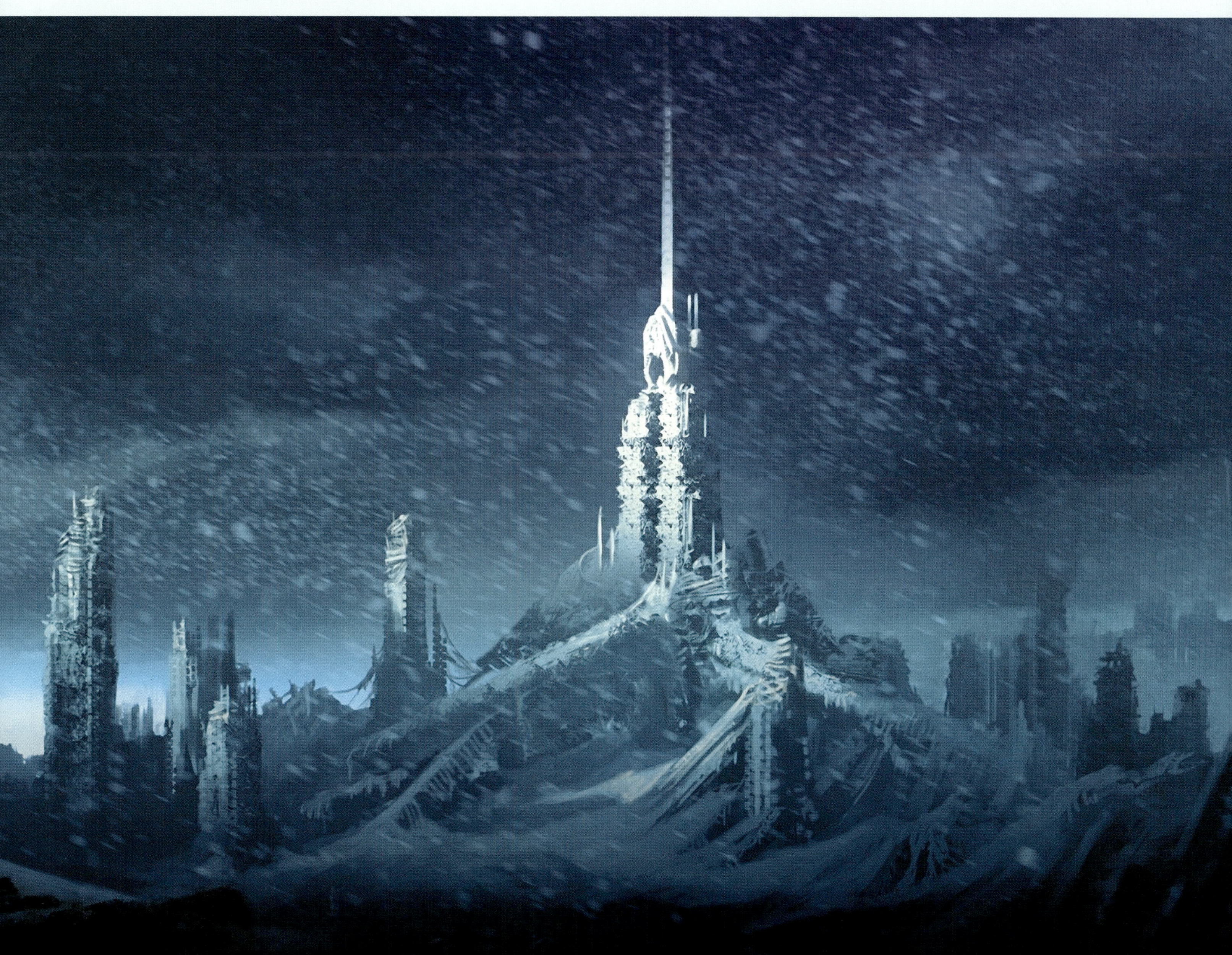

DARK SHEPHERD SCREENPLAY

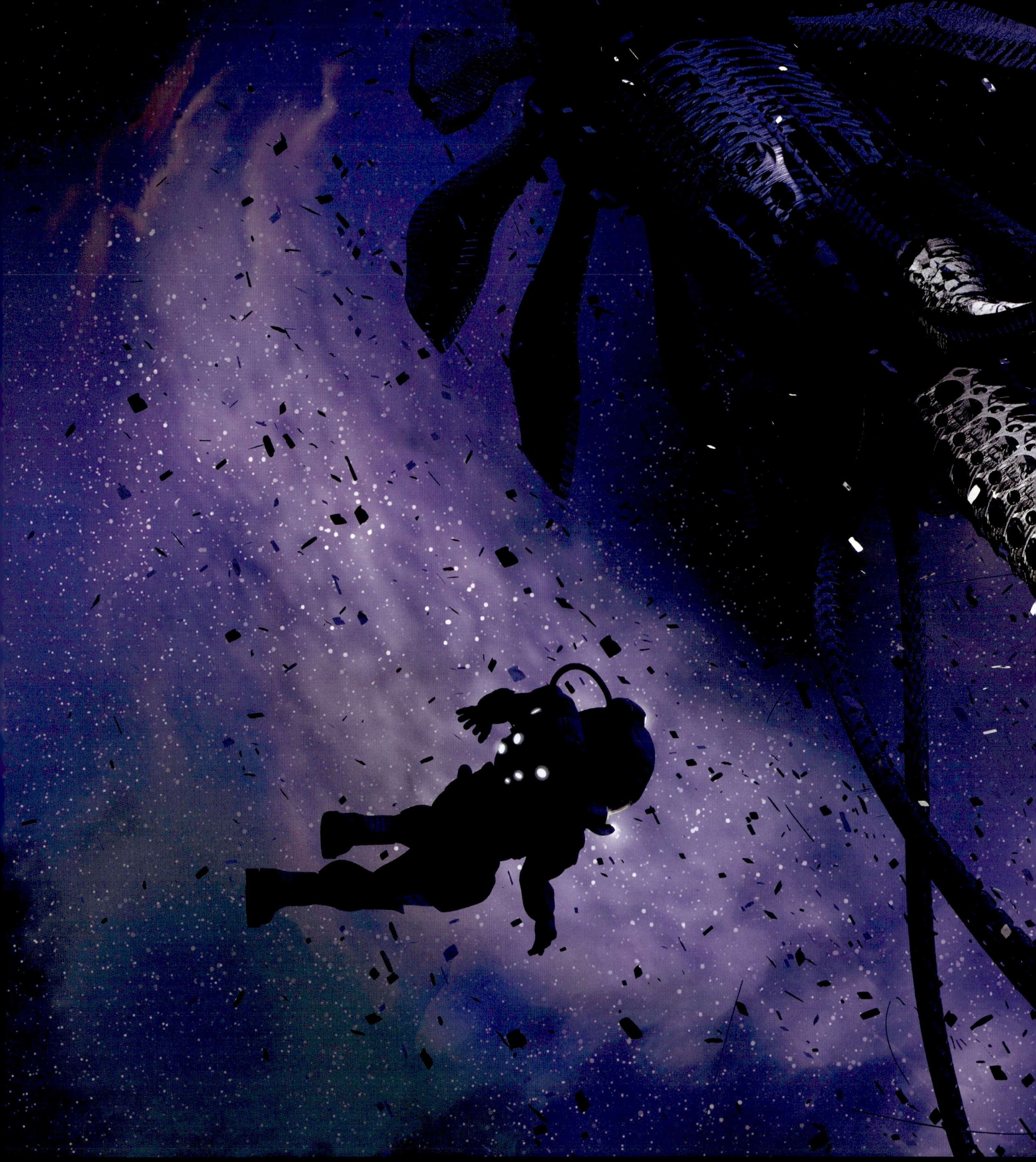

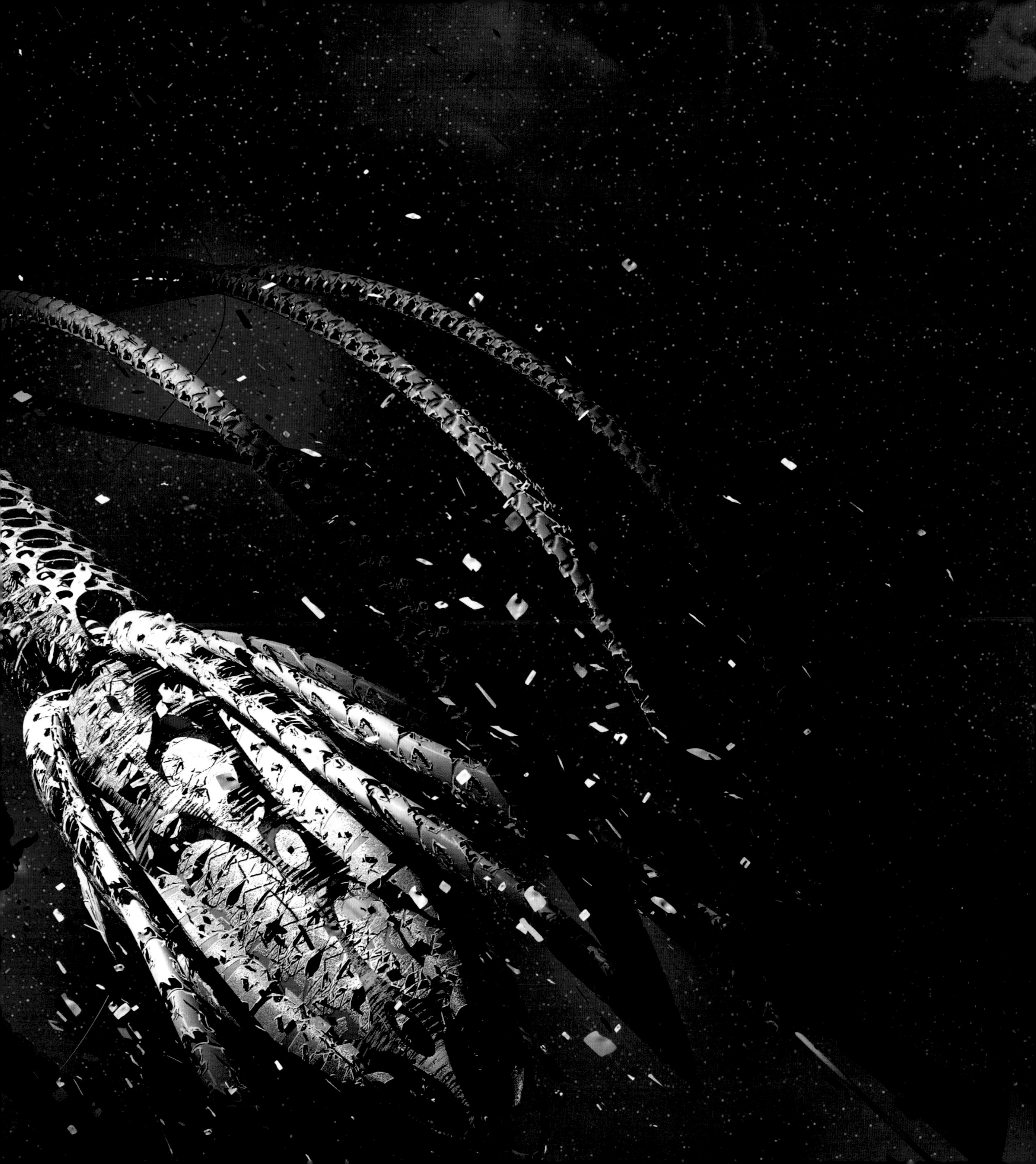

Dark Shepherd
by Fred Gambino
(With Contribution By John A. Lewis)

FADE IN:

EXT. DEEP SPACE - SOMETIME IN THE FUTURE

A huge nebula fills the view: it is a gaudy dramatic display 1000 light years across, filling the heavens with dripping colour and light. A dark spot appears against the glowing patterns, rapidly expanding.

Here in interstellar space it is perfectly black, the light from the multitude of distant stars so weakened by the unthinkable distance that it fails to illuminate in any way.

The object appears to be changing shape, first squarish, now a distorted octagon. It moves in complete silence.

CUT TO:

Another squat dark shape against the infinite night. This is the Claimer prospecting STARSHIP WINDFALL Its running lights illuminate a hull clustered with equipment and antenna arrays. Her engines vent blue flames as she passes.

INT. MAIN BRIDGE

A no-frills workspace jammed with viewscreens and readouts, and about a dozen command crew in low seats. The bridge has a worn, makeshift look about it, a patchwork of different design sensibilities strung together in a seemingly ad-hoc way.

The crew have a similar care worn look with a tough, no nonsense air.

Large windows fill the foredeck and the ship's captain, TANAKA, stands before the stars with a cup of coffee.

TANAKA
Yuric, what's our status?

Yuric consults a screen. Dozens of readouts and complicated graphics.

YURIC
Two minutes until we match velocity. I've got three tugs prepped and ready to go. Boarding crews are suiting up.

INT. AIRLOCK

Here we find the BOARDING CREW: nine astronauts pulling on suits and checking equipment. A klaxon sounds and the hissing of air leaves us in the silence of the vacuum. The astronauts' breathing is loud over an open mic channel.

NEVIS and SIRI, a husband and wife team, are helping each other crosscheck. They touch faceplates and share a moment.

The airlock door opens onto the blackness of space and the astronauts cross the Windfall's main hull towards a trio of smaller ancillary spacecraft clamped nearby - the TUGS.

They are the size of a regular van, a squat framework of struts and thrusters with a rudimentary cockpit. Nevis and Siri follow their pilot FALIAN to the nearest Tug.

INT. MAIN BRIDGE

Tanaka and Yuric watch live feed of the teams climbing aboard the tugs.

TANAKA
Make sure the cameras are rolling. We're making history here, I want backups of everything.

YURIC
Velocity matched. Boarding crews launch when ready.

FALIAN (V.O.)
Roger that. Launching now.

EXT. SPACE

The tugs lift off with three astronauts aboard, one at the controls and the others clinging to the framework. Nevis and Siri hold on as their pilot manoeuvres the tug out into the void.

WIDER

The three tugs pull away from the Windfall and we follow them around to reveal...

THE DERELICT

A massive dark shape looming ahead of the tugs, utterly dwarfing both them and the Windfall. Sudden bursts of light give the object form, throwing planes and facets into sharp relief. Brilliant metallic surfaces cast completely black shadows. Now and again, an escaping puff of gas

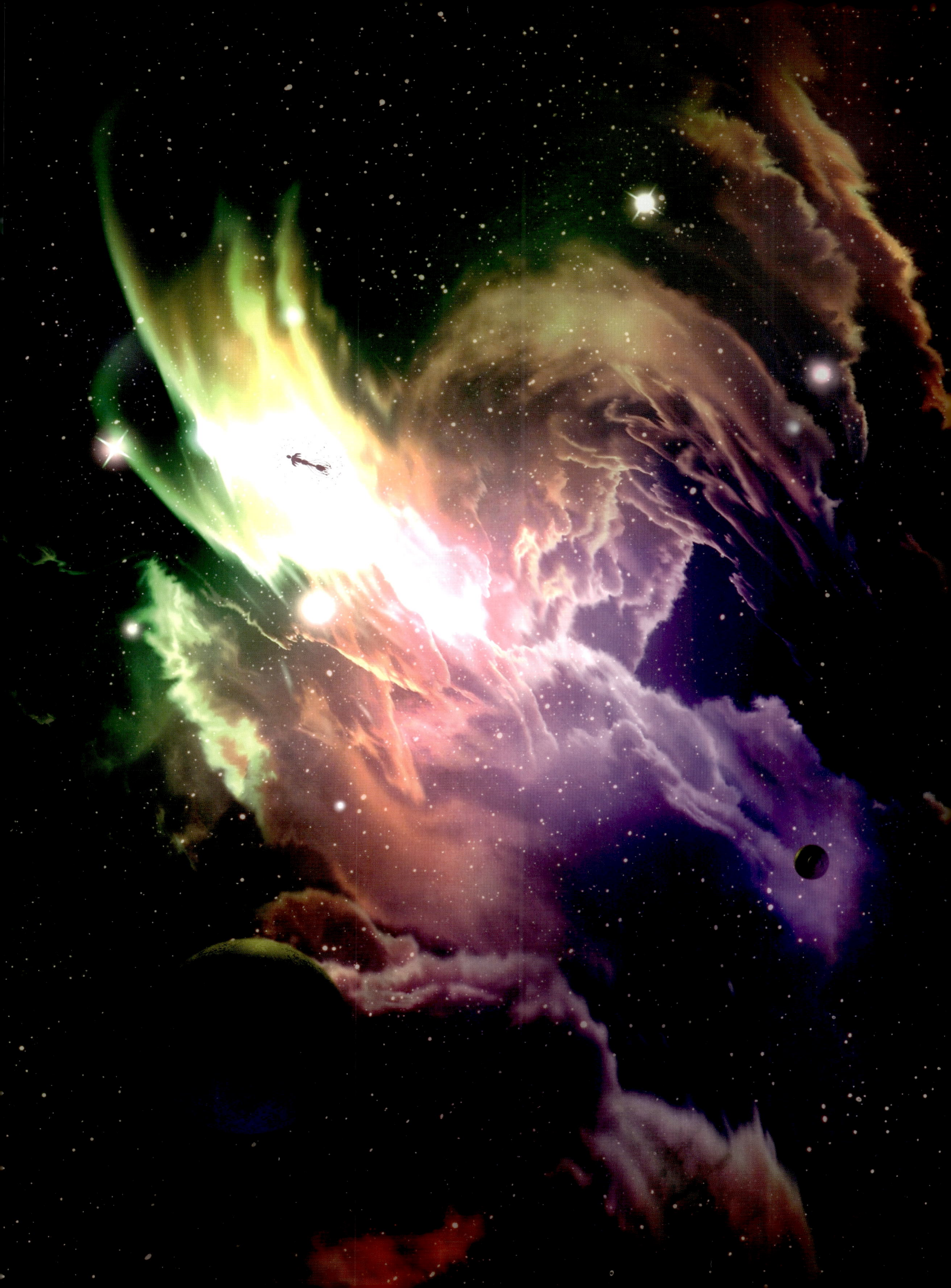

adds a new wobble to the tumbling motion, turning instantly into a cloud of ice crystals in the almost absolute zero of space.

The object is surrounded by a spherical halo of glittering particles, tumbling with it in perfect unison.

This is a craft unlike anything we have seen before, unmistakably alien. The derelict resembles some kind of nightmarish sea creature, a tangle of shapes and trailing sectional fuselage hang like tentacles. As the ship slowly rotates, details appear and disappear in shadows as the flood lights from the Windfall play across the surface.

The tugs leave formation and move closer to the alien ship, using powerful searchlights to examine the wreckage. Large sections are damaged and twisted, the metallic surfaces littered with holes and missing panels. Countless tumbling pieces of debris surround the main bulk of the ship.

FALIAN

Looks like it's taken quite abeating. What's holding it together?

SIRI

Hull is open to the vacuum, interior is as cold as space. No signs of life.

INT. MAIN BRIDGE

Tanaka and Yuric watch the mission feed on the main screen.

YURIC

It's like no ship I've seen before.

TANAKA

No one has seen anything like this before.

YURIC

Hold on. Sensors are picking up a hotspot near the bow. Tug 3, you're the closest. Can you see anything?

FALIAN (V.O.)

Roger that. Moving in for a closer look.

EXT. THE DERELICT

Falian brings the tug around closer to the main fuselage, passing into the debris field. The searchlight illuminates the dark recesses of the alien ship.

NEVIS

There. Looks like a hatch. Could be a way inside.

A hatchway is revealed by the searchlight, dented but apparently serviceable.

SIRI

Falian, get us in closer. Can you match the rotation?

FALIAN

No problem. Hold on.

Falian manipulates the controls and arcs the tug safely past some tumbling debris, bringing the small ship within reach of the hatch.

SIRI

Let's do this.

Nevis and Siri detach their safety lines and jump across the void towards the hatch.

INT. MAIN BRIDGE

Tanaka and Yuric watch the video feed, multiple angles from helmet cameras, tug mounted cameras and long range scans.

TANAKA

We need to stabilise that rotation.

YURIC

I've got Tugs 1 and 2 looking at that.

NEVIS (V.O.)

We're at the hatch.

TANAKA

Can you get it open?

NEVIS (V.O.)

I don't think we need to.

Next to the hatch Nevis examines a rip, as if the panels of the ship have been blown apart by some massive force. Nevis and Siri peer inside.

INT. MAIN BRIDGE

Tanaka and Yuric move closer to the monitors, trying to see anything in the blackness. The entire bridge crew is watching the video feed.

YURIC
What do we do now? Send in a drone?

TANAKA
Maybe. Tug 3, do you have a drone on board?

EXT. DERELICT - THE HATCH

Nevis looks across at Falian in the cockpit of the Tug. He is nodding. Yes they have a drone.

NEVIS
Negative captain, we don't have a drone.

Siri gives him a 'what are you doing?' look.

TANAKA (V.O.)
Ok. Stand down Tug 3, let's get another team over there.

NEVIS
Uh... I think we need the human touch here, captain.

TANAKA (V.O.)
Negative Tug 3, it's too much of a risk.Tug 2 can you get over there and take over?

TUG 2 PILOT (V.O.)
Roger that, en-route now.

NEVIS
Dammit captain, this is our shout. We're going in.

TANAKA (V.O.)
Negative Tug 3, you are to stand down. Over.

Nevis and Siri turn to see the rival tug inbound. There are only seconds until it reaches them. They look at each other and make a decision. Holding hands they step off the edge of the tear in the derelict's hull and freefall into the blackness.

TANAKA (V.O.)
Tug three what the hell are you doing? Nevis I told you to stand down!

Nevis and Siri fall into the dark interior of the alien ship. Their helmet lights are the only illumination.

TANAKA (V.O.)
Nevis? You... are... to... stan...do... resp... tha... order...

The radio signal is lost. Nevis and Siri are alone.

INT. MAIN BRIDGE

Tanaka is incandescent with rage. He throws his coffee mug on the deck, shattering it.

TANAKA
Godammit! Can't anyone on this ship follow a simple order?

YURIC
Tug 2, do you have a visual on them?

TUG 2 (V.O.)
Negative control. No sign. Shall we deploy the drone?

TANAKA
No. We can't risk it. Hold until we know what's going on.

YURIC
Tug 1 and 2, concentrate on getting that wreck stabilised. Tug 3, stand station and wait for Nevis to return. Over.

Tanaka kicks the remains of his coffee mug, enraged.

INT. DERELICT

Nevis and Siri continue to freefall through the blackness. Their helmet lights pick out vague shapes around them, the interior structure of the ship is vast.

SIRI
What are we doing?

NEVIS
We're making history.

Massive struts and framework lattice loom up out of the darkness.

NEVIS
Look out.

Using their suit thrusters, Nevis and Siri manoeuvre through the obstacles, still freefalling.

SIRI
This place is a mess. No sign of a conventional deck structure.

NEVIS
There has to be some kind of control centre in here.

A faint glow is forming below them.

SIRI
Do you see that?

NEVIS
Yeah, something is still drawing power, must be the source of the hot spot.

Nevis and Siri drift closer to the glow, now revealed to be coming from a cluster of machinery as they land on a deck, alone in the depths of the alien craft.

SIRI
What is it?

The machinery is connected with pipes and tubes, in the centre is a sarcophagus. It looks like a metal casket, like something from an ancient Egyptian tomb.

NEVIS
I don't know, hibernation chamber maybe?

SIRI
You mean...

NEVIS
Could be.

SIRI
Alien life?

NEVIS
Let's find out.

They approach the sarcophagus warily. Suddenly, there is a blast of sound and light that leaves both astronauts senseless.

SIRI
What was that?

NEVIS
Suit tech is going haywire. I think we just got scanned by something.

The noise increases, alien technology straining to restart after a millennia of inactivity. Rattling and creaking noises as vapour of some kind bursts out of the pipes, a cloud of white gas surrounding them.

NEVIS
Siri!

SIRI
I can't see, what is this stuff?

Nevis checks his suit readouts.

NEVIS
It's... it's oxygen?

SIRI
Oxygen? How is that possible?

The cloud of oxygen swirls into a bubble around them and the sarcophagus, becoming a breathable atmosphere. The noise level increases, machinery stuttering and grinding, it is clear that the alien systems are only just holding together. The Sarcophagus splits open to reveal a pool of black liquid, iridescent in the light, ripples sending unnatural colours across the surface.

SIRI
What is this?

NEVIS
Don't touch it Siri. Stay back.

The machinery is glowing, the black liquid beginning to bubble. A small shape forming in the centre of the pool. Suddenly there is a tremor... the boom of an explosion somewhere deep in the ship.

EXT. DERELICT

The explosion blows up through a section at the rear of the derelict. One of the trailing fuselage sections is ripped loose and begins to spin away from the ship.

INT. MAIN BRIDGE

Tanaka and Yuric can only watch as their prize begins to self destruct.

TANAKA
What the hell was that?

YURIC
Shit! It's overloading. The readouts are off the scale.

TANAKA
Get them out of there.

YURIC
All Tugs abort abort! Abort! Get out of there now!

EXT. DERELICT

Another explosion, and debris flies in all directions. A large chunk hits Tug 1, causing it to spin out of control.

TUG 1 PILOT (V.O.)
We're hit, we're hit, mayday may...

The stricken tug is enveloped in the debris and explodes.

INT. DERELICT - SARCOPHAGUS ROOM

The floor shakes, several pipes spring loose from the machinery. More tremors as one of the massive girders comes loose overhead.

NEVIS
The ship's coming apart. We have to get out of here.

At the pool, the black liquid continues to coalesce, forming into something, almost like a small figure curled up on the surface. Movement within the liquid.

SIRI
Look, Nev... I think it's alive.

NEVIS
No time. We have to get out of here now.

A section of deck nearby is ripped apart by a secondary explosion, buckled girders punch through the metal. Nevis pulls Siri away. They begin to rise back towards the surface, leaving the sarcophagus room.

Suddenly, their suit speakers erupt with an ear deafening screech. Nevis and Siri stare at each other dumbfounded as the nature of the sound becomes clear. It is the unmistakable sound of a baby crying.

Siri stops, then turns and begins to float back down to the sarcophagus.

NEVIS
Siri!

The black liquid is peeling back, the small figure revealed to be a newborn human, a tiny life created somehow by this alien technology. Siri stares at the child in wonder. The derelict continues to disintegrate around them but this moment of contact between the woman and the child overrides her instinct for survival. Siri reaches into the black gunk, cradling the child in a gloved hand.

SIRI
It's a girl.

Nevis reaches them, he stares at the child.

NEVIS
How is this possible?

SIRI
It's a miracle, Nev.

Another explosion rips through the deck nearby. The oxygen cloud begins to dissipate as the dubious integrity of the ship worsens. The child begins to wheeze and cough.

NEVIS
(Realising) The oxygen is gone – it's choking.

SIRI
What do we do?

Nevis is already on it. He pulls a pack from his suit marked 'EVAC SHROUD' and opens it. The pack inflates in a few seconds, forming a transparent protective cocoon. Nevis tries to lift the child but it's clear that it is still connected to the machinery – who knows what pulling her loose might do. Quickly, he starts to pull pipes and connections out of the Sarcophagus, releasing more vapour and steam, momentarily thickening cloud around them. With Siri's help, he pulls the evac shroud around the alien object. It's a tight fit, but it'll do. More explosions nearby. Nevis and Siri are already moving, using their suit thrusters to fly up and out of the derelict, carrying the evac shroud between them.

EXT. DERELICT

Nevis and Siri reach the hatch where Falian is waiting with Tug 3.

FALIAN
What is that?

NEVIS
A survivor.

Falian stares at her without answering and looks back at the controls, getting the tug moving.

Nevis and Siri watch as the derelict recedes behind them.

NEVIS
It's going!

More explosions rip through the derelict's hull, the ancient ship ripping apart as the tug races away. Safe in the evac shroud, the alien child stares up at her new parents through coal black eyes...

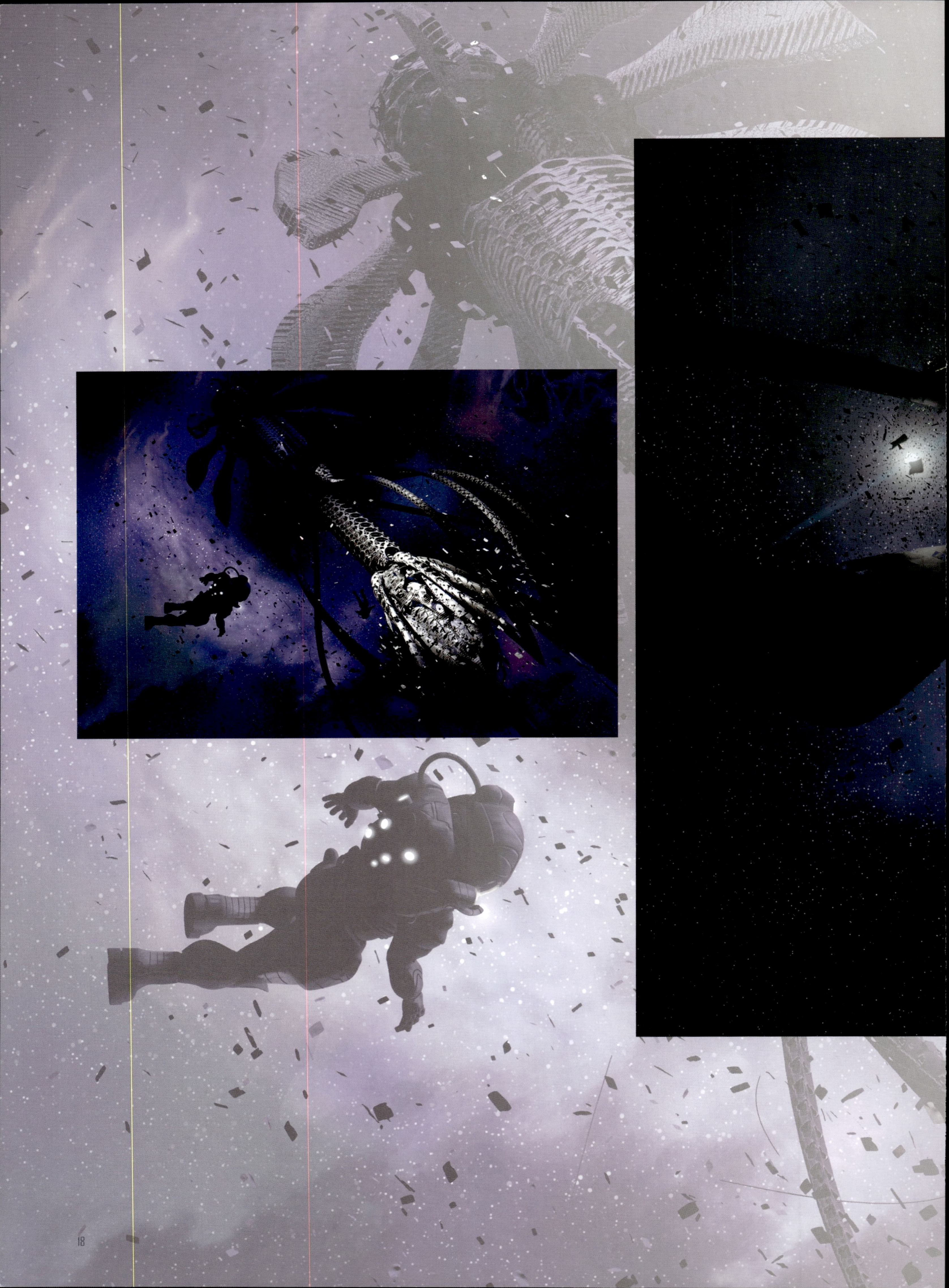

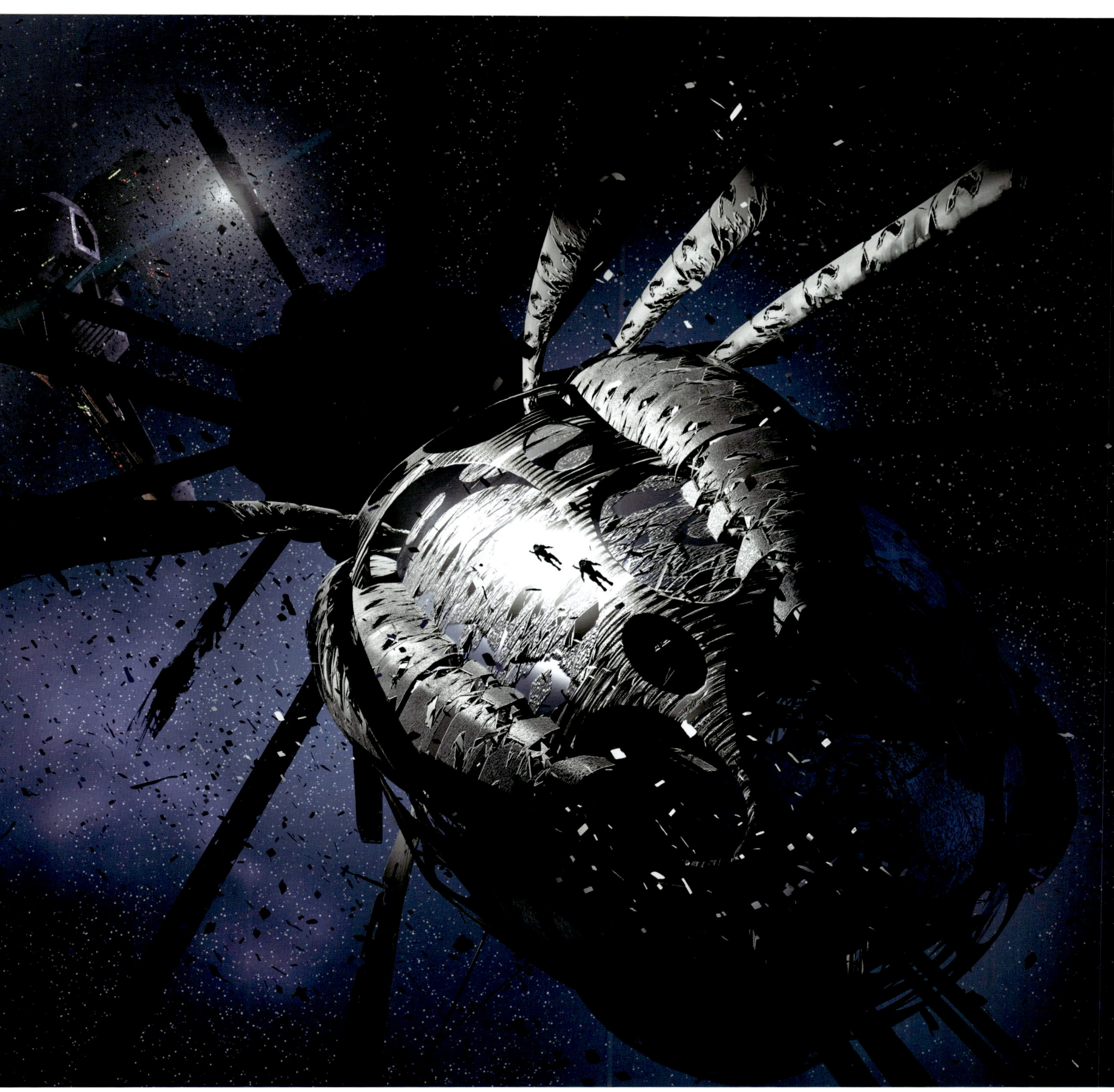

▽ Suddenly a burst of light gives the object form, throwing planes and facets into sharp relief. Brilliant metallic surfaces cast completely black shadows, the shape-shifting revealed to be a product of an erratic, uncontrolled tumble.

△ Falian brings the tug around closer to the main fuselage, passing into the debris field. The searchlight illuminates the dark recesses of the alien ship.

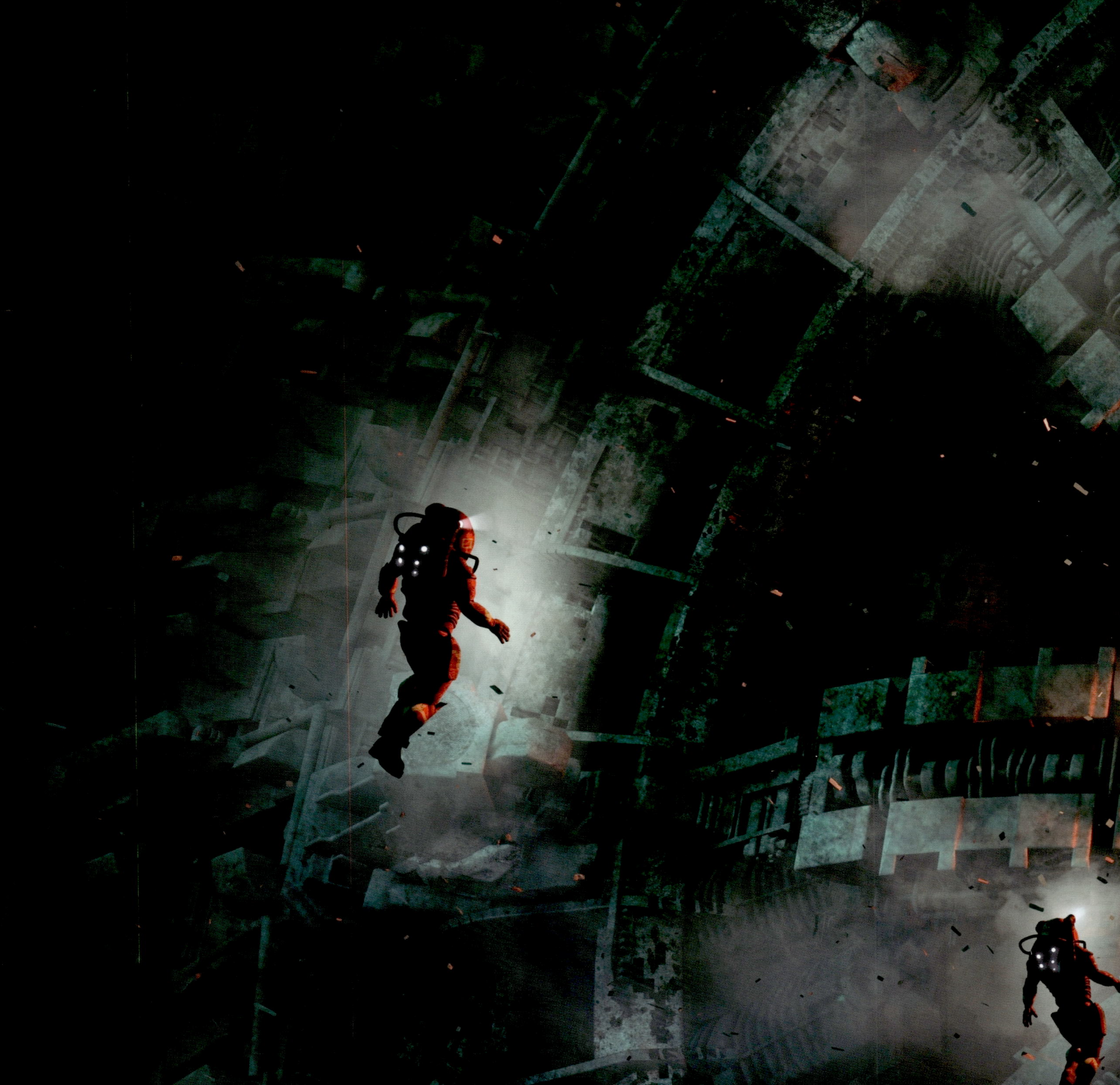

▽ The noise increases, alien technology straining to restart after millennia of inactivity. The ancient alien machinery is coming to life. Rattling and creaking noises begin, as vapour of some kind bursts out of the pipes, a cloud of white gas surrounding them.

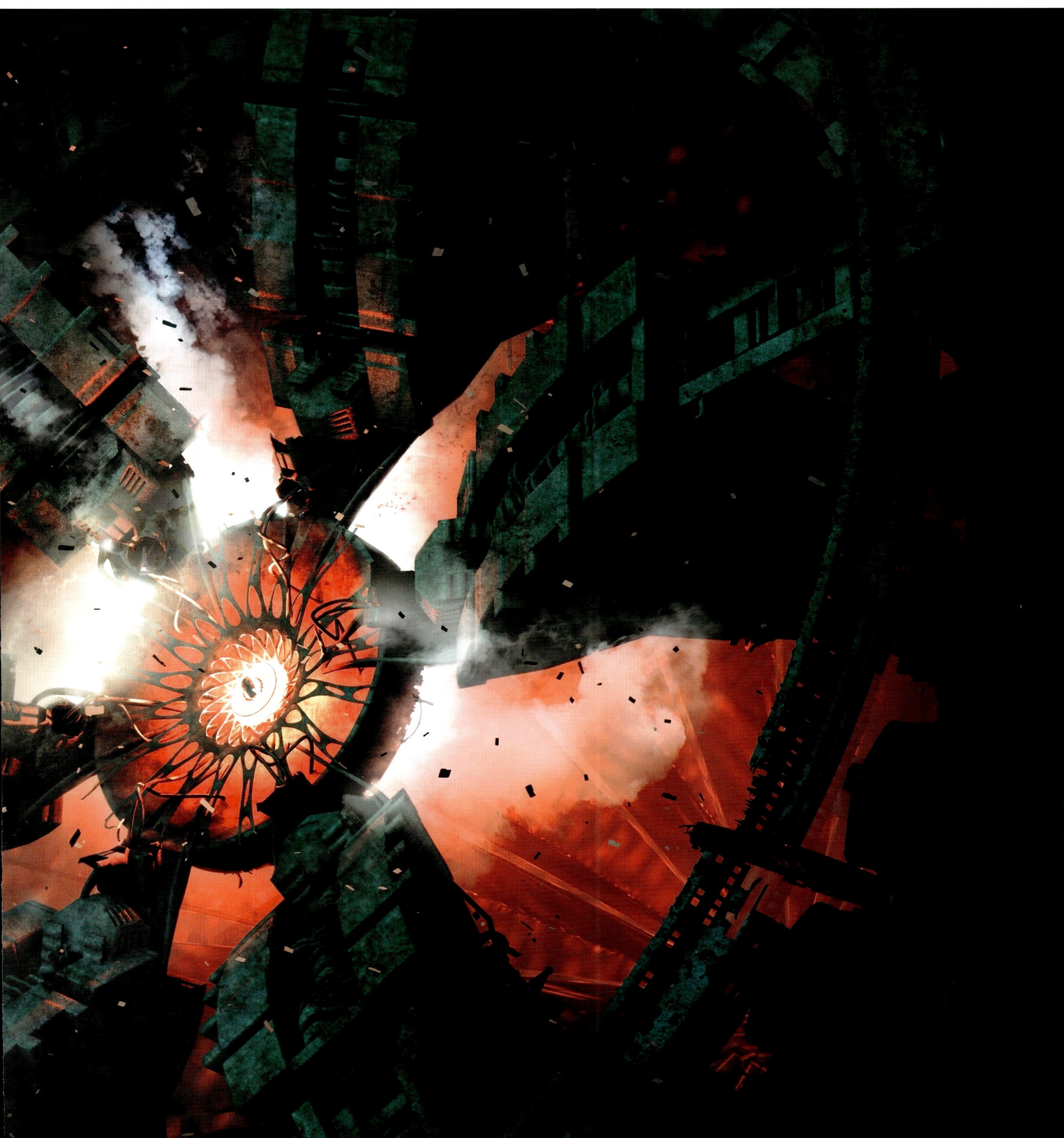

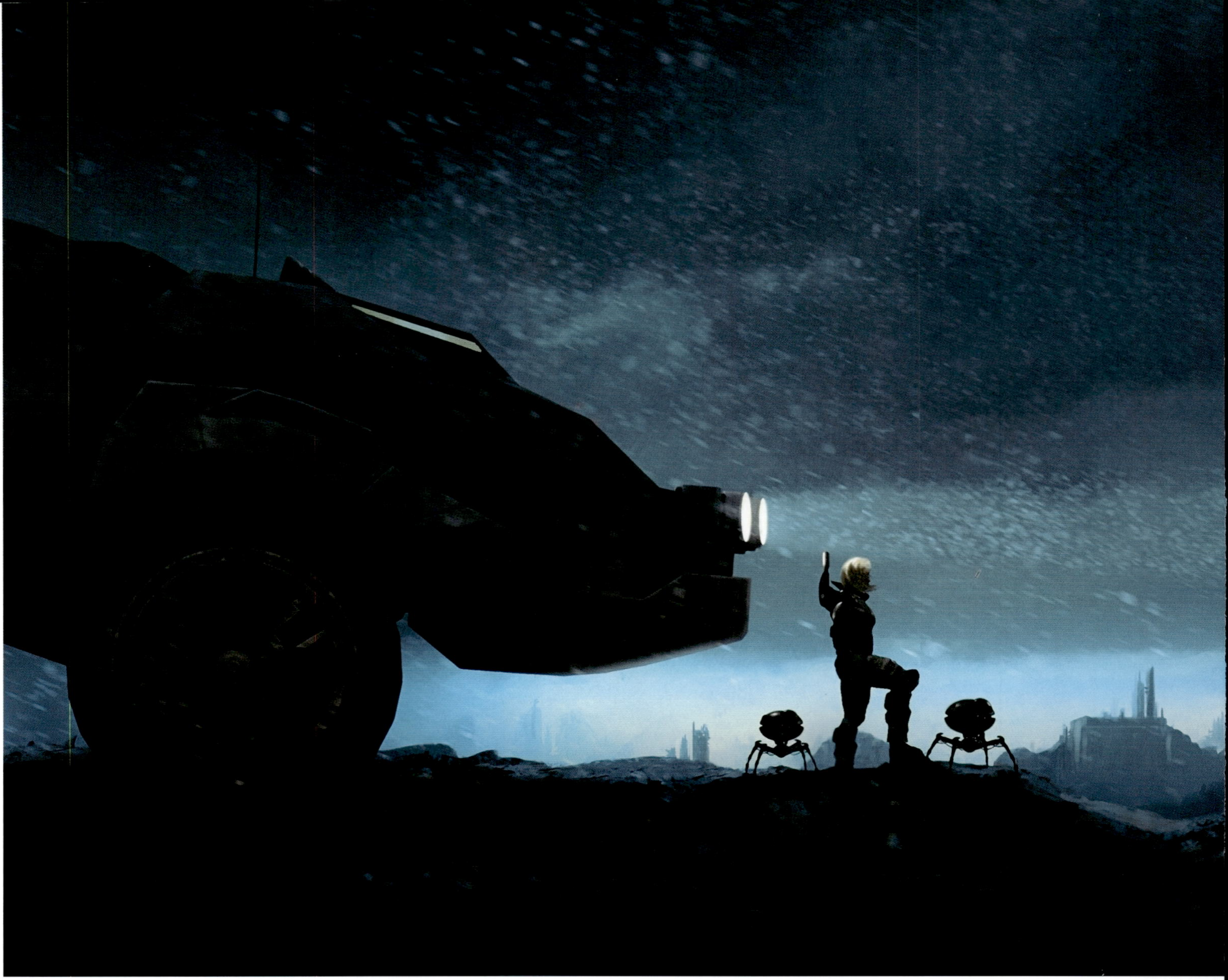

△ A snow covered wasteland scoured by wind blown icy particles. Partially buried in the ice and snow are the remains of an ancient, once high tech city, stretching as far as the eye can see, speared by a huge tower at its centre.

▷ Just outside, an aggressive looking wheeled vehicle waits...

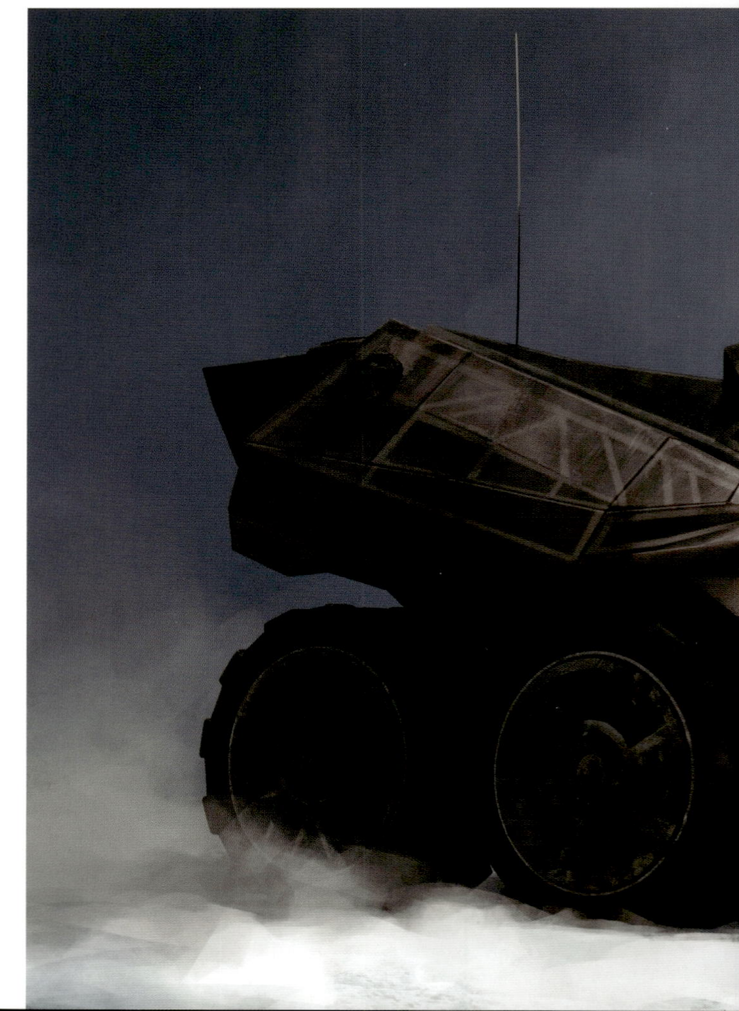

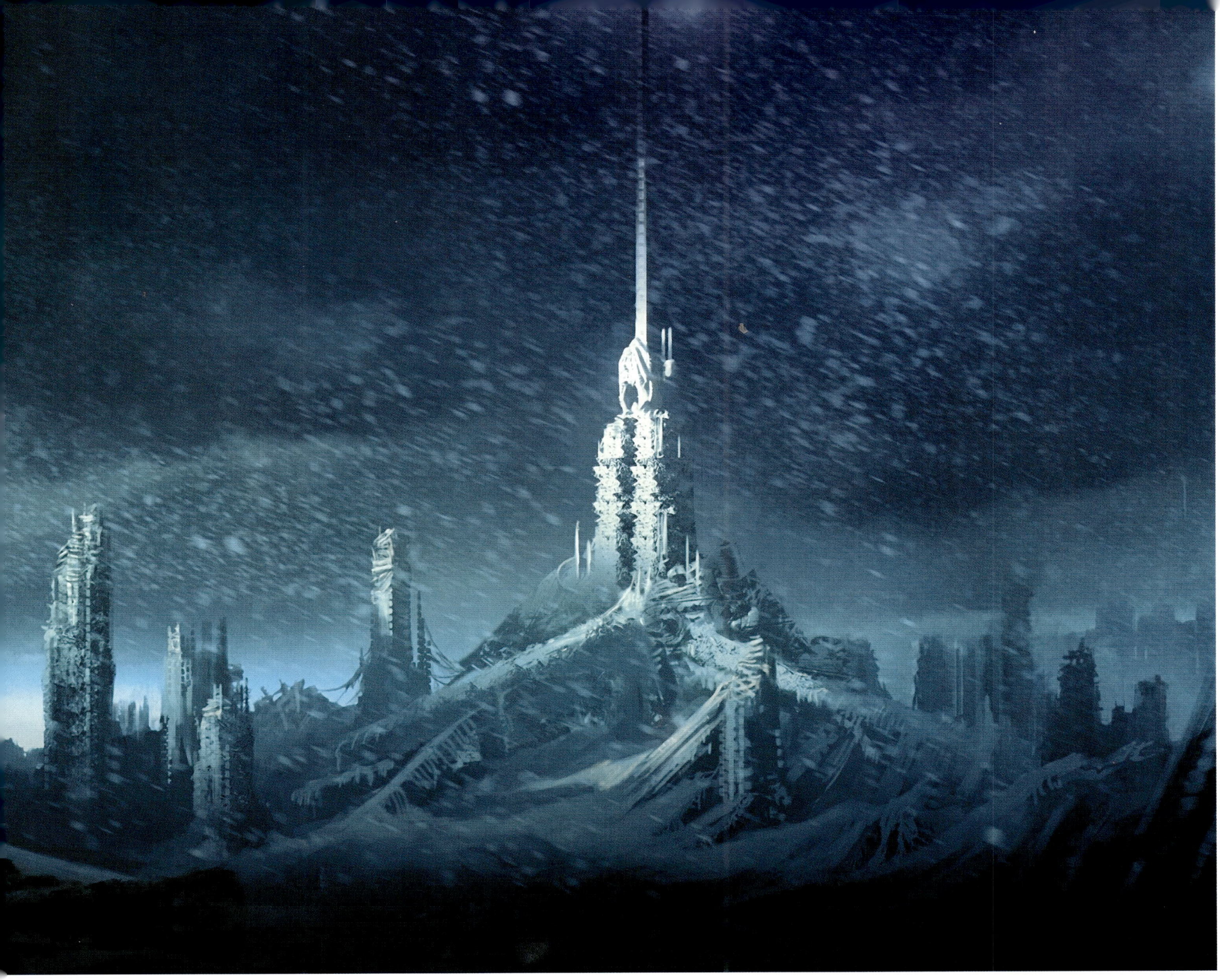

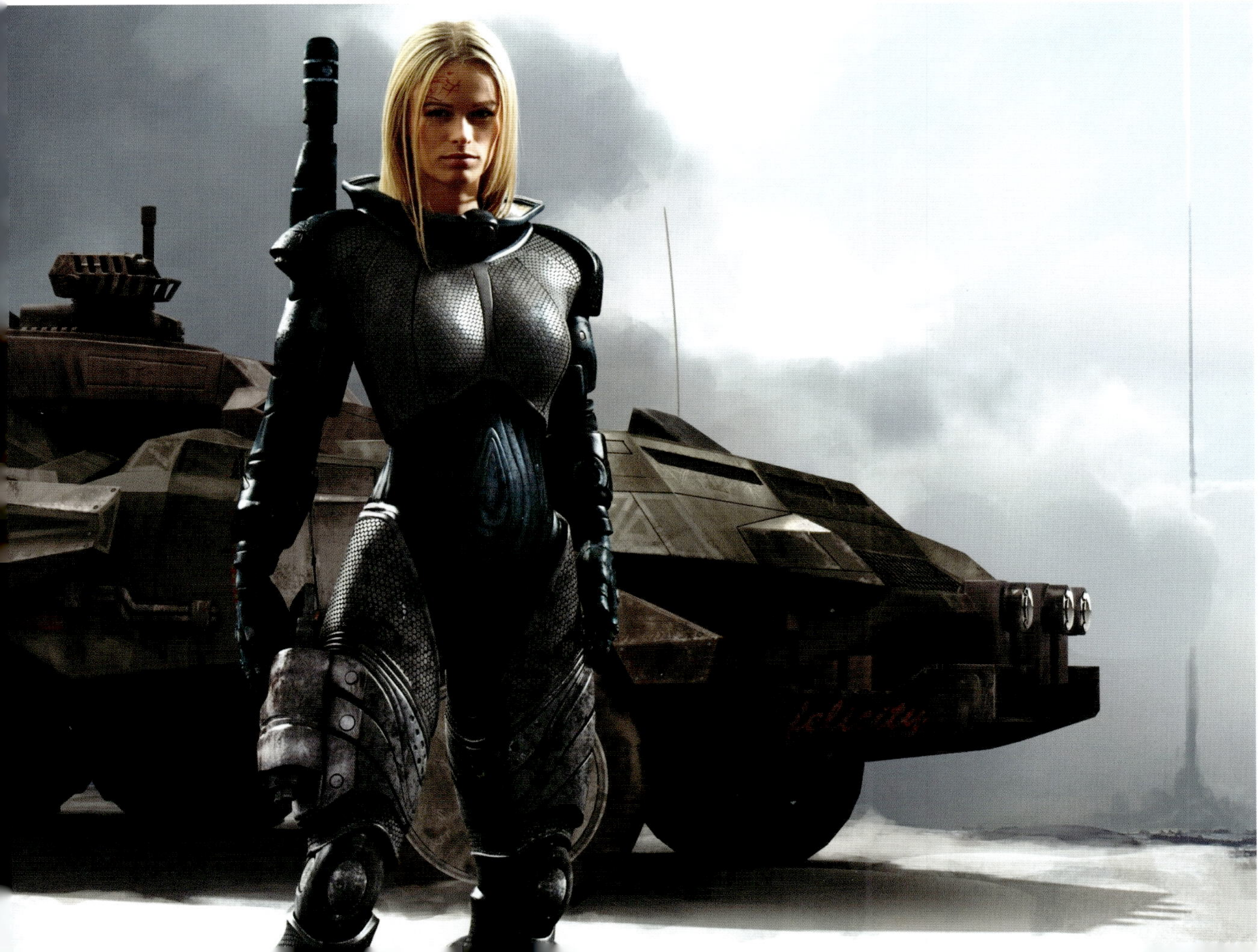

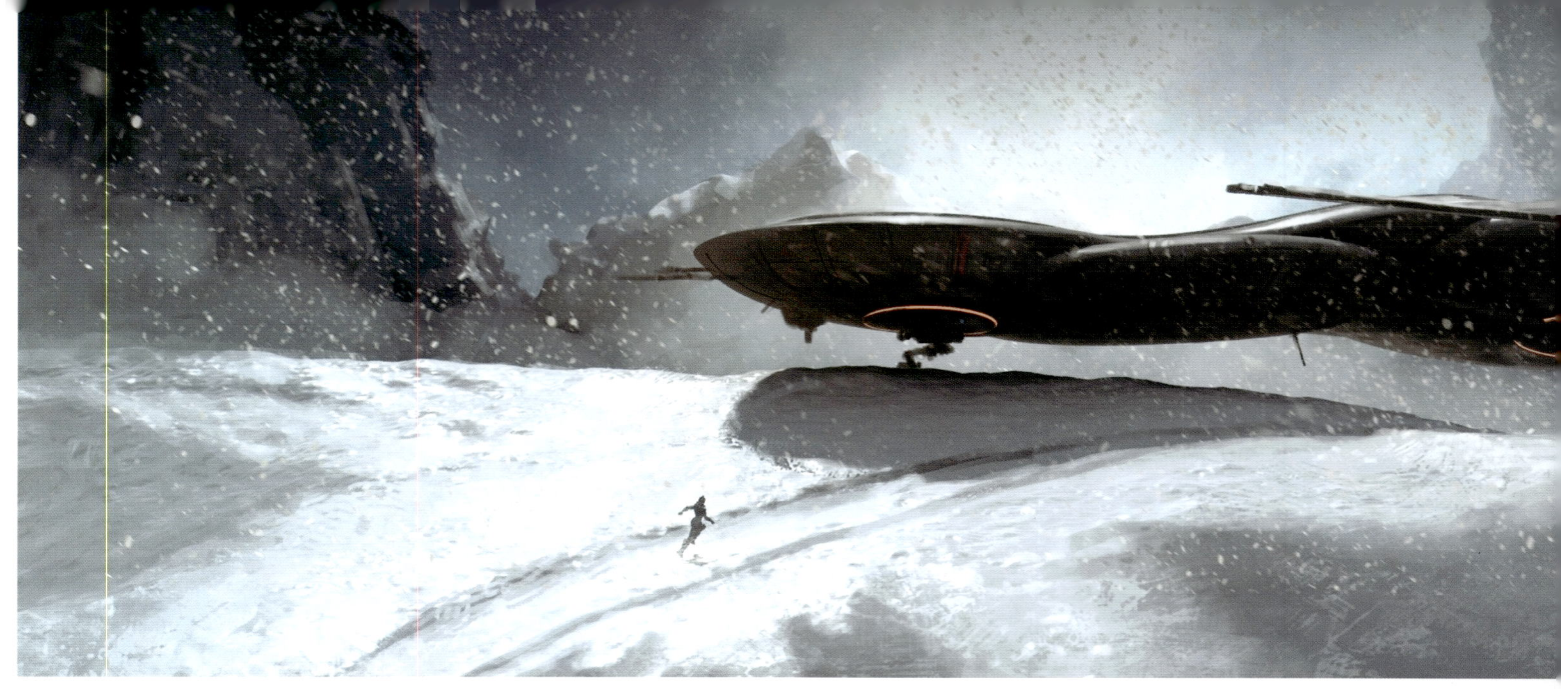

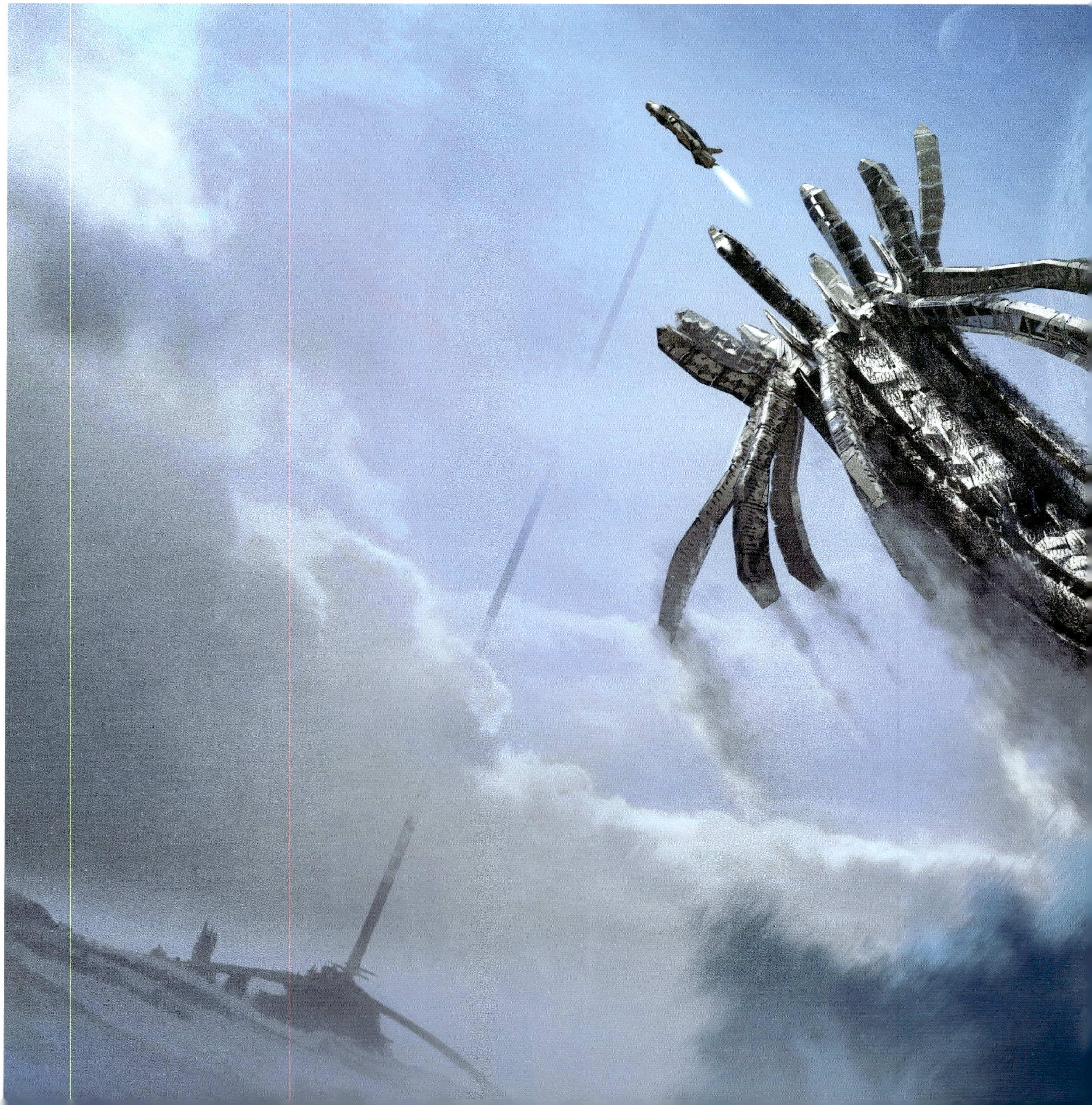

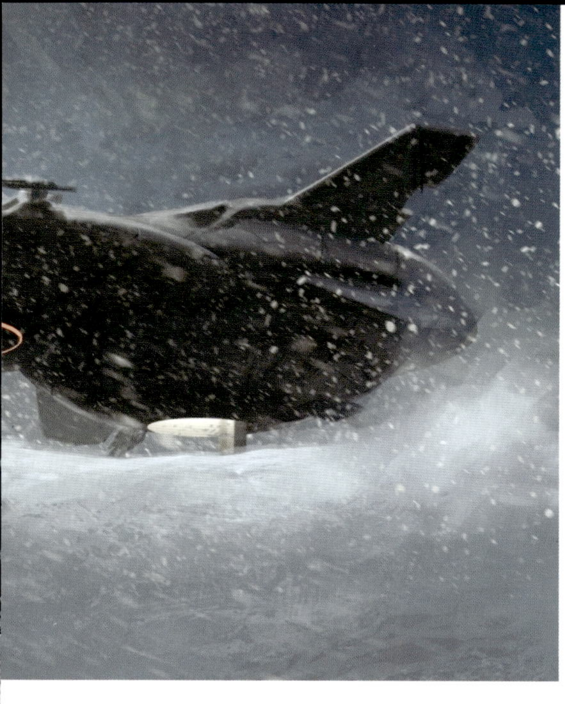

◁ There is a small pause as the selfless robots are consumed but it gives Breel just enough extra time to reach the ship and get aboard.

▽ For a moment it seems like Breel has made good her escape but then a monstrous serpent like creature, halfway between organic and machine erupts from the cloud. A maw filled with meshing metal snaps shut, missing the space craft by feet.

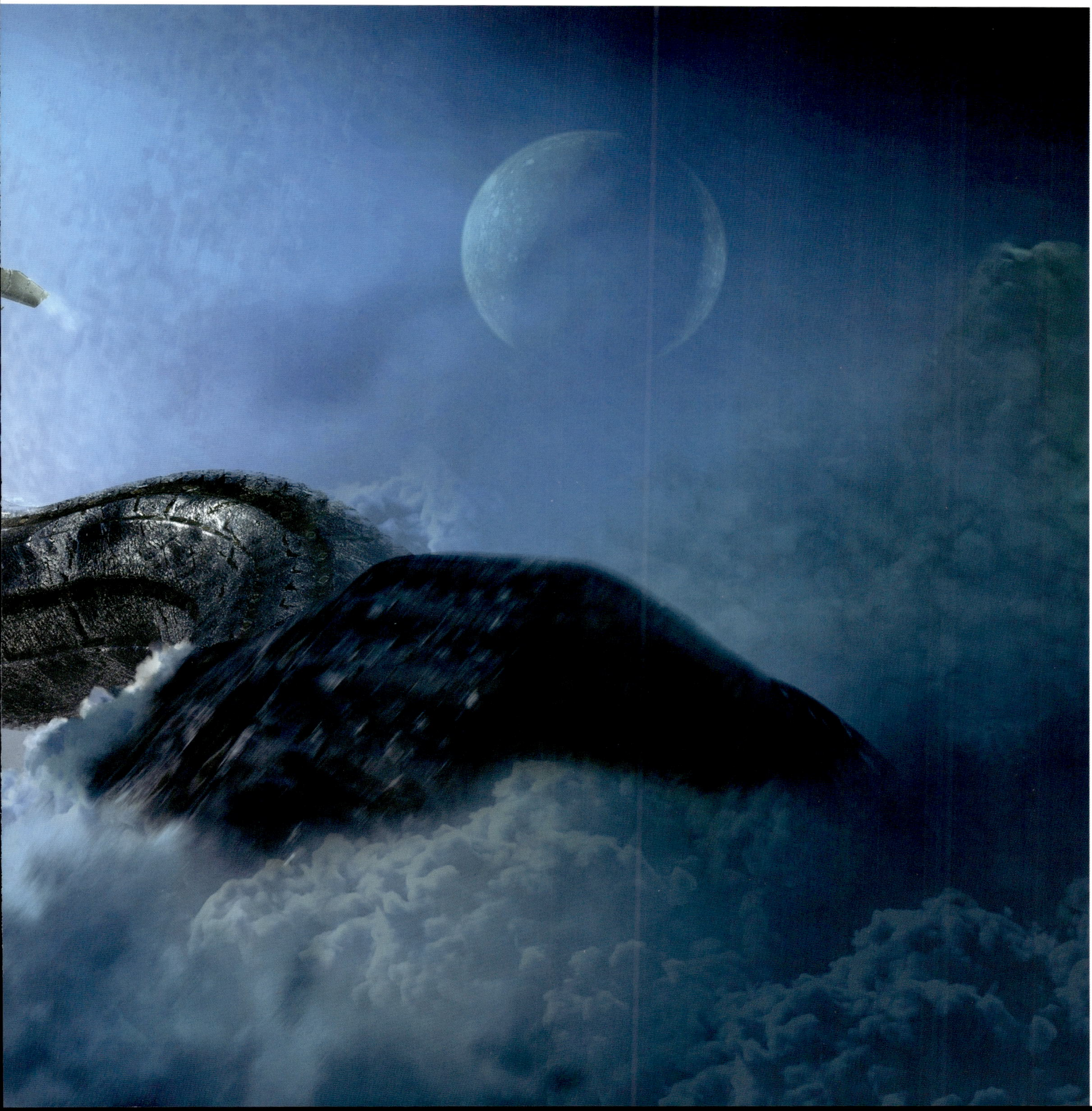

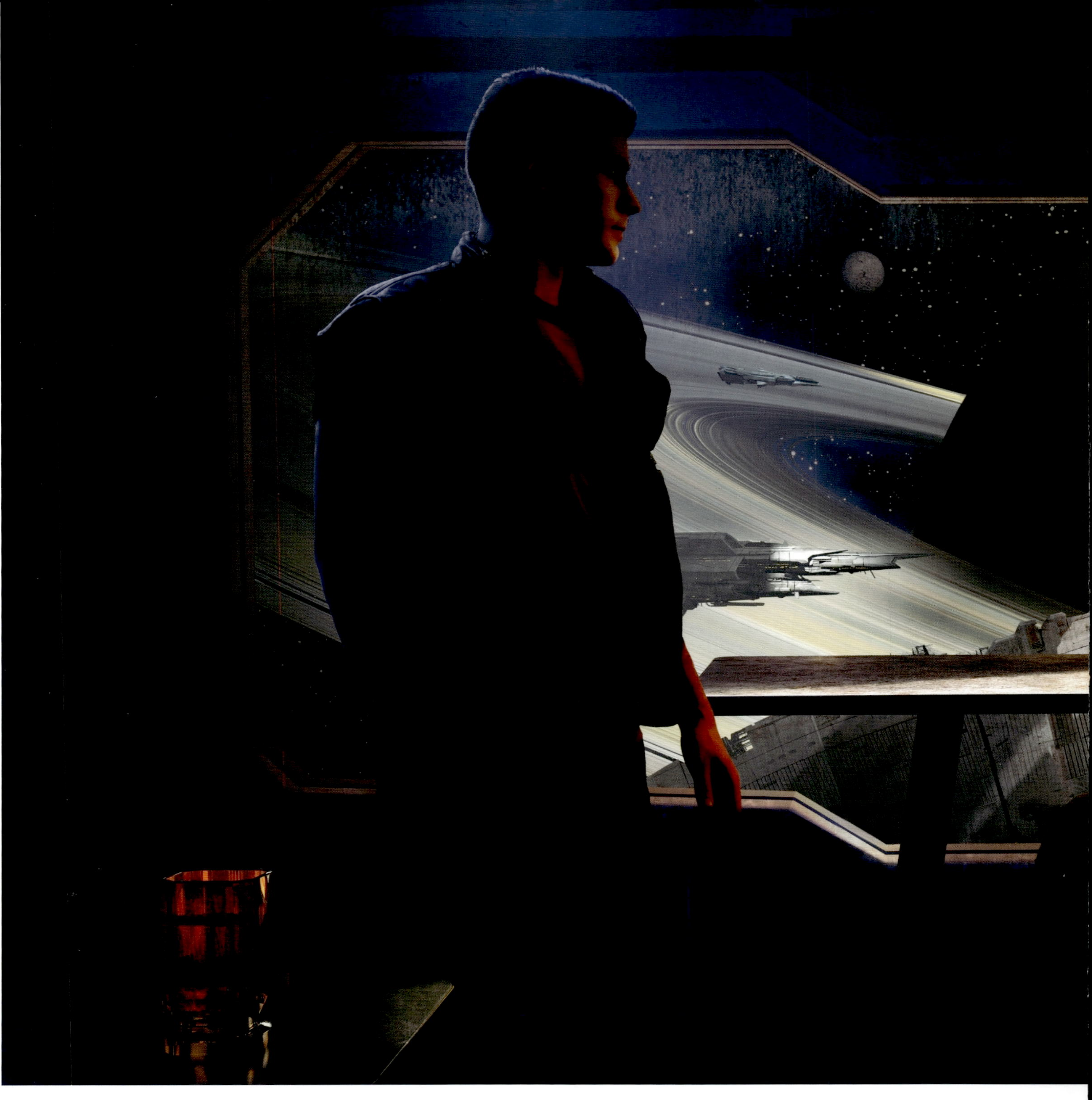

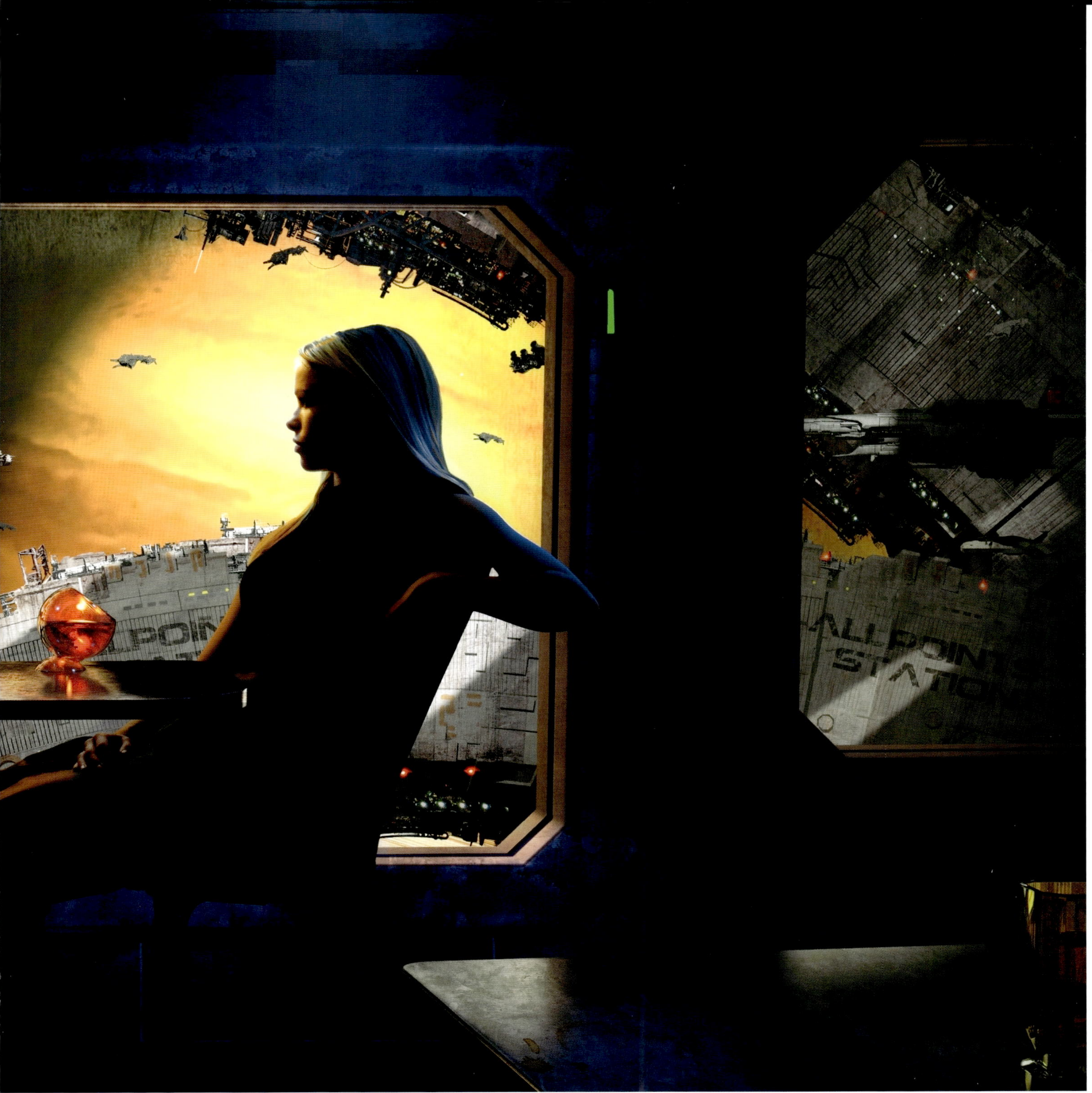

△ She is sitting seemingly in rapt concentration of the view outside, her single drink barely touched on the table before her.

A shadow crosses the table.

MALE VOICE.OS

Quite a view.

Breel continues to stare out of the window.

BREEL

I'm not looking for company. There are plenty of other seats free in the room.

A figure comes into view: he is athletic looking with short blond hair. This is Matt Harken-Court (32). He pulls up a chair and sits anyway.

Breel doesn't look round but continues to stare out at the concentric bands of ice surrounding the gas giant.

BREEL

What part of 'get lost' did you fail to understand?

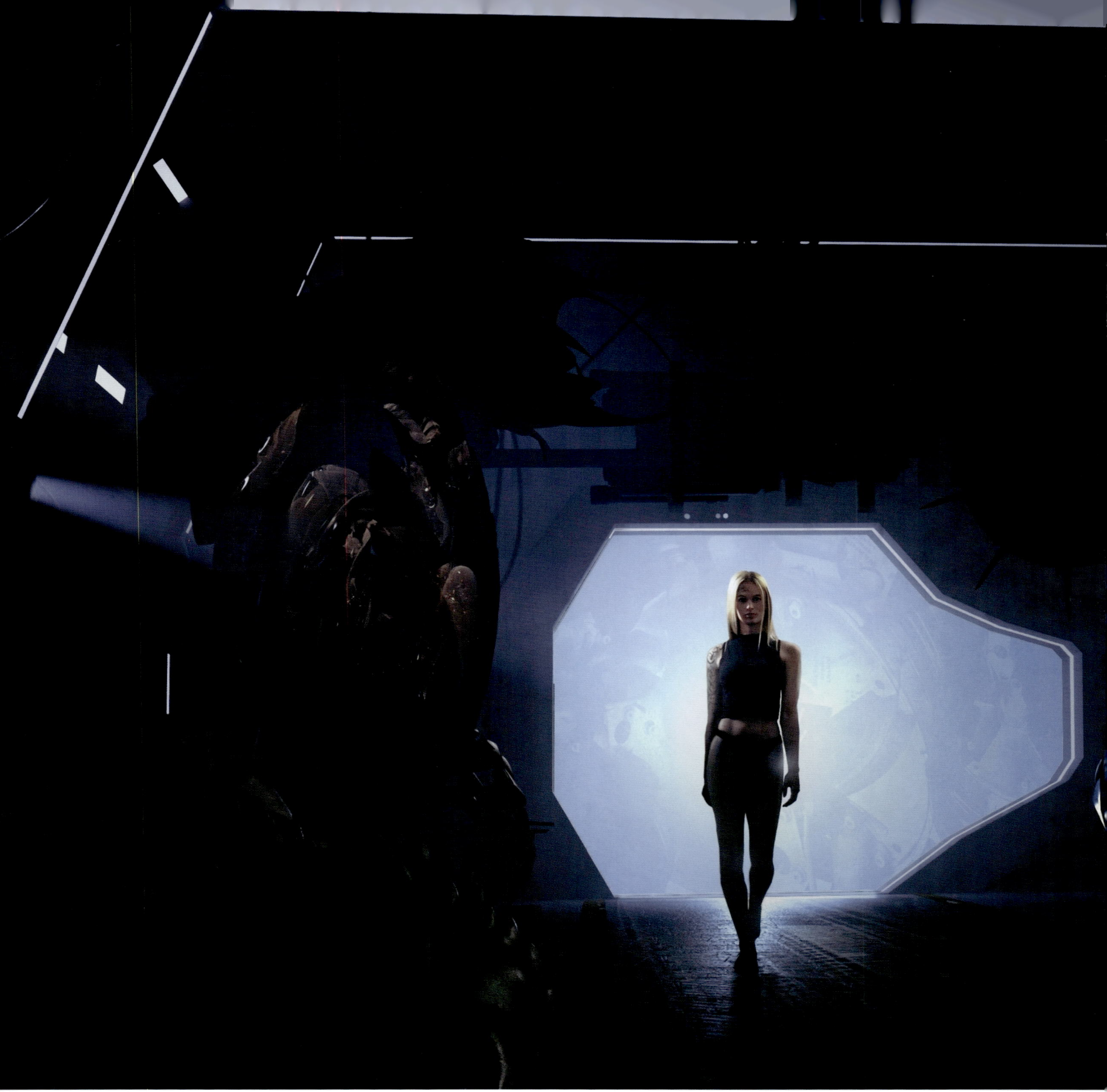

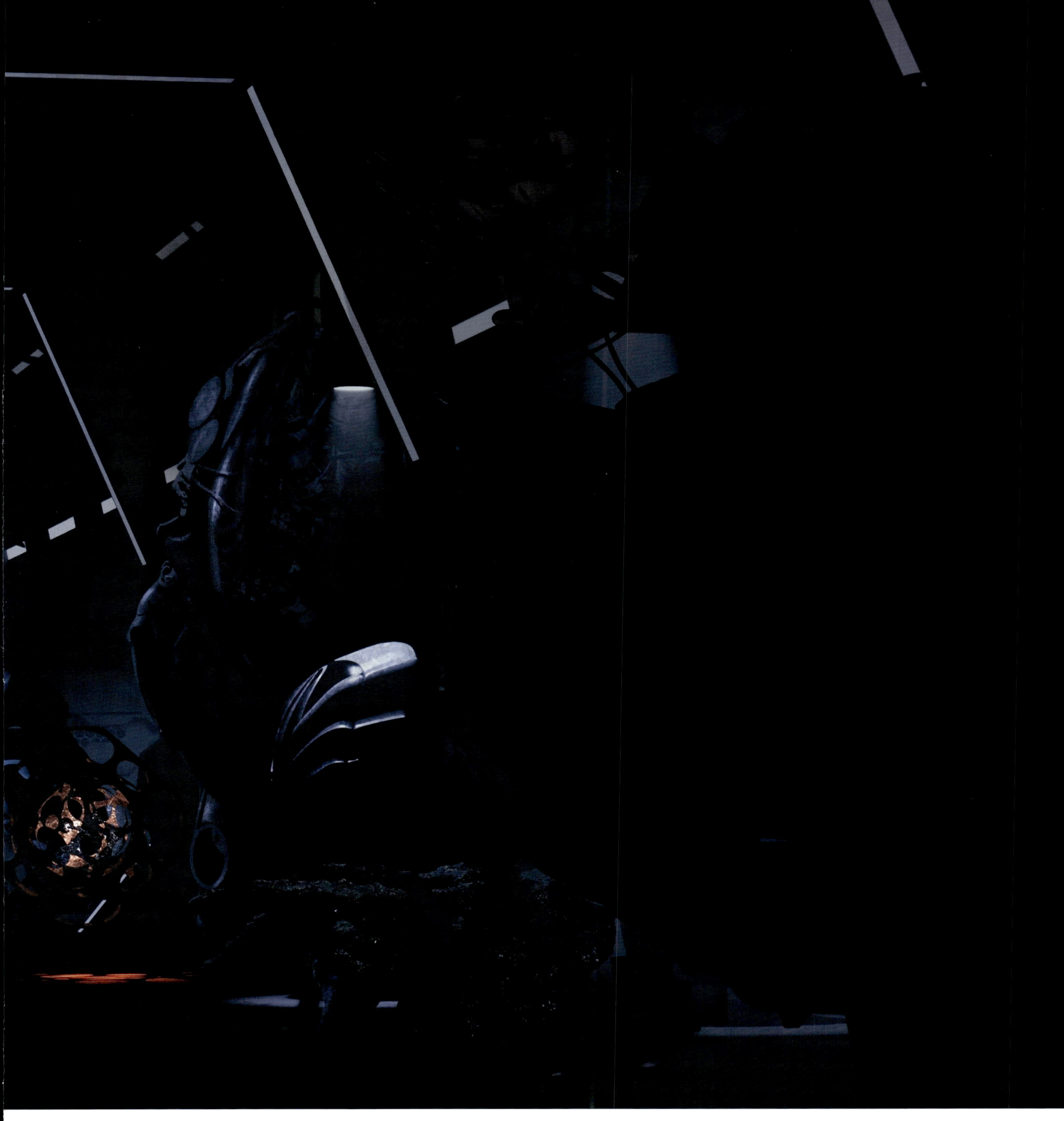

△ The bay is dark. As Breel steps into it, lights flicker on down its length to reveal a room about sixty feet long and about twenty feet high, divided into two storeys by a steel gantry. Both floors are packed full of strange equipment and vehicles. They are all neatly arranged and stowed and have a very different look to each other, as if they have come from many different design sensibilities and cultures. The space feels part storage area and part art gallery.

▷ Matt watches the crater pass beneath them. It's not pretty, a deep central cone like a Russian uranium mine, 'The Pit' houses the living quarters and main landing area.

The bright neon of the casinos and red light districts add splashes of bright colour to the tightly packed buildings in the shadows of the crater.

MATT
What a dump.

NEVIS
That's the pit. It's the best part of Asylum.

MATT
That's the best part? I'd hate to see the worst.

BREEL
Well that's unfortunate. We're going to the beach.

MATT
The beach? There's an ocean here?

BREEL
Not exactly.

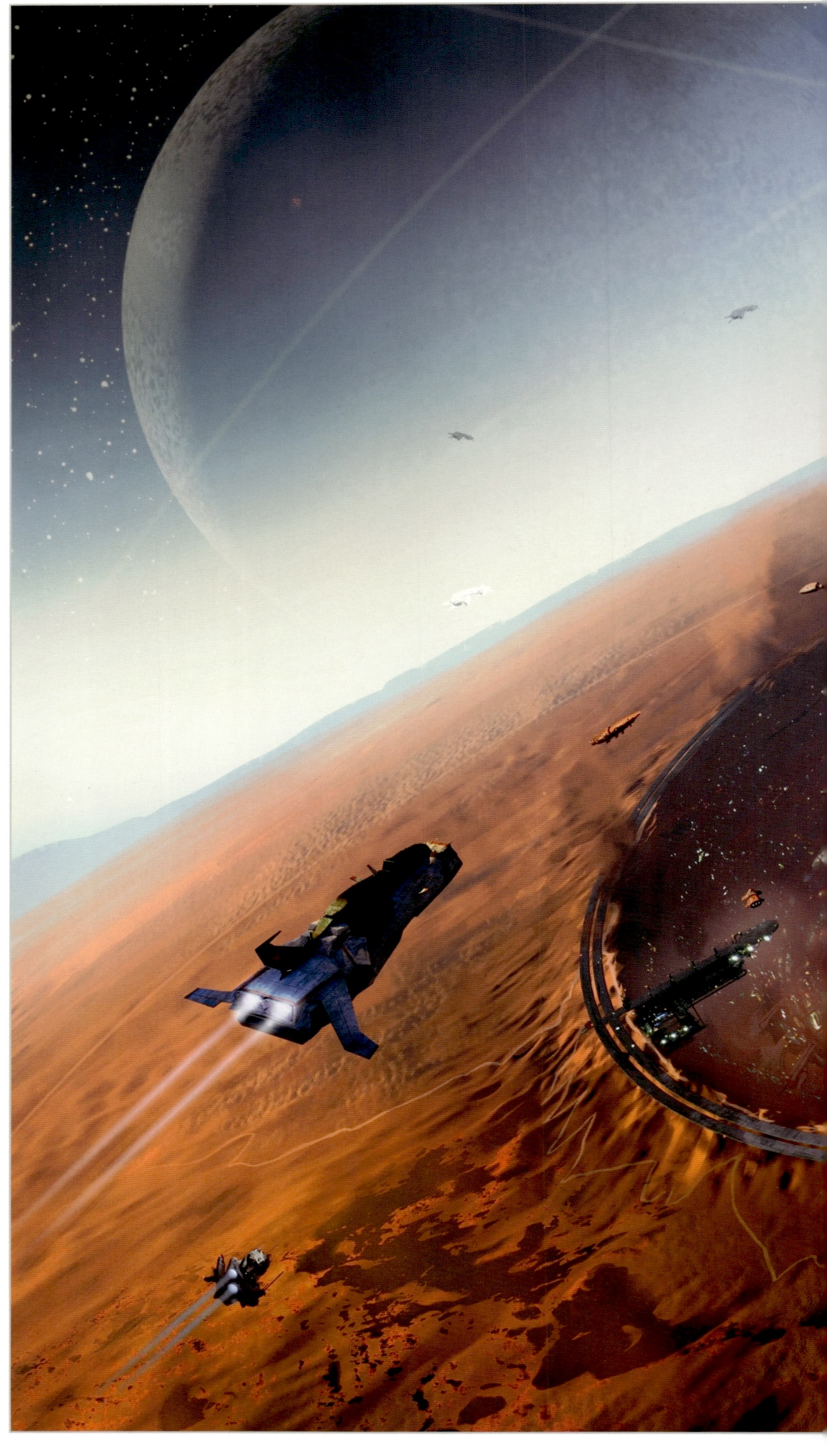

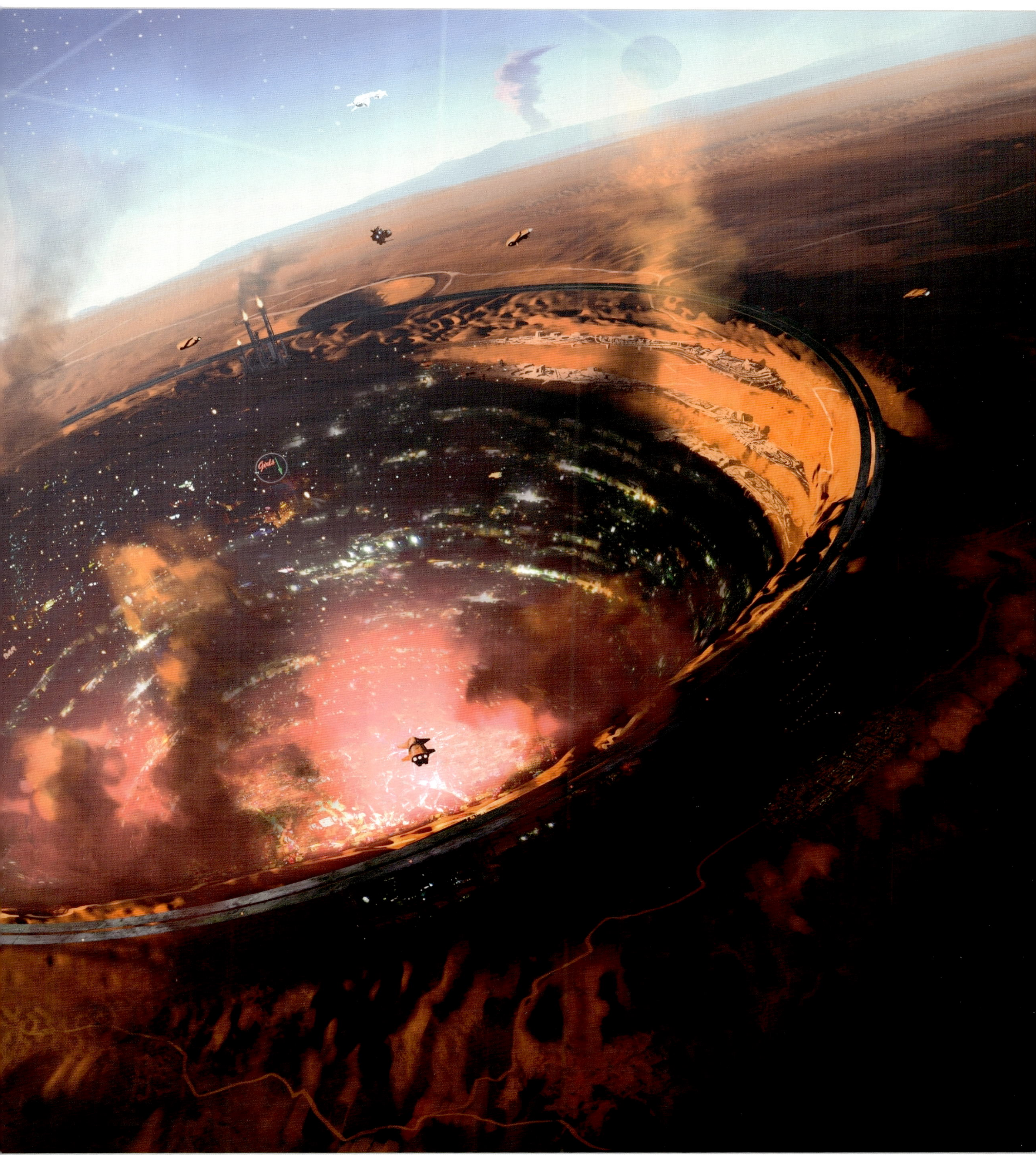

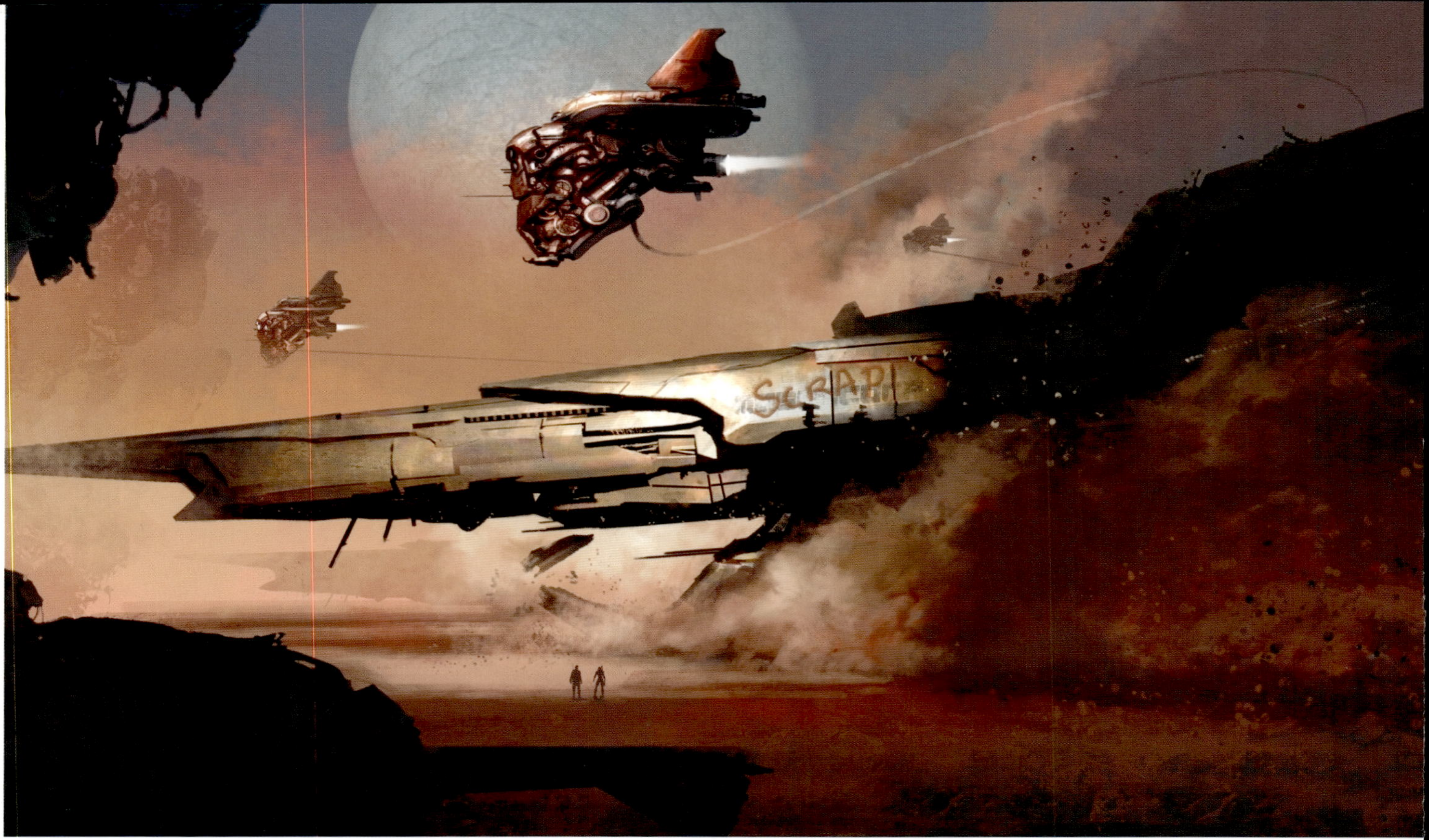

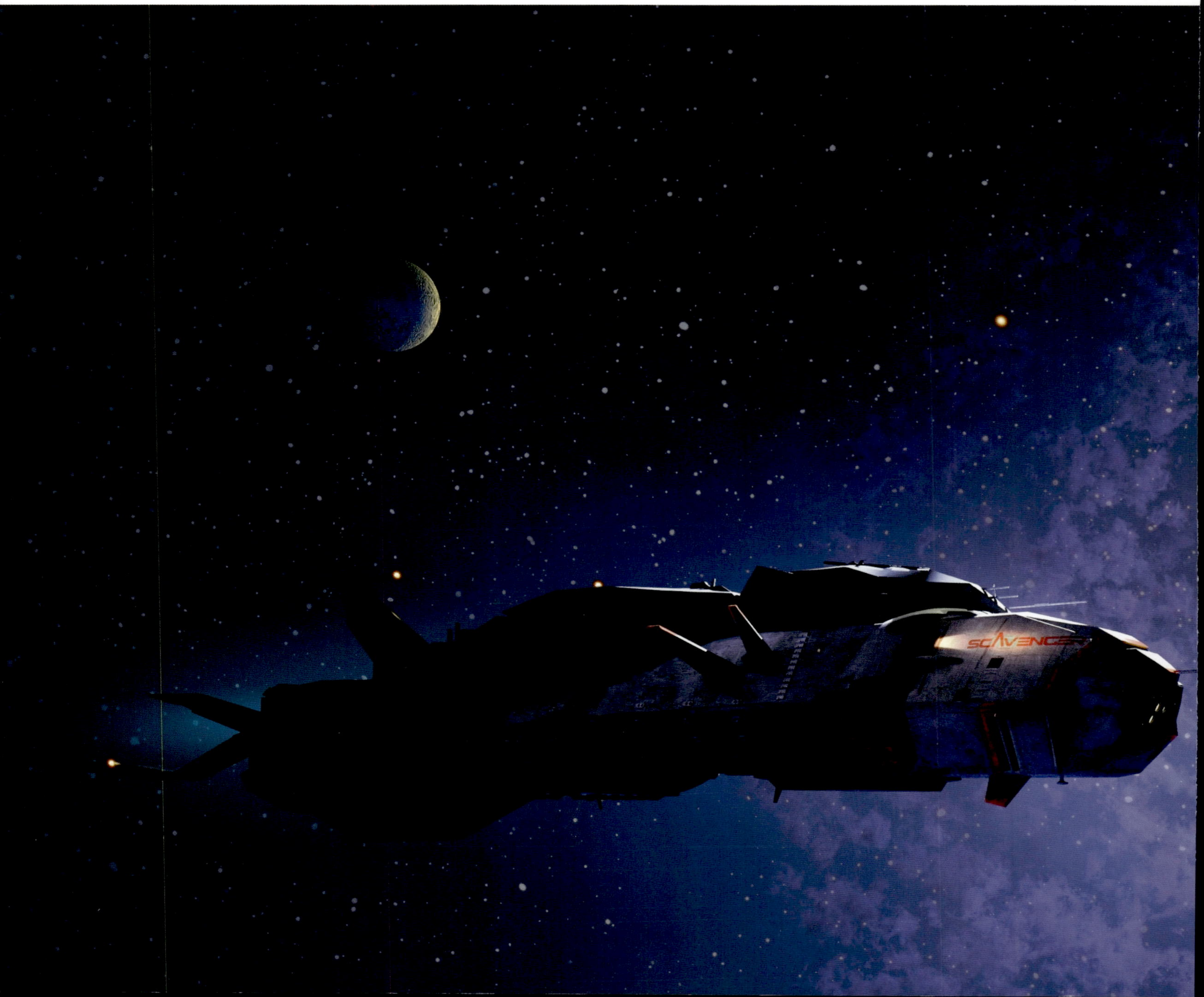

◁ The freighter is less than two thousand yards away, coming on like an express train. Nevis shuts off the systems in his tug and checks his seat harness, bracing himself.

The freighter is only a few feet from impact. The ship casts a shadow across the beaching area.

BREEL

Come on dad.

The freighter's nose hits at a shallow angle. Like a plough through heavy snowfall, the massive fuselage gouges rock and dirt from the surface.

The ship noses down into a belly skid that throws up a bow wave of dirt as she begins to scrub speed.

▽ Behind them, the blue smudge on the screen has expanded into a swirling mass of blue matter. A tremendous whirlpool with a hot blue-white centre burns as compressed wavelengths of light try to escape the fierce hidden object in the middle. An object without size but with infinite mass. A black hole.

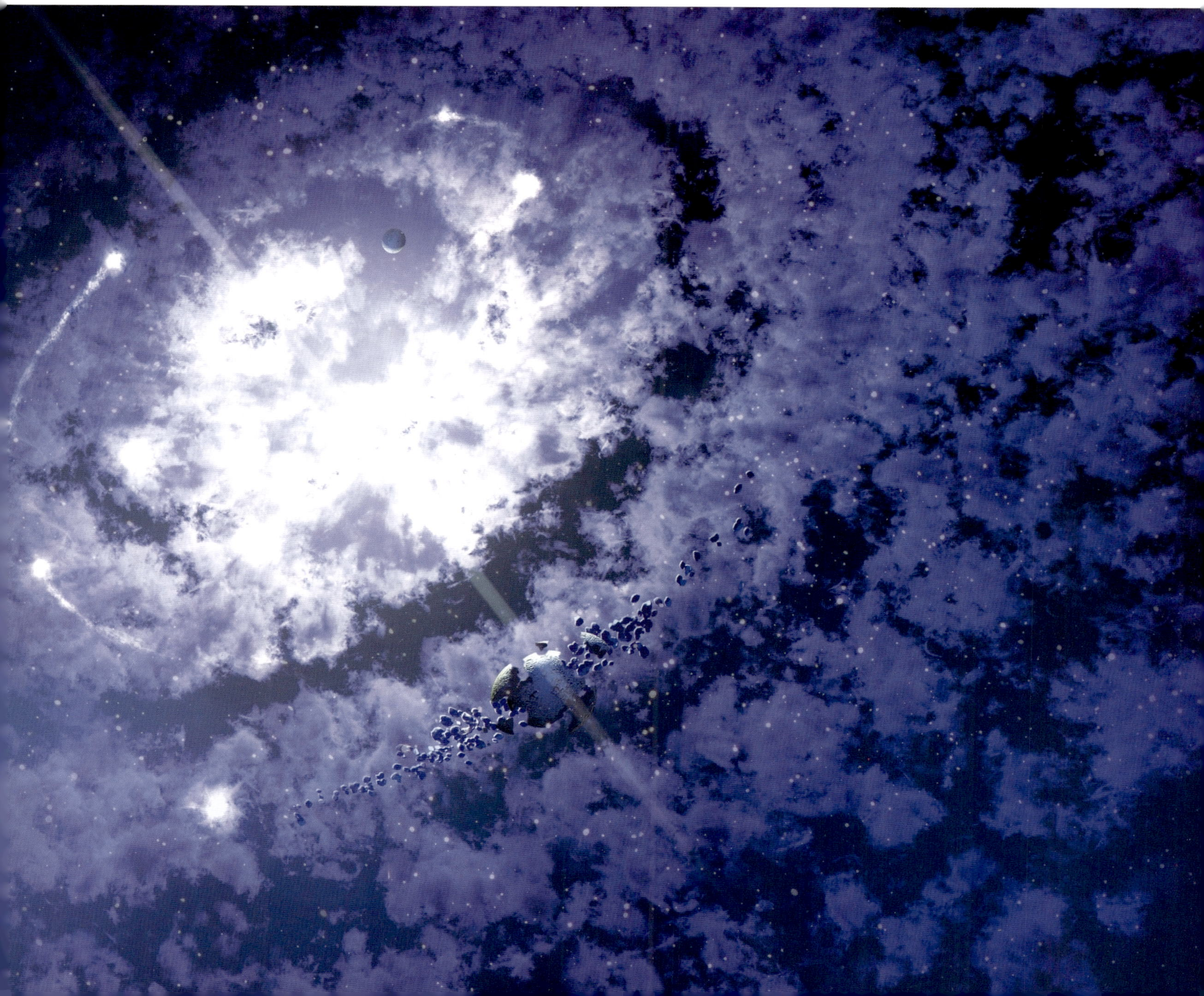

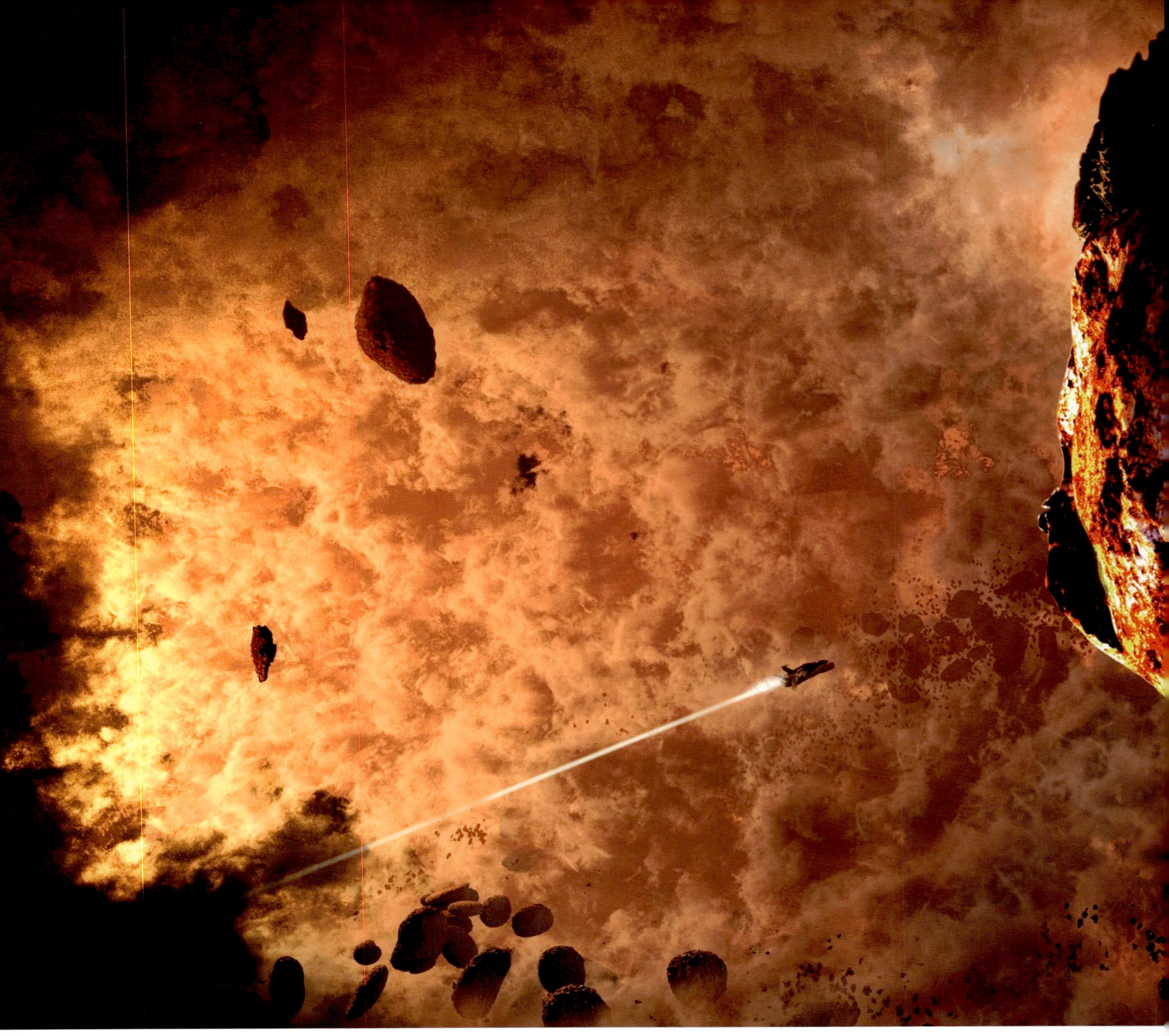

△ Ahead now, a truly ominous lump of rock, battered and twisted by endless collisions during countless millennia, its shadowed side etched black against the golden wall of the canyon. Every part of it is covered by the scars of massive collisions. Craters nestling within craters sit next to swirling rivers of one-time molten rock.

▷ Then, as the Scavenger moves around, the spindle the second ring comes more clearly into view – and this one is blue. The Scavenger's scope shows clouds, mountains and rivers wrapped around in an endless circle.

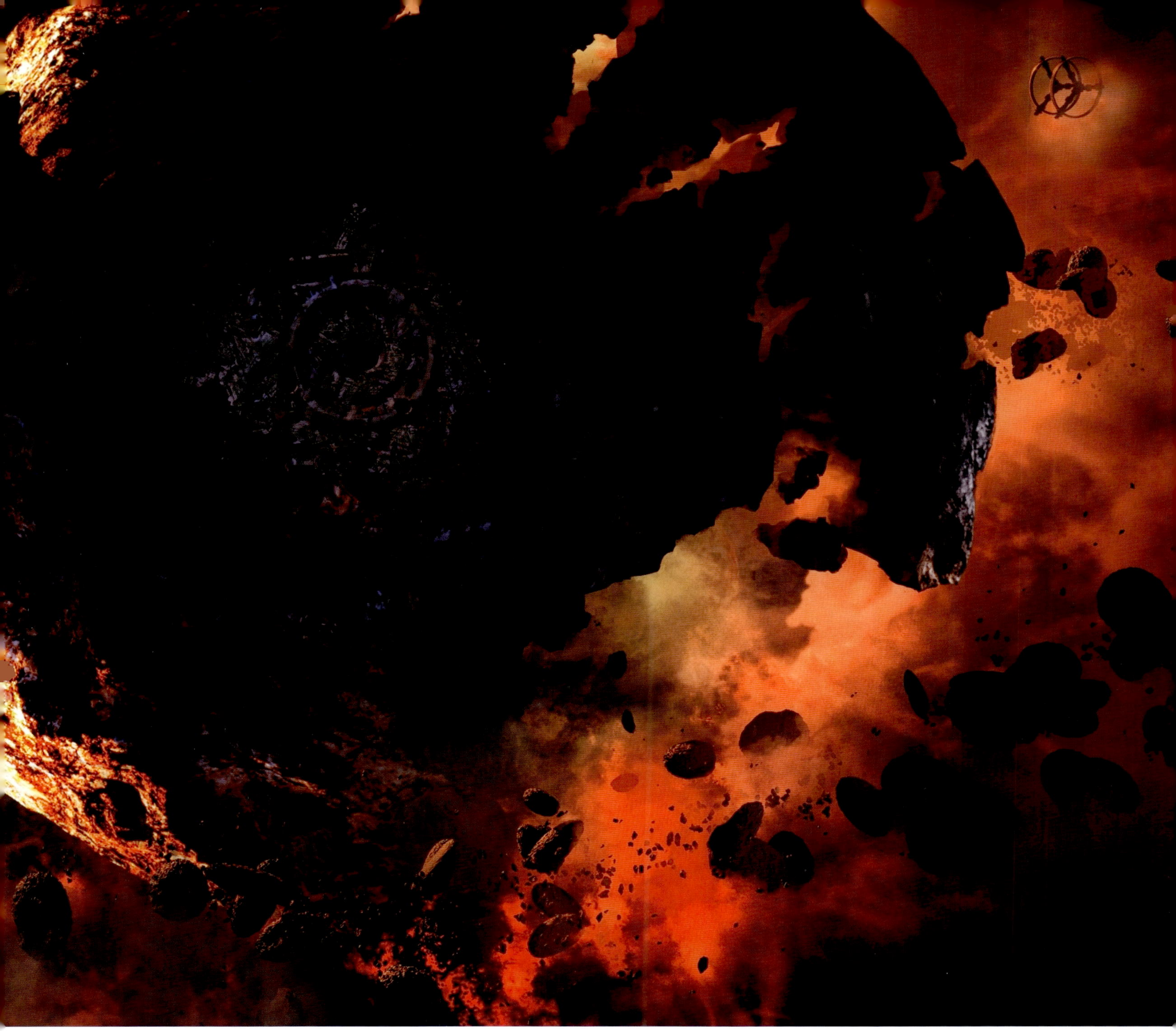

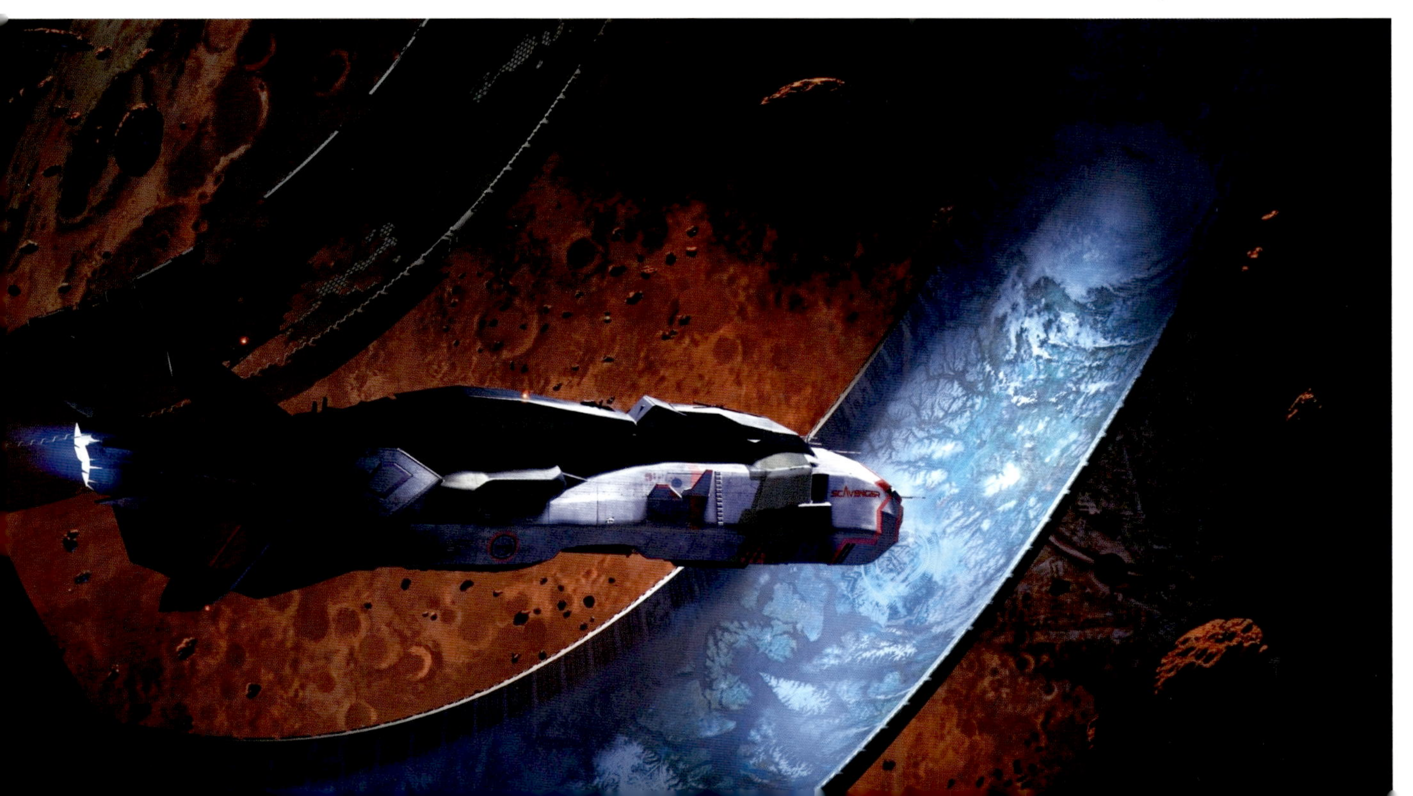

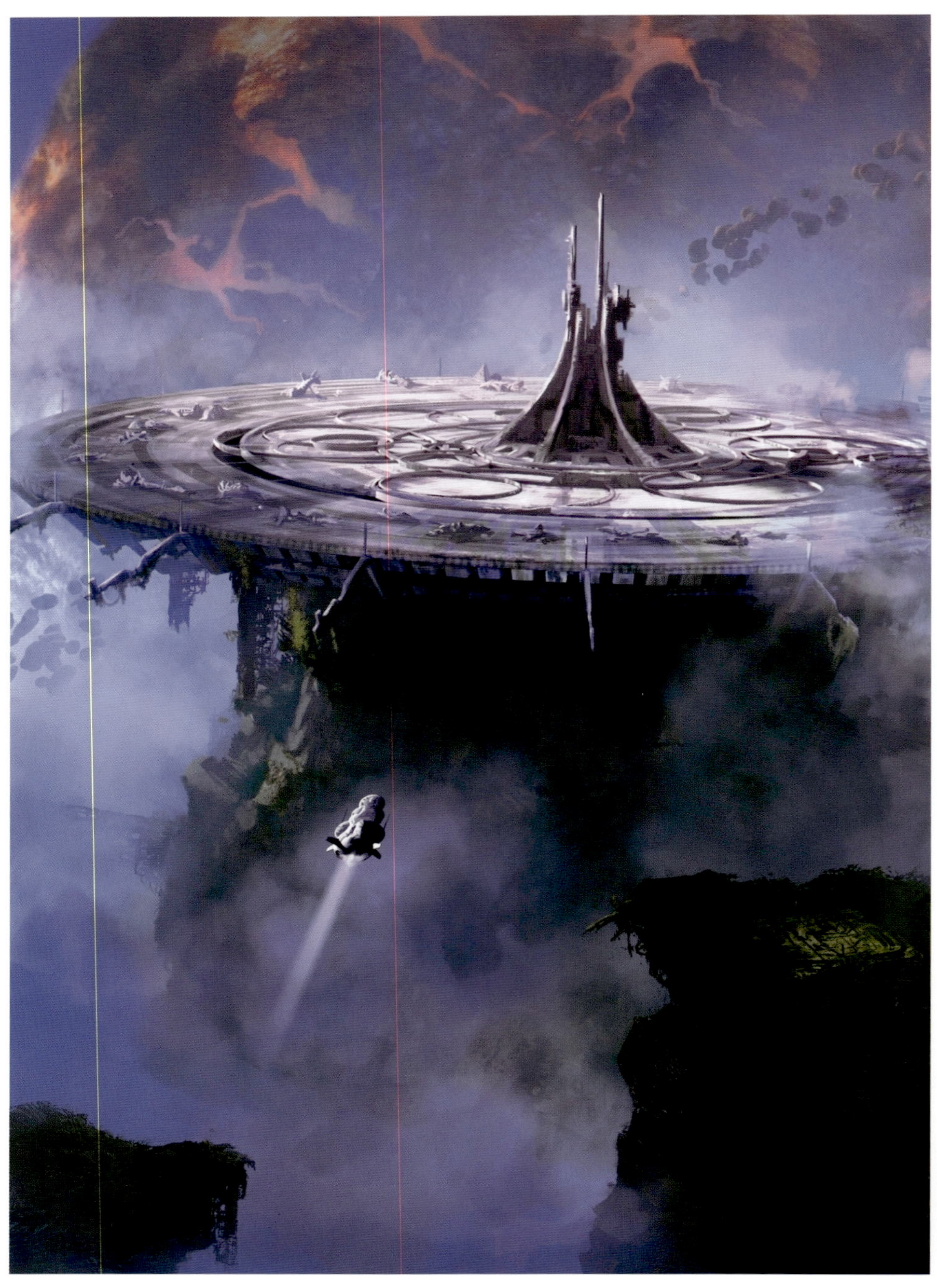

△ Below them a structure is fast resolving into detail: a huge alien complex, taking the form of a series of concentric rings. Around the structure is a massive apron of what looks like concrete, littered with alien ships and vehicles of all kinds.

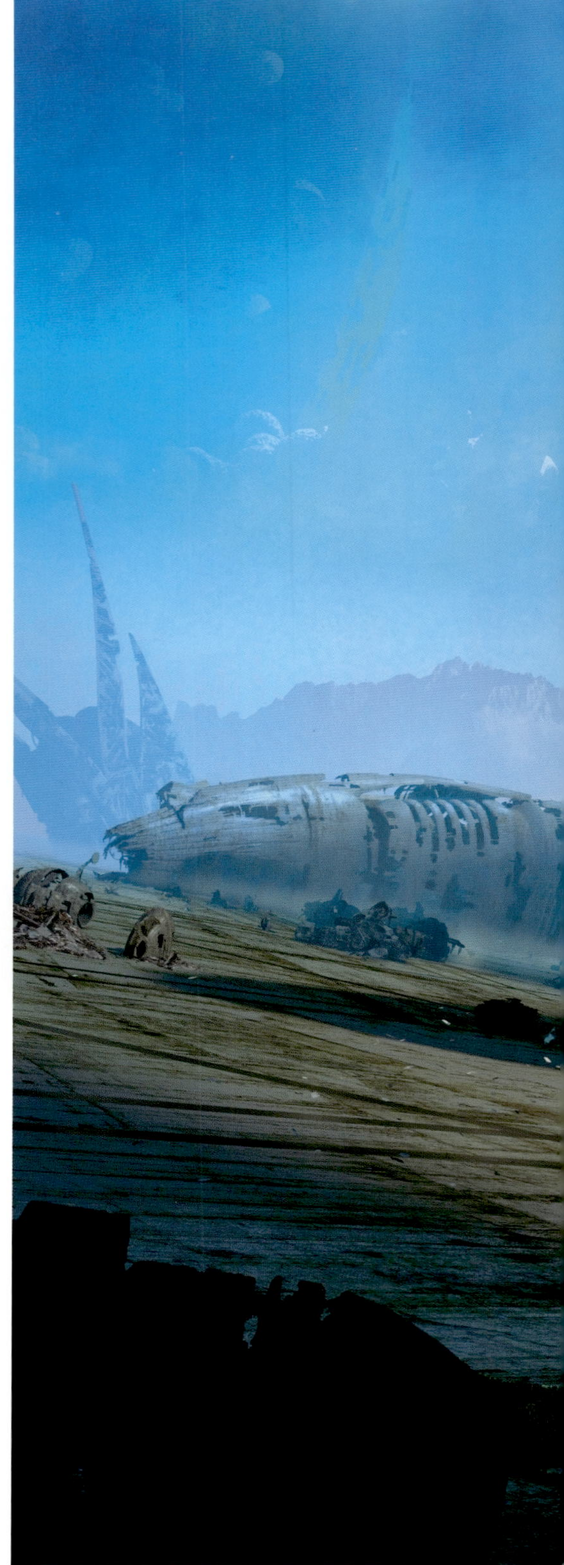

▽ A ramp at the rear of the Scavenger swings open and a wheeled vehicle emerges.

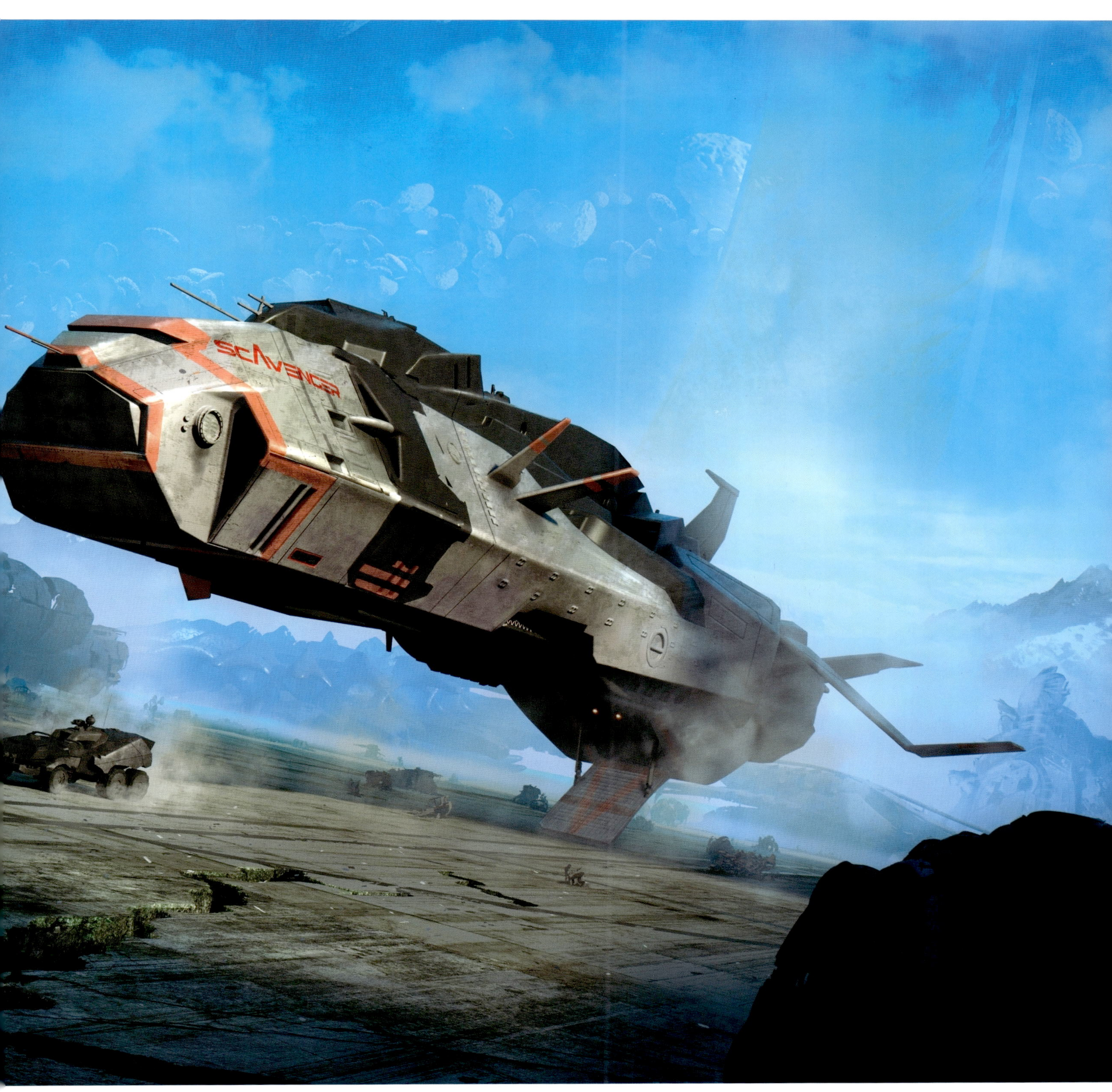

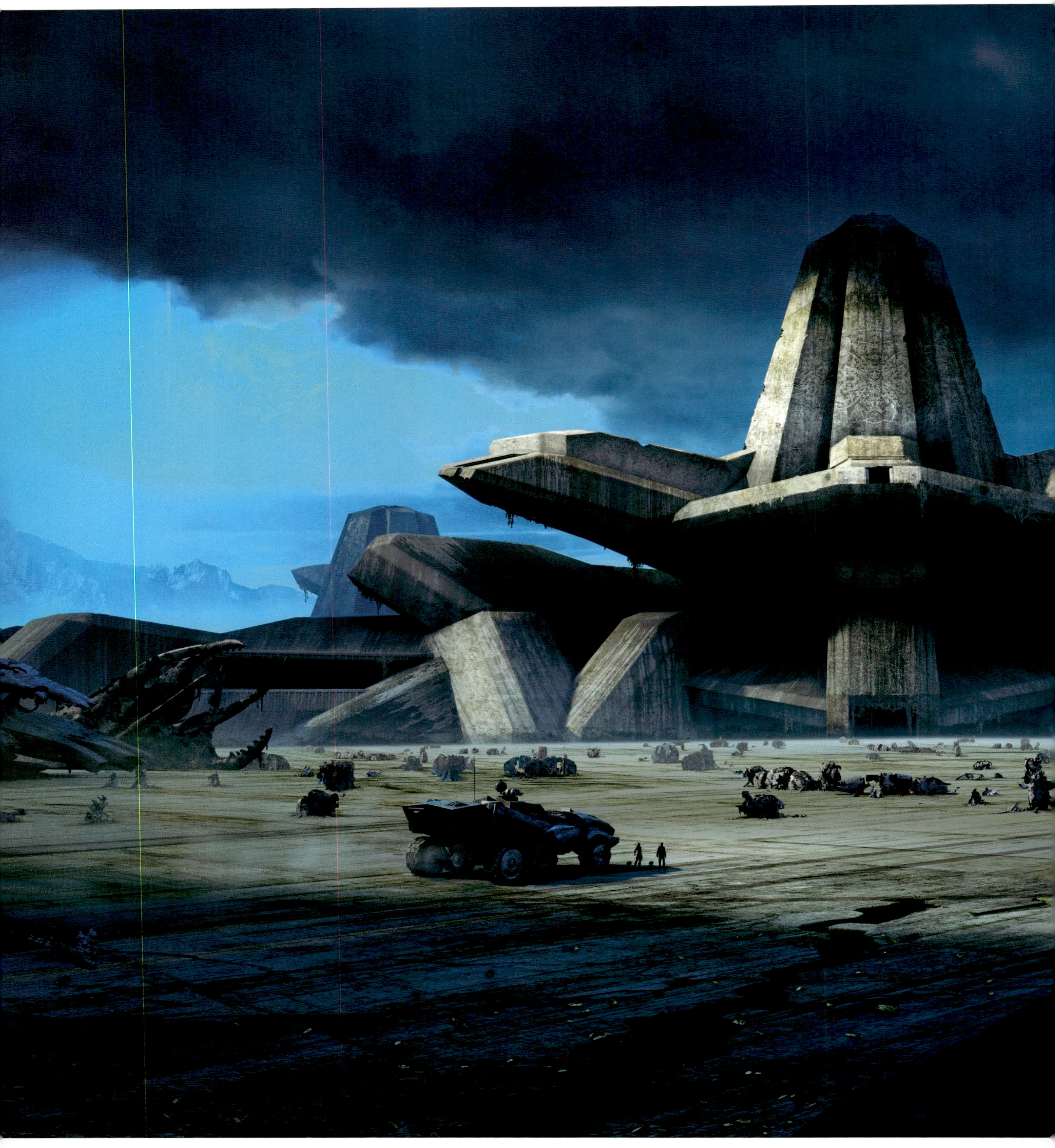

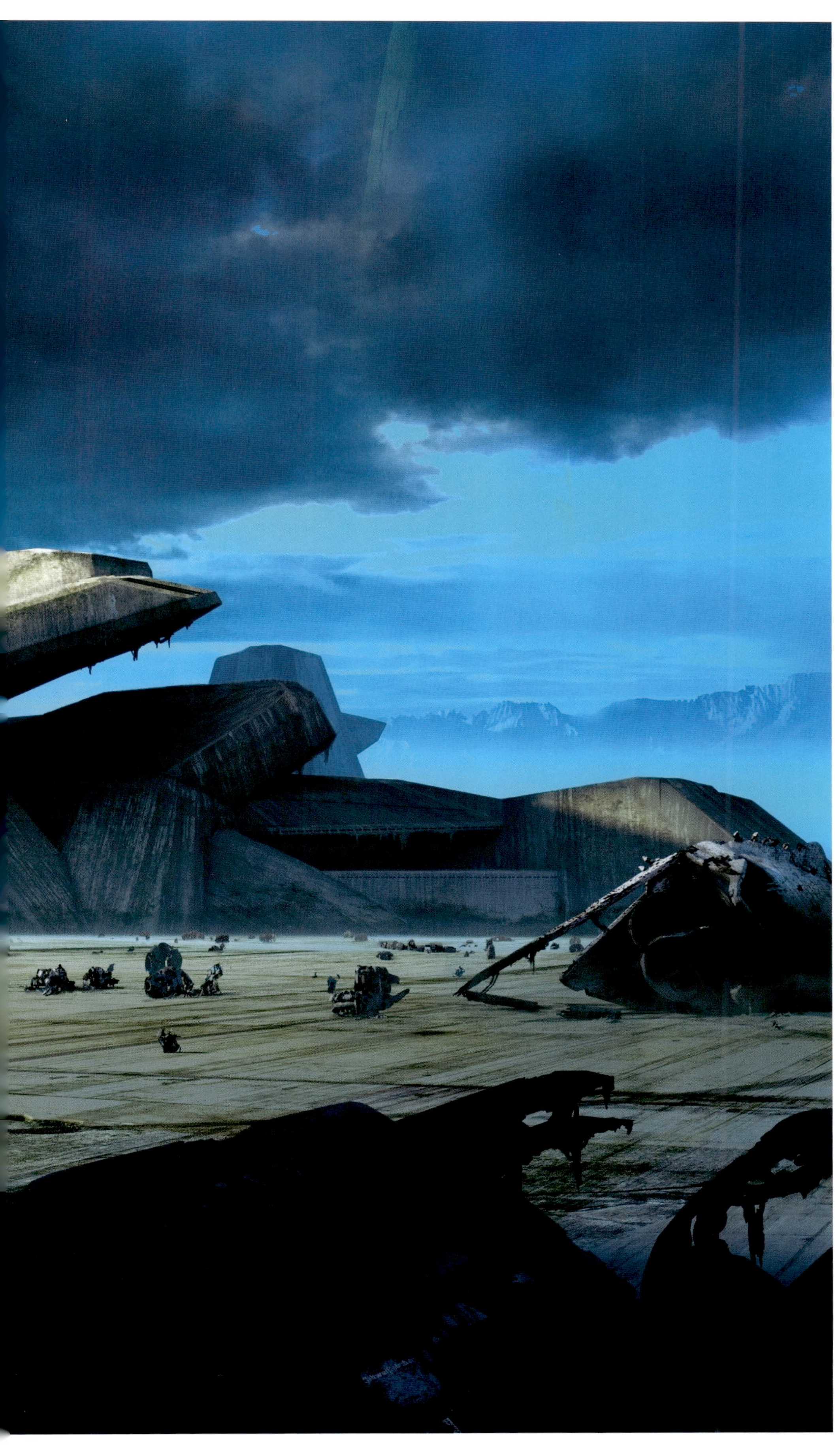

◁ They walk to the front of the vehicle and look towards the monolithic maze entrance. It sits there like a squat spider on a monumental scale. A large tapering tower rises from its centre.

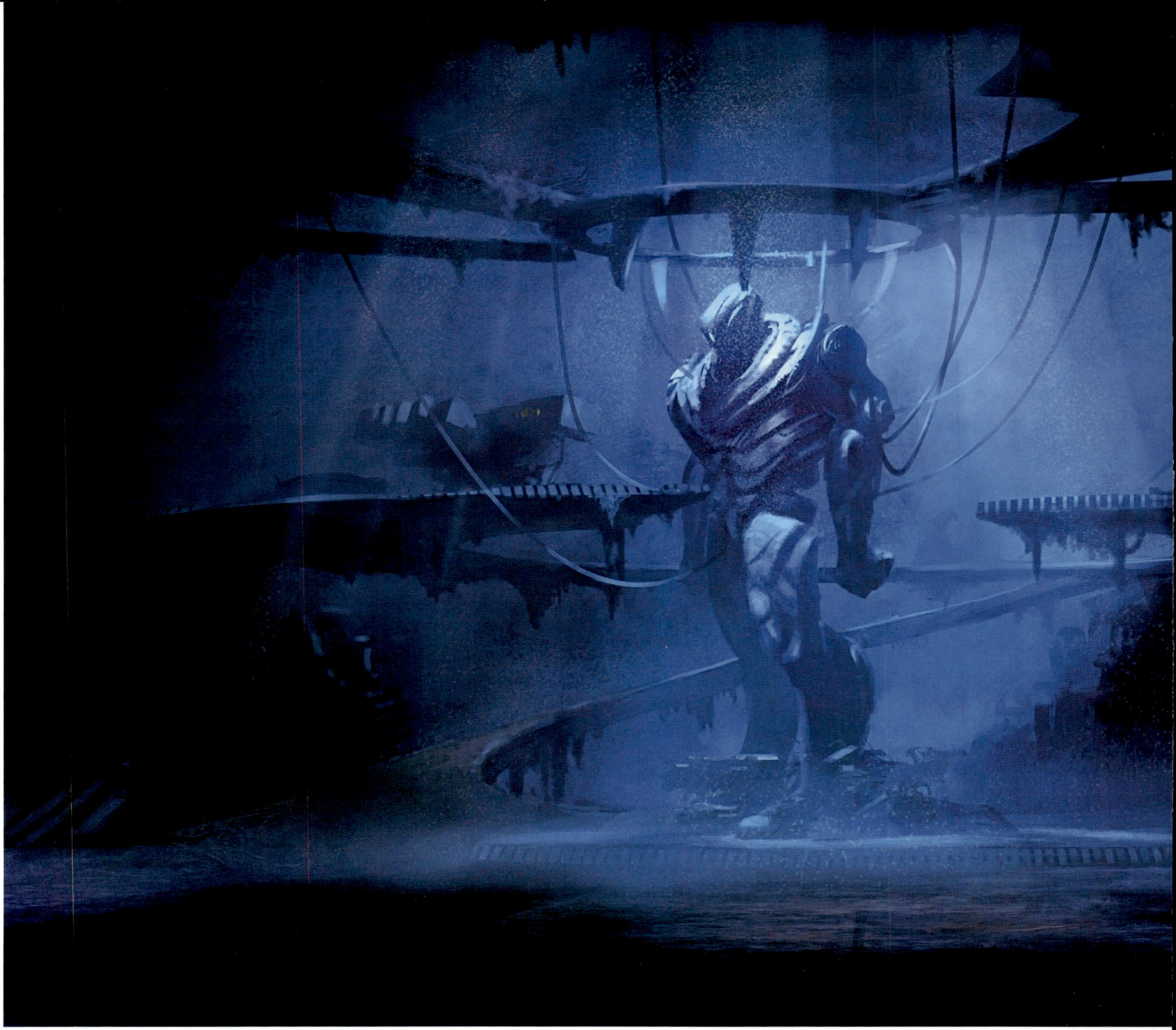

△ Breel has already noticed that one of the niches is occupied. Standing with head down on massive chest, hands resting loosely at its side is a huge mechanoid, roughly humanoid in form.

▷ The view pulls back as more and more ships arrive to join the fight. Light starts to pour out of the planet as it starts to break up under hundreds of sustained impacts. Spirals of atmosphere and debris thousands of miles high spin into space.

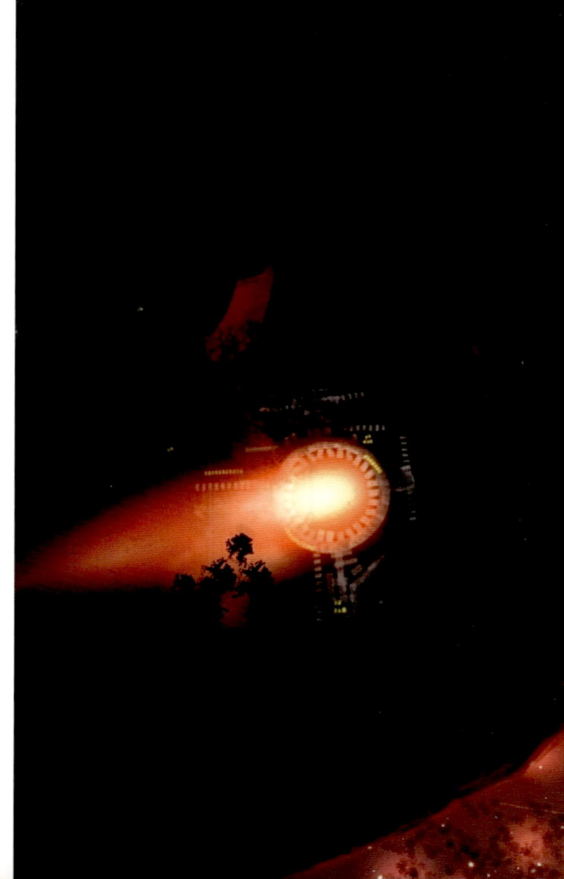

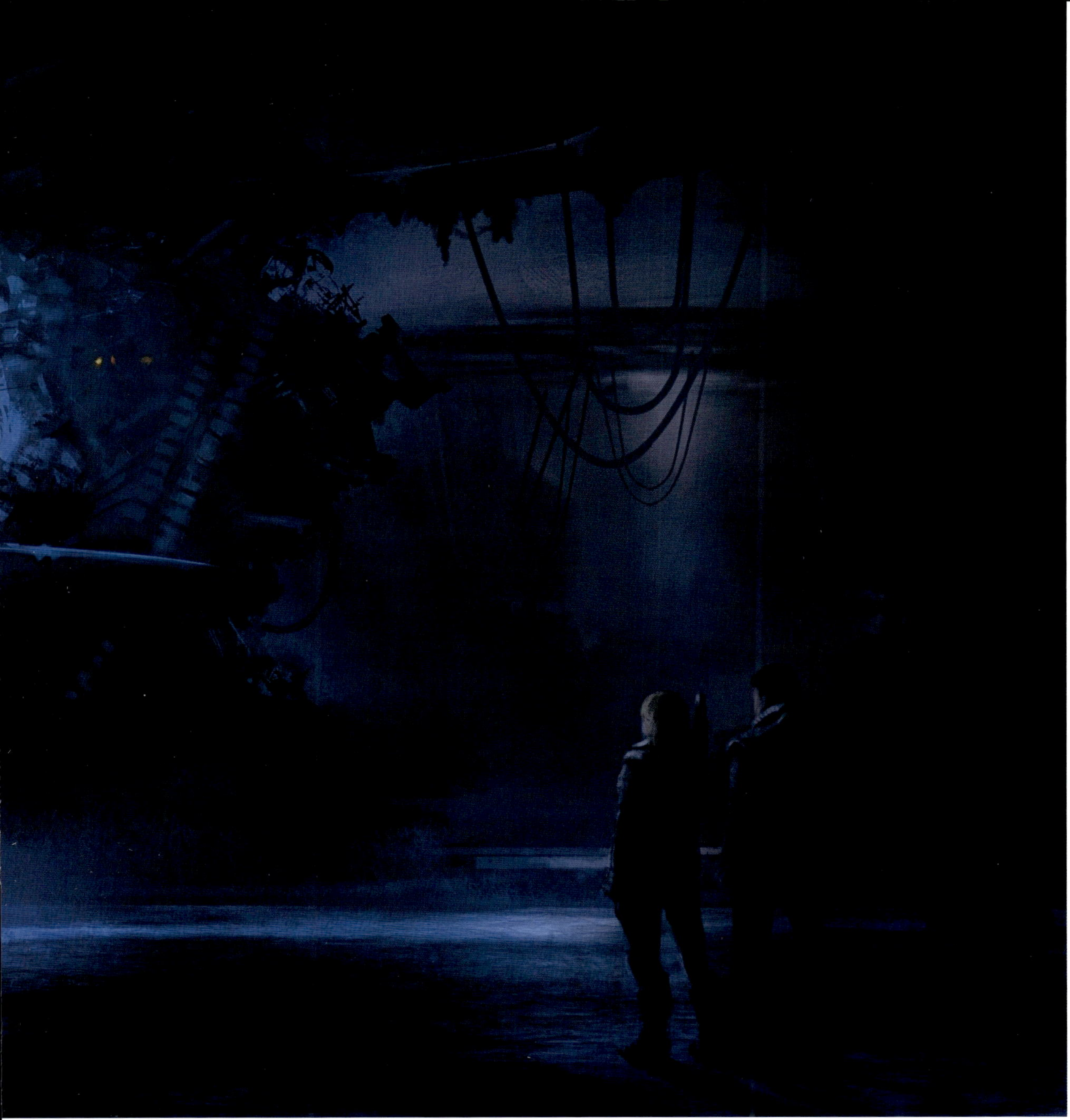

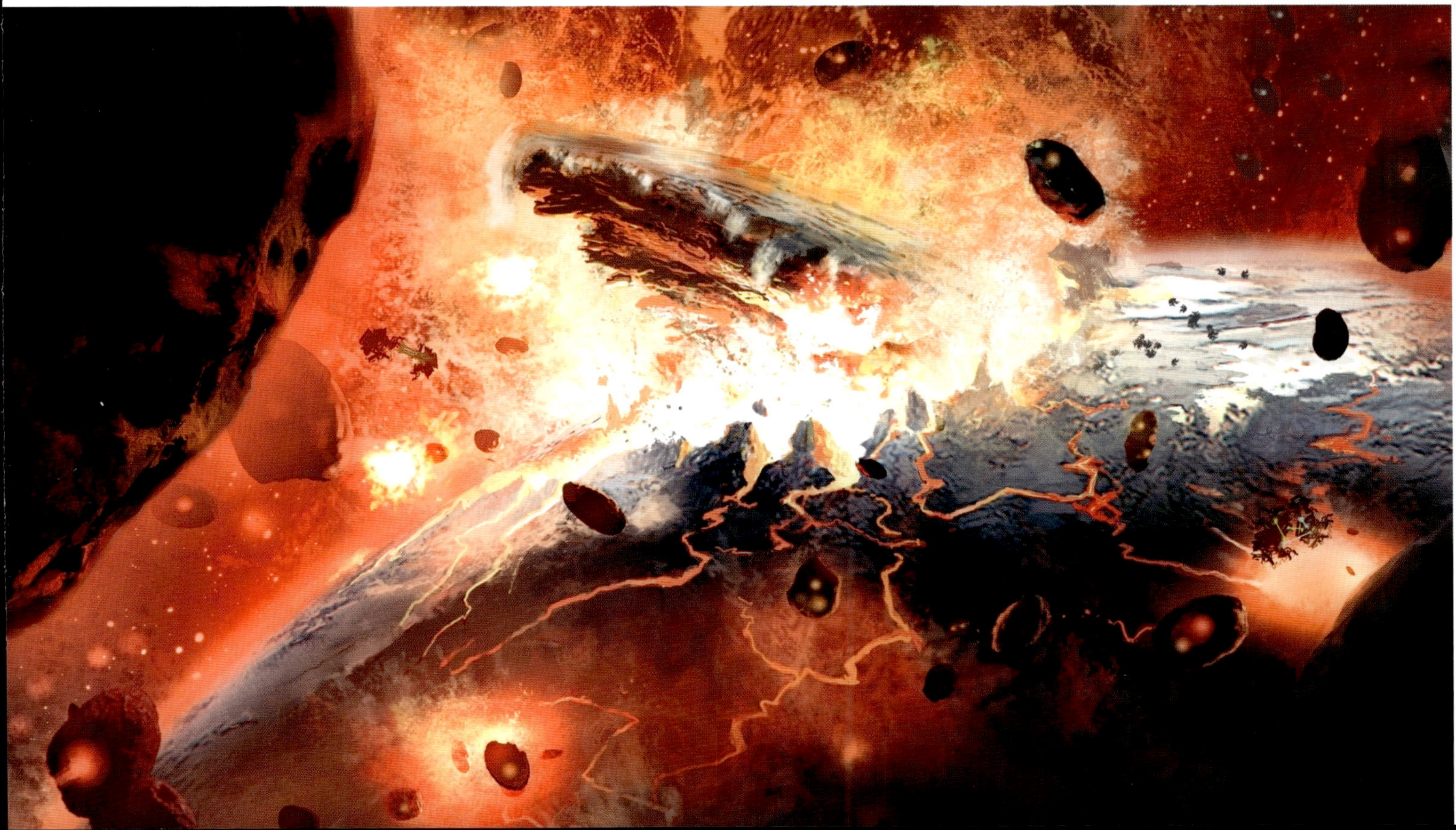

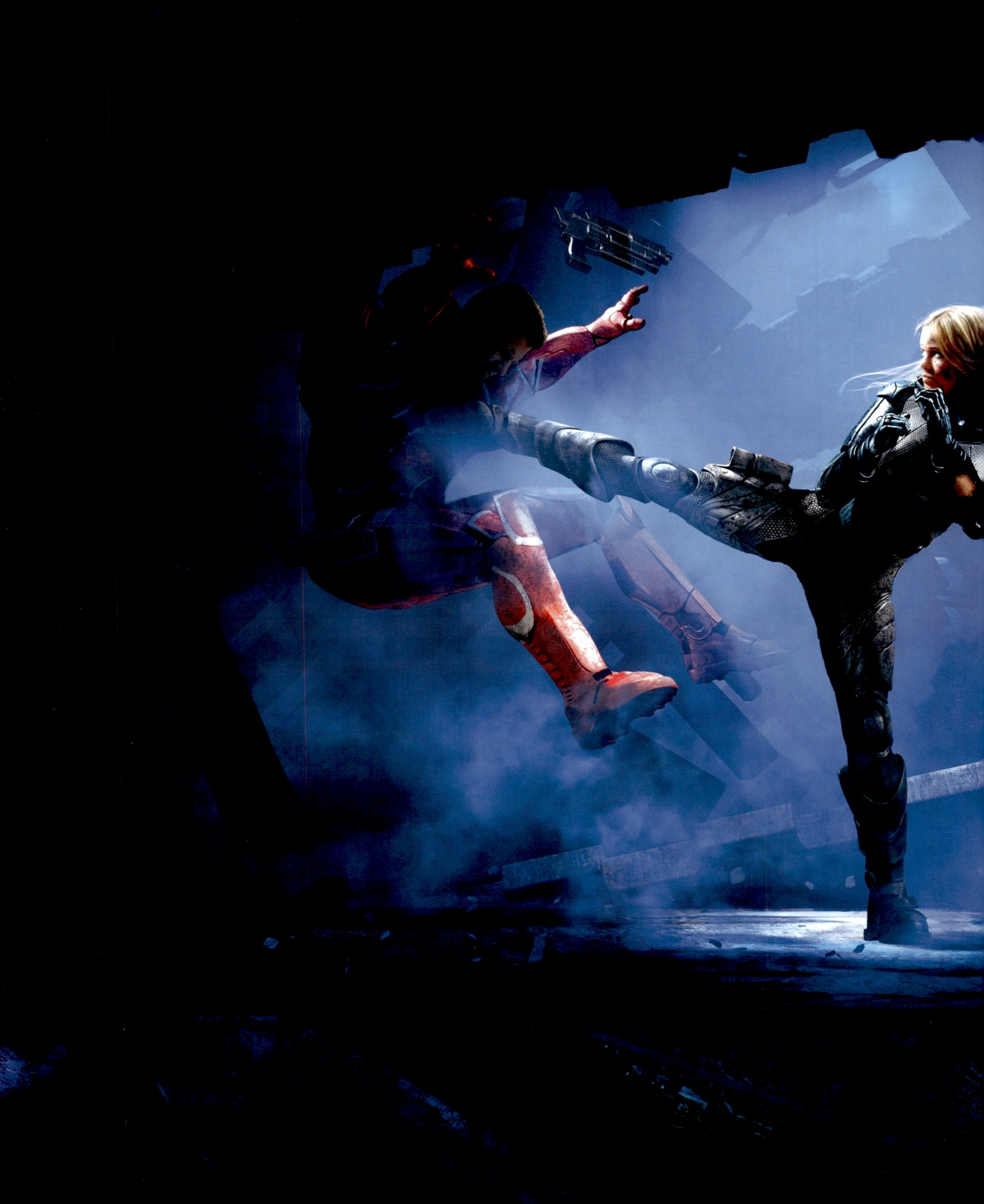

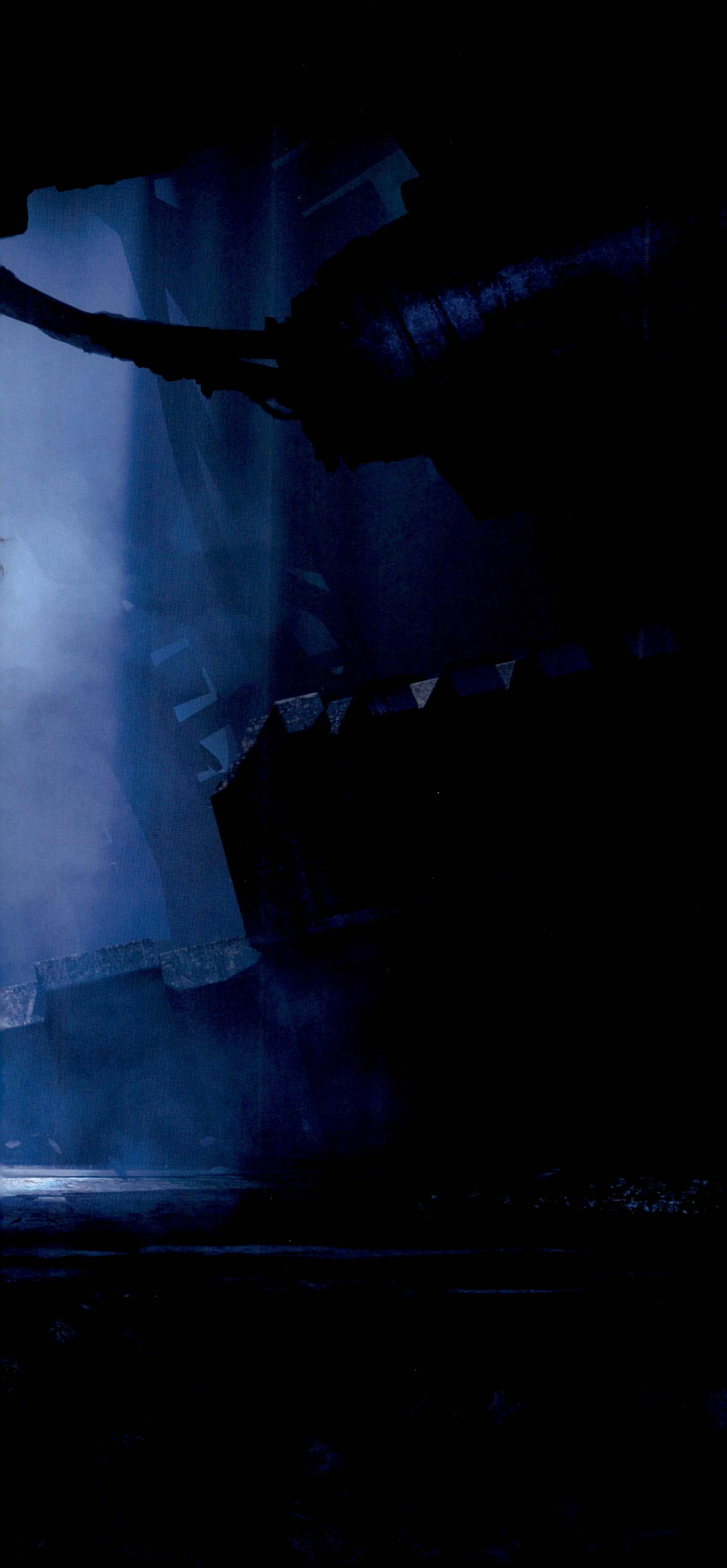

◁ Breel isn't in the mood for further discussion: she steps in suddenly and swings a blow. Matt blocks the first but three more hit home followed by a kick to his solar plexus that sends him flying back.

MATT
Had a little training, have we?

Regaining his composure, he steps forward, aiming a blow to the side of her head. Breel blocks and follows with a palm heel to his solar plexus. The servos in her suit whine as they multiply the impact of her blow, making him stagger back despite the protection of his own suit. As Matt tries to regain his balance, Breel aims a kick to the side of his leg, just above the knee. The impact, again multiplied by the servos in her suit, causes Matt's leg to give way, whereupon Breel spins around and lands a spinning back kick on his temple. Matt's reflexes are good, he manages to lean back enough to reduce the impact to a glancing blow. He lands on his backside at the foot of the ruined ramp. He isn't smiling now, shaking his head to clear it. Turning, he vaults up the slope of shattered metal onto the platform. With a final leap he reaches the control deck and puts his hands into the interface.

MECH

What do you think you can achieve? Without my help, you will never leave. If you kill the girl, you will never leave.

MATT

Names will never hurt me, make your choice. As you say, I have nothing to lose... either way.

The mech's weapons systems move in deployment, Matt flinches involuntarily and Breel seizes her chance: she twists free, the metal shard leaving a bloody trail across her neck. Matt throws himself backwards as Mech's weapons open up, turning the area where he was standing into molten ruin. The smoke clears: there is no sign of Matt, but Breel is lying in a crumpled heap.

Mech turns and moves towards her. Human eyes and alien sensors meet. Mech's weapons deploy. Breel closes her eyes and waits for the blast. Almost too fast to follow, Mech scoops her up, his weapons discharge upwards and a gaping hole appears in the roof just as he leaps into the air. Breel finds herself cradled in his arms flying past the glowing red hot edges. He lands just outside the complex and another bound lands them at the Scavenger.

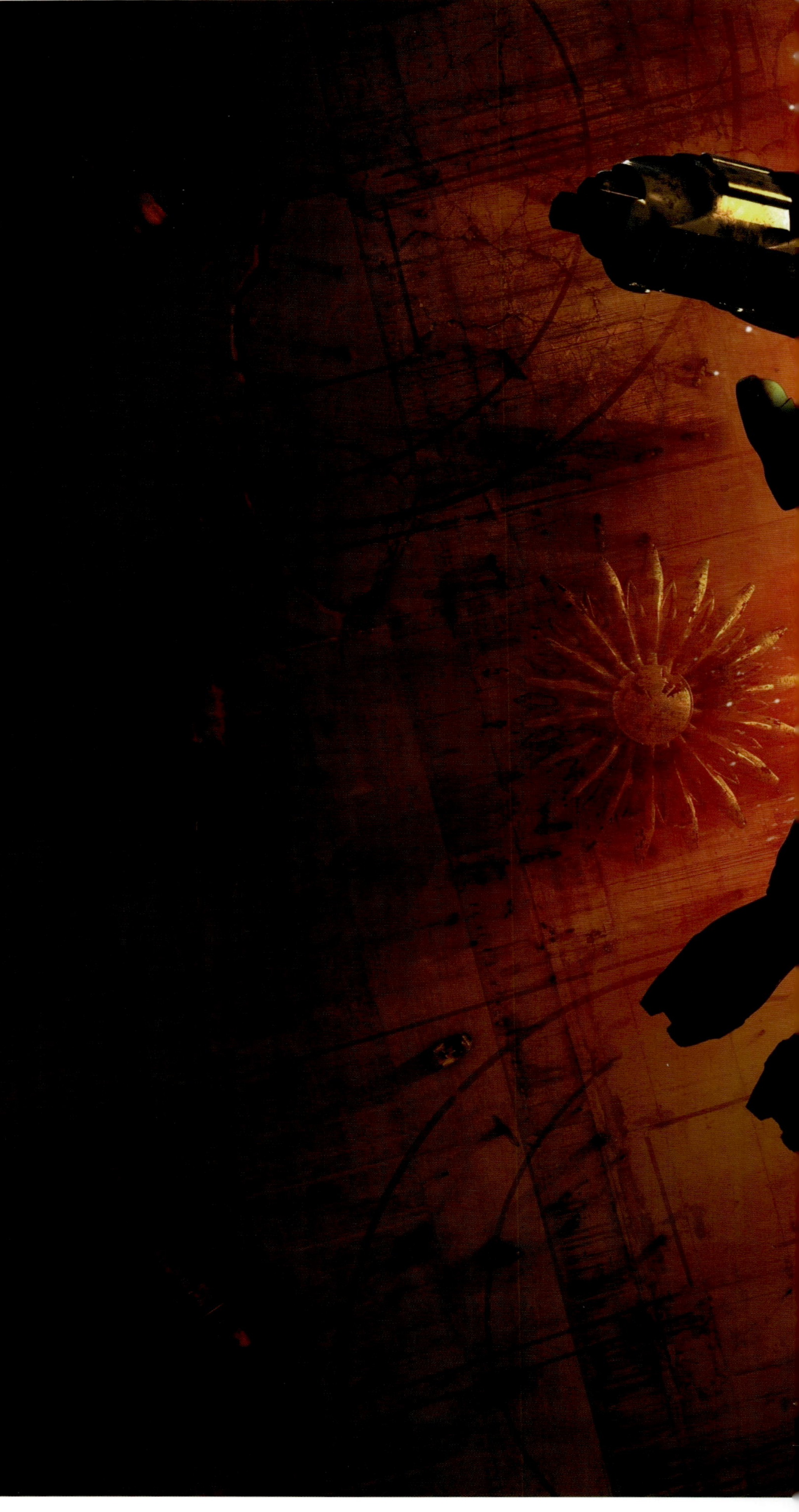

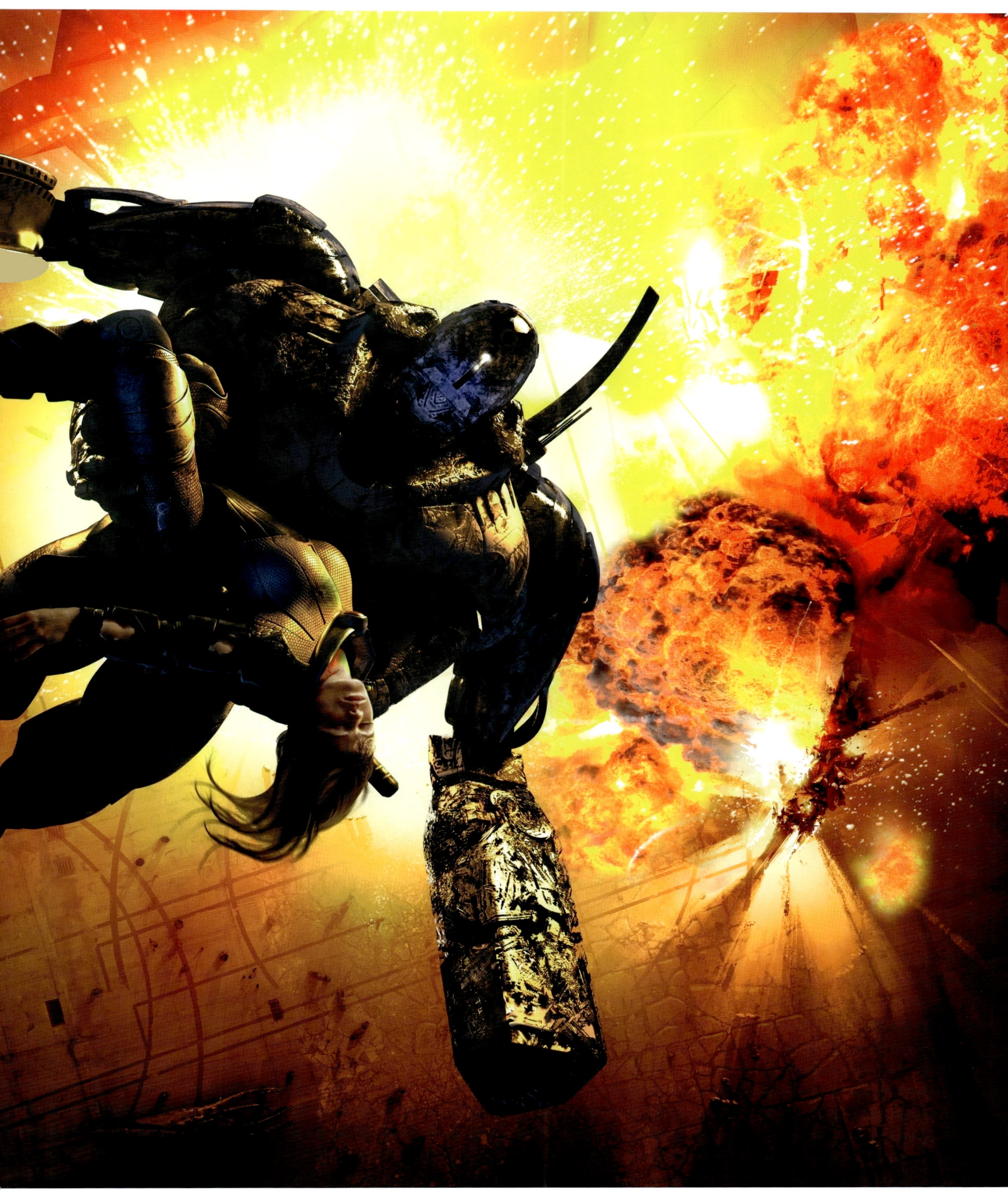

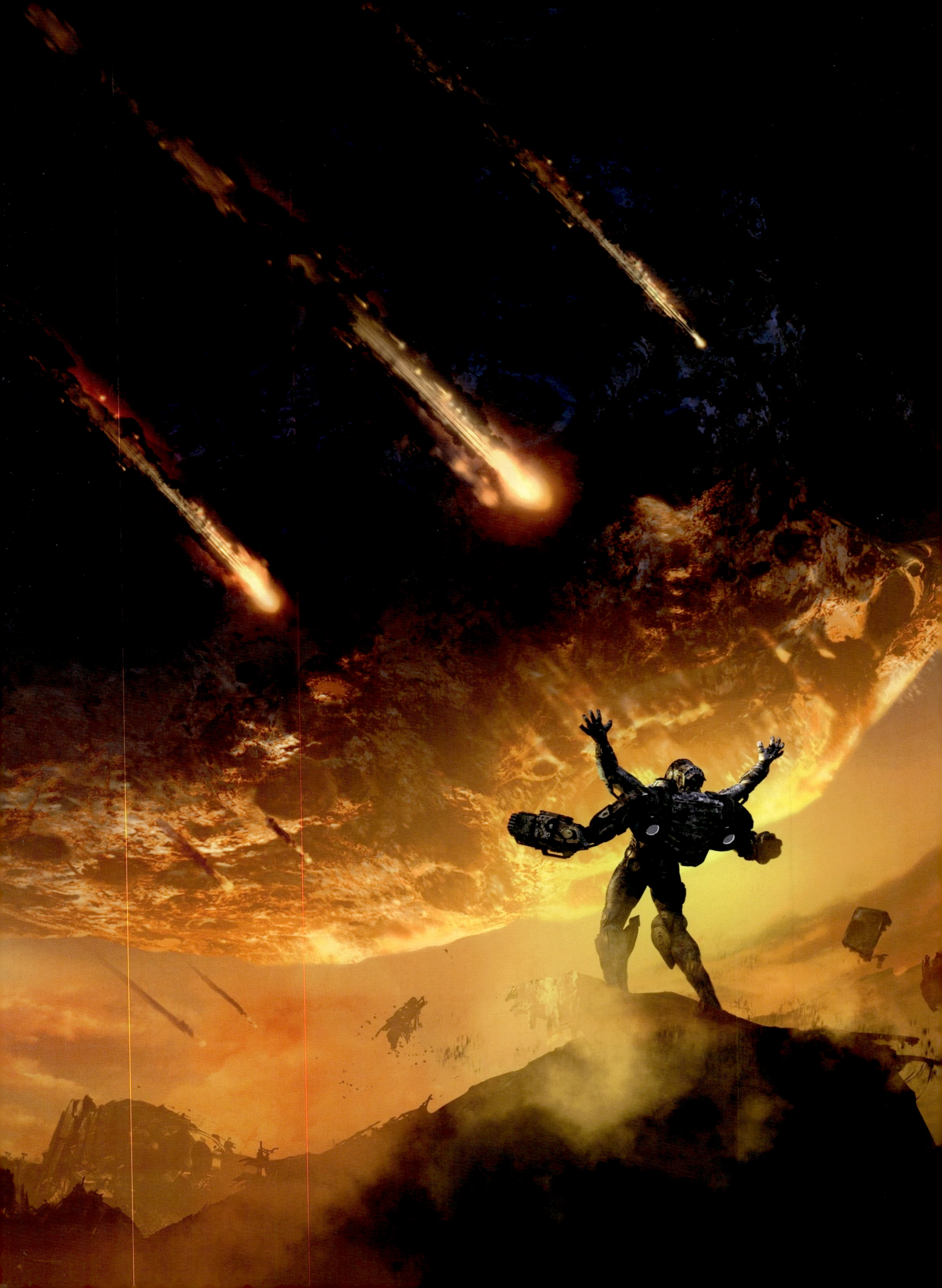

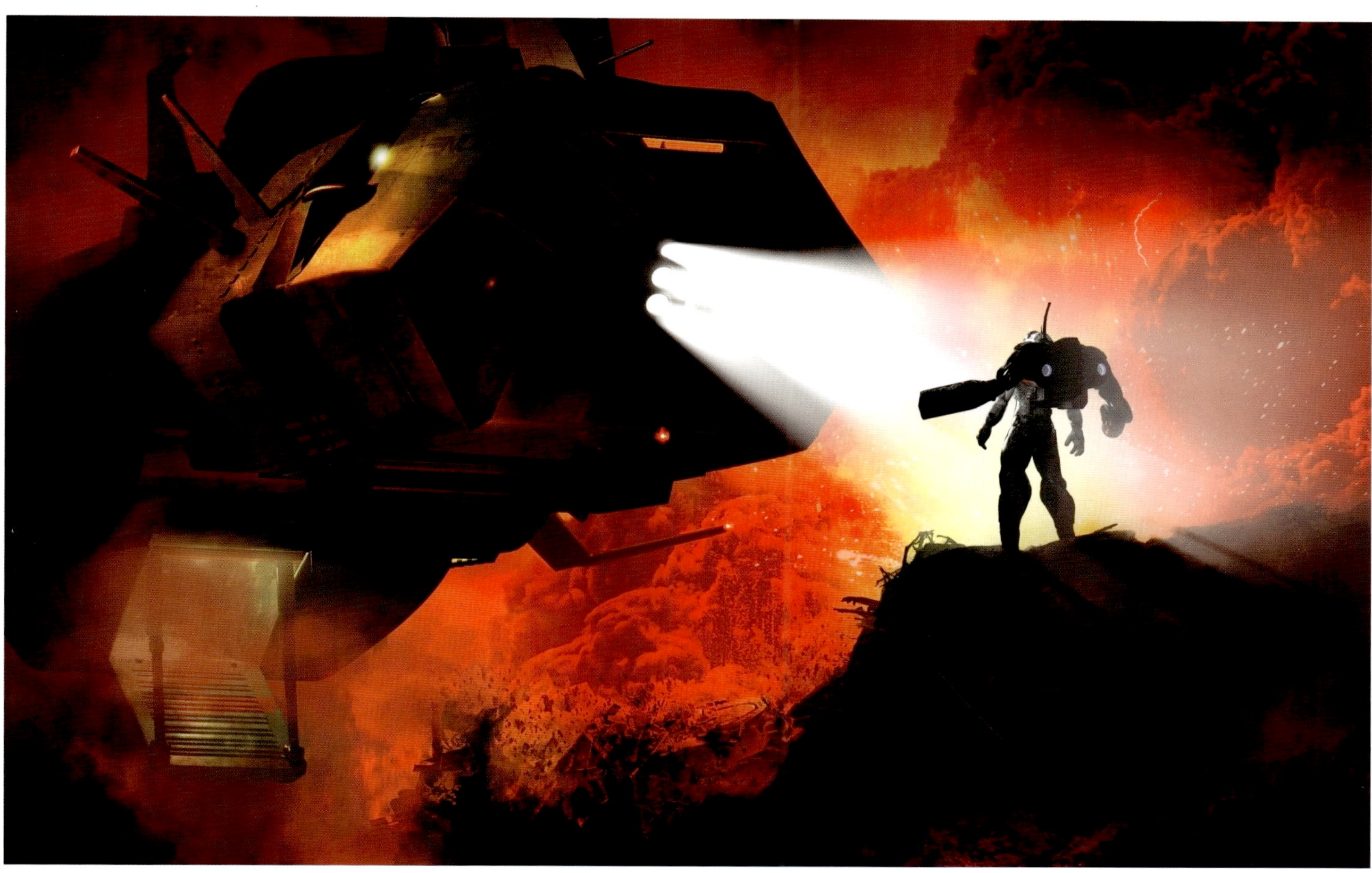

△ EXT. HABITAT MAZE ENTRANCE

The sky is completely filled by the Shepherd moon, its rotating, battered surface seemingly close enough to touch. The wind howls as the habitat loses its integrity, its atmosphere pouring into space. Large and dangerous chunks of debris are being catapulted into the air, one crashes down, narrowly missing the ship. Mech releases Breel. She staggers away from him as the ramp lowers from the back of the Scavenger. Reaching the ramp she hangs on the struts, struggling to stay upright in the wind as she looks back.

The ancient alien war machine and human share a long stare. The machine makes a very human gesture, nodding once. Breel holds his gaze for a second longer then quickly walks up the ramp into the ship. The landing gear retracts and the ship lifts off, raising a cloud of dust, momentarily obscuring Mech. The view clears. Mech stands motionless, silhouetted against the terrifying spectacle of the descending Shepherd moon. He raises his arms as if to embrace the object of his imminent destruction.

Around him, objects and whole buildings are starting to move and lift into the air as the gravitational pull of the moon overcomes the centrifugal force of the habitat ring. The very ground he stands on starts to ripple and buckle rising into the air.

Then, a high pitched whine and the Scavenger drops back into view, hovering just in front of the robot. The ramp lowers and an amplified voice temporarily drowns out the surrounding sounds of destruction.

BREEL

Time to go.

▽ Breel keeps the Scavenger close to the spindle connecting the two wheel habitats, the safest route as debris is being thrown into space away from the centre by the habitats' spins. She dodges the many structures studding the massive pillar. Behind them the first part of the alien station crashes into the moon, a blinding white light silhouettes the ship and starts racing up the station after them. The Scavenger zooms through the dead ring, over the black landscape, followed almost immediately by the blinding light: a false and final sunrise on a dead world.

As the habitat power systems fail and give up their energy, the Shepherd moon starts to split. It explodes into light, sending whirling chunks of molten debris in all directions. The Scavenger stays just ahead of the shock wave and debris front.

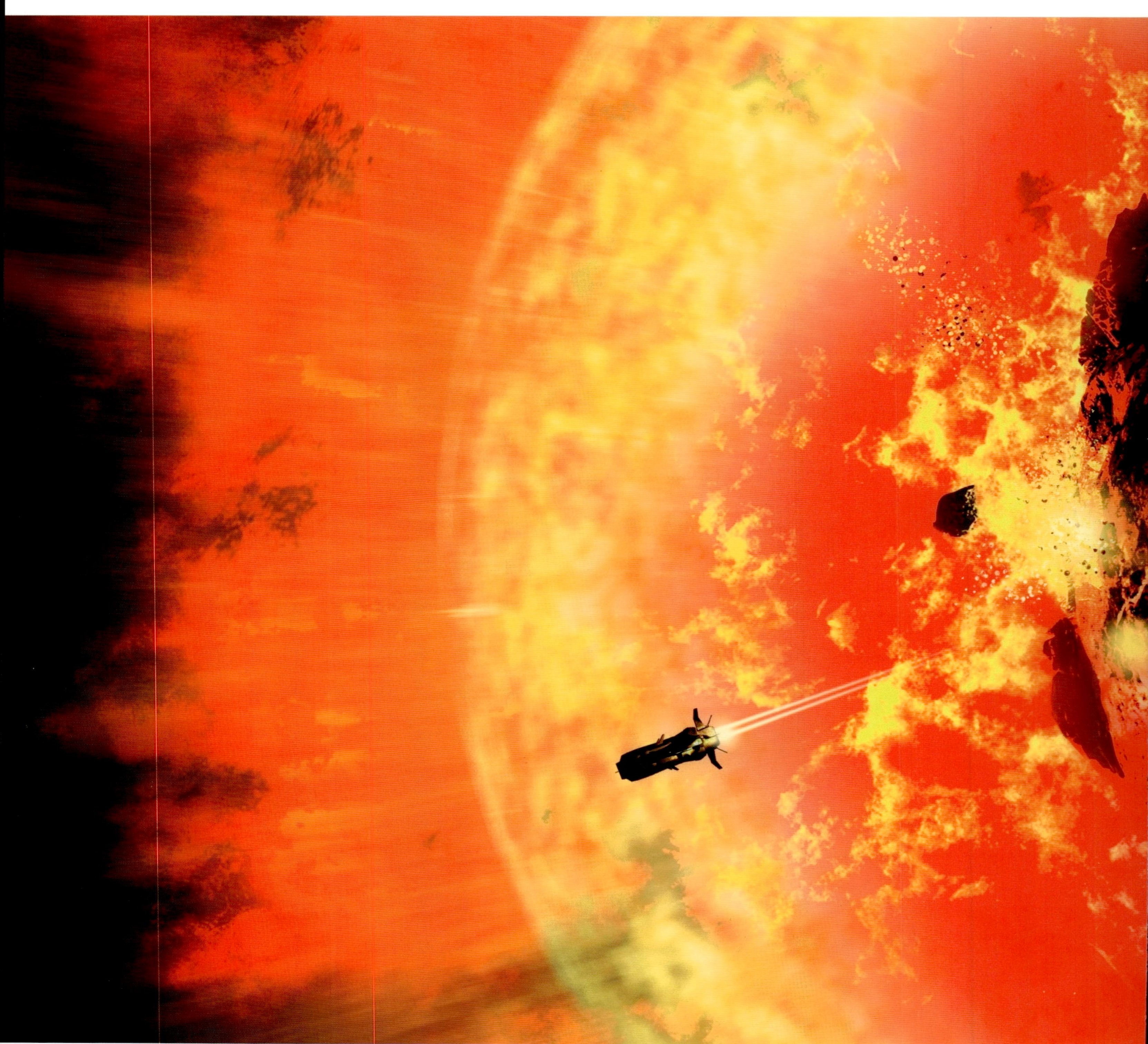

From outside, the golden disc appears to have acquired a second sun as light from the exploding habitat momentarily outshines the system's primary and then quickly fades. Debris tumbles outwards into space...

One piece is the Scavenger.

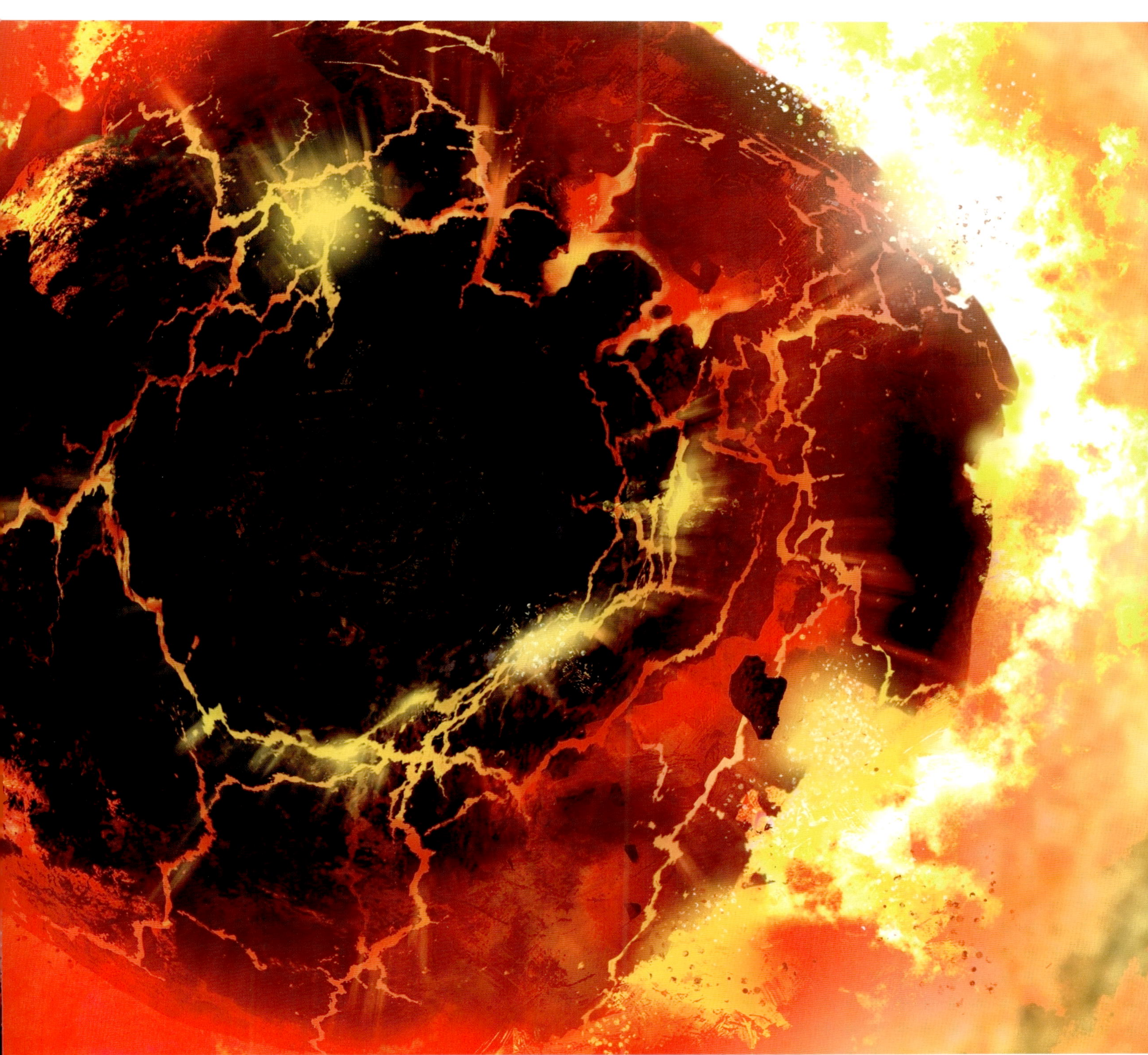

DARK SHEPHERD CONCEPTS

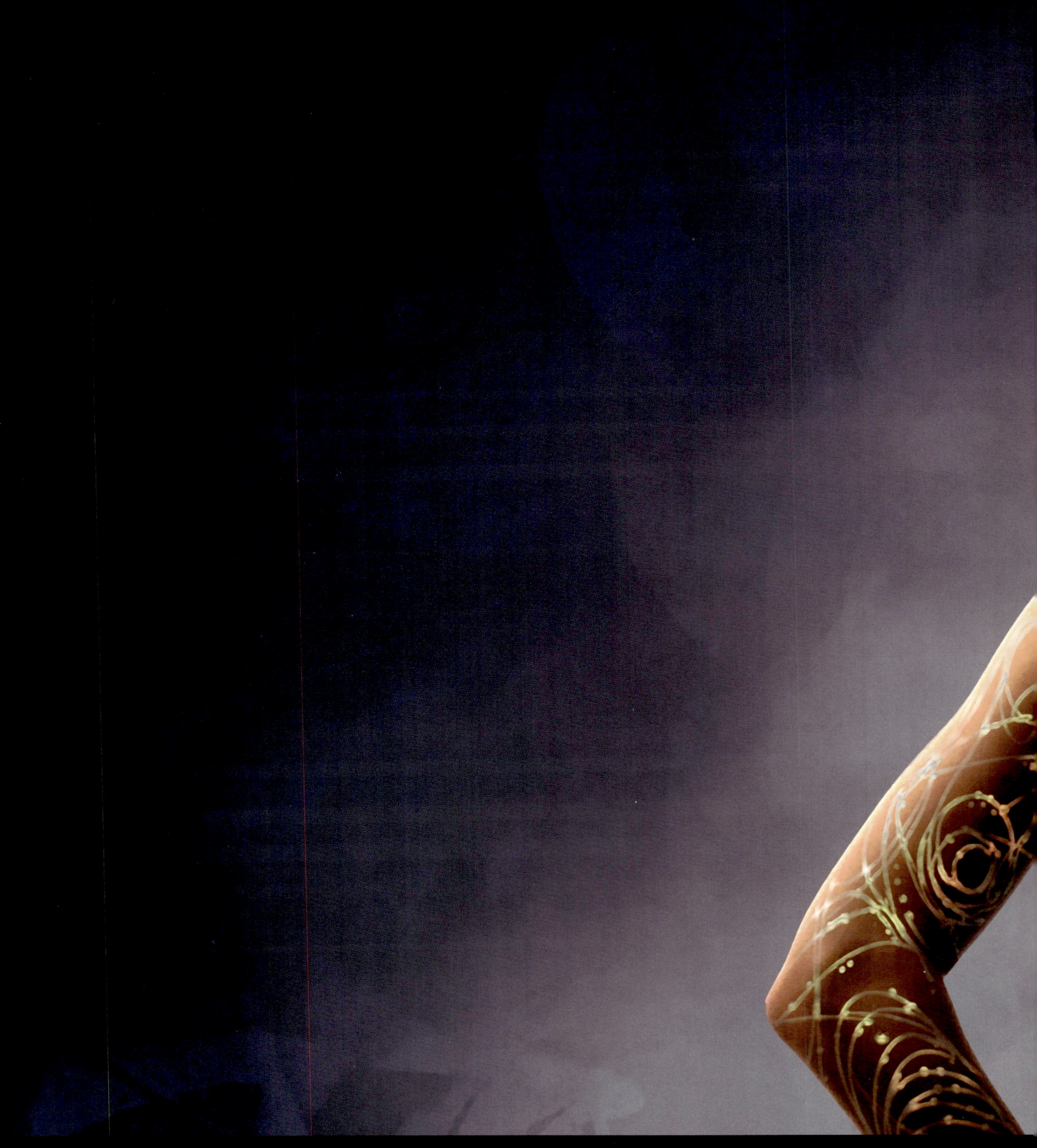

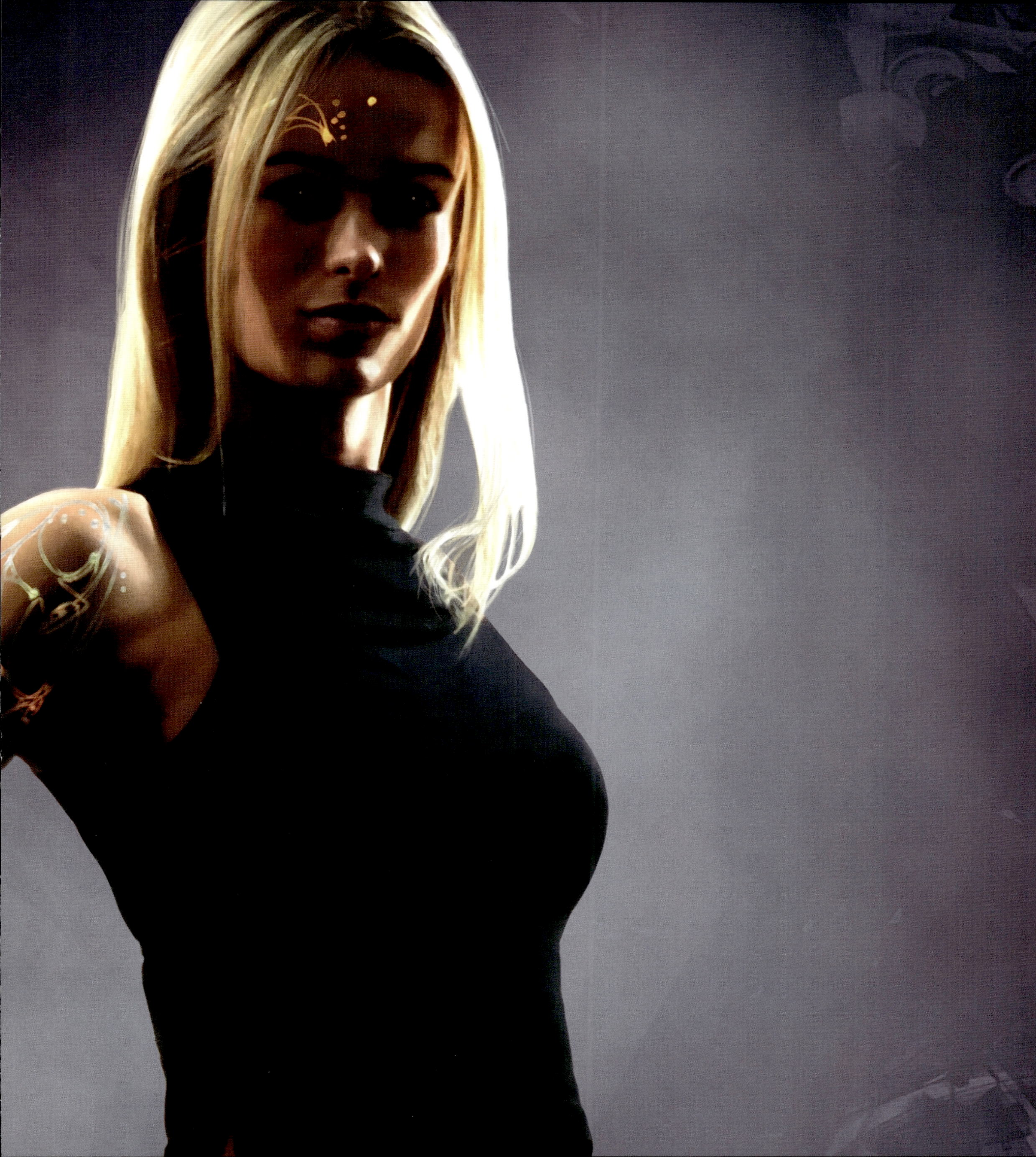

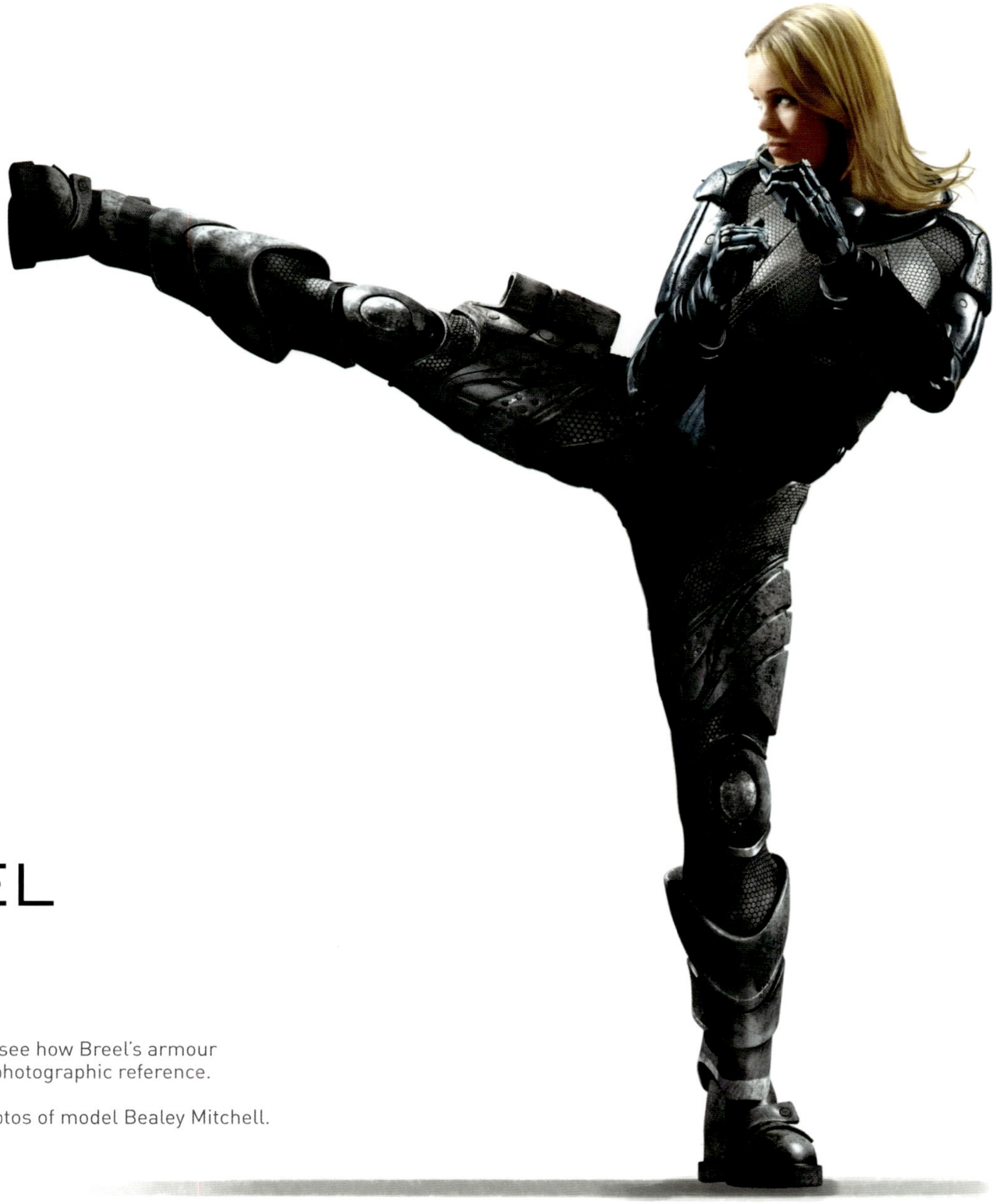

BREEL

Above: Test image to see how Breel's armour would fit around the photographic reference.

Below: Reference photos of model Bealey Mitchell.

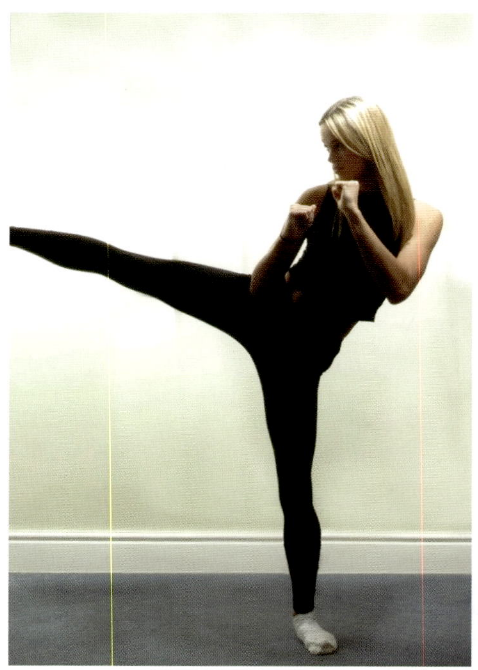

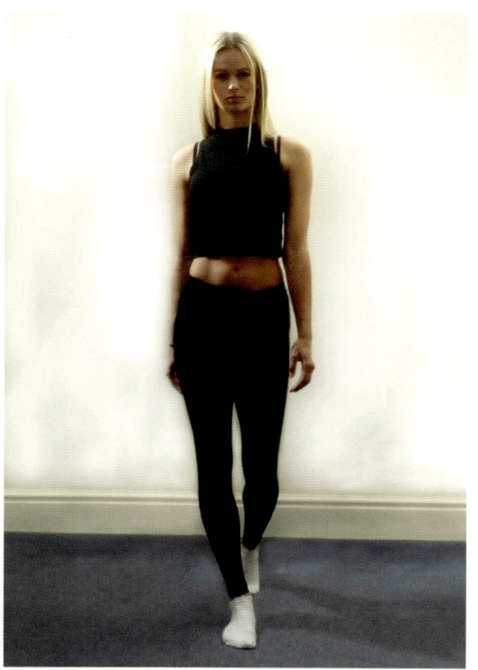

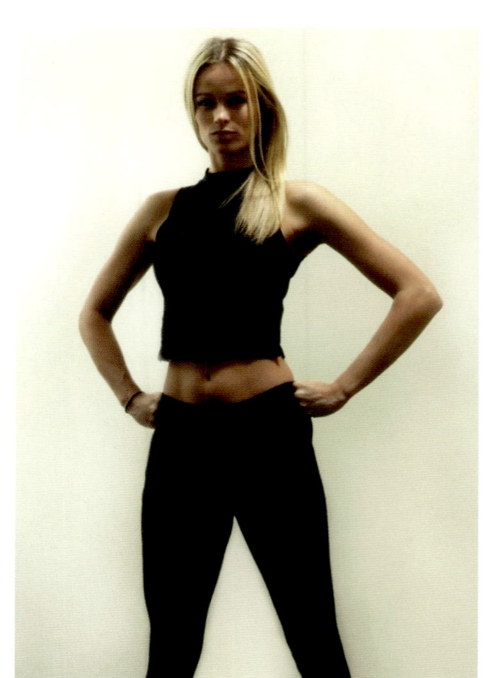

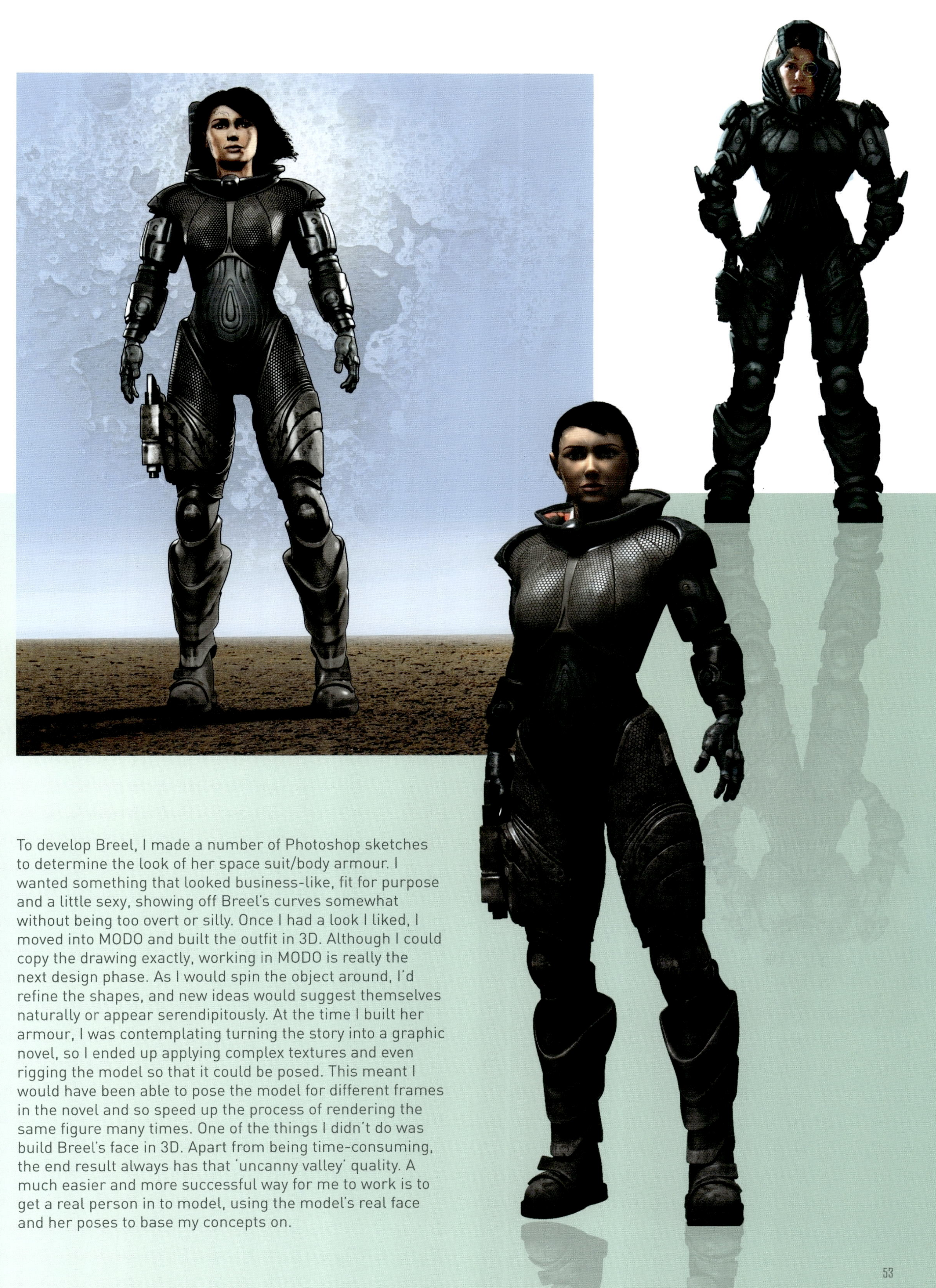

To develop Breel, I made a number of Photoshop sketches to determine the look of her space suit/body armour. I wanted something that looked business-like, fit for purpose and a little sexy, showing off Breel's curves somewhat without being too overt or silly. Once I had a look I liked, I moved into MODO and built the outfit in 3D. Although I could copy the drawing exactly, working in MODO is really the next design phase. As I would spin the object around, I'd refine the shapes, and new ideas would suggest themselves naturally or appear serendipitously. At the time I built her armour, I was contemplating turning the story into a graphic novel, so I ended up applying complex textures and even rigging the model so that it could be posed. This meant I would have been able to pose the model for different frames in the novel and so speed up the process of rendering the same figure many times. One of the things I didn't do was build Breel's face in 3D. Apart from being time-consuming, the end result always has that 'uncanny valley' quality. A much easier and more successful way for me to work is to get a real person in to model, using the model's real face and her poses to base my concepts on.

Right: Screen grabs of the 3D model of Breel's suit.

Right bottom: 3D model of Breel's ubiquitous robot helpers, the MARRVs. MARRV stands for Multi Appendage Reconnoissance and Remote Viewing.

Bottom left: Early concept sketch of Breel's tattoos.

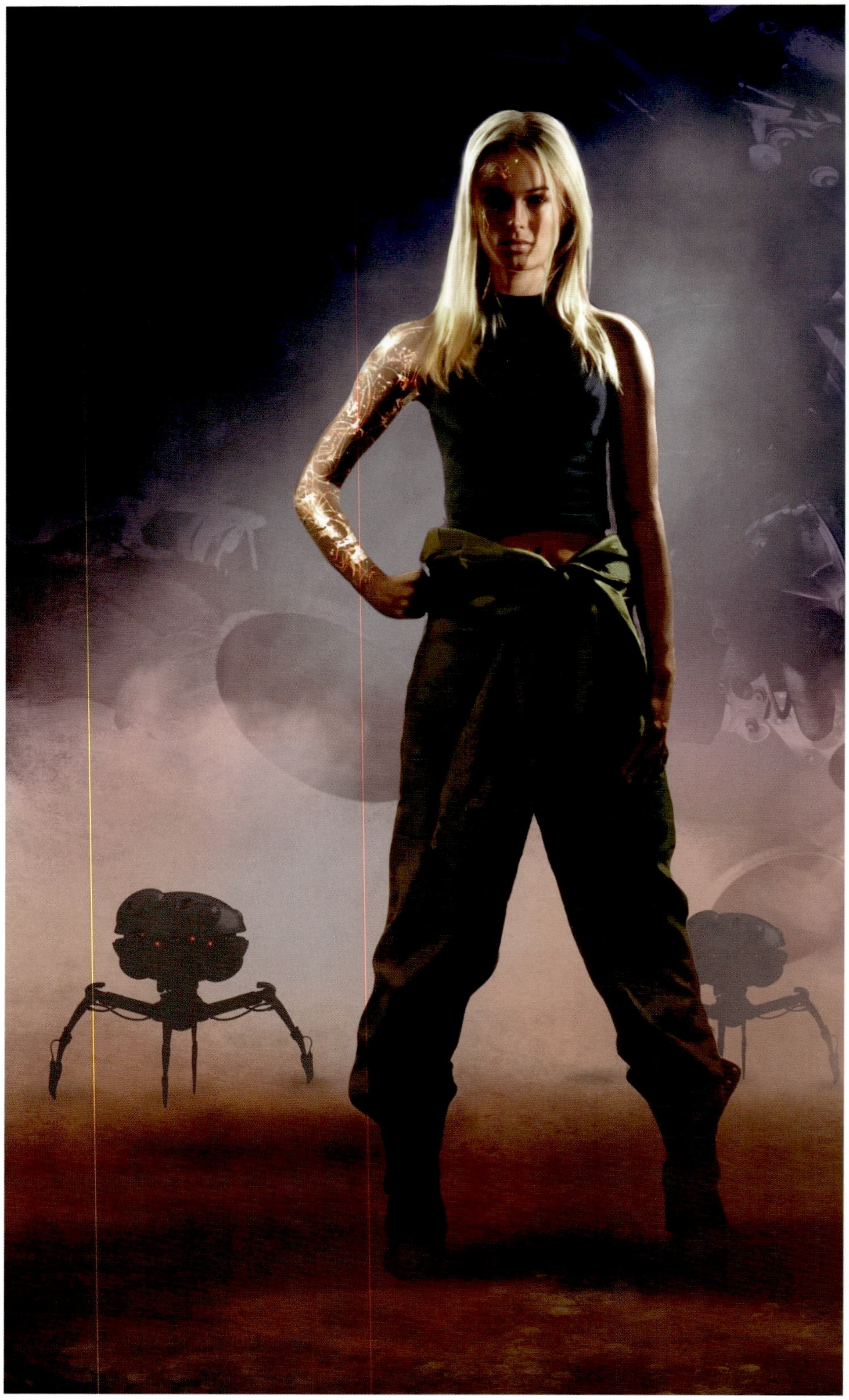

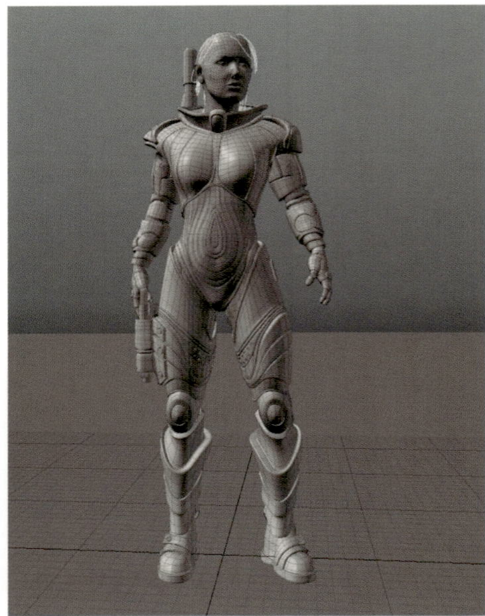

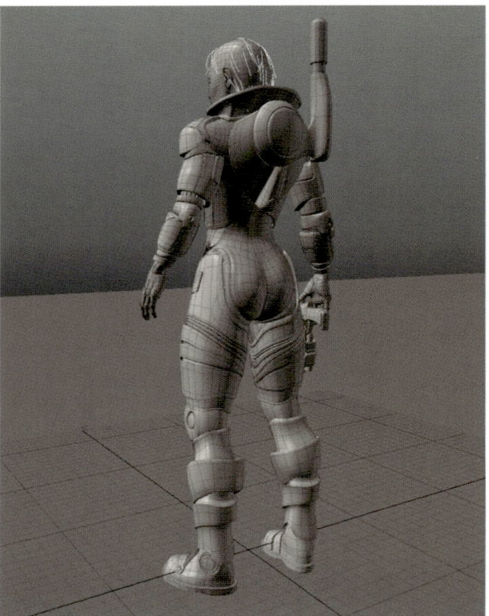

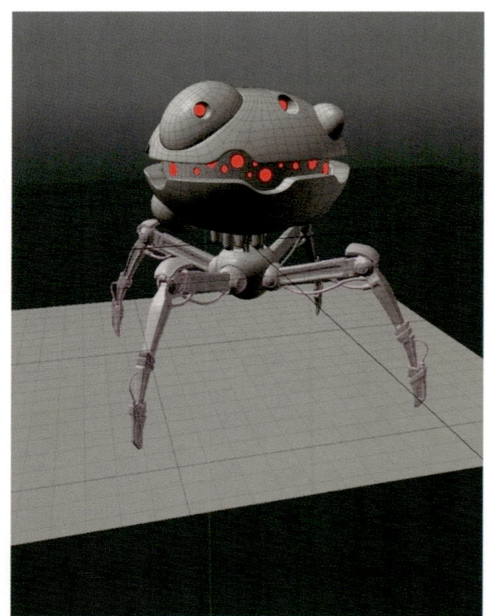

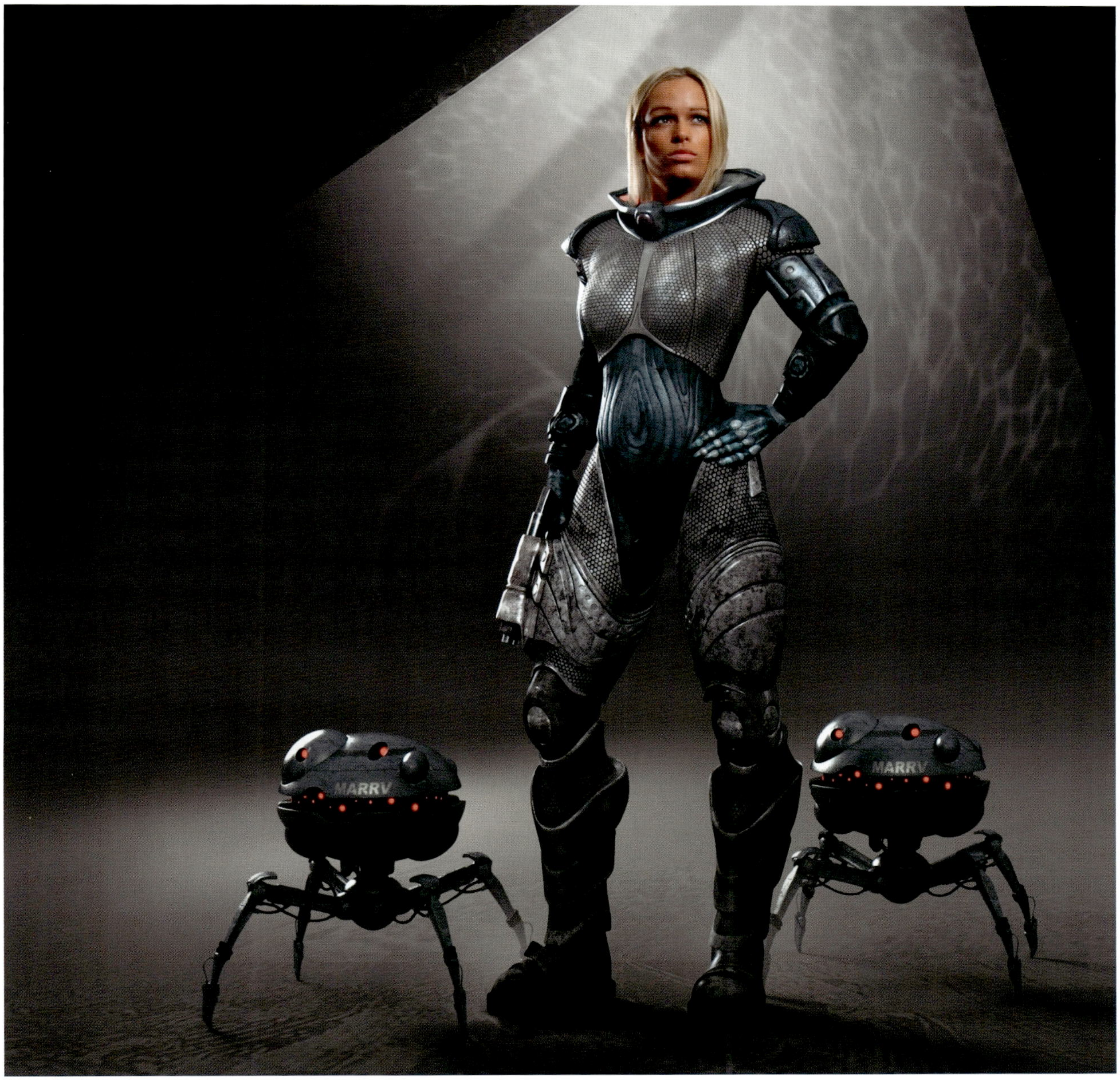

The model I used for Breel is Bealey Mitchell. I had used her for book cover commissions in the past and so already had some nice images I could test the 3D model out with. She seemed to fit the bill perfectly, tough-looking but with a certain vulnerability, so when it came to creating the *Dark Shepherd* images, I hired her again. This image (*above*) was the first test piece I made, using the 3D model and the already existing picture I had of Bealey. I took the lighting and pose from the photograph and matched it virtually, swapping out the generic 3D head I'd used for lighting and shading reference for Bealey's real head. Where the 3D model failed because I hadn't time to rig it properly, I simply took the render and cut it up in Photoshop to fit the reference, painting in or otherwise manipulating the image to fill the gaps.

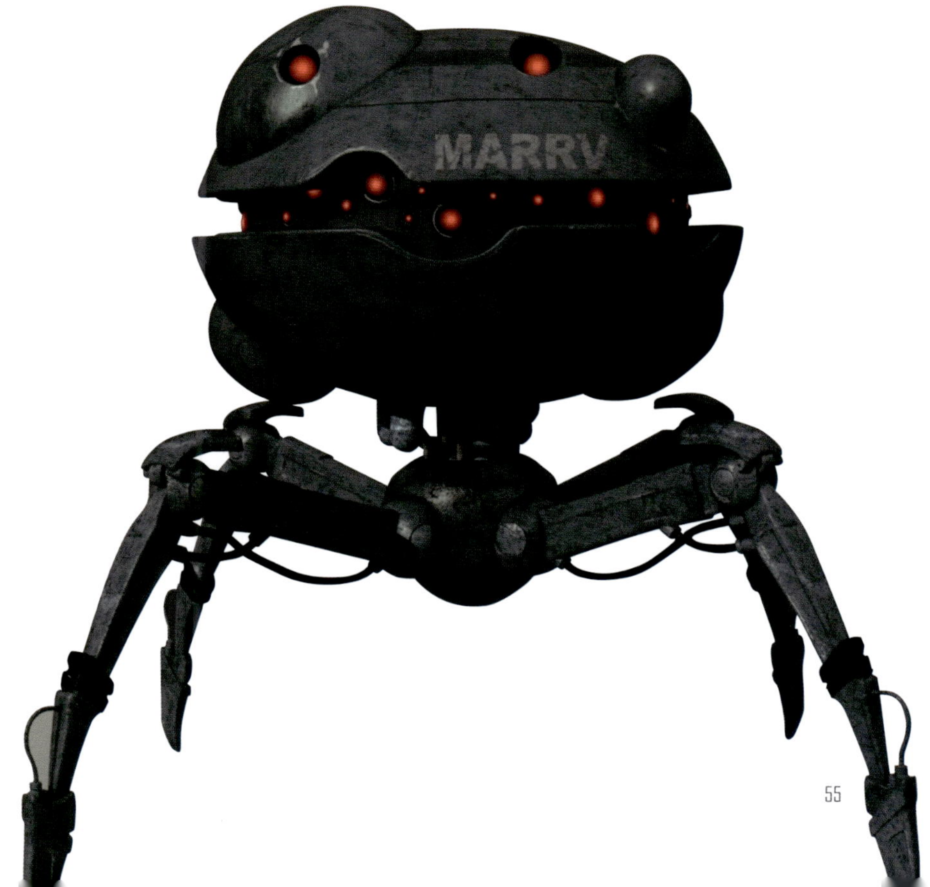

THE MECH

Right: Early sketch ideas for Mech.

Below: Fully realised test render of Mech.

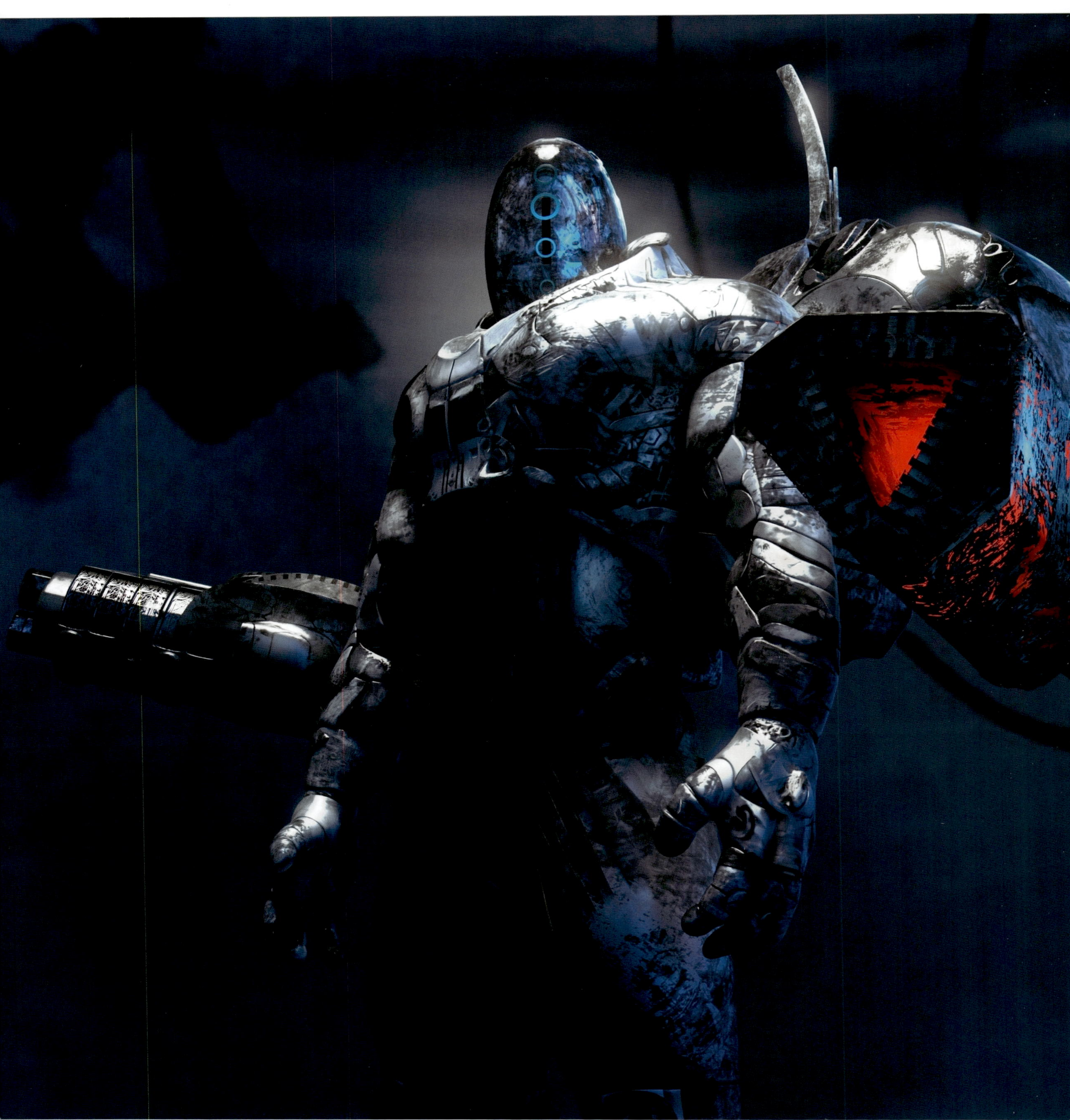

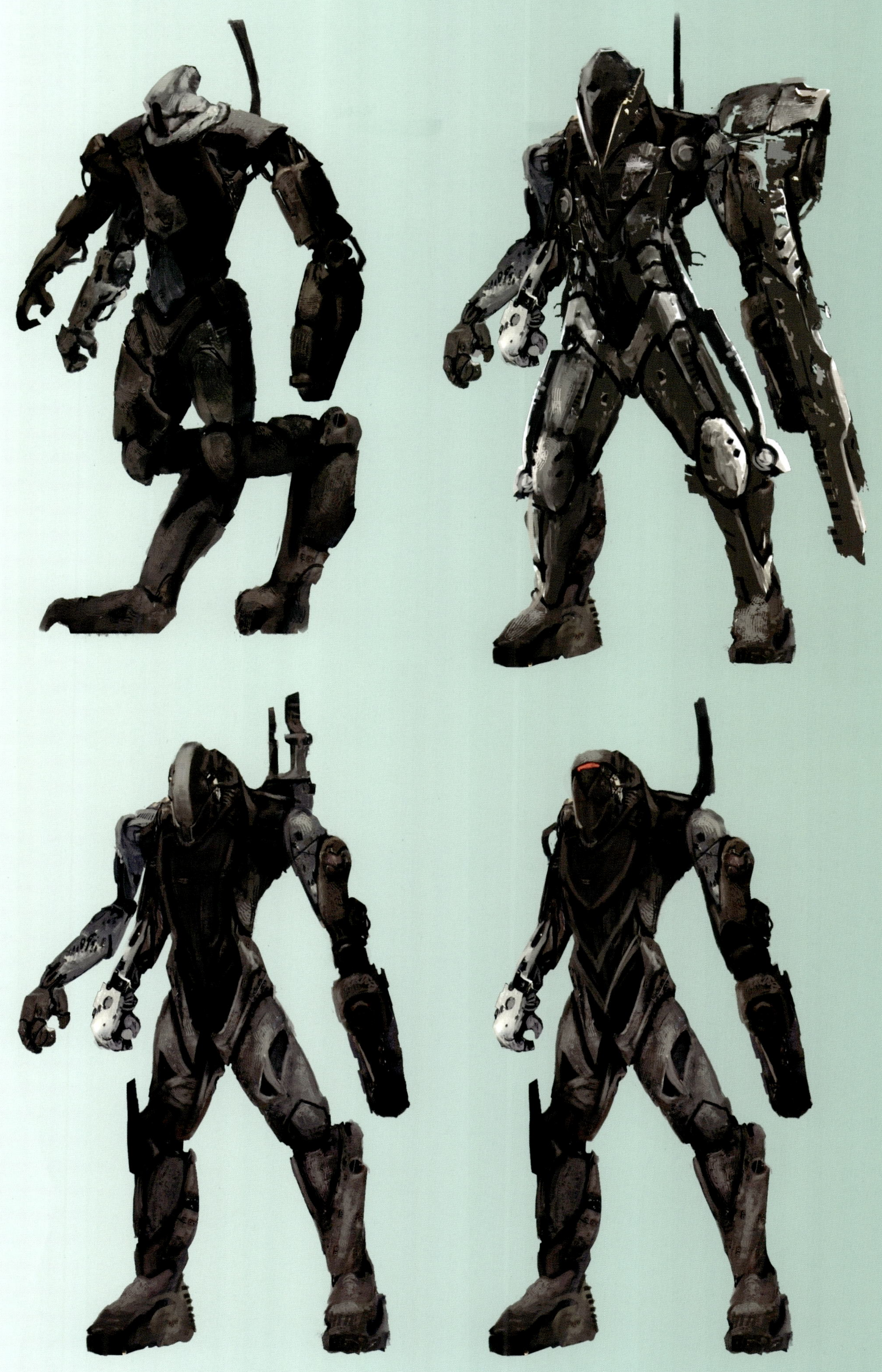

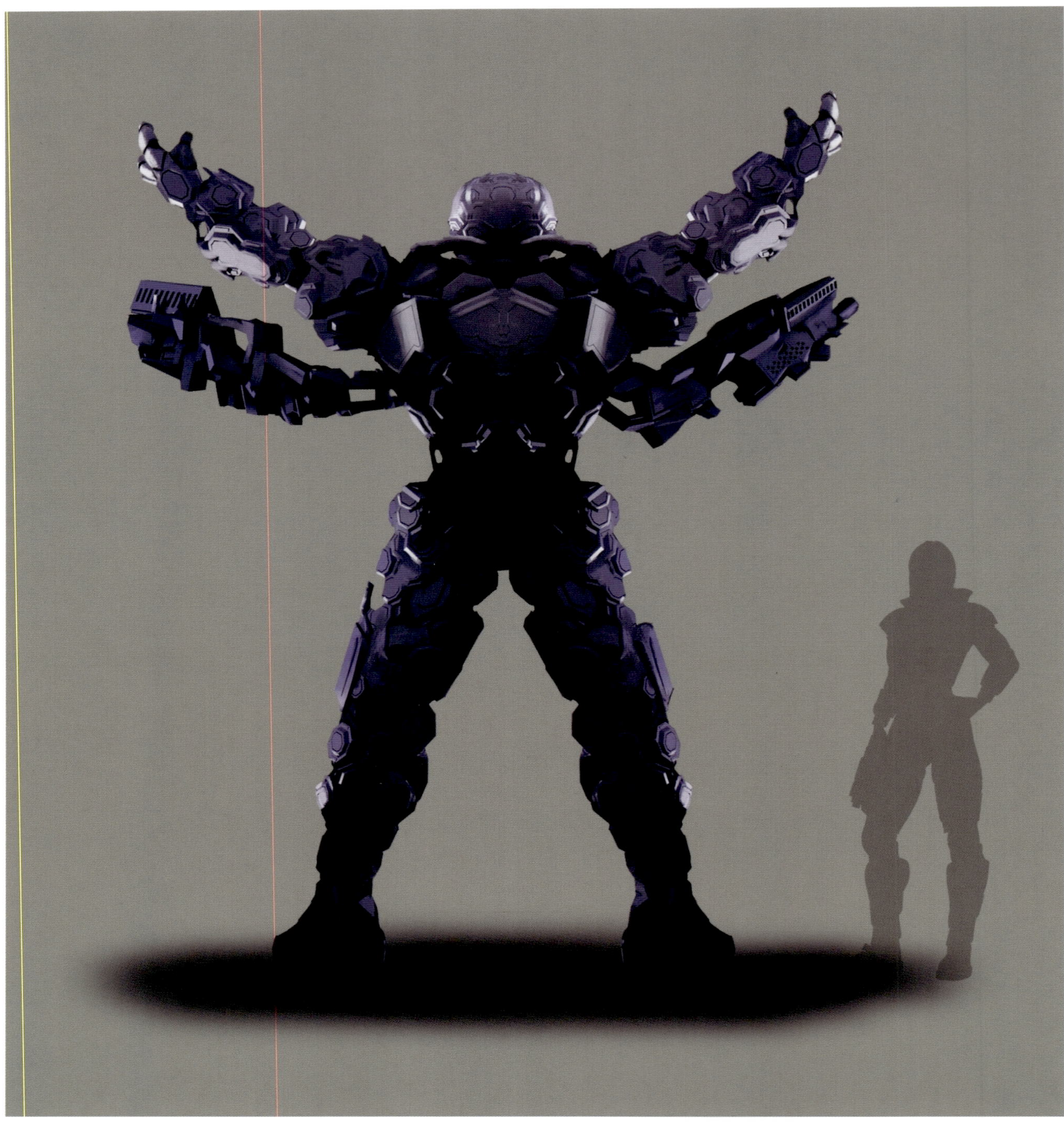

The Mech was always going to be an enjoyable creative challenge. I quickly realised I didn't want him to look like a traditional robot. He had to look dangerous, but also to have some empathic qualities – as he is, however ambiguously, one of the good guys. He is the 'Dark Shepherd' of the title. I also didn't want him to have a conventional skull or humanoid face. In the script I developed the idea that the patterns you see on his face move about in an oily way and become more agitated as he gets more emotional, although always in a pattern that emulates a face.

I also didn't want hydraulics and pistons. He is, after all, the product of an advanced technology, more advanced than Breel's. At the end of the script, he has access panels open and Breel notices that nothing inside is remotely recognisable, a soft honeycomb, hard to focus on. Mech asks, 'What did you expect, pistons and hydraulics?'

I tried to imply some kind of nano tech or otherworldly construction in the patterning on his body. At the same time though, he is destined to become Breel's partner, and so the humanoid form helps to make him more empathetic. The weapons system gives him a multi-armed alien appearance, but I figured that he would shed his weapons and be even more accessible when not in combat or otherwise at rest.

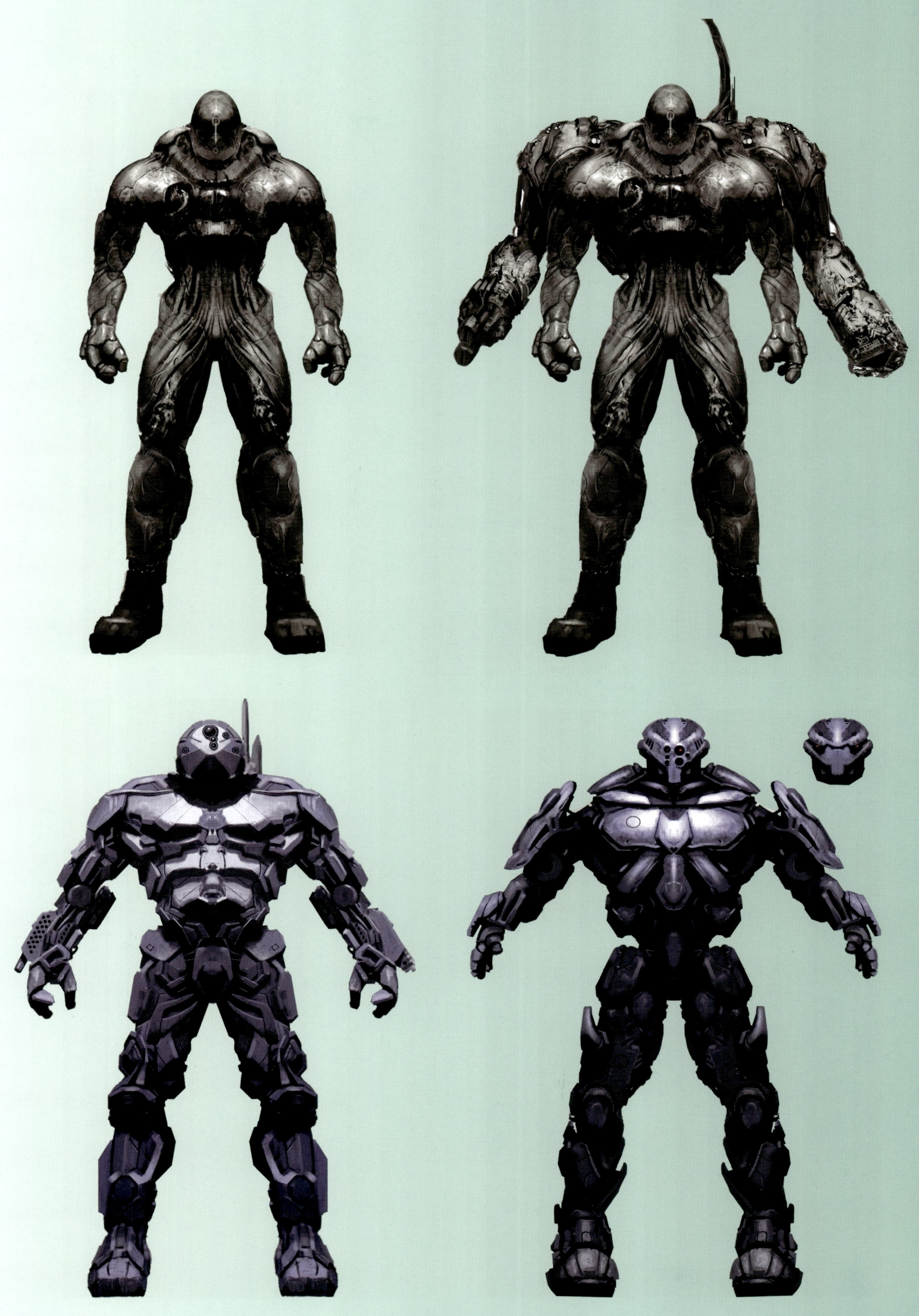

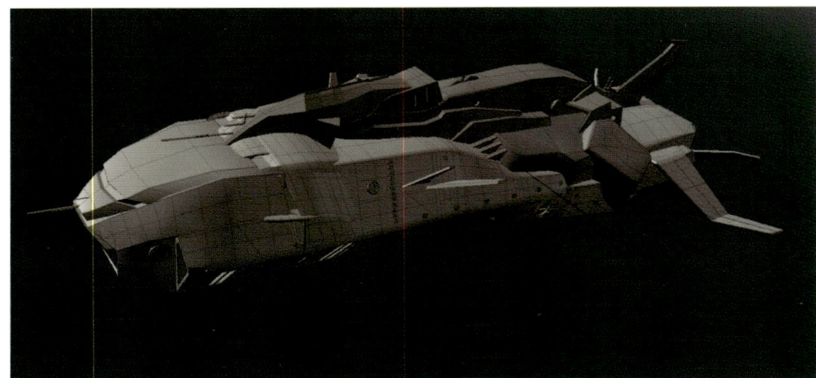

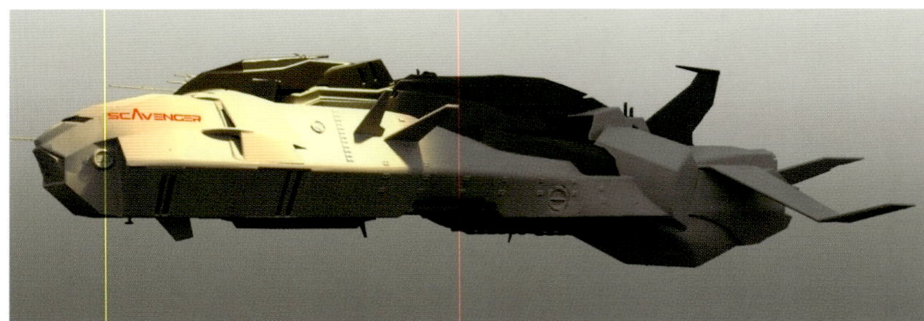

Left: Screen grab of Scavenger MODO model; Render of Scavenger.

Opposite: Concept for Masencorp cruiser; Concept for Matt's gun; Concept for the Claimer's tugs.

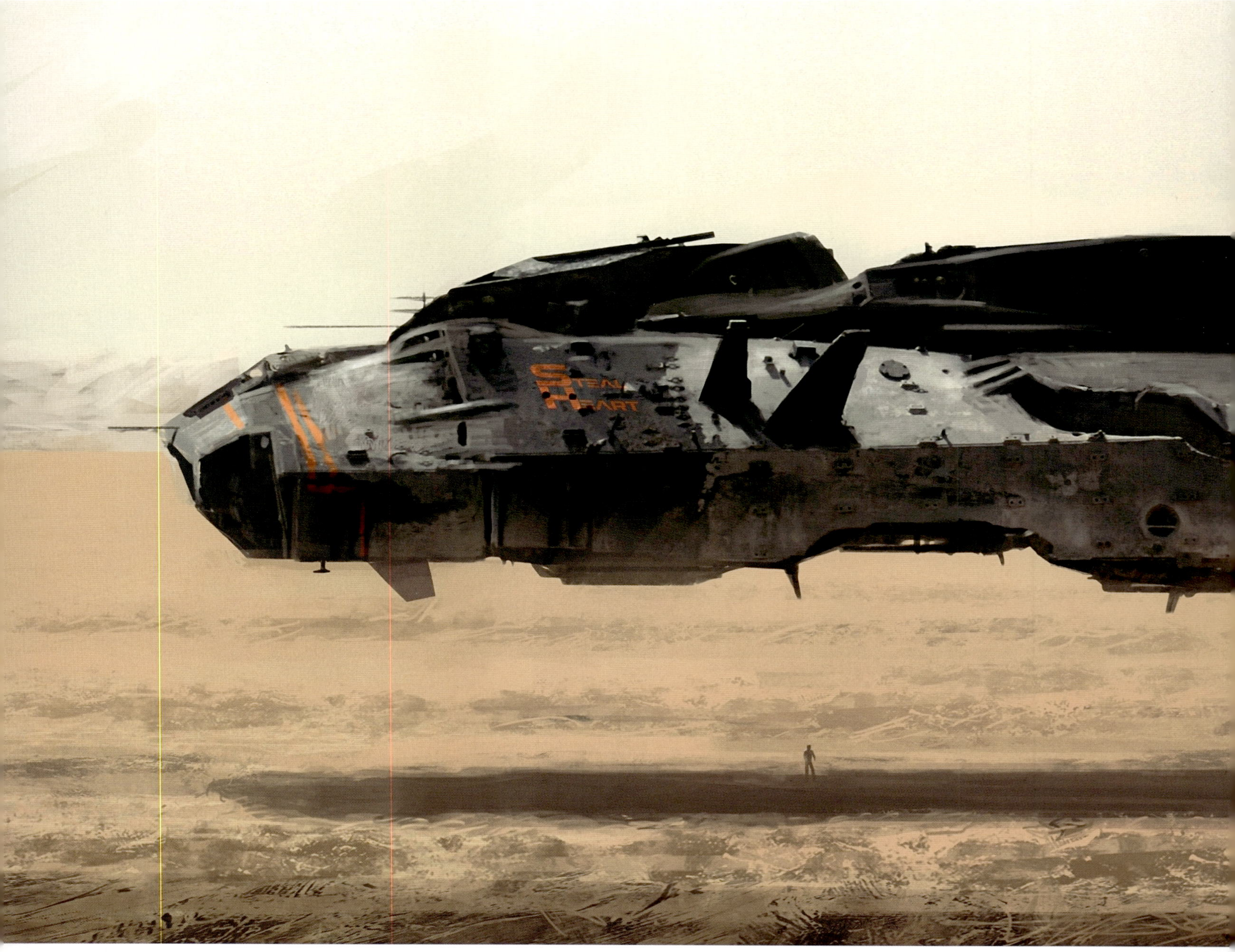

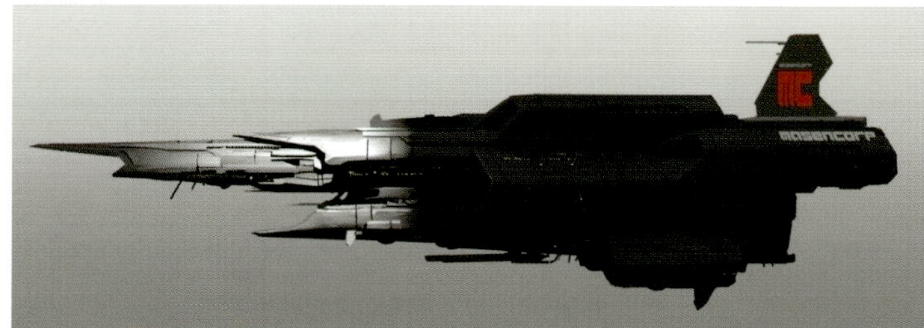

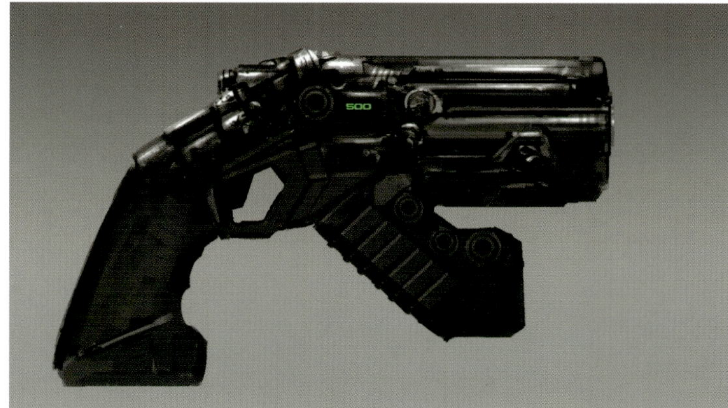

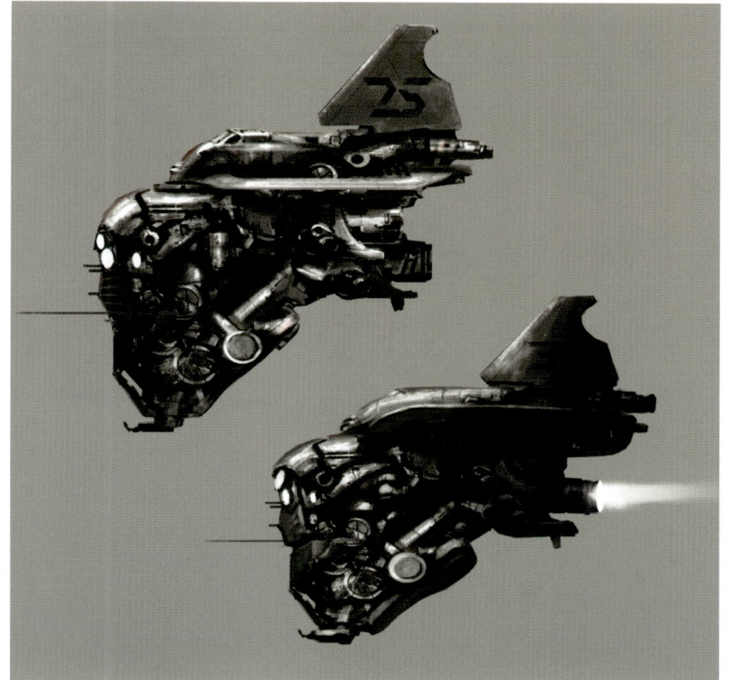

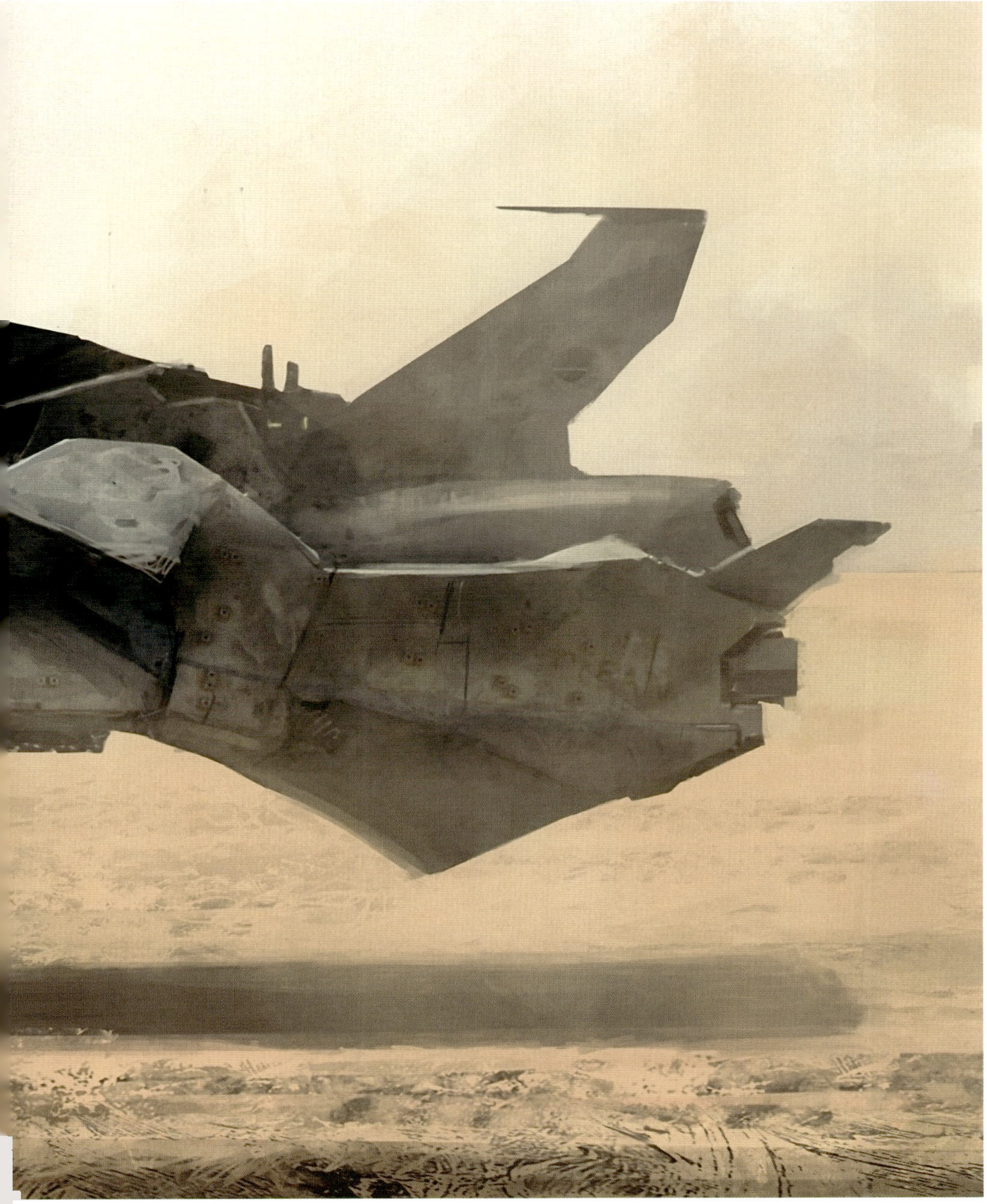

THE SHIP

This ship evolved through a number of versions. Originally, it was curvaceous (as on page 24, *top*), but I decided upon a more angular and aggressive look in the end. Whilst searching for inspiration on the internet, I was scrolling through the thumbnails of an image search for military vehicles and one caught my eye. At thumbnail size I couldn't see what it was, but it seemed to have spaceship-like qualities about it. It turned out to be a photo of a wrecked tank in Iraq. I took that image as a starting point and painted the ship around and over it. The figure on the ground was put in for scale; I always feel the introduction of a human figure helps to ground the audience in this kind of image, giving them something familiar to latch on to.

I liked the result, but felt that it looked a bit 'junky' at first. As Breel's background developed and it became clear her adopted people were scavengers, it made more sense. During the MODO design phase, the shapes became more refined and so lost some of that junky feel anyway.

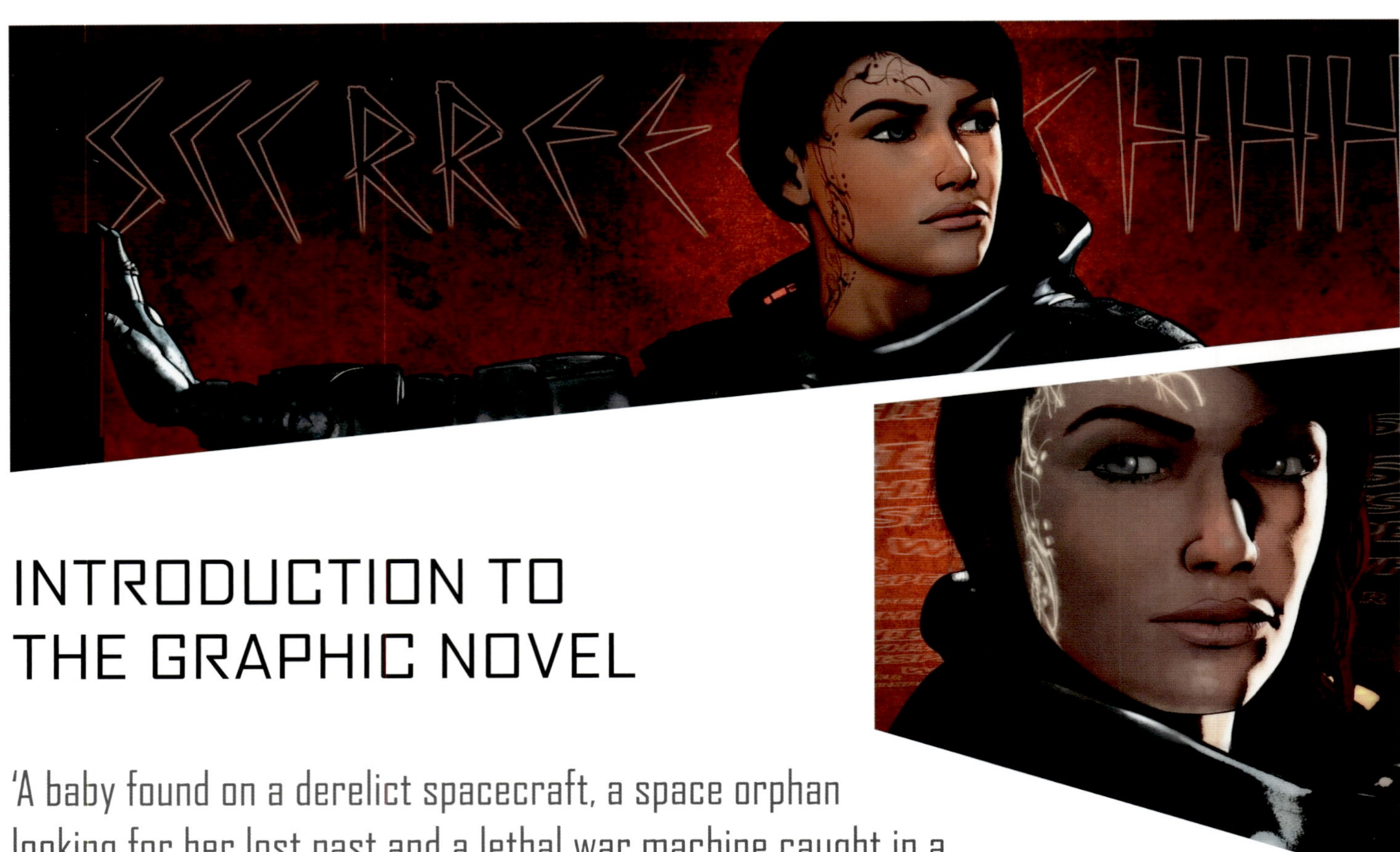

INTRODUCTION TO THE GRAPHIC NOVEL

'A baby found on a derelict spacecraft, a space orphan looking for her lost past and a lethal war machine caught in a deadly maze, trapped by the last order given to it millennia ago.'

When I wrote the initial treatment for *Dark Shepherd*, I wasn't sure what it was going to be. One of the reasons I wrote it was to give myself a brief for some personal pieces. I find it difficult, faced with a blank canvas and an infinite possibility of images, to settle on just one. At first, I thought I could use *Dark Shepherd* to create a series of images or maybe even a graphic novel. This seemed a good option, as there would be plenty of images required to tell the story – but never having attempted a graphic novel before, I had to do a bit of R&D.

These pages are my attempt to define a style and tell the opening sequence as described in the introduction. I created a fully rigged and textured suit of body armour for Breel. Although this was a time consuming process, the idea was that it would save me time later, as I could render the figure with different lighting and perspectives many times – and end up with a good reference for each frame to paint over. I also created simple background geometry for each scene, to give me lighting and perspective cues, with all of this based on a black and white storyboard.

It was an interesting exercise, but other work soon forced me to put the whole project on the back-burner to await the day I either find myself at a loose end or until, just possibly, someone commissions it.

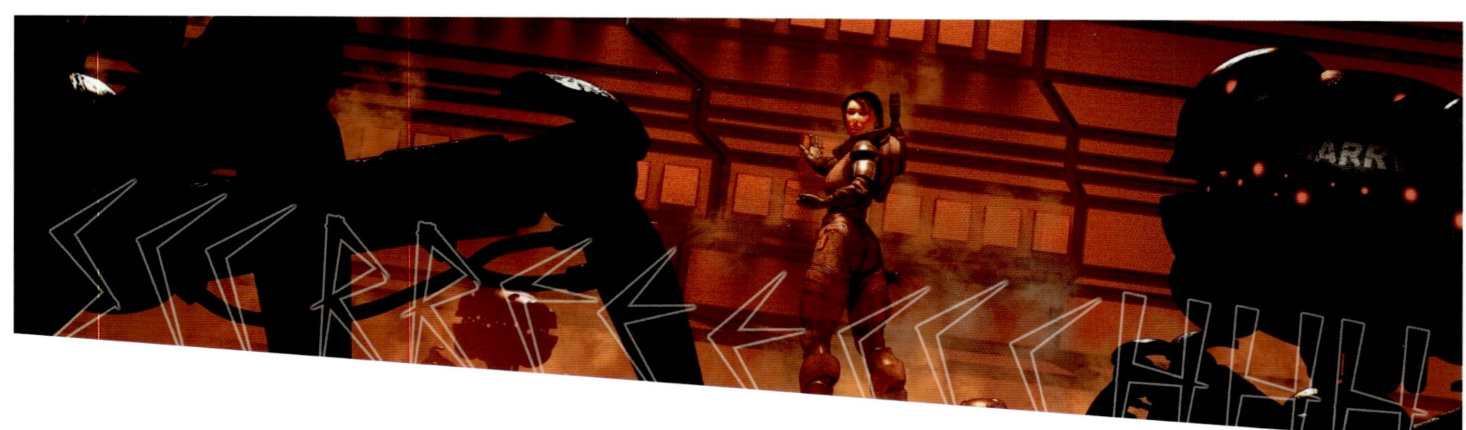

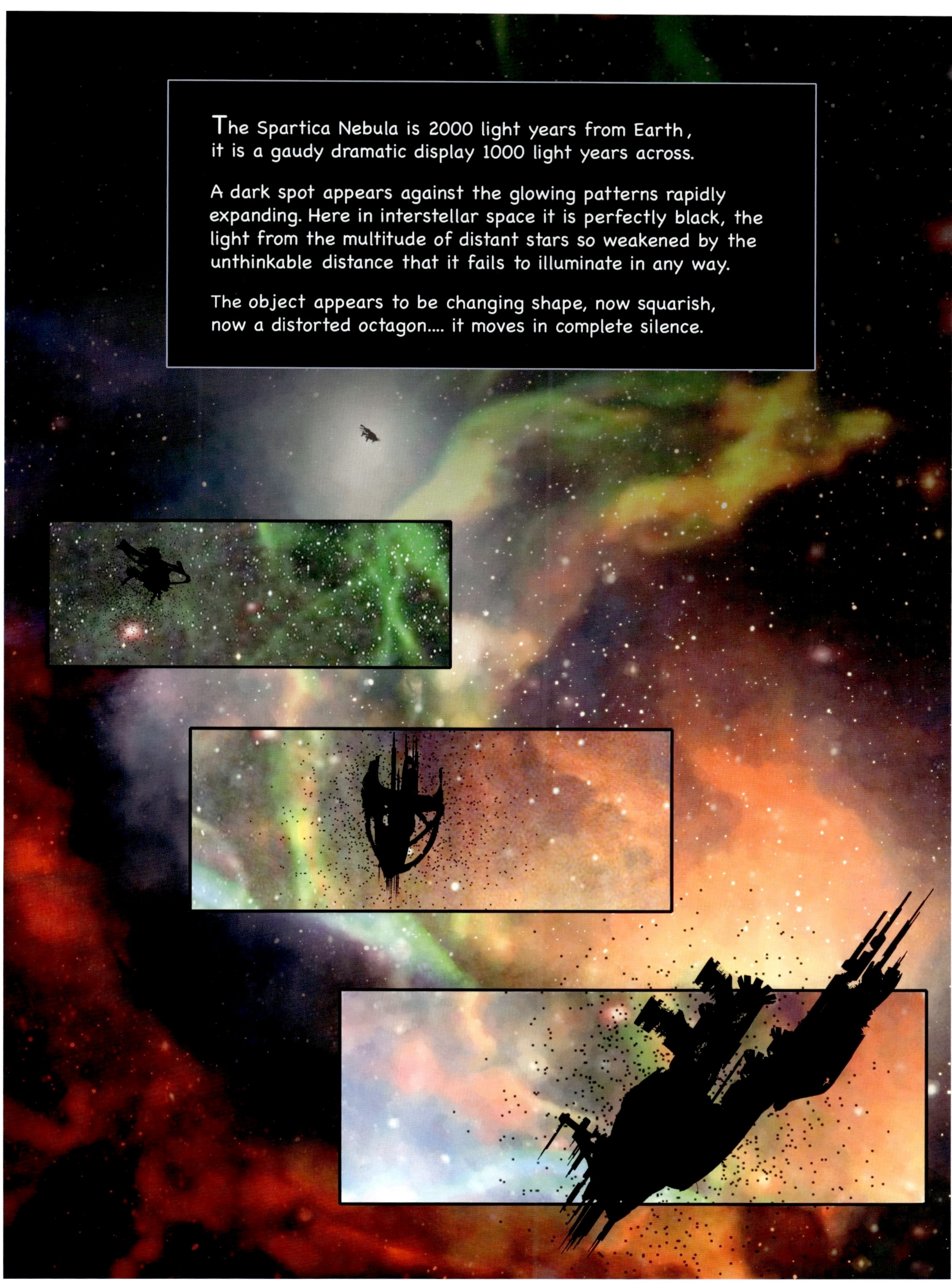
The Spartica Nebula is 2000 light years from Earth, it is a gaudy dramatic display 1000 light years across.
A dark spot appears against the glowing patterns rapidly expanding. Here in interstellar space it is perfectly black, the light from the multitude of distant stars so weakened by the unthinkable distance that it fails to illuminate in any way.
The object appears to be changing shape, now squarish, now a distorted octagon.... it moves in complete silence.

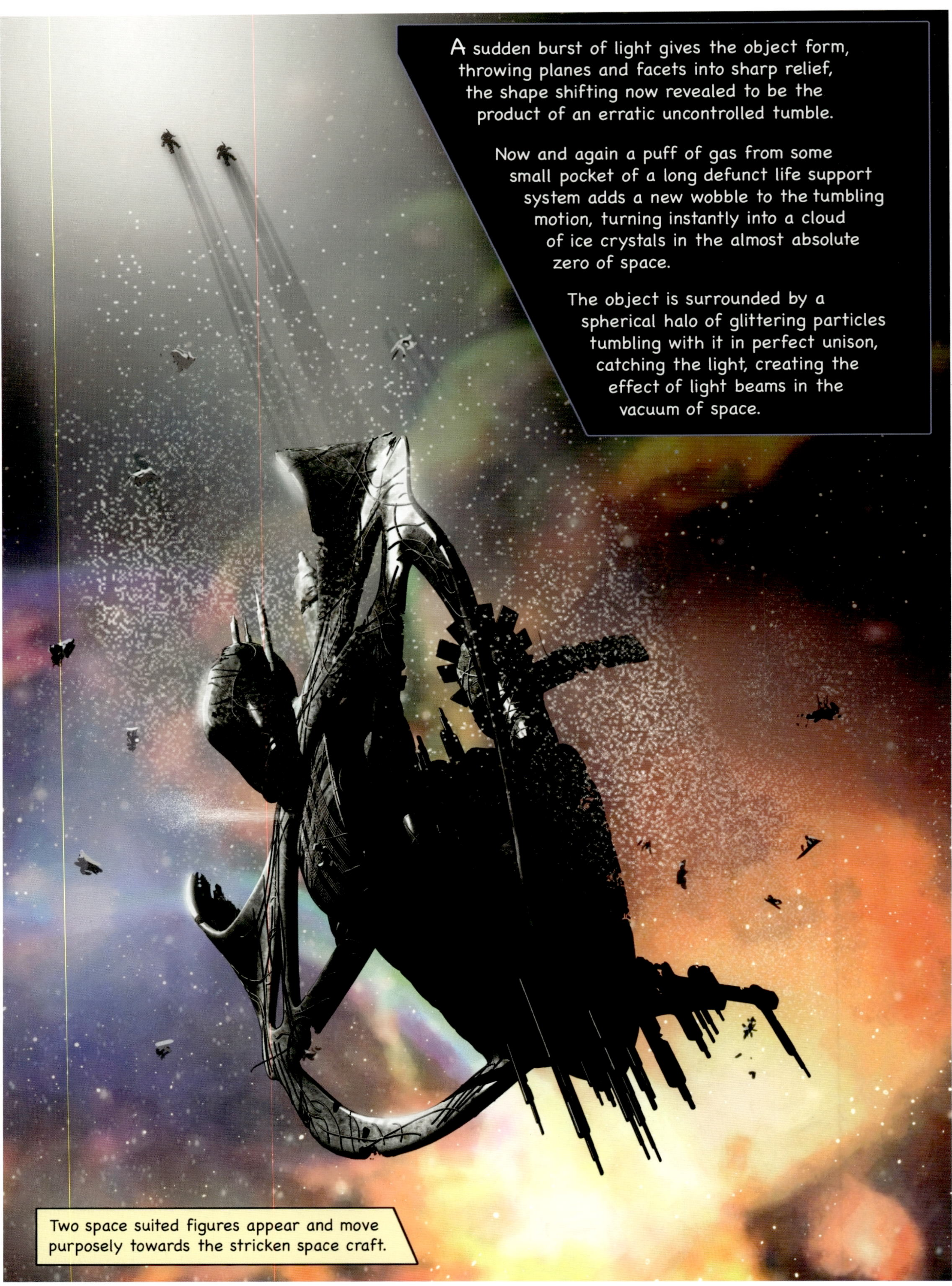
A sudden burst of light gives the object form, throwing planes and facets into sharp relief, the shape shifting now revealed to be the product of an erratic uncontrolled tumble.
Now and again a puff of gas from some small pocket of a long defunct life support system adds a new wobble to the tumbling motion, turning instantly into a cloud of ice crystals in the almost absolute zero of space.
The object is surrounded by a spherical halo of glittering particles tumbling with it in perfect unison, catching the light, creating the effect of light beams in the vacuum of space.
Two space suited figures appear and move purposely towards the stricken space craft.

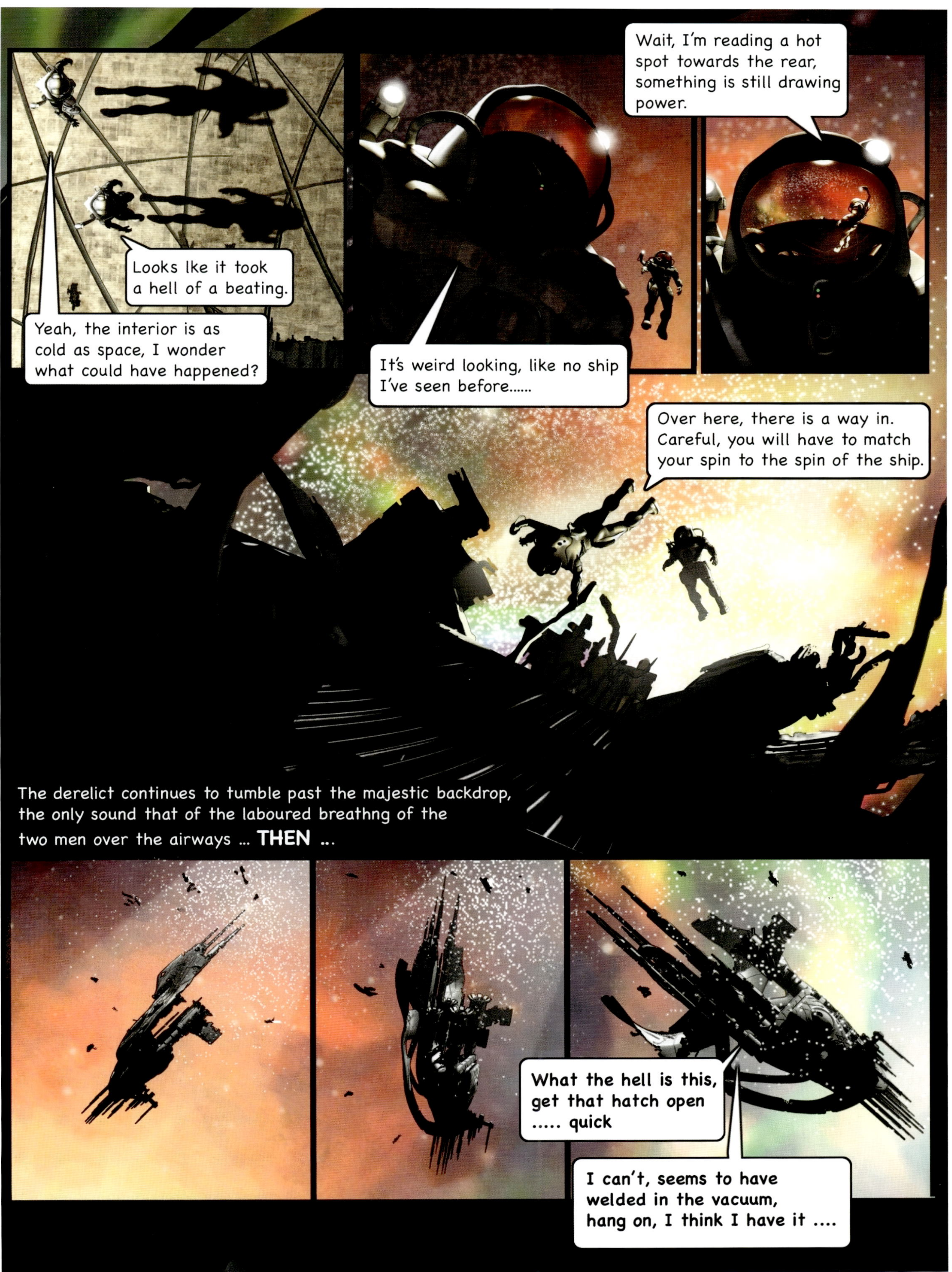
Looks lke it took a hell of a beating.
Yeah, the interior is as cold as space, I wonder what could have happened?
It's weird looking, like no ship I've seen before......
Wait, I'm reading a hot spot towards the rear, something is still drawing power.
Over here, there is a way in. Careful, you will have to match your spin to the spin of the ship.
The derelict continues to tumble past the majestic backdrop, the only sound that of the laboured breathng of the two men over the airways ... **THEN** ...
What the hell is this, get that hatch open ..... quick
I can't, seems to have welded in the vacuum, hang on, I think I have it ....

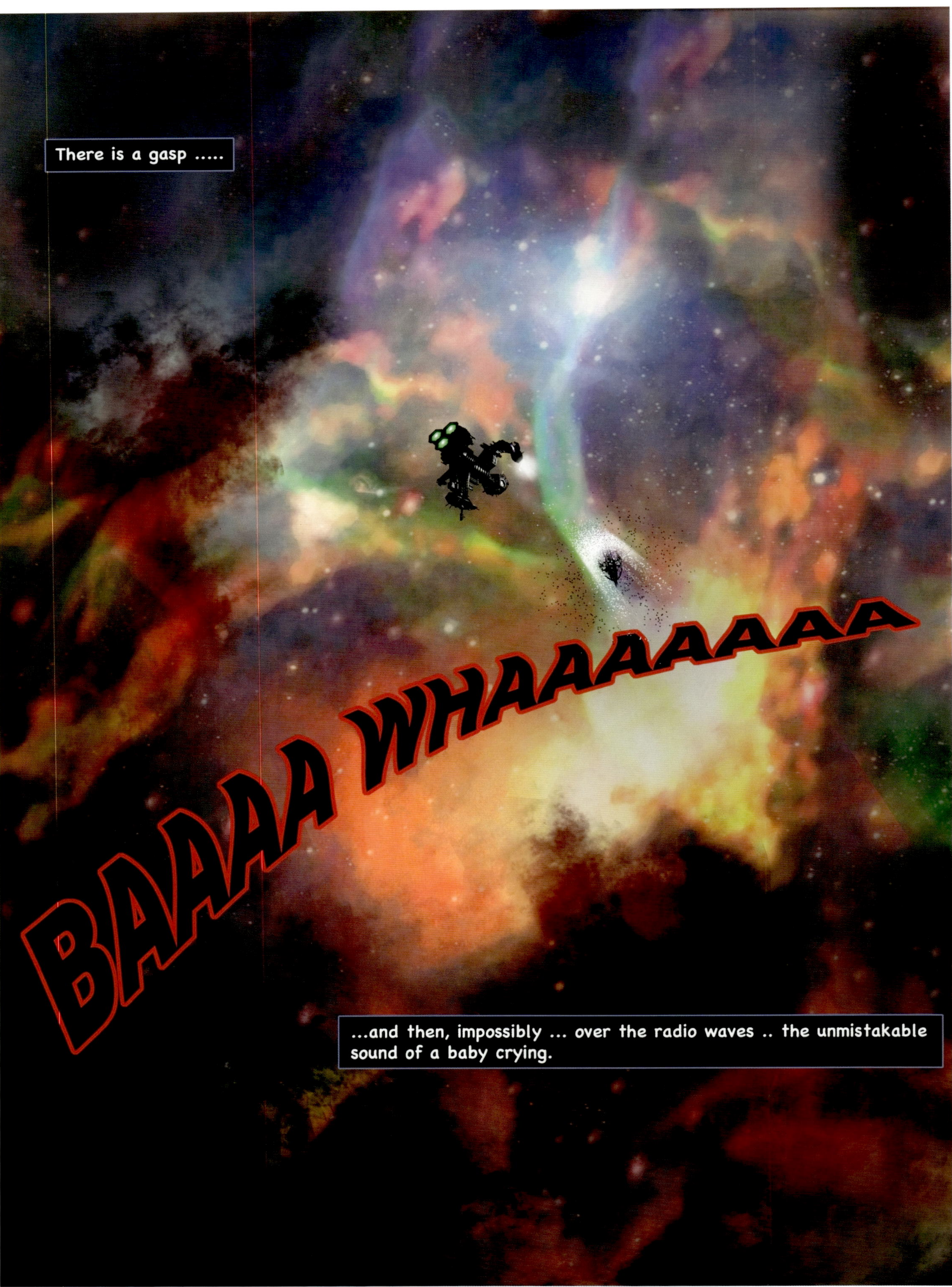
There is a gasp .....
BAAAA WHAAAAAAAA
...and then, impossibly ... over the radio waves .. the unmistakable sound of a baby crying.

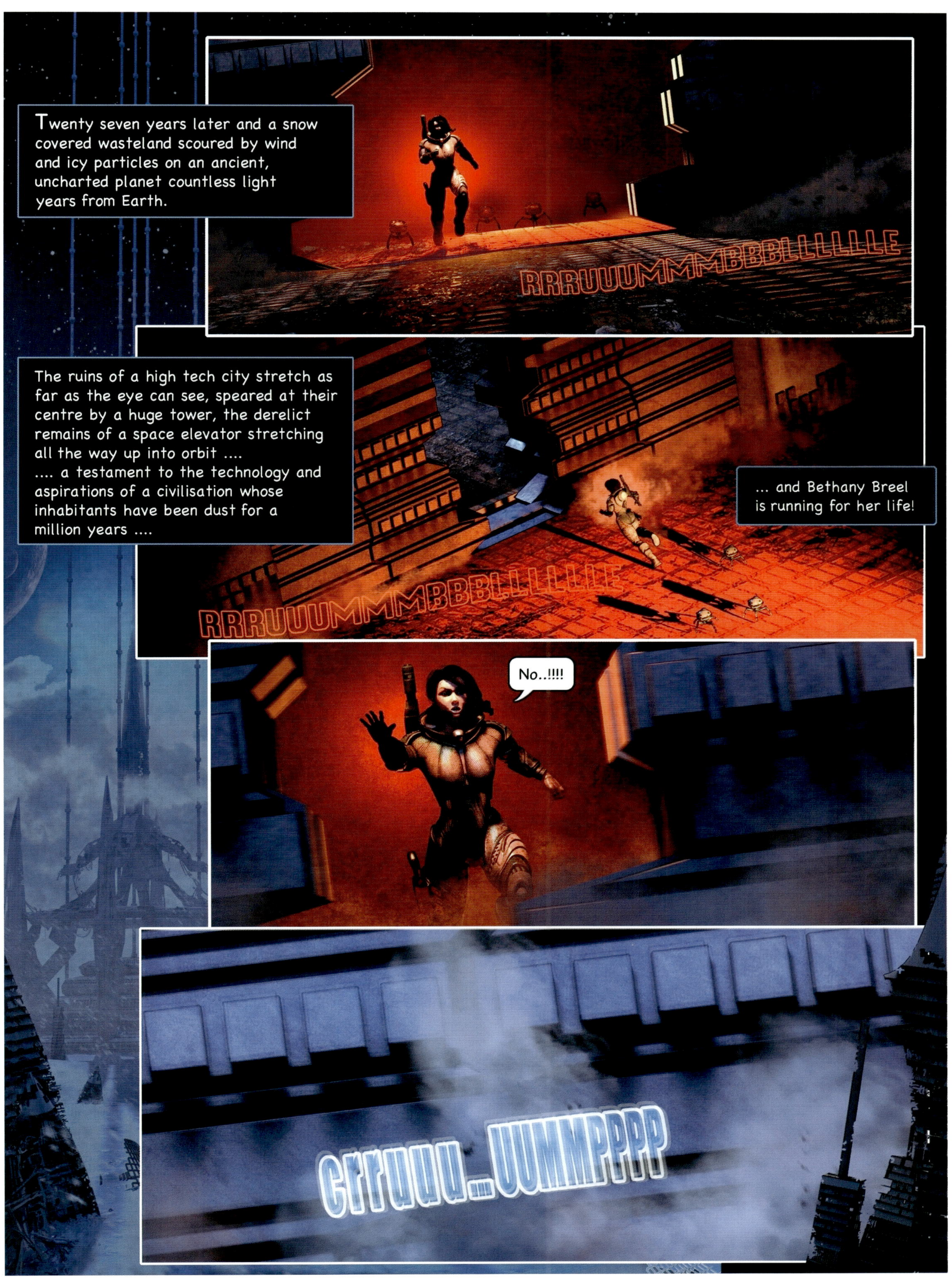

Twenty seven years later and a snow covered wasteland scoured by wind and icy particles on an ancient, uncharted planet countless light years from Earth.
RRRUUUMMMBBBLLLLLLE
The ruins of a high tech city stretch as far as the eye can see, speared at their centre by a huge tower, the derelict remains of a space elevator stretching all the way up into orbit ....
.... a testament to the technology and aspirations of a civilisation whose inhabitants have been dust for a million years ....
... and Bethany Breel is running for her life!
RRRUUUMMMBBBLLLLLLE
No..!!!!
Crruuu...UUMMPPPP

PUBLISHING

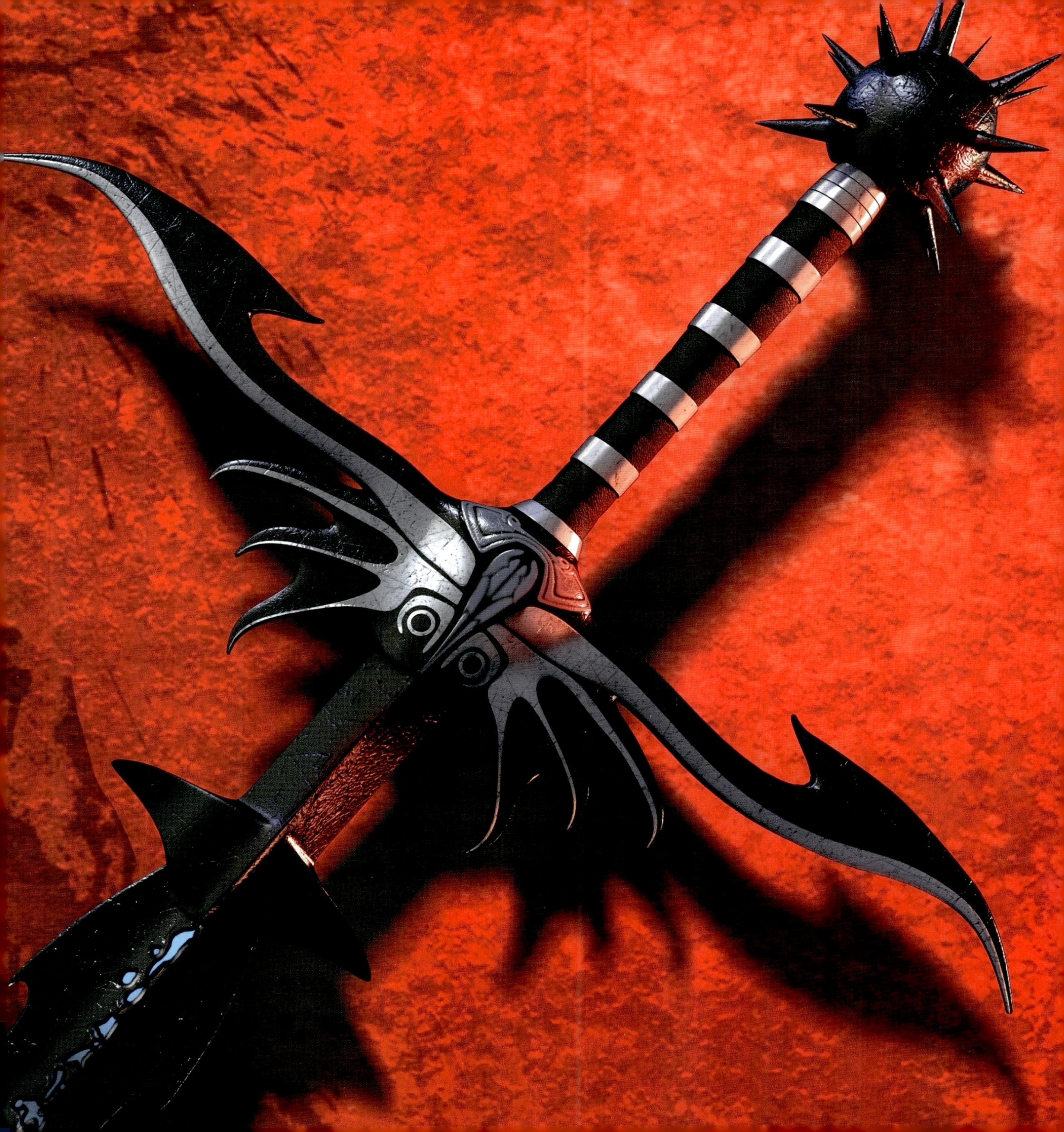

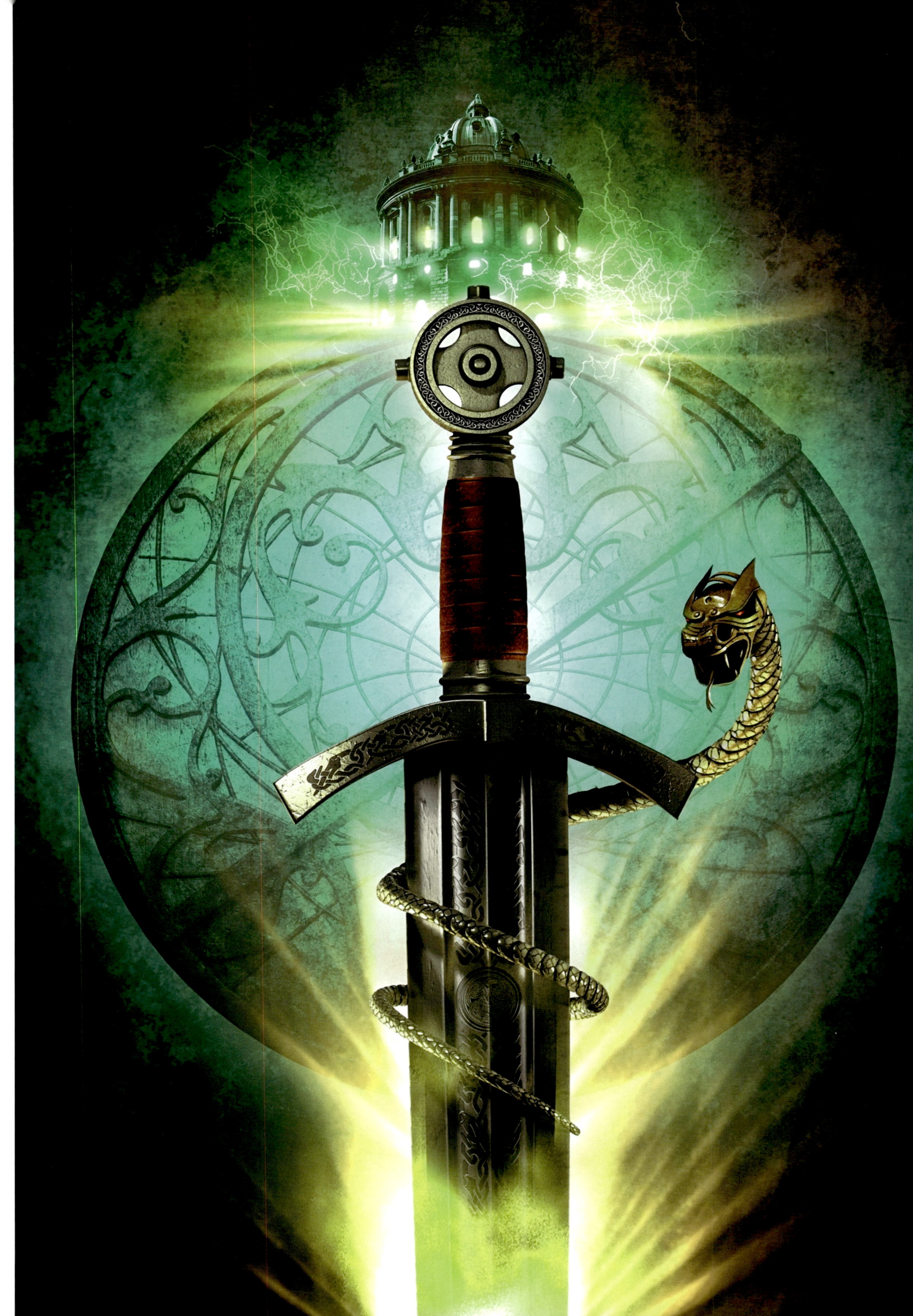

Previous page: *The Warlord's Legacy*, by Ari Marmell.

Opposite: *Dark Spies*, by Julia Golding.

This page, clockwise from right: *Shadow of the Conquerer*, by Ari Marmell; *I Am The Blade*, by J P Buxton; *Heartless Dark*, by J P Buxton.

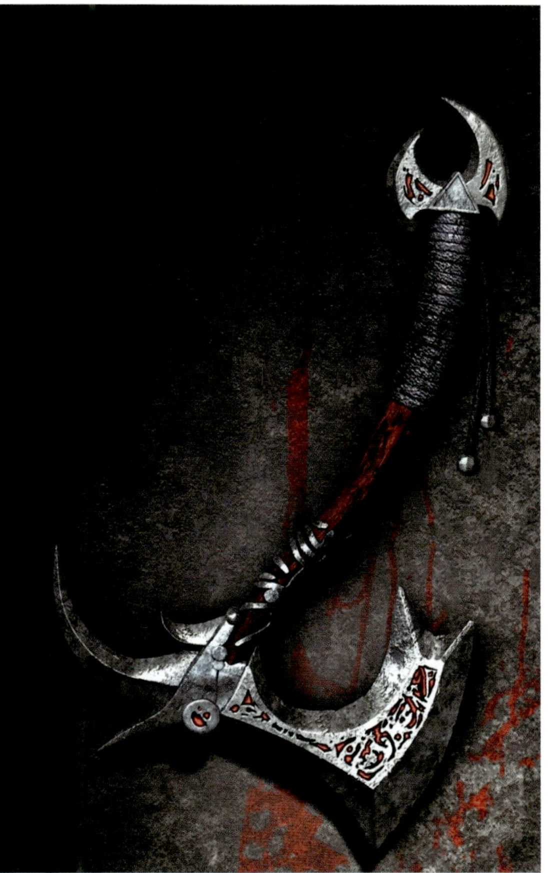

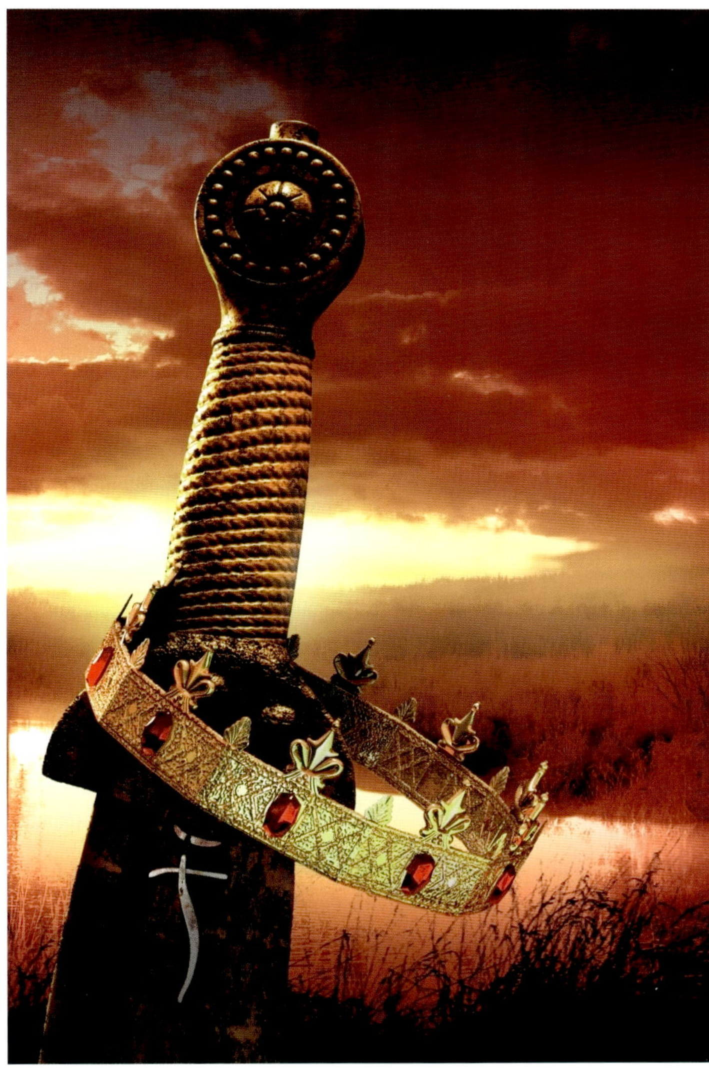

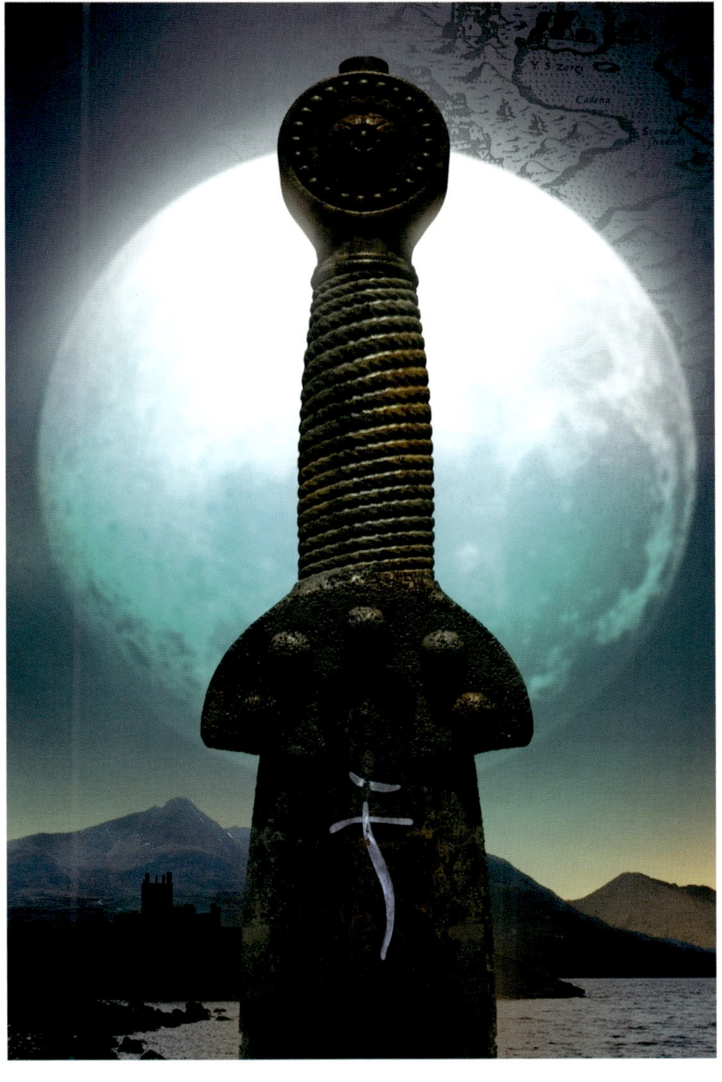

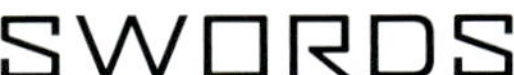

SWORDS

Swords are fantasy icons, symbols of status and power and more than a little Freudian. As such, they are often used to represent the genre. A sword on a cover, especially combined with an atmospheric background, tells the would-be-reader what they are letting themselves in for. This page shows a selection of fantasy weaponry realised using a combination of 3D modelling and photography. To get the background blood spatters on the *Shadow of the Conqueror* cover, I took a piece of board out into the garden and splashed black paint onto it, photographed the results and then comped them into the image, layering the paint into the background texture.

MODELS

One often gets commissions for a series of covers featuring a single main character. I mainly use professional models, but also use friends and people I run into – including, once, the barmaid at the local pub. Using models has its advantage and disadvantages. On the one hand, any input is helpful, and sometimes they'll drop into a pose I hadn't considered, which actually ends up looking much better than my original idea. On the other hand, I might need a very exaggerated pose, or the character might be floating weightless. The trick is not to be slavish to the reference but use it as raw material to get the desired effect.

Below left, top to bottom: *Changelings (The Twins of Petaybee)*, by Anne McCaffrey and Elizabeth Ann Scarborough; *Throne of Fire*, by Rick Riordan; *Mark of Athena*, by Rick Riordan.

Below right, top to bottom: *The Rebel Prince*; *The Crowded Shadows*; *The Poison Throne*. Speculative covers for the book series by Celine Kiernan.

Opposite: *Mist*, by Susan Krinard.

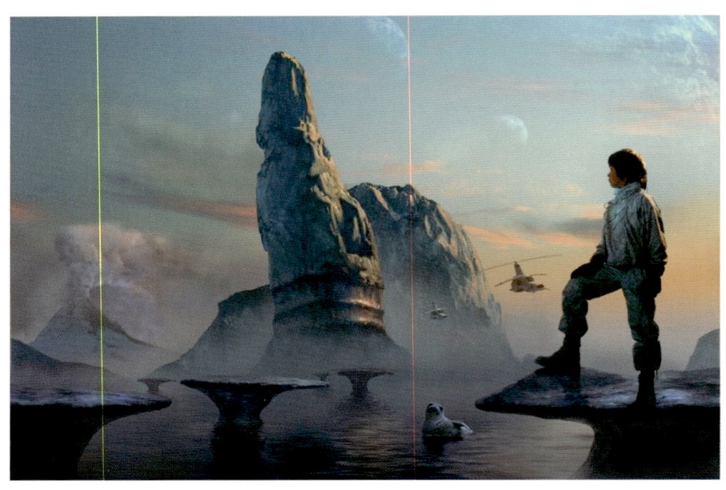

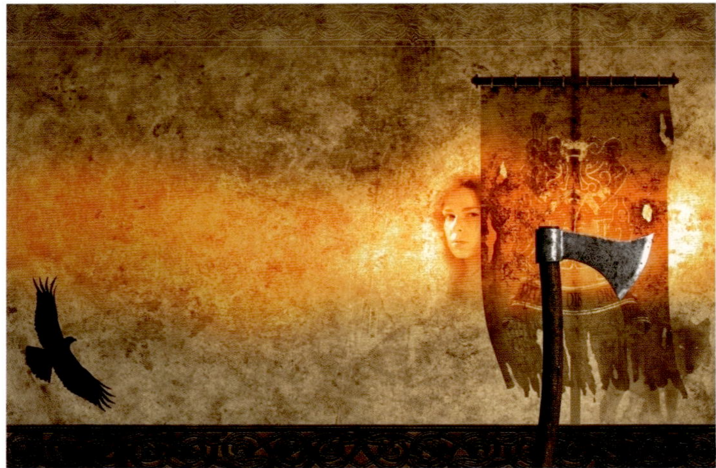

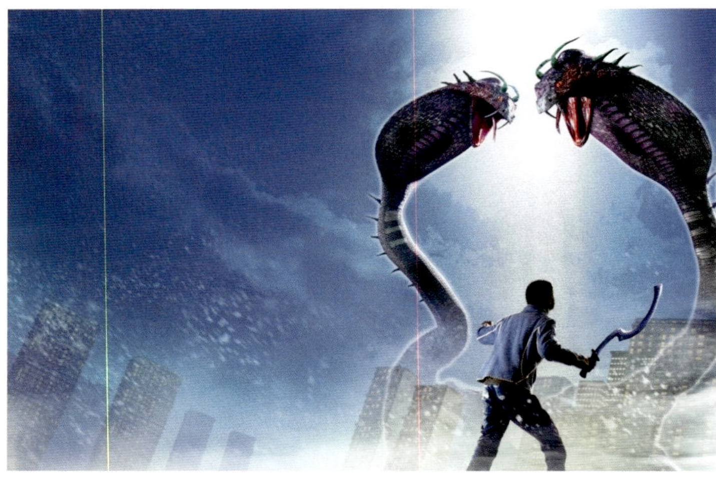

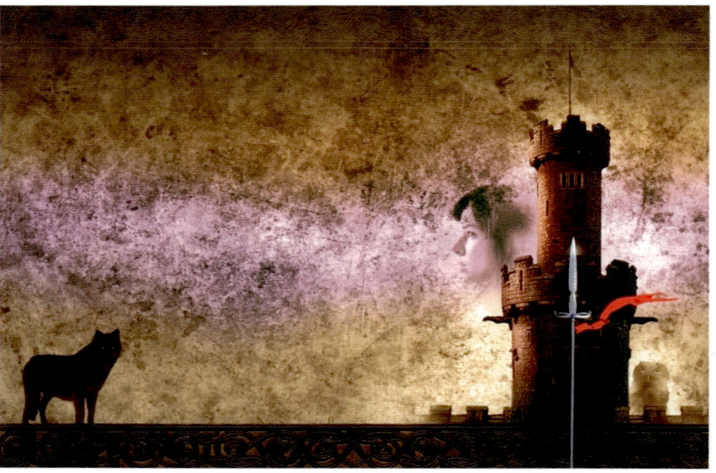

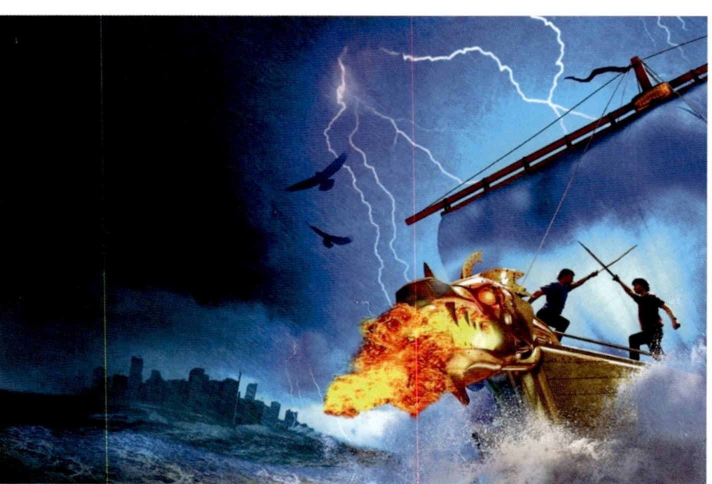

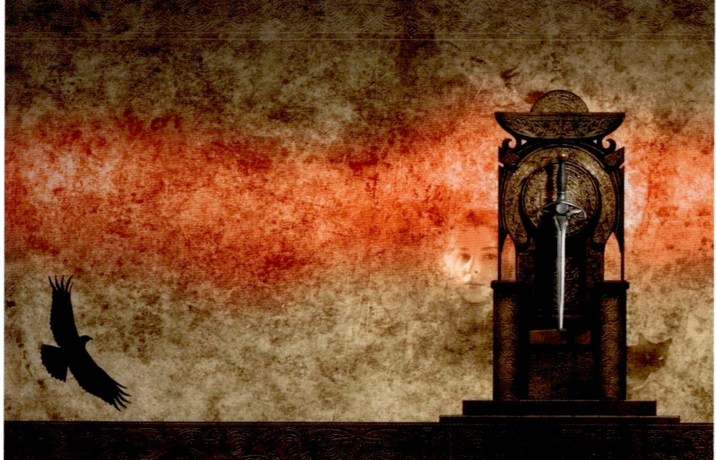

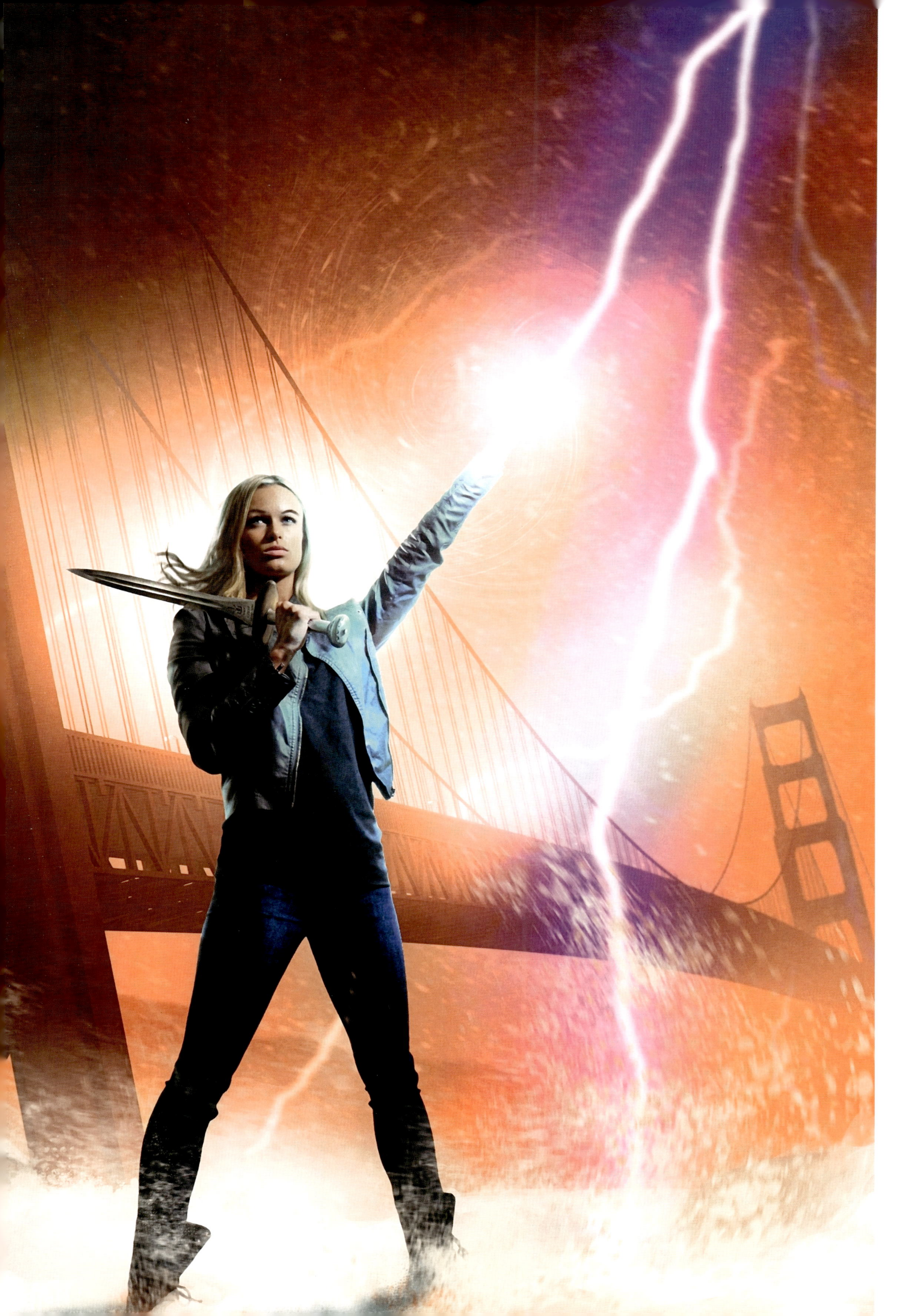

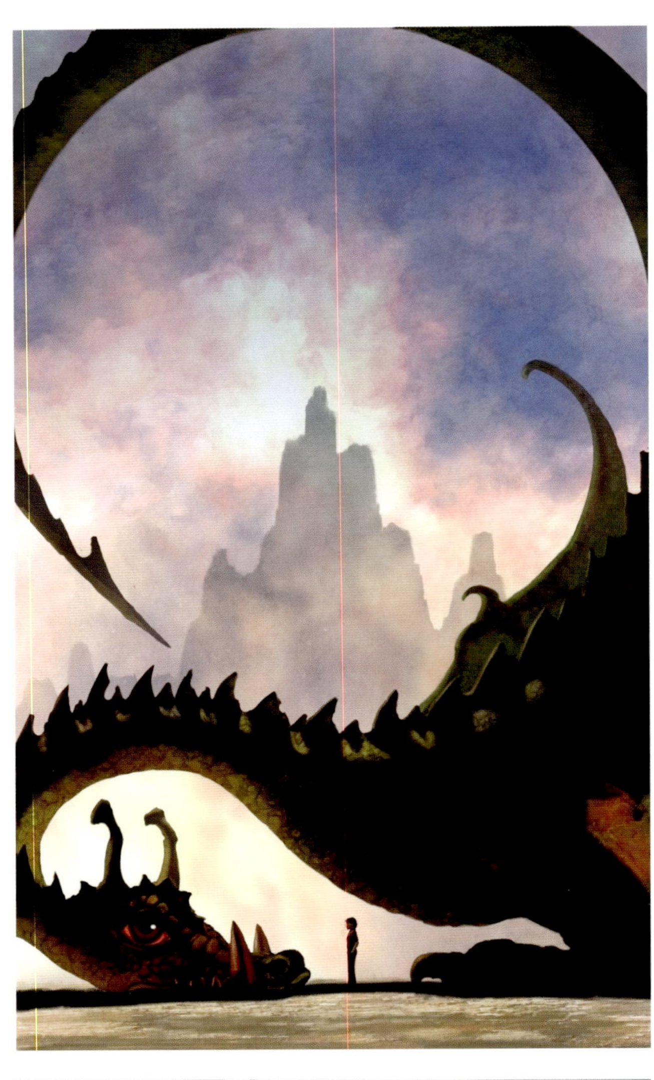

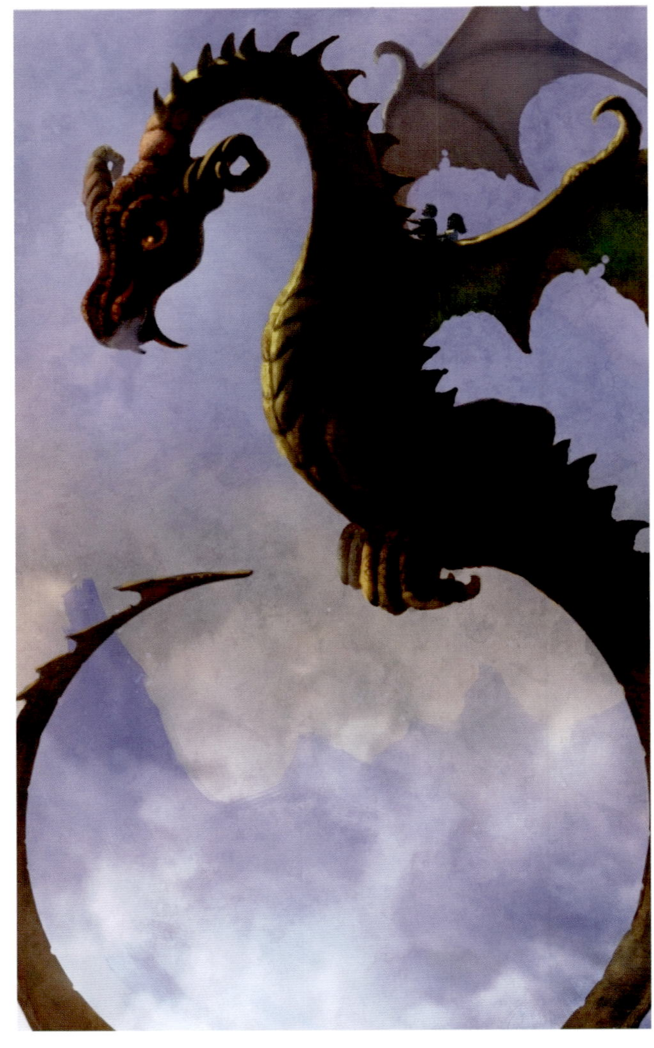

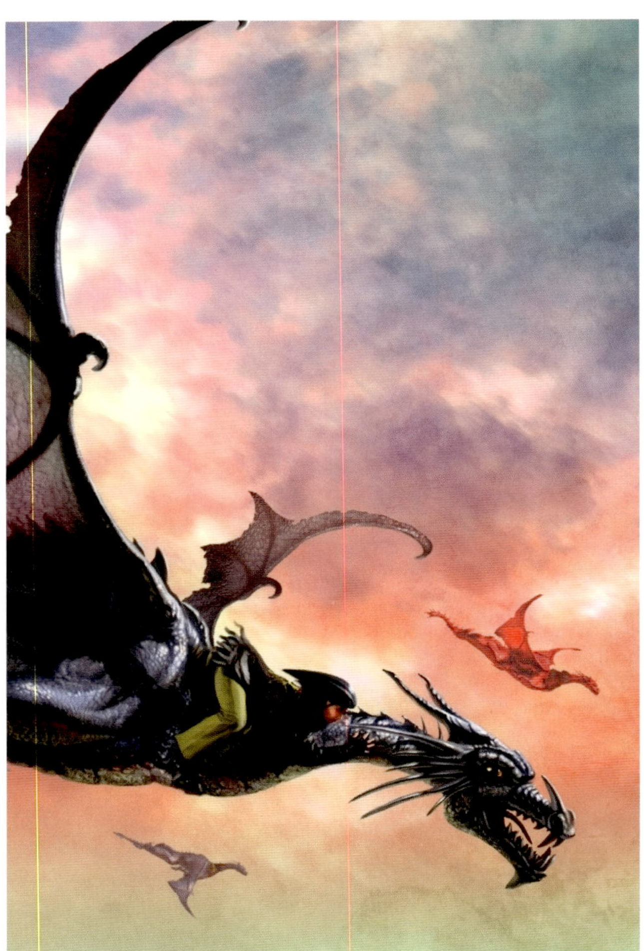

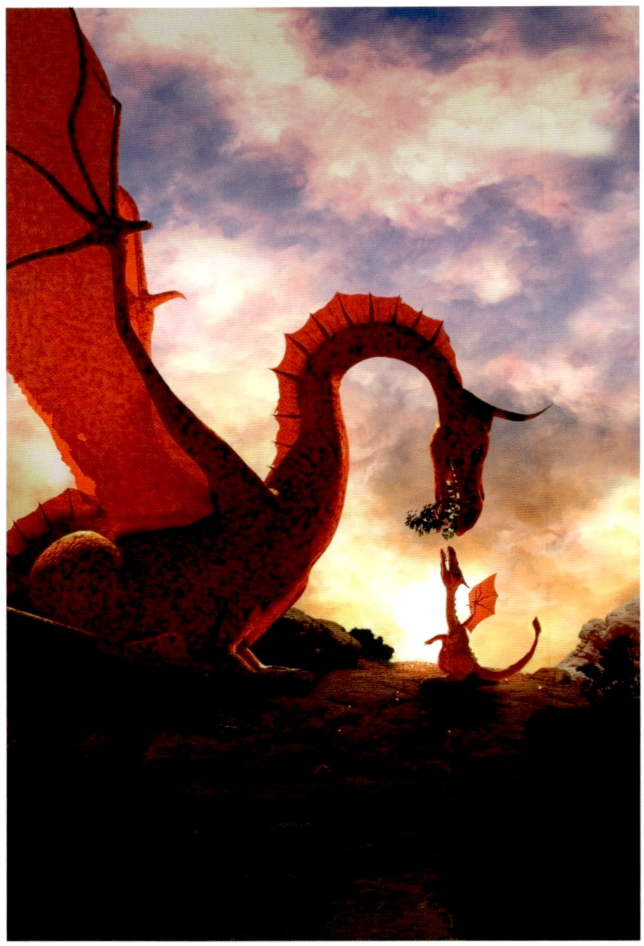

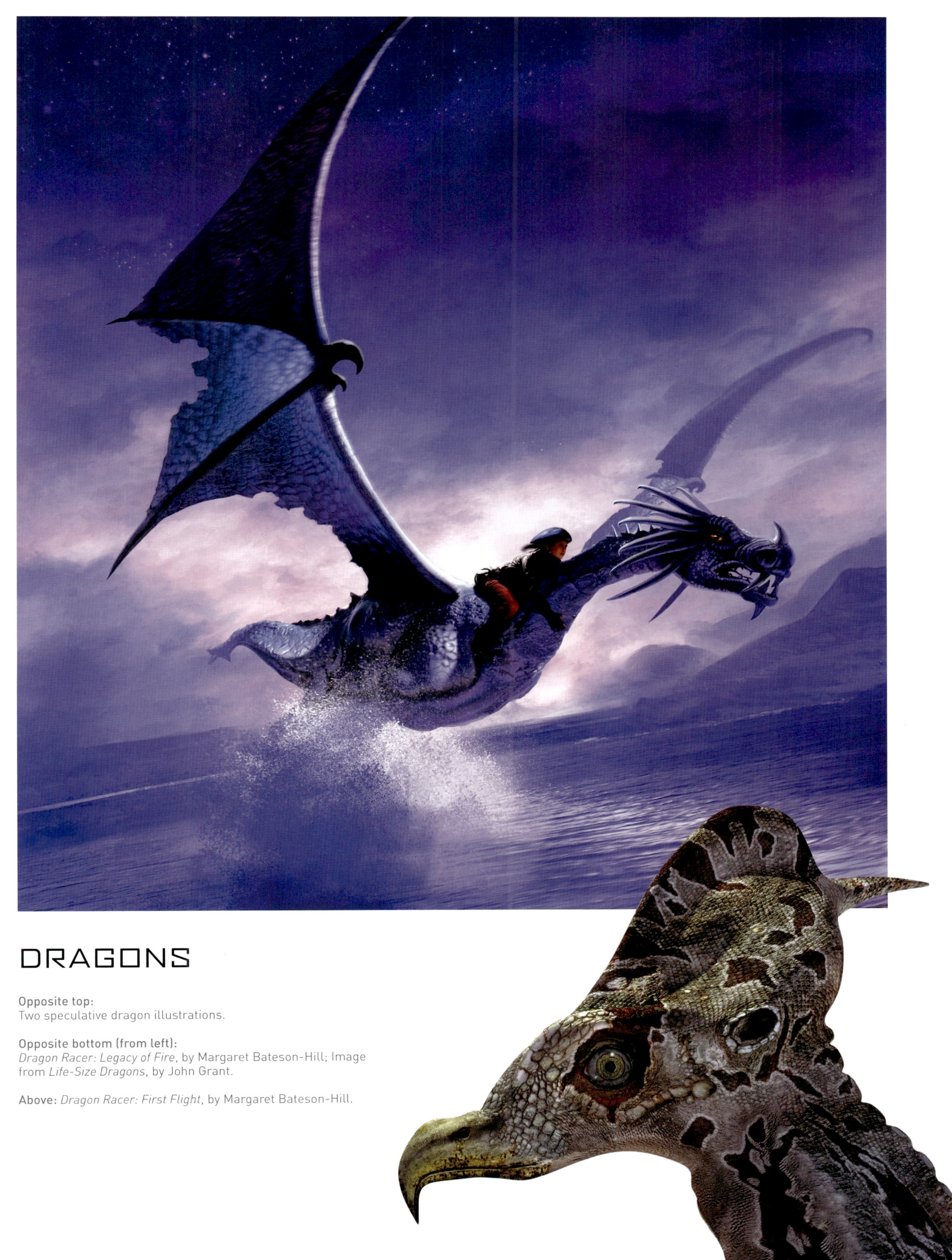

DRAGONS

Opposite top:
Two speculative dragon illustrations.

Opposite bottom (from left):
Dragon Racer: Legacy of Fire, by Margaret Bateson-Hill; Image from *Life-Size Dragons*, by John Grant.

Above: *Dragon Racer: First Flight*, by Margaret Bateson-Hill.

3D WORK & PHOTOGRAPHY

These covers all use a combination of 3D work and photography. *Legend* has my great niece Charlotte and *Patriot* my friend's son, Arthur. The backgrounds for both were generated in MODO using buildings from Google's sketch up library and then heavily worked over in Photoshop. The characters on *Starcorpsman* and *Bloodstar*, however, were wholly computer generated with a lot of atmospheric effects layers in Photoshop, whilst the *Alien in Battlespace* image was largely digitally hand painted.

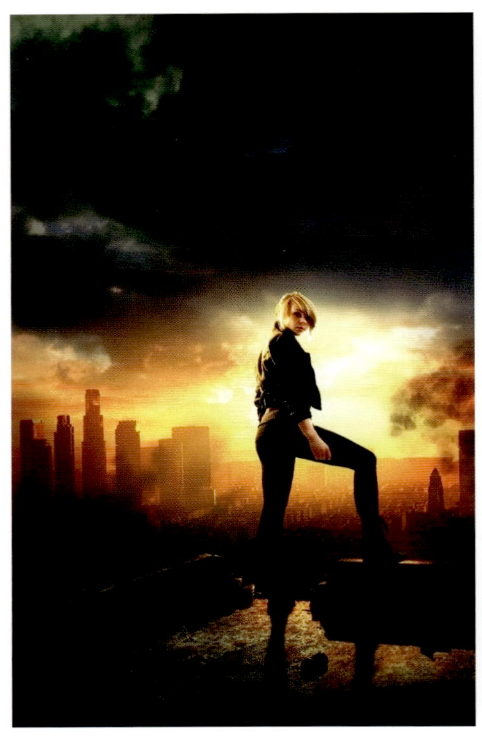

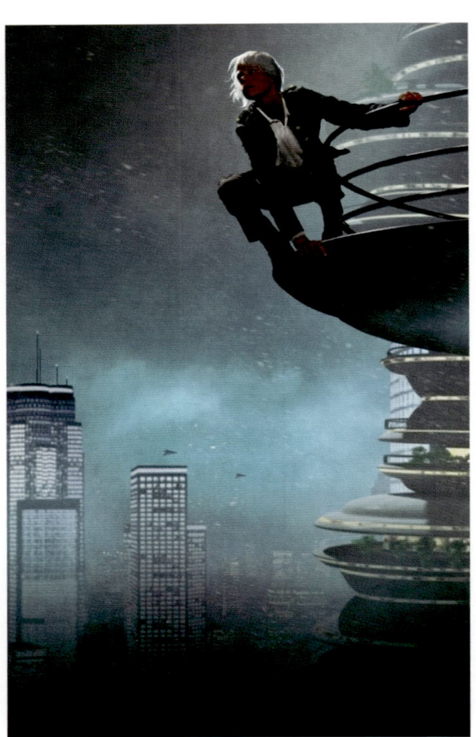

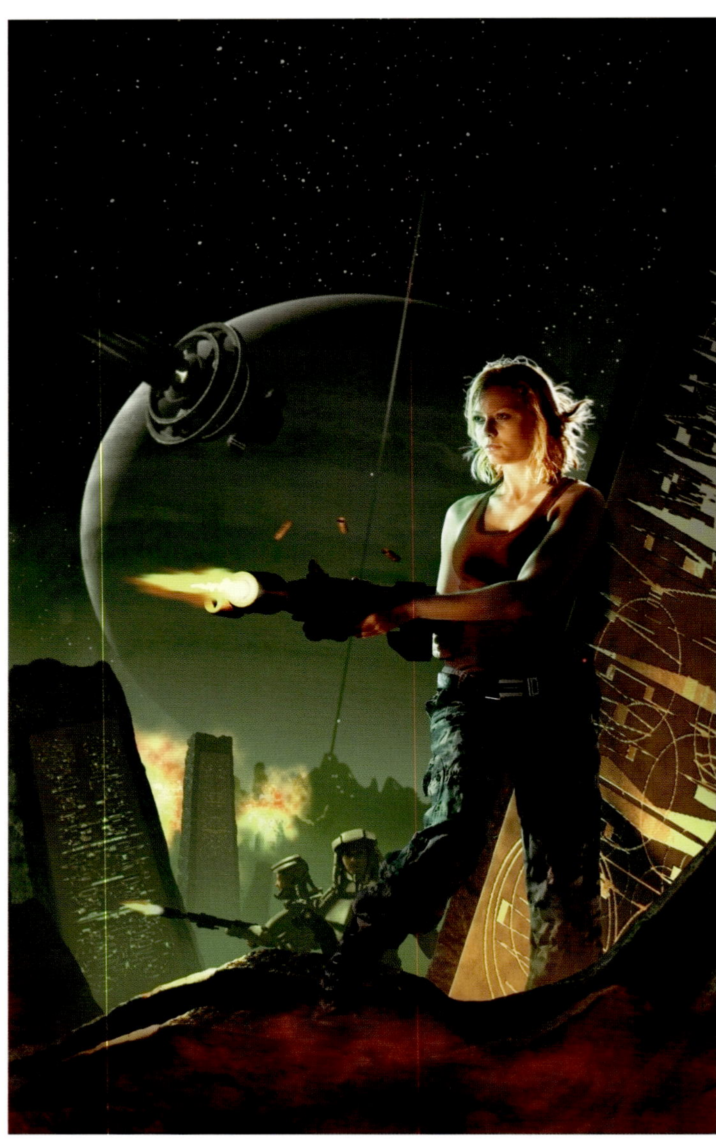

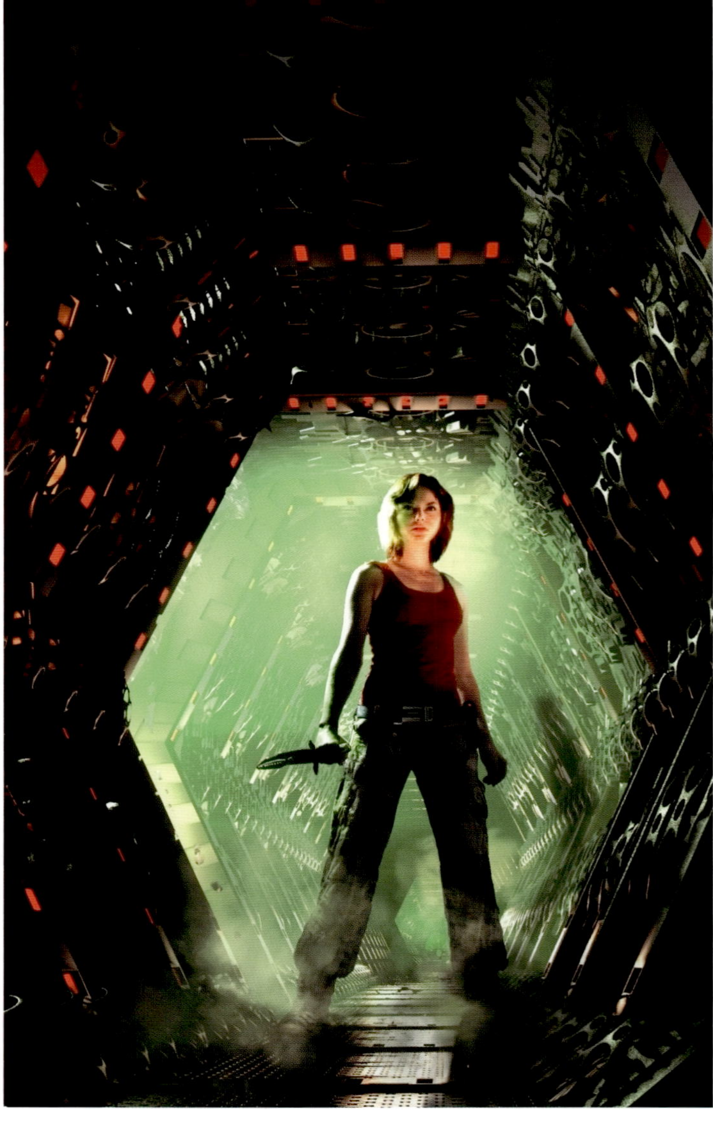

Opposite, clockwise from far left: *Legend* and *Patriot, by Marie Lu*; *Pathfinder* and *Vigilante*, by Laura E Reeve.

Below: *Battlespace*, by Ian Douglas.

Right, top and bottom: *Starcorpsmen Book 1: Bloodstar* and *Starcorpsmen Book 2: Abyss Deep*, by Ian Douglas.

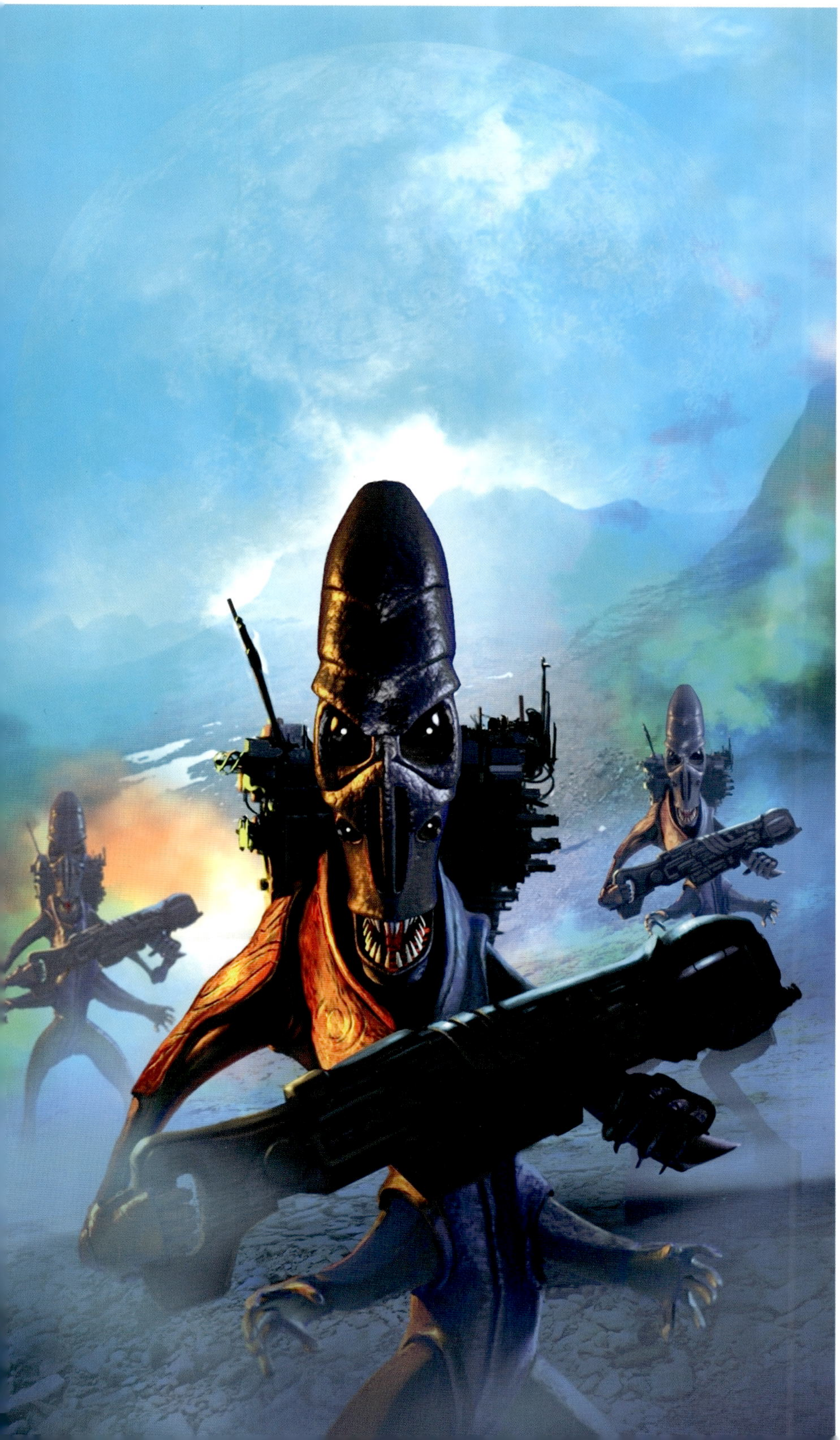

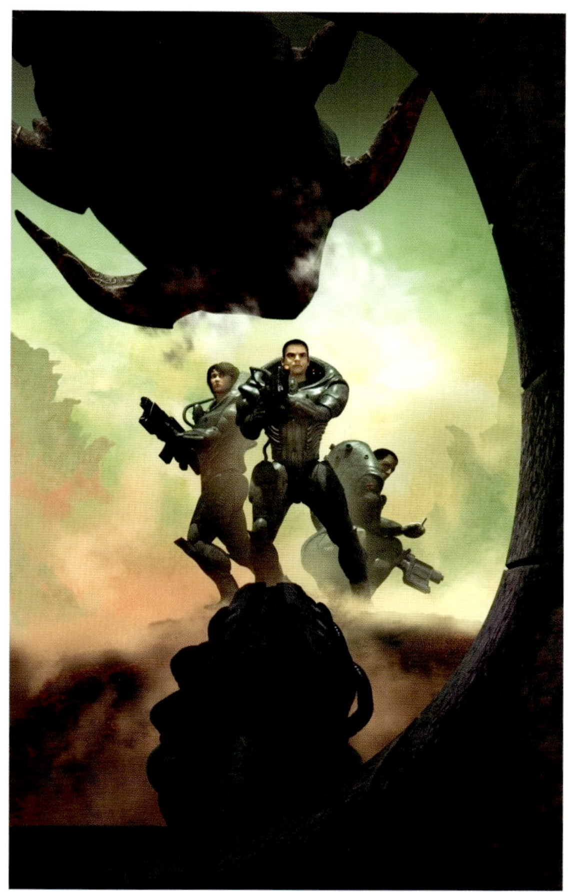

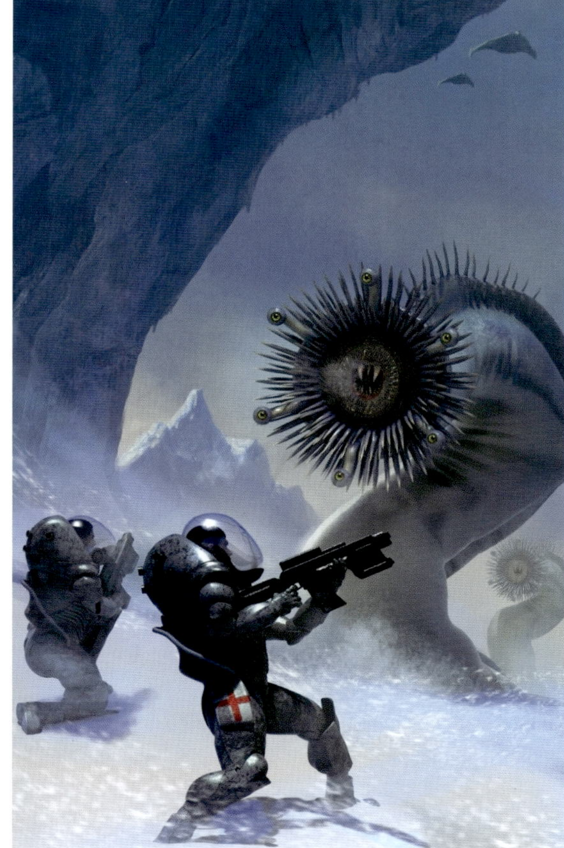

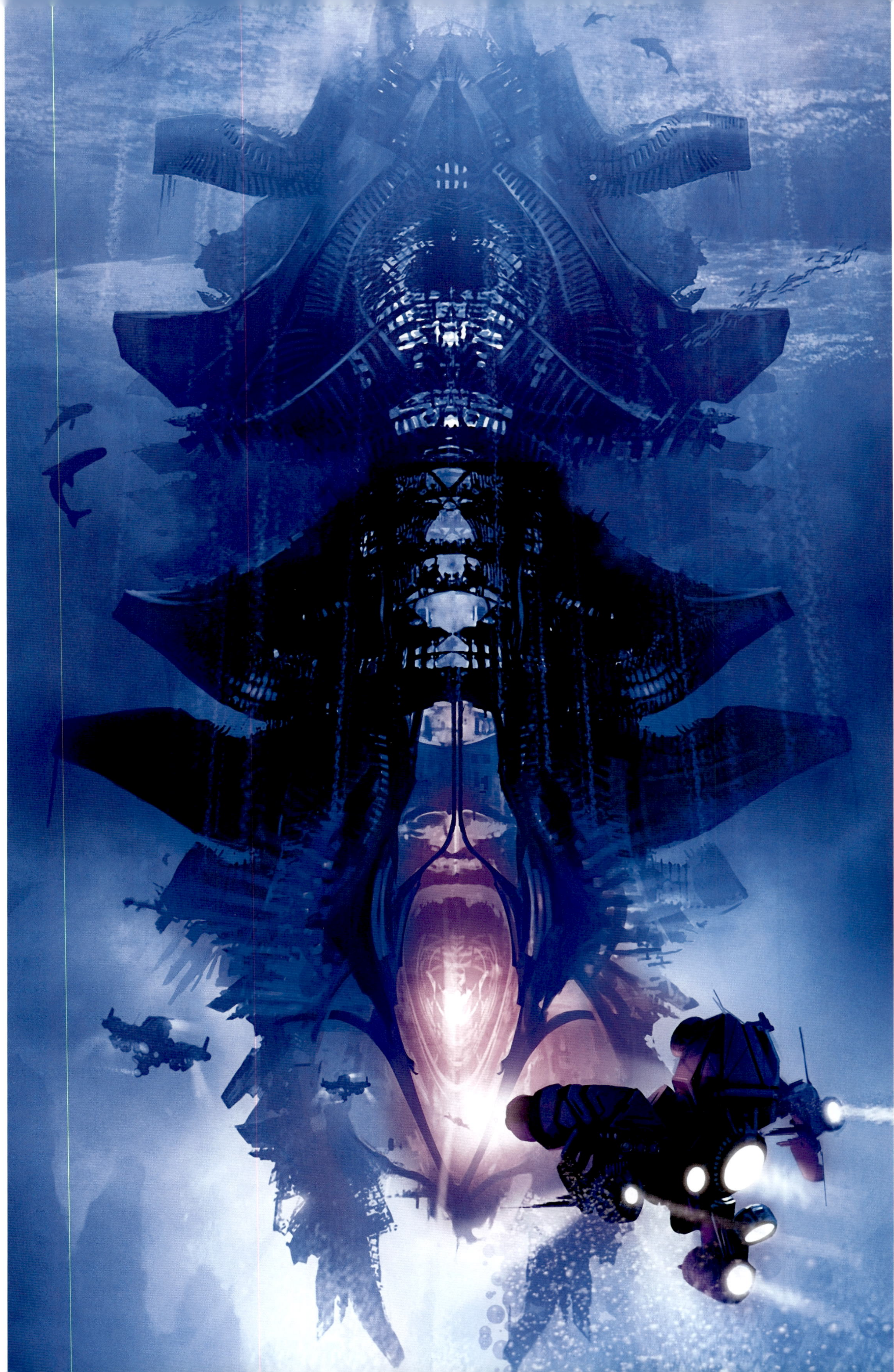

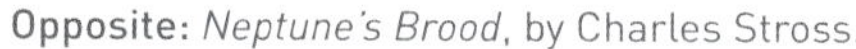

Opposite: *Neptune's Brood*, by Charles Stross.

Clockwise from left: *Old Twentieth*, by Joe Haldeman, Ace Books; Unused cover for *Jinx*, by Sage Blackwood; *Monster Odyssey: The Eye of Neptune*, by Jon Mayhew.

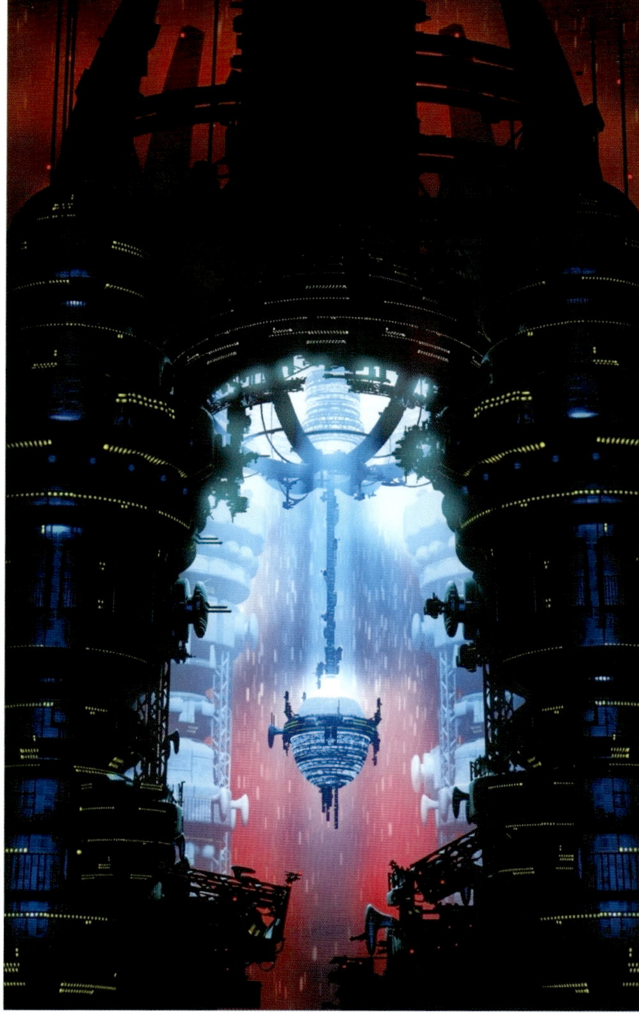

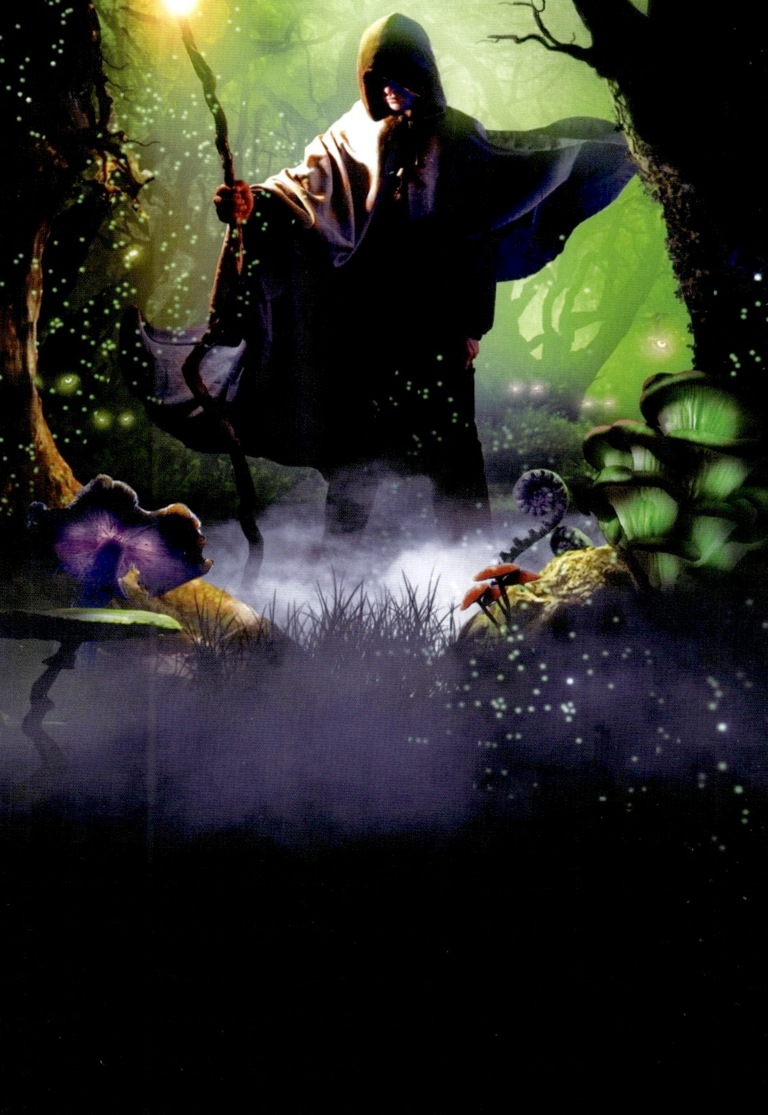

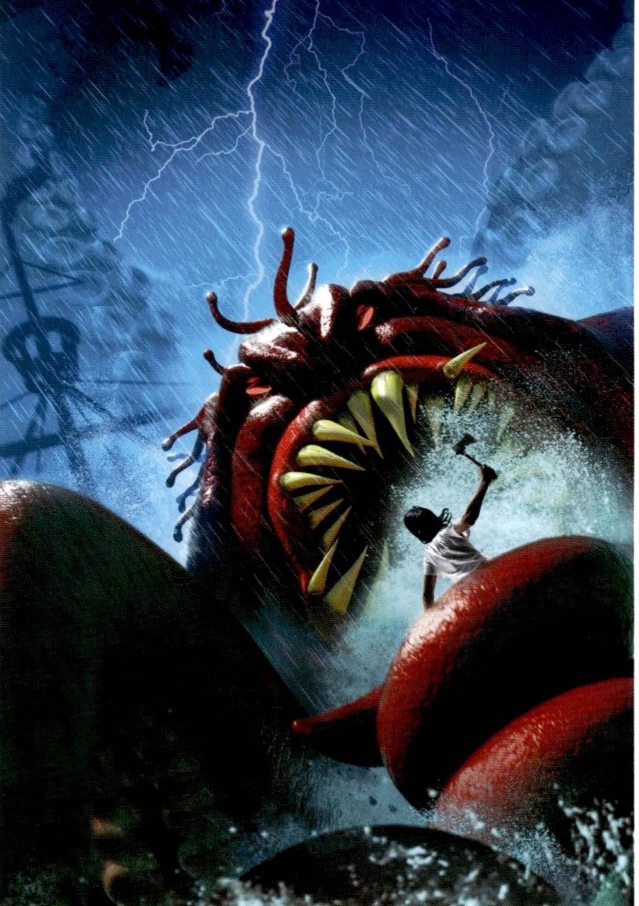

PHOTOSHOP

It's possible to make your own brushes using found or made black and white shapes in Photoshop. These shapes can be anything: bits of cars, buildings, something more organic or something I've drawn myself. By changing the parameters of the brush, you can get Photoshop to stamp out the shapes in unexpected ways, and use them as the starting point of a spaceship, an alien landscape or a creature. It's a way to escape the muscle memory that tends to make you repeat yourself despite your best efforts, and a way to generate shapes that you may not have thought of.

The ships in *Neptune's Brood* were created using this randomised method. I took the raw shapes and used them as a starting point, and ended up with the gothic looking submerged spacecraft and its ancillary vehicles.

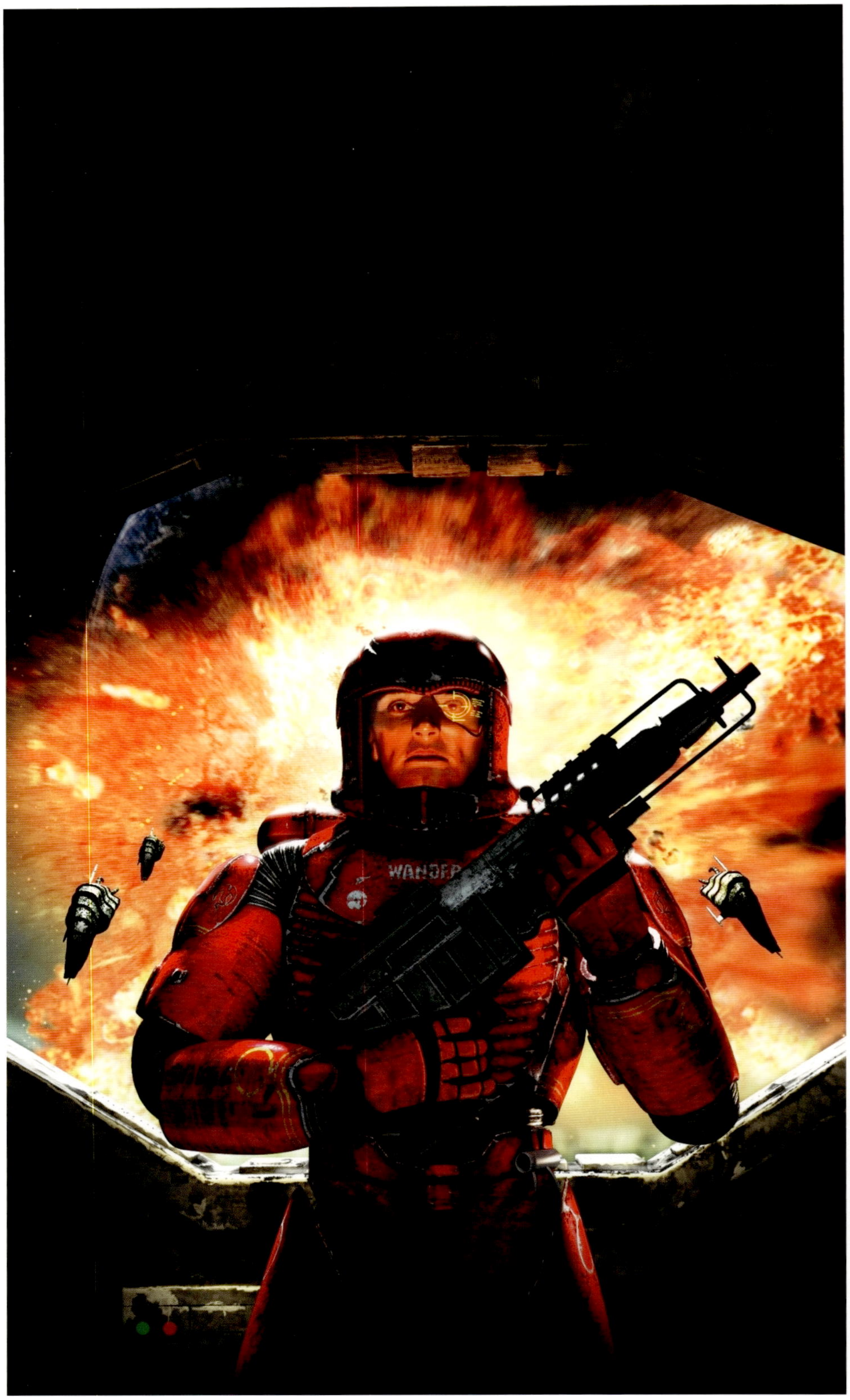

Left: *Orphanage*, by Robert Buettner.

Opposite: *Sten 8: Empire's End*, by Allan Cole and Chris Bunch.

Below: *Sten 5: Revenge of the Damned*, by Allan Cole and Chris Bunch.

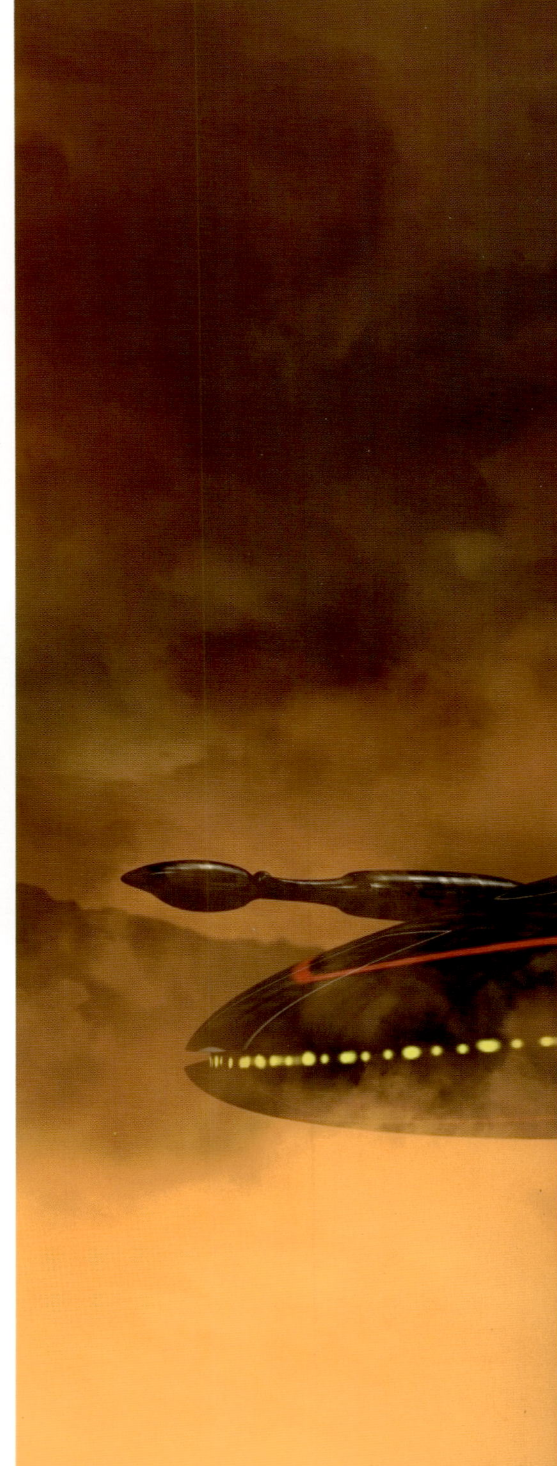

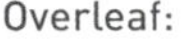

Overleaf:

Page 82, clockwise from top left: *Vatta's War: Victory Conditions*; *Vatta's War, Book 1: Trading in Danger*; *Vatta's War (unused version)*; *Vatta's War, Book 3: Engaging the Enemy*. Books by Elizabeth Moon.

Page 83:
Vatta's War Book 4: Command Decision, by Elizabeth Moon.

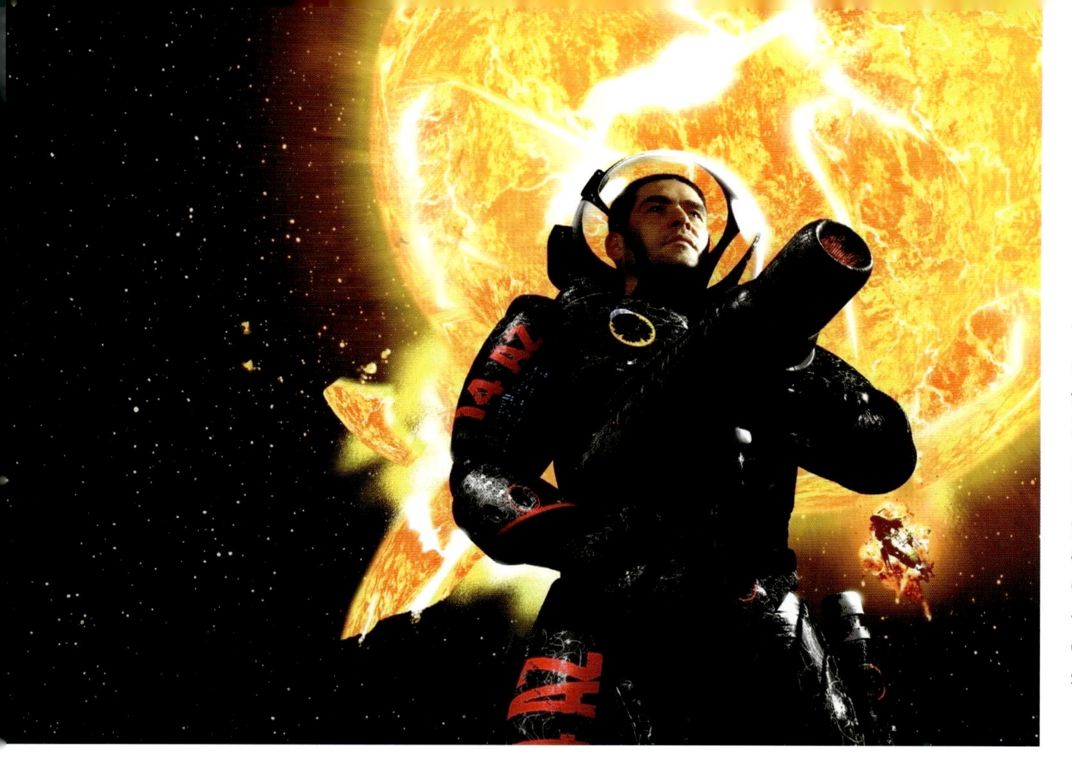

MILITARY SF

The character Sten appeared on six covers. My friend's brother Jamie, who I happened to meet at a party, looked the part and – like so many of my friends and acquaintances – found himself the eponymous hero of a galactic quest. The level of destruction amped up with each cover, from crashing spacecraft to destroyed cities – until I got to destroy an entire planet on the final cover. The planet and space suit were realised in MODO.

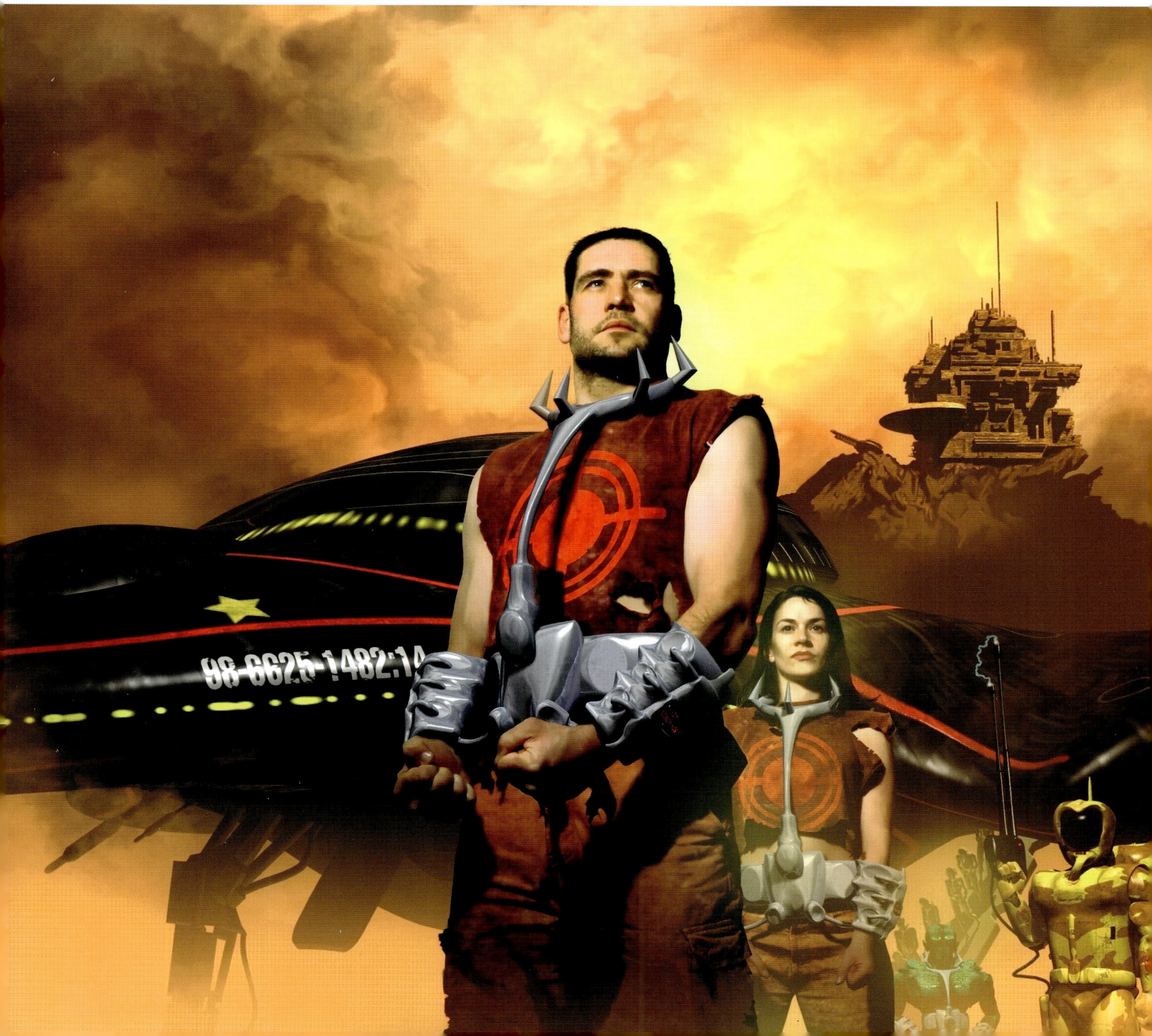

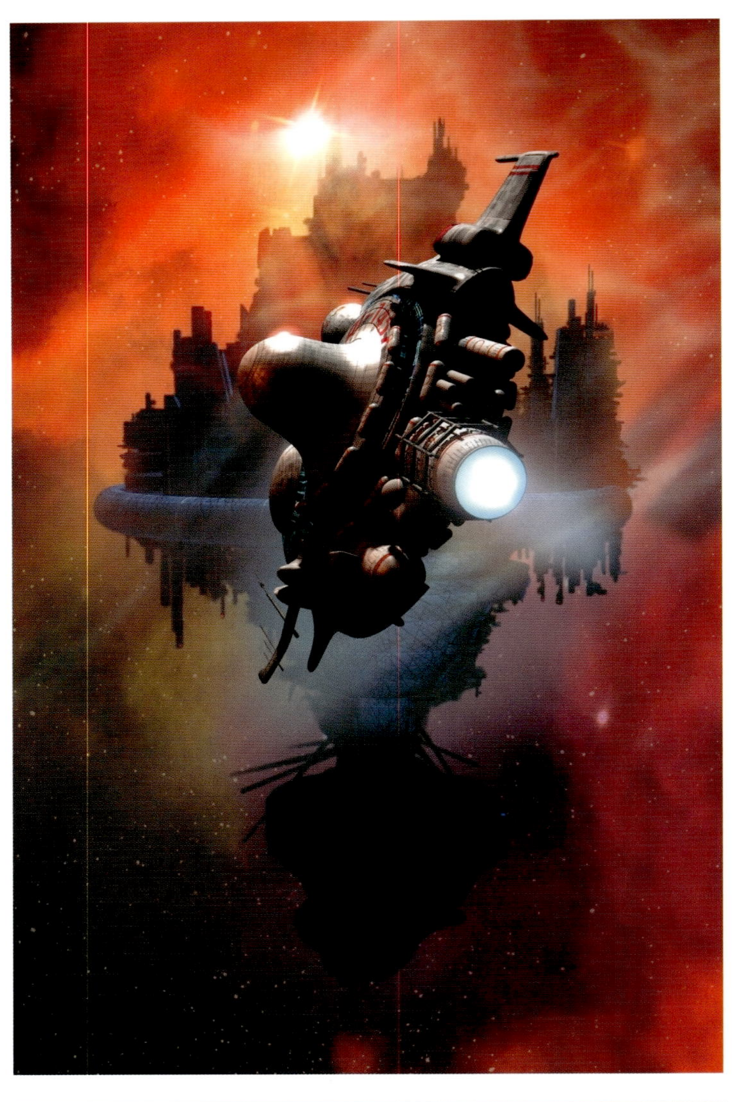

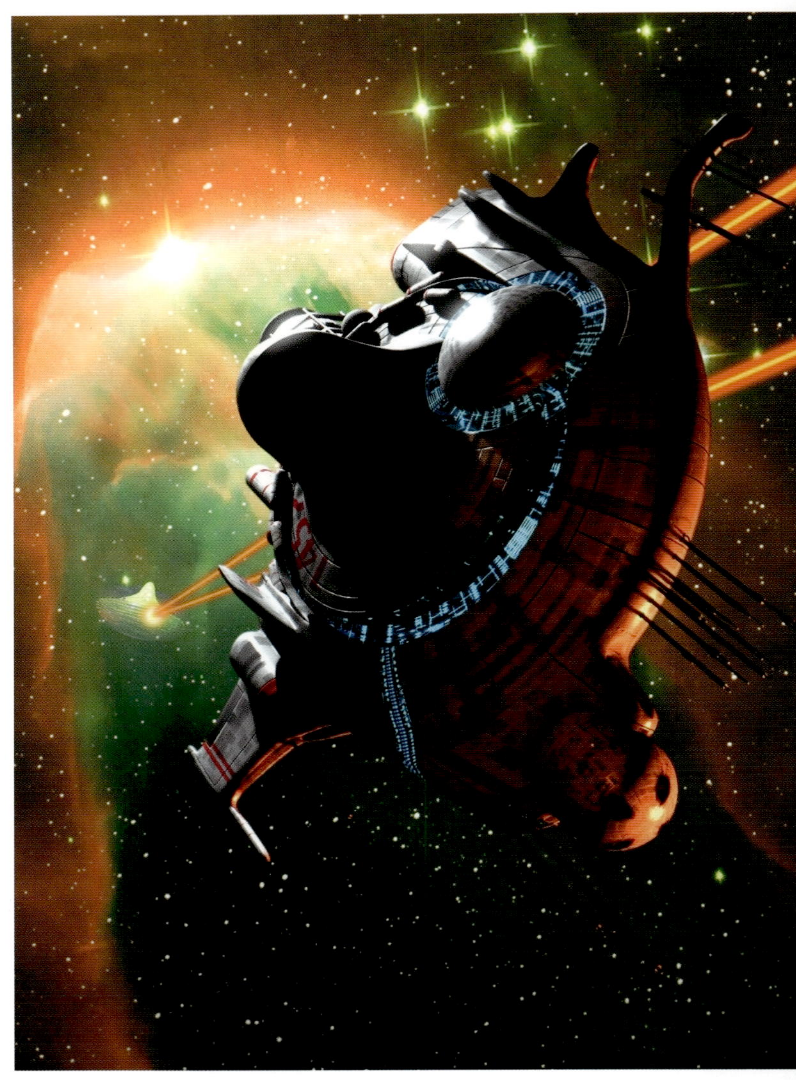

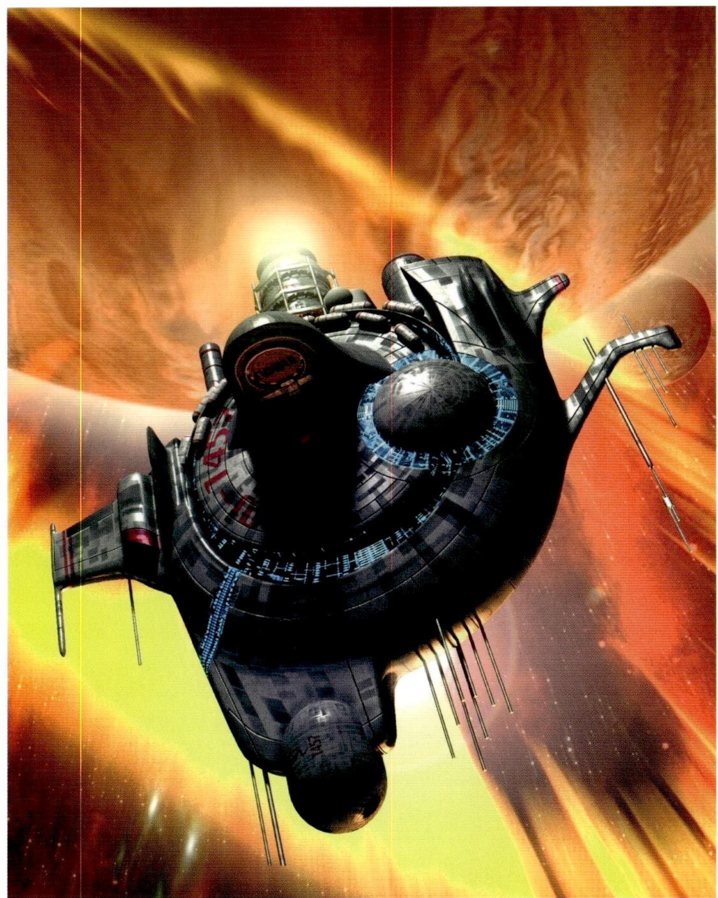

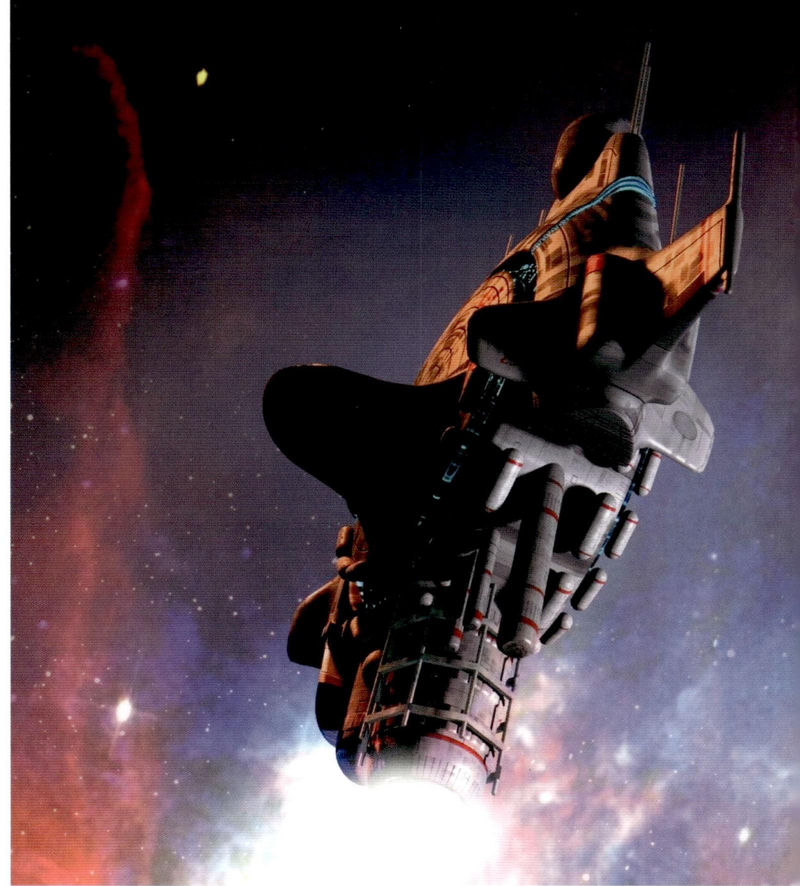

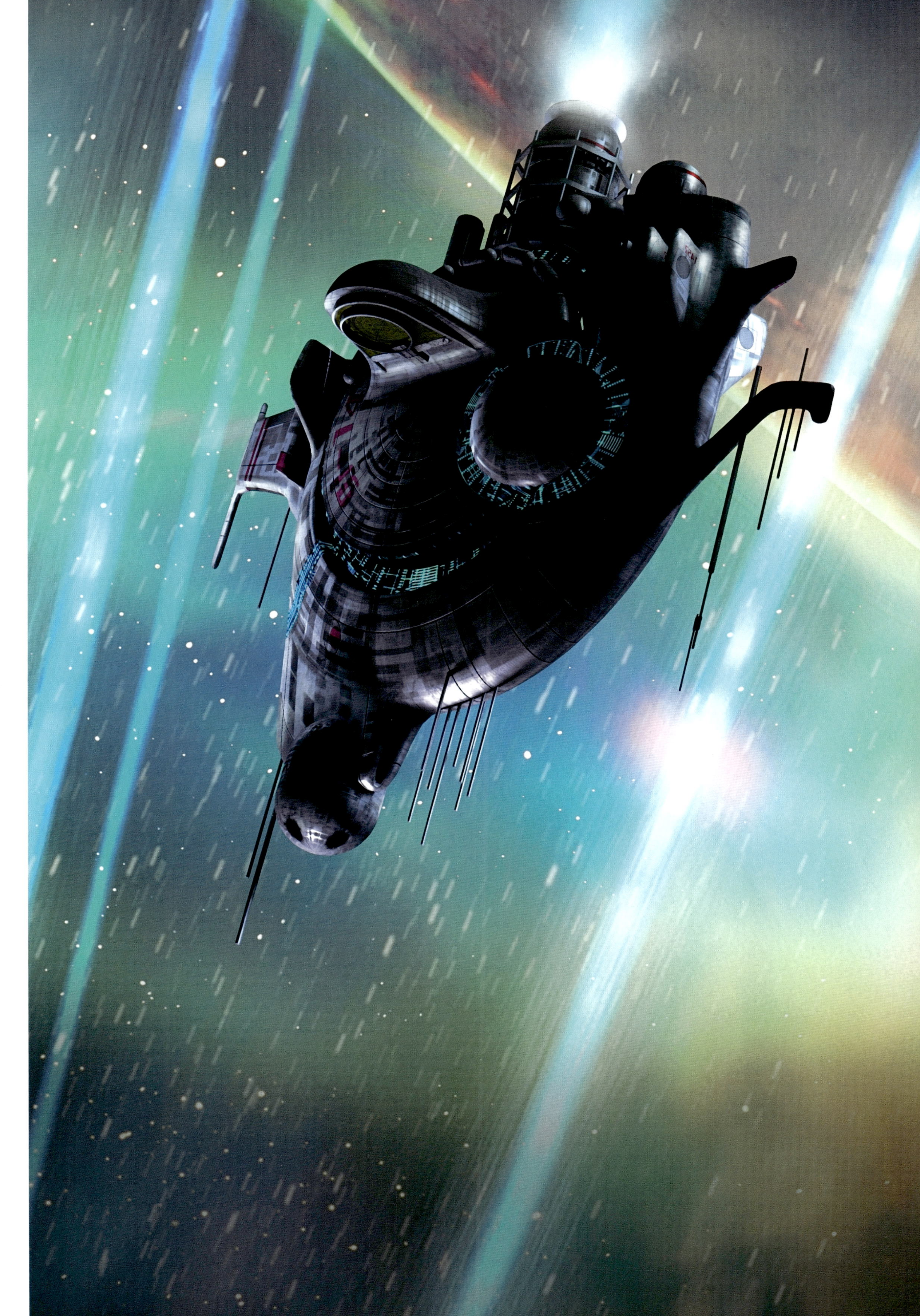

BATTLETECH AND MECHWARRIOR

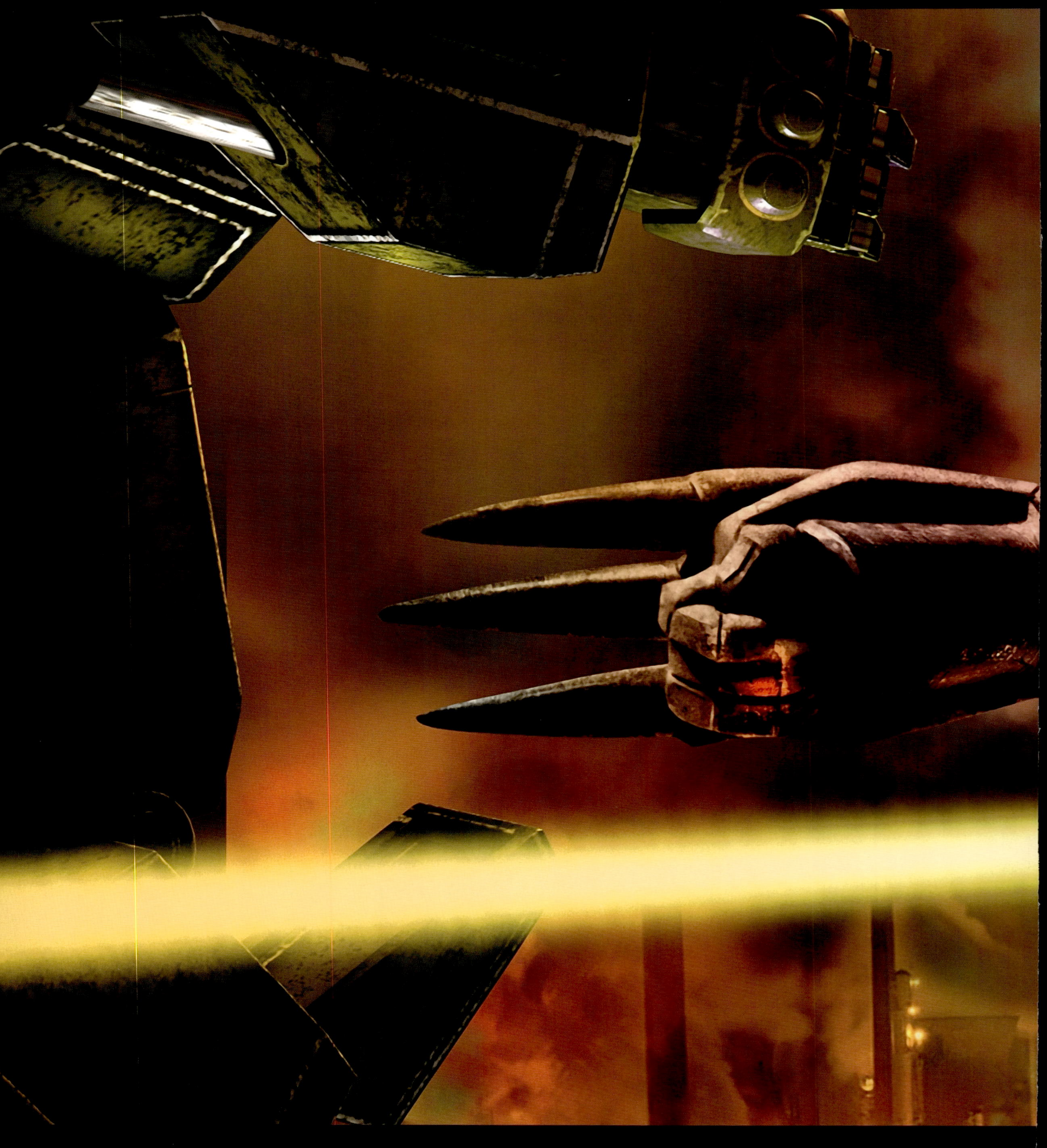

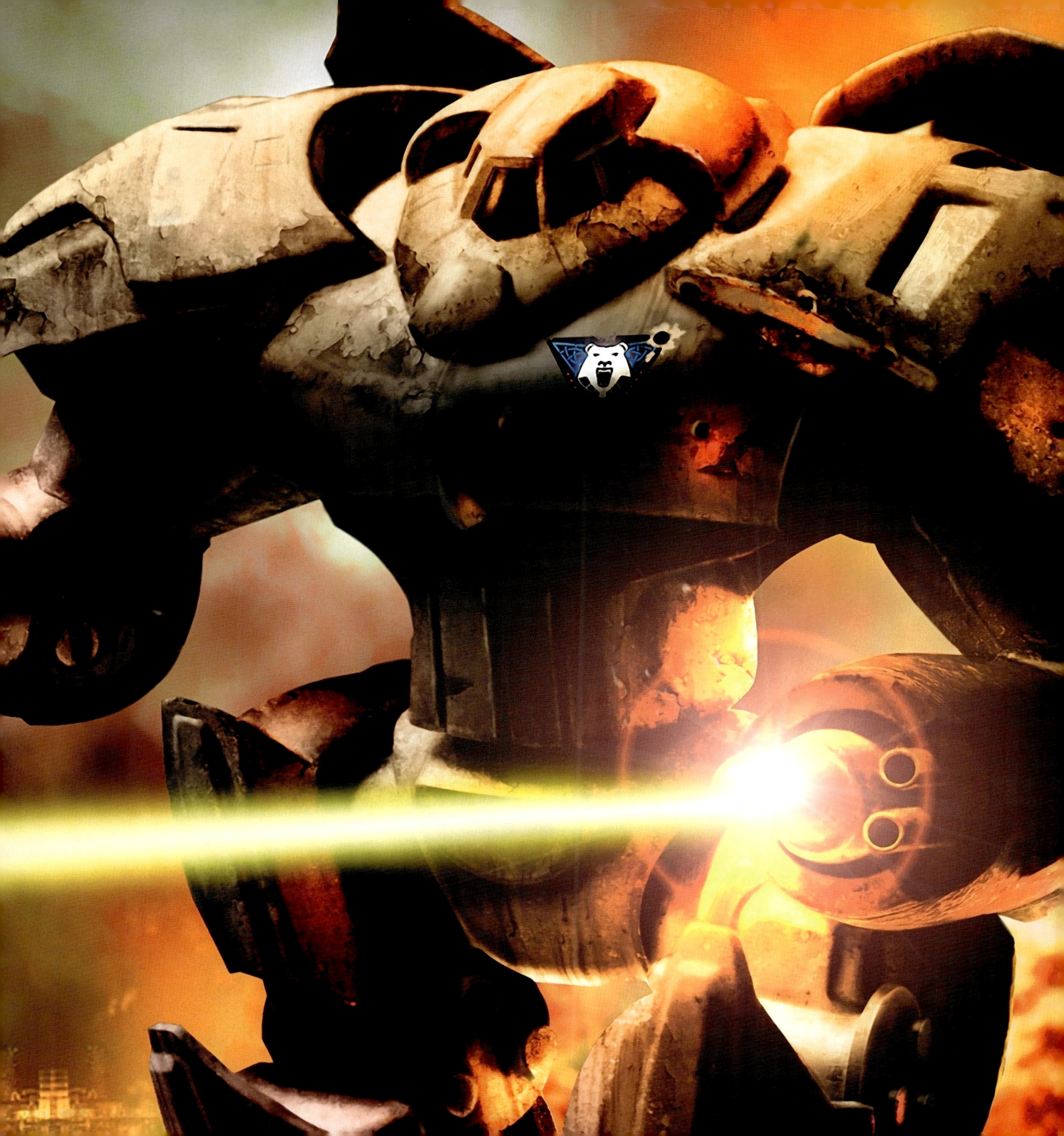

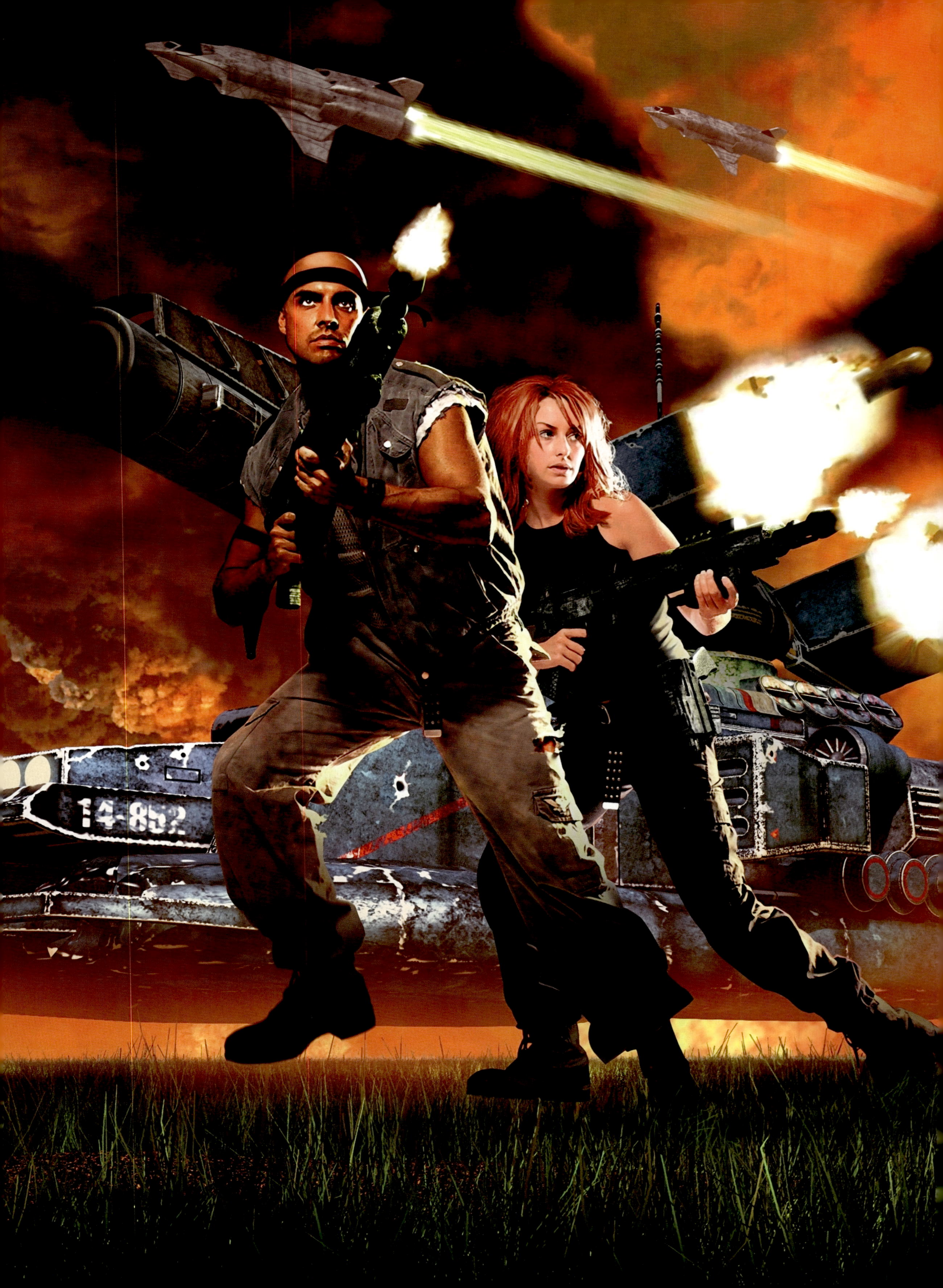
14-852

Previous page: *Trial by Chaos*, the book by J. Steven York, Roc, an imprint of New American Library, a division of Penguin Group (USA).

Opposite: *Patriot's Stand*, the book by Mike Moscoe, Roc, an imprint of New American Library, a division of Penguin Group (USA).

This page, clockwise from top left: *Target of Opportunity*, the book by Blaine Lee Pardoe, Roc, an imprint of New American Library, a division of Penguin Group (USA).

The Scorpion Jar, the book by Jason M Hardy, Roc, an imprint of New American Library, a division of Penguin Group (USA).

Service for the Dead, the book by Martin del Rio, Roc, an imprint of New American Library, a division of Penguin Group (USA).

A Silence in the Heavens, the book by Martin del Rio, Roc, an imprint of New American Library, a division of Penguin Group (USA).

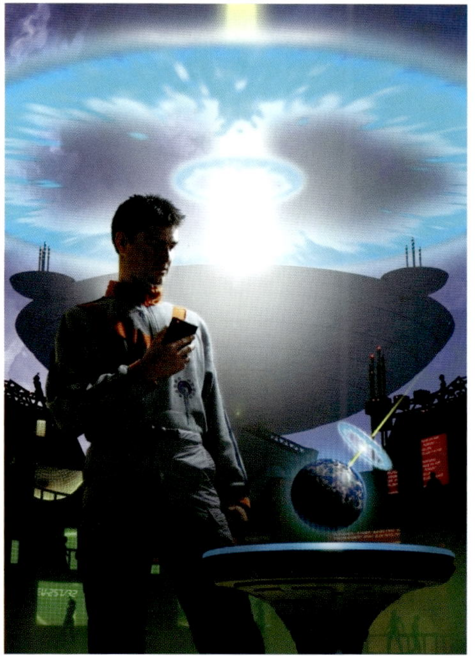

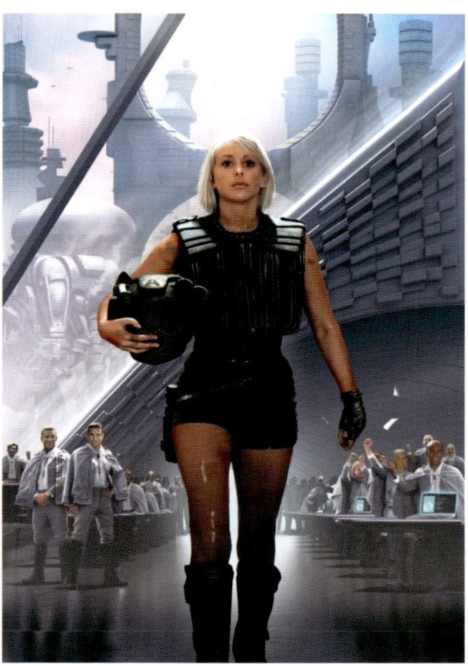

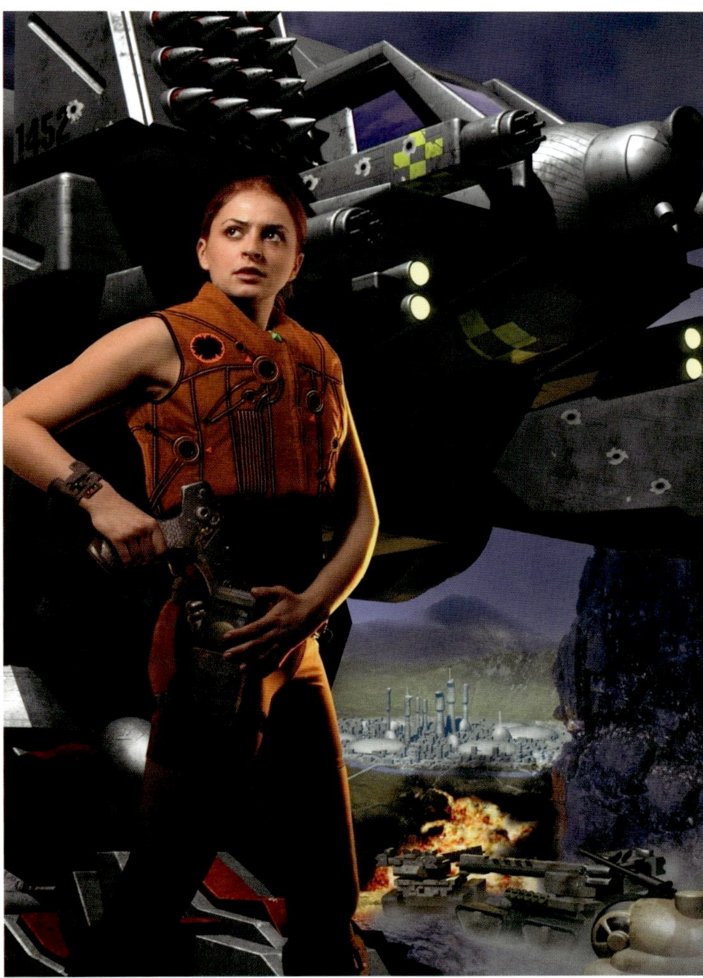

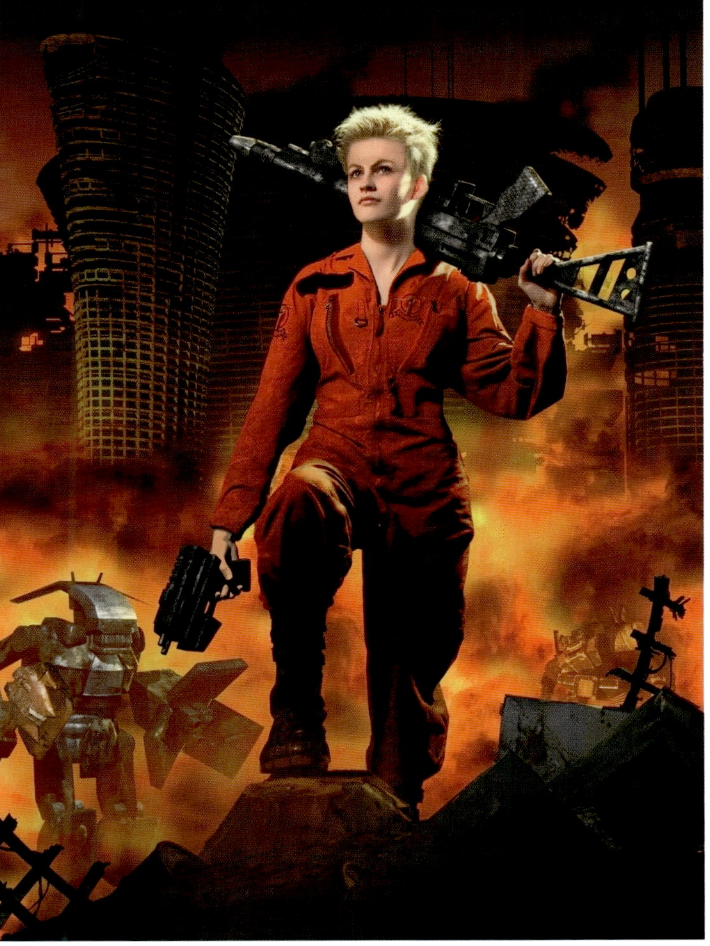

The *Battletech* series was a mainstay for me for about six years until the series was finally terminated. Originally titled *Battletech* but later renamed *Mechwarrior*, I cut my digital teeth on this series, so to speak.

These covers had always featured two battling robots but as the *Mechwarrior* series progressed they wanted to include more of the human characters. My partner Jenny can be seen toting a gun on *Wolf Hunters* (page 91, *top left*). Most of the mechs were modelled in Lightwave and later MODO.

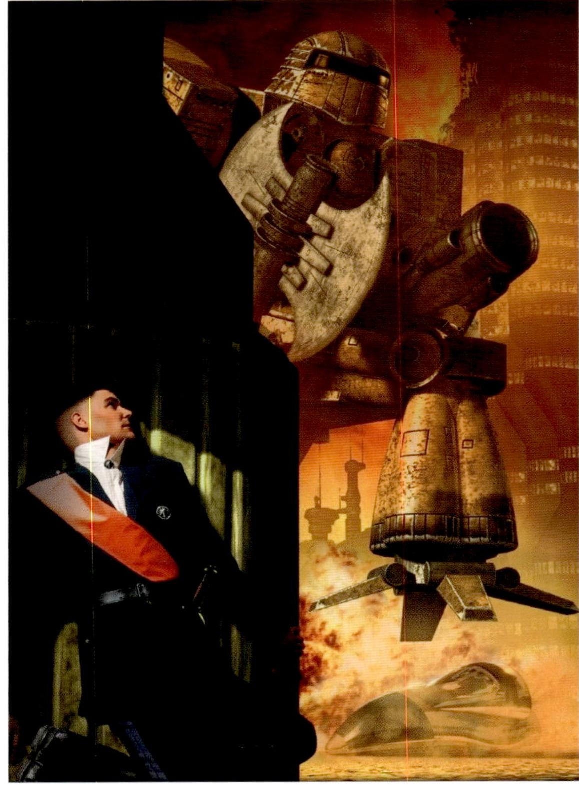

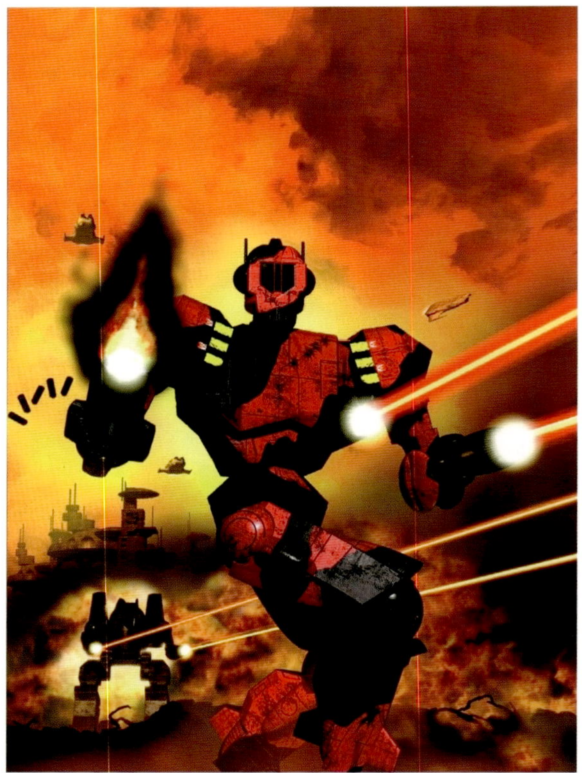

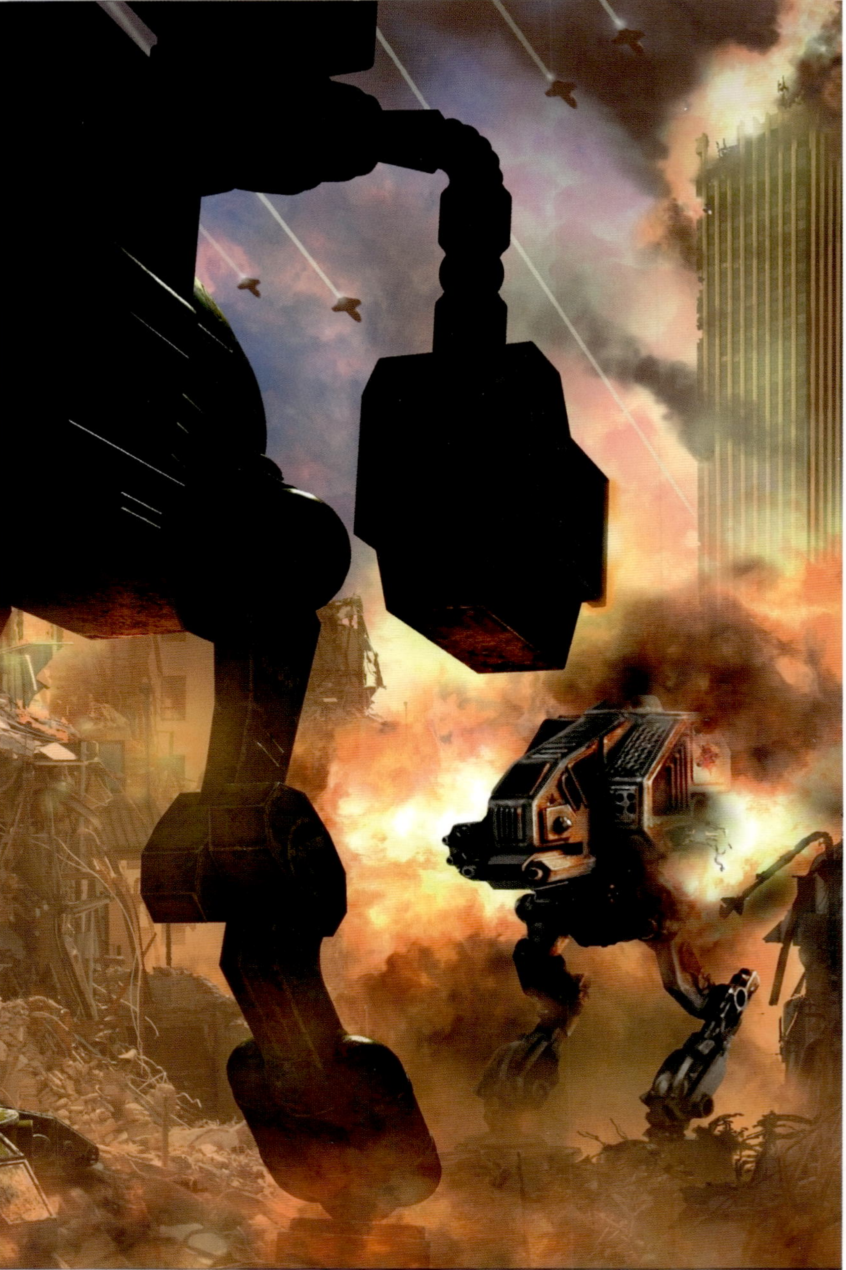

I really taught myself a lot about 3D modelling, texturing and lighting on these commissions and probably went to more trouble than was strictly necessary, but it was an enjoyable learning curve.

For reference, I usually had line drawings to work to. Most of the mech designs were *Battletech* designs, but occasionally they sent me small, two-inch tall action figures. When I got these, I often photographed them and took them into Photoshop for a lot of painting and texture work. As you can imagine, a photo of a two-inch model requires a lot of work to make it look like a one-hundred foot mech in a battle-torn environment.

Clockwise from top:
Fortress of Lies, the book by J Steven York, Roc, an imprint of New American Library, a division of Penguin Group (USA).

The Last Charge, the book by Jason M Hardy, Roc, an imprint of New American Library, a division of Penguin Group (USA).

Patriots and Tyrants, the book by Loren L Coleman, Roc, an imprint of New American Library, a division of Penguin Group (USA).

Opposite: *A Call to Arms*, the book by Loren L Coleman, Roc, an imprint of New American Library, a division of Penguin Group (USA).

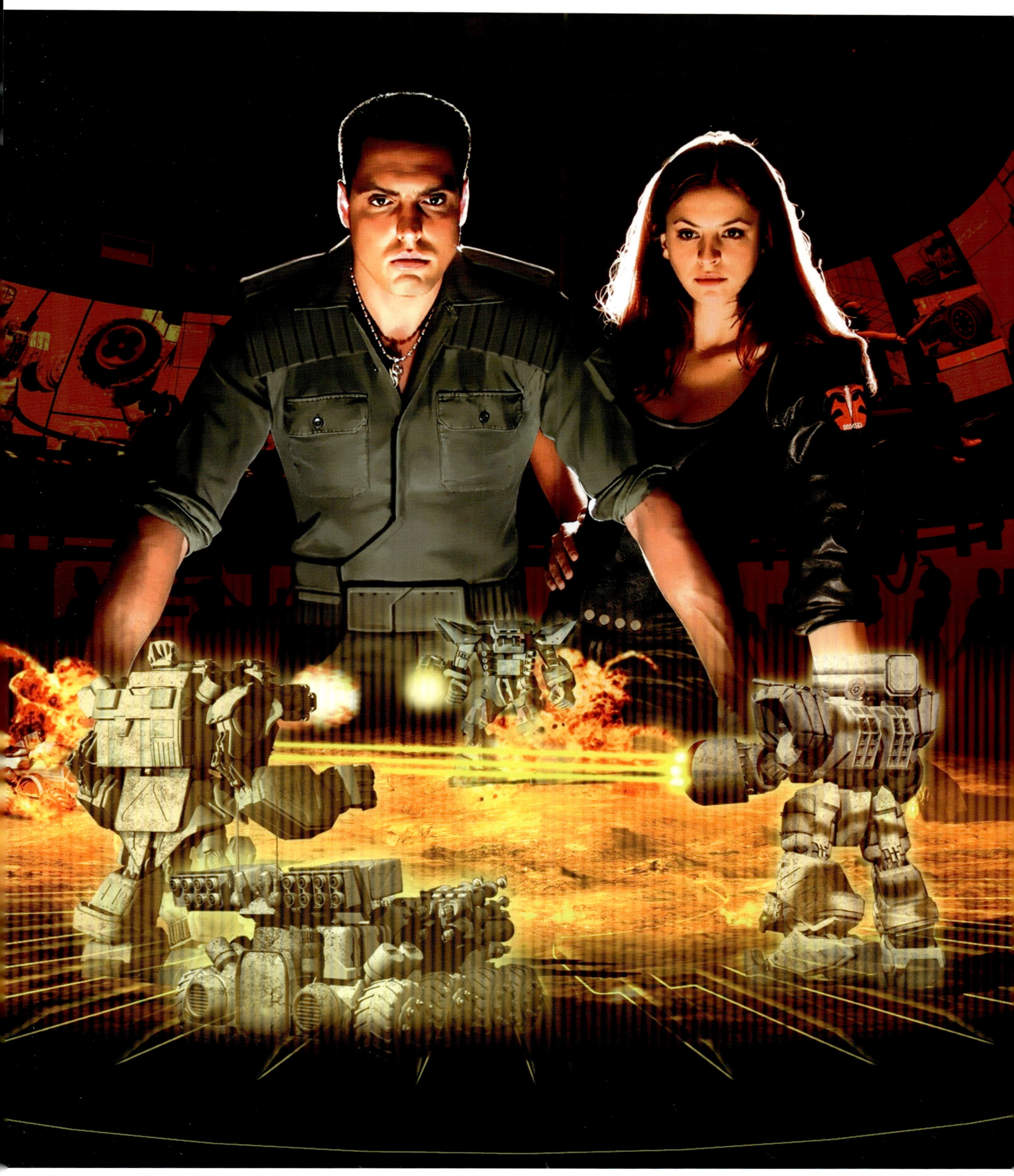

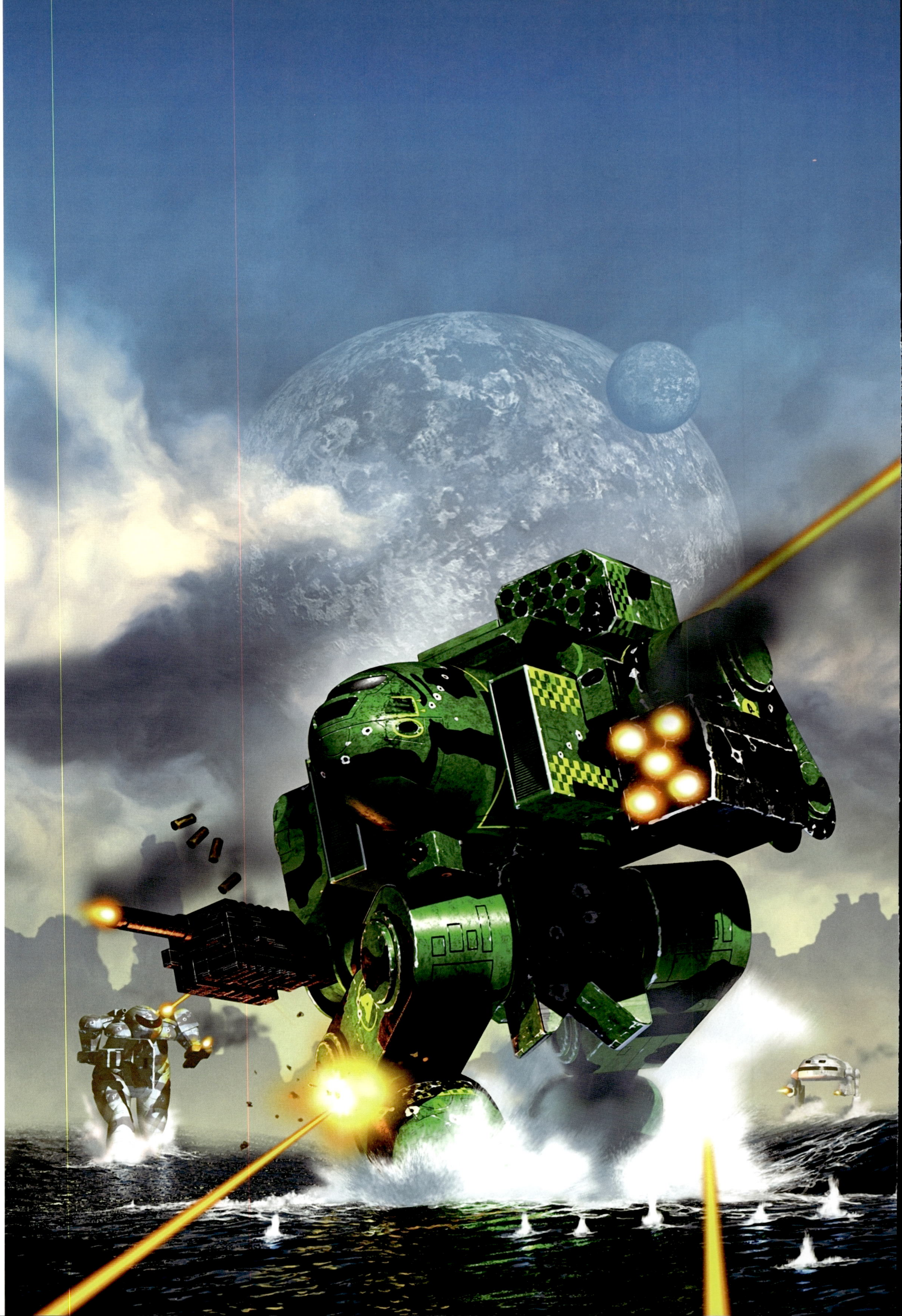

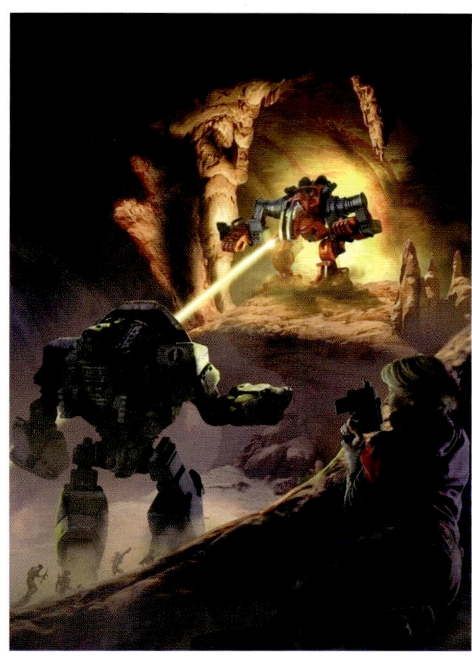

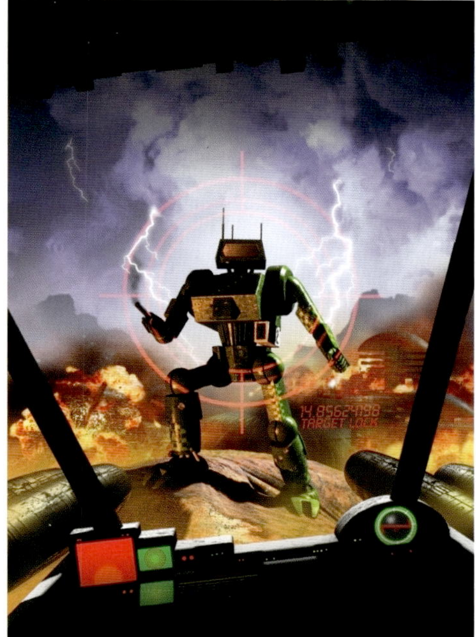

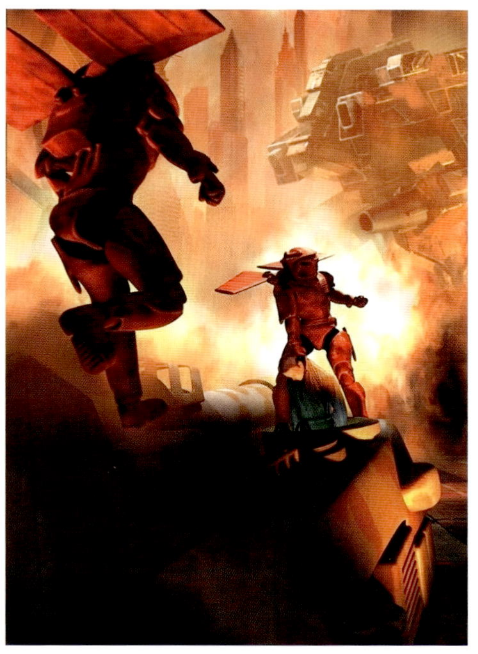

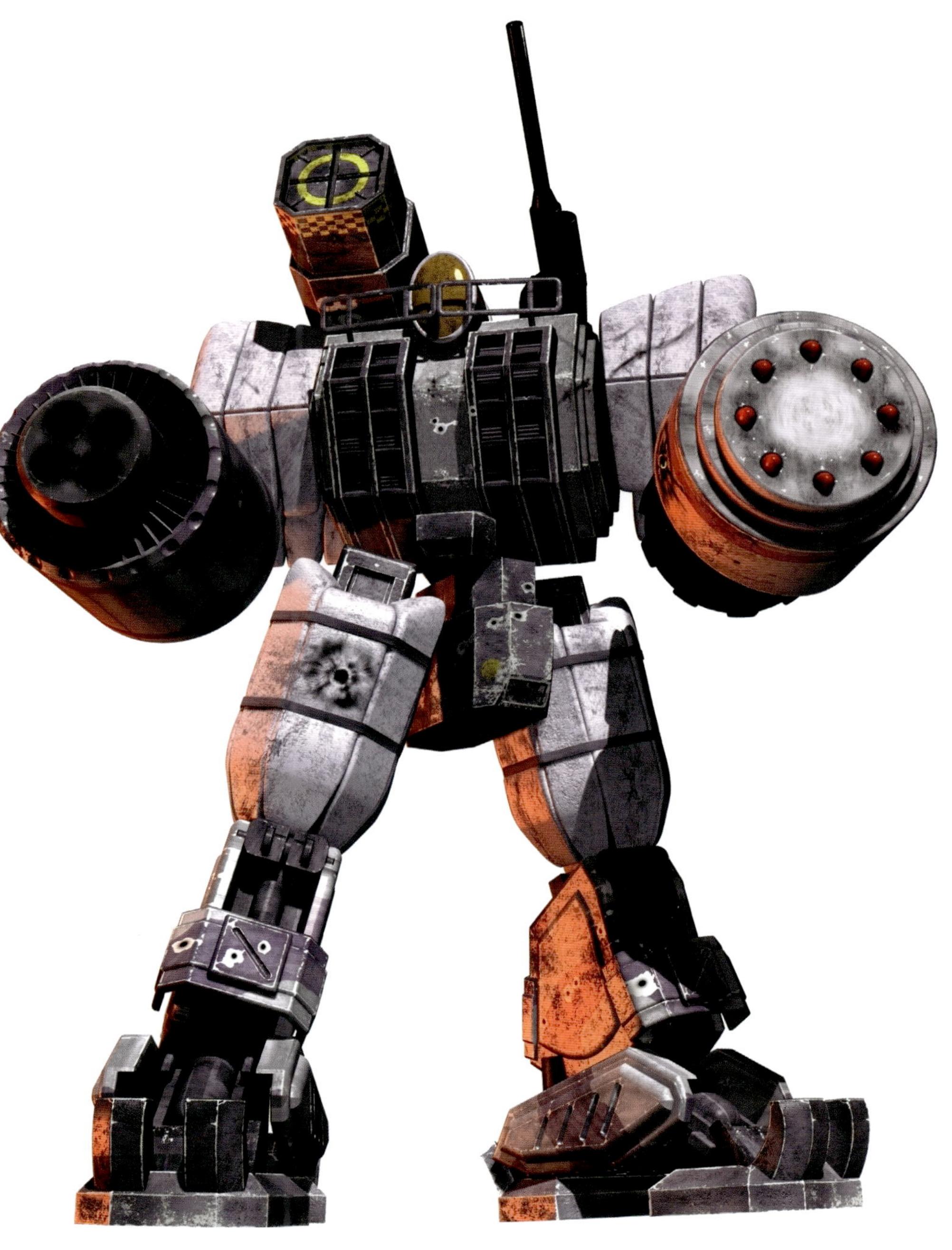

Opposite:
Storms of Fate, the book by Loren L Coleman, Roc, an imprint of New American Library, a division of Penguin Group (USA).

Above, left to right:
Wolf Hunters, the book by Kevin Killiany, Roc, an imprint of New American Library, a division of Penguin Group (USA).

The Dying Time, the book by Thomas S Gressman, Roc, an imprint of New American Library, a division of Penguin Group (USA).

Surrender Your Dreams, the book by Blaine Lee Pardoe, Roc, an imprint of New American Library, a division of Penguin Group (USA).

Right:
Ghost War, the book by Michael A Stackpole, Roc, an imprint of New American Library, a division of Penguin Group (USA).

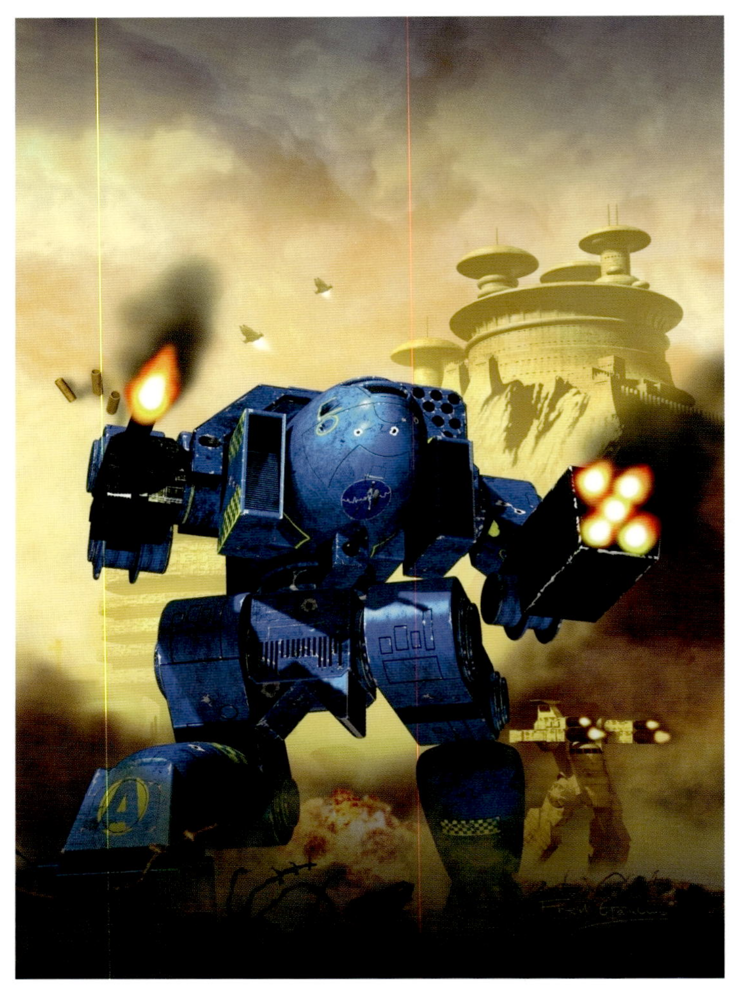

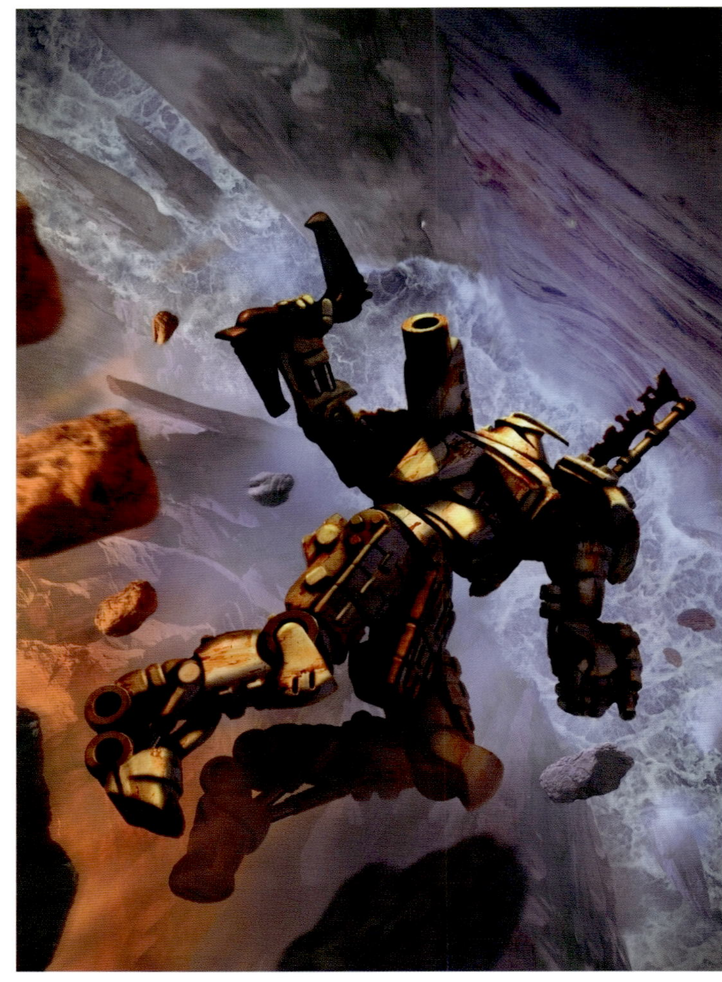

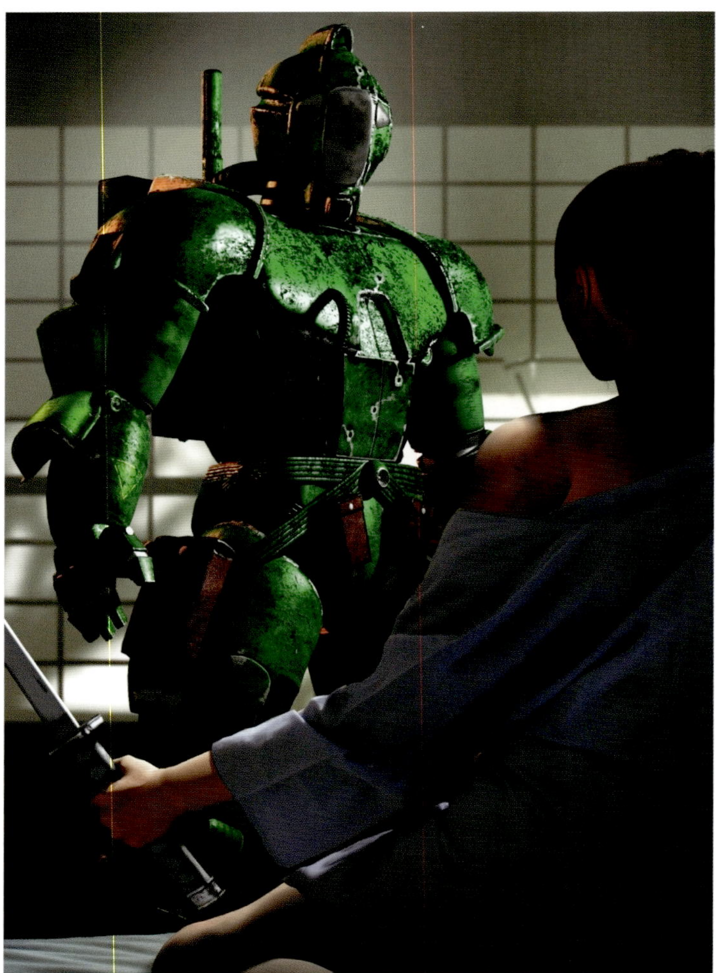

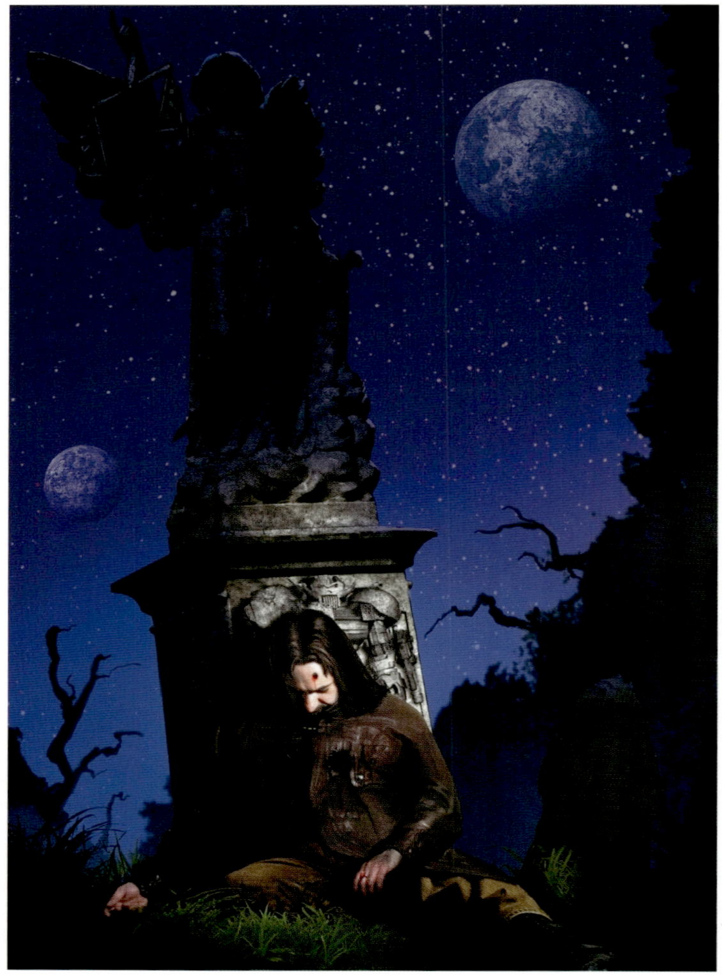

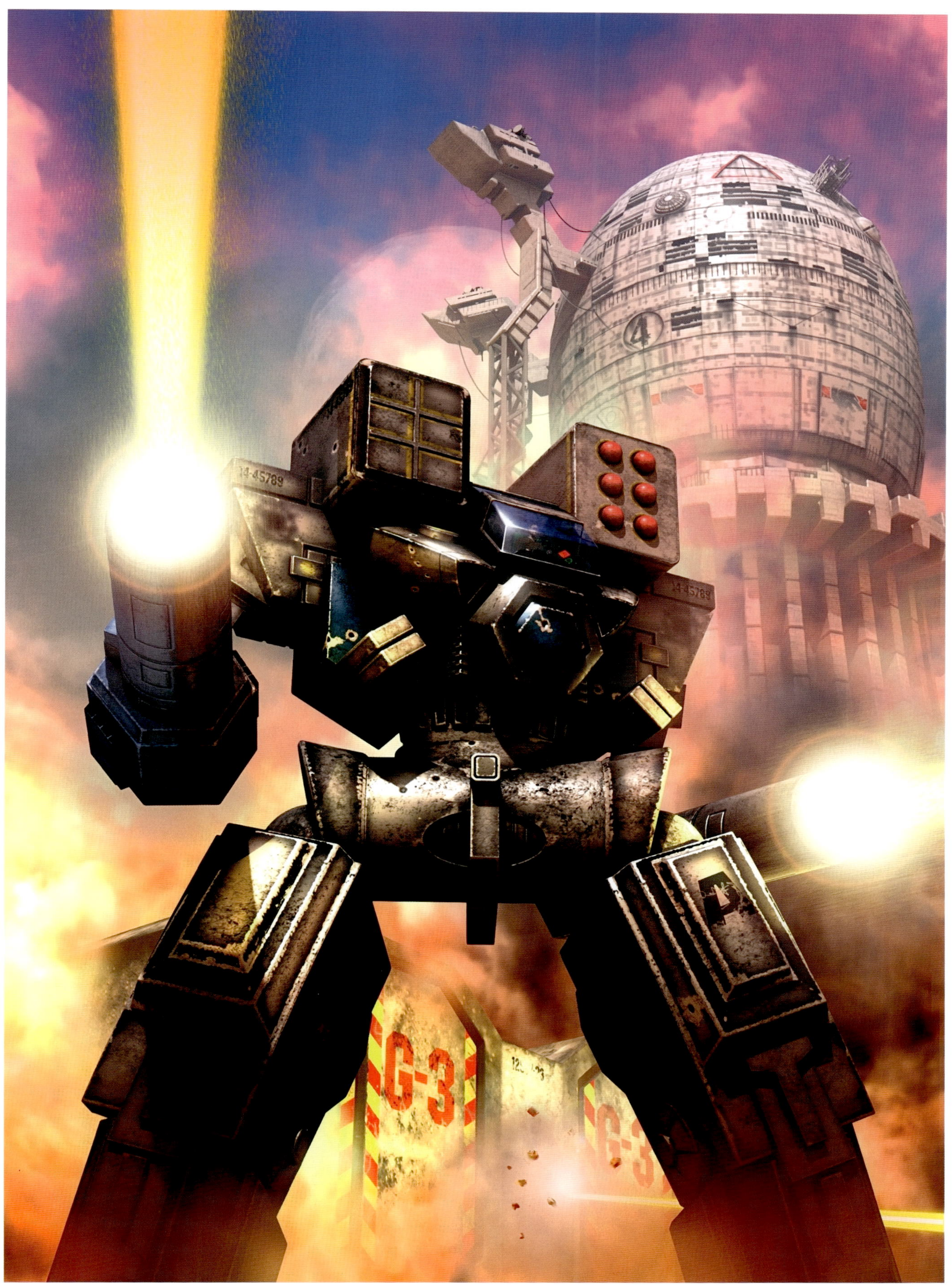

Opposite, clockwise from top left: *Endgame*, the book by Loren L Coleman; *Dragon Rising*, the book by Ilsa L Bick; *Blood Avatar*, the book by Ilsa L Bick; *Daughter of the Dragon*, the book by Ilsa L Bick. Reprinted with permission of Roc, an imprint of New American Library, a division of Penguin Group (USA).

Above: *Blood of The Isle*, the book by Loren L Coleman. Reprinted with permission of Roc, an imprint of New American Library, a division of Penguin Group (USA).

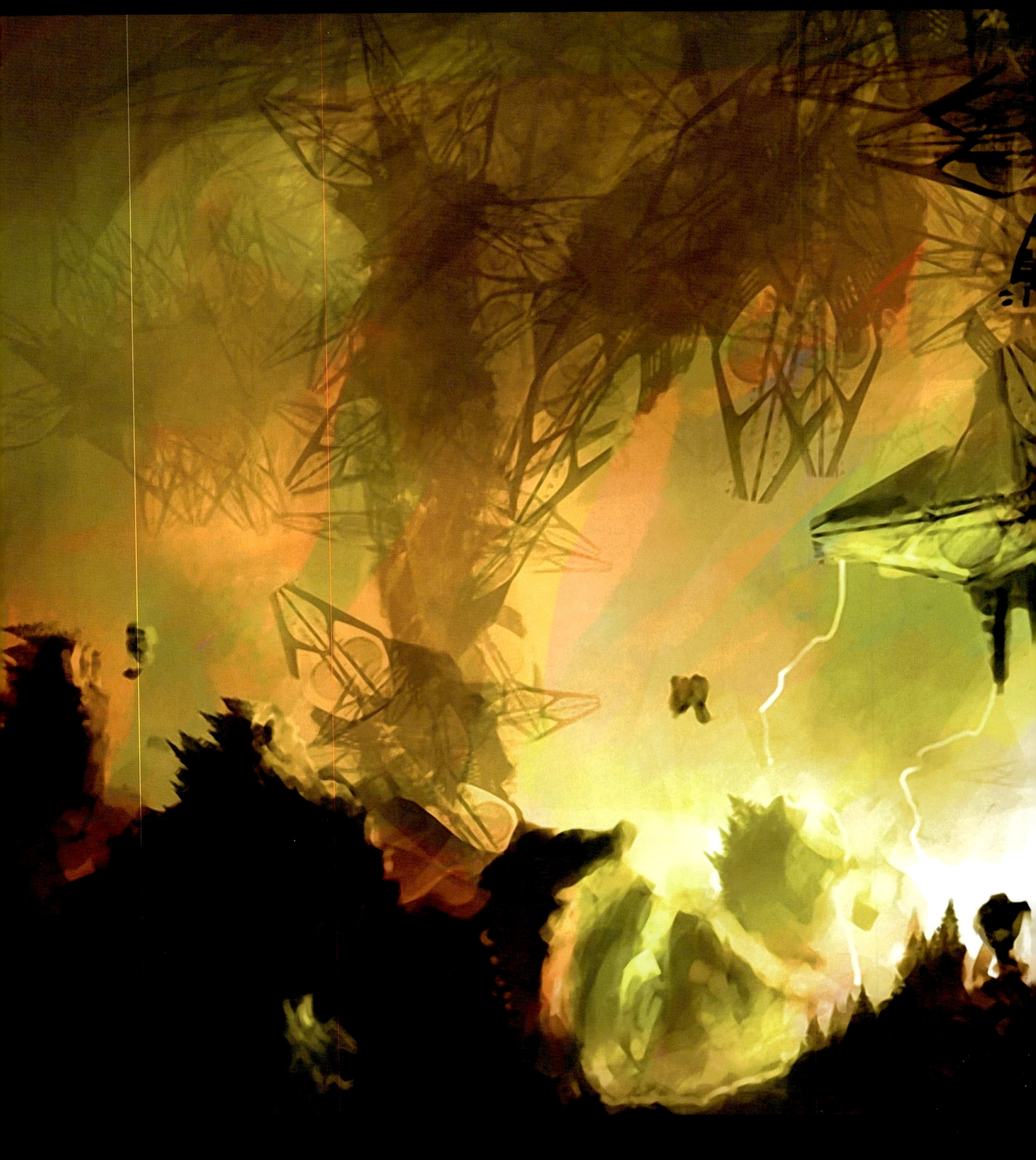

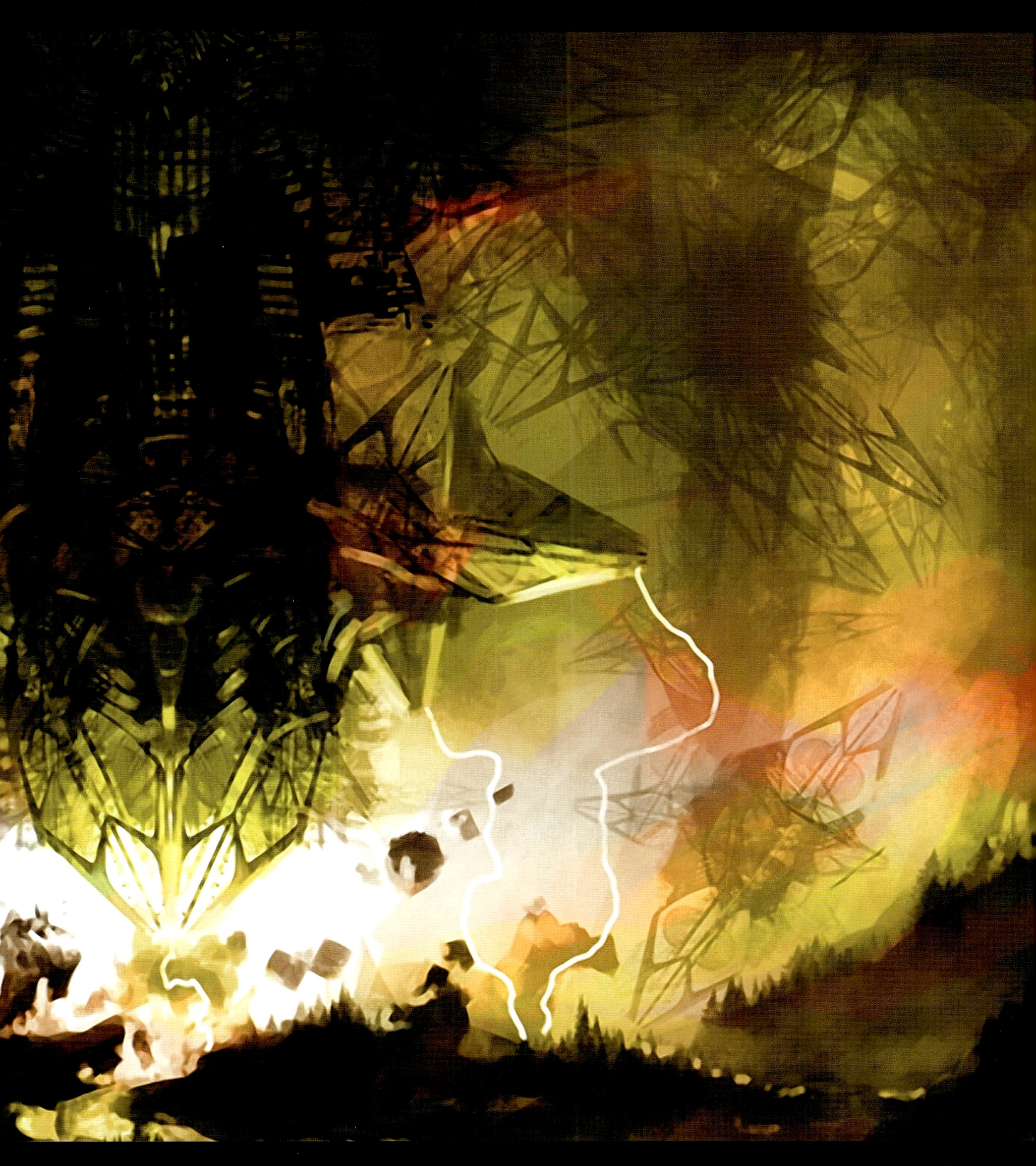

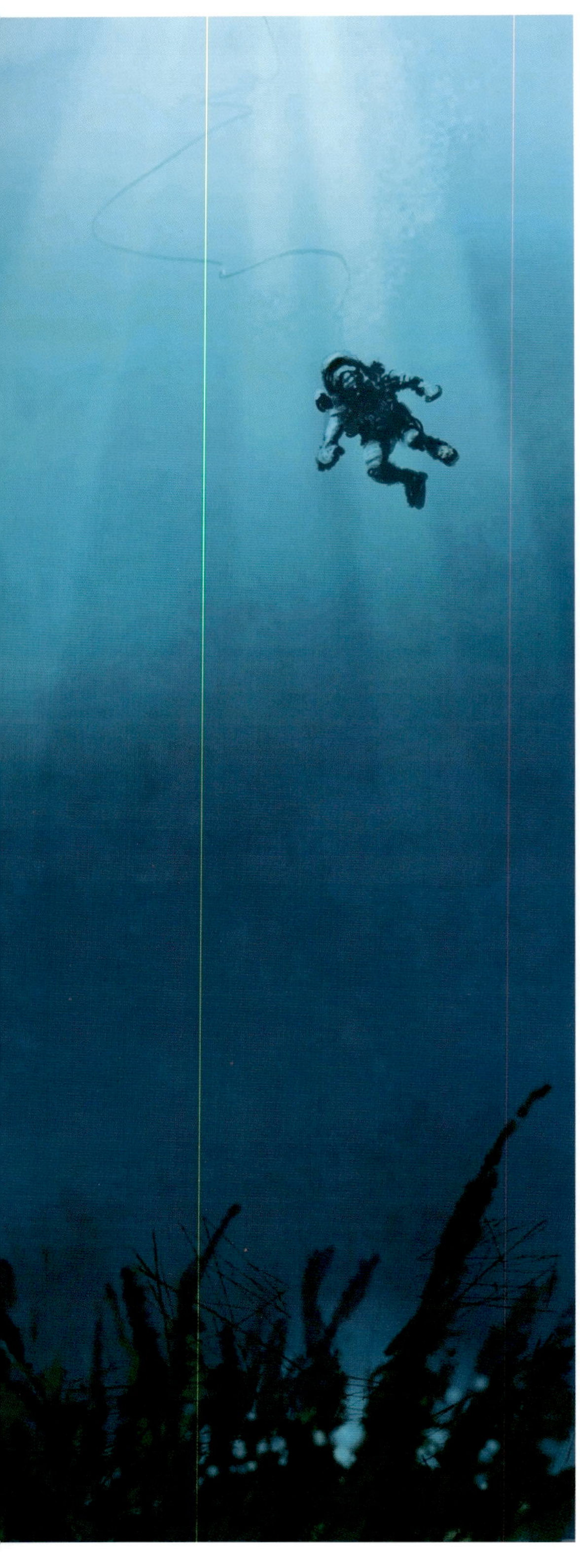

Whilst working as principal artist at a video game company, the only 'real' job I've ever had, part of my remit was to stoke up enthusiasm and keep the creative juices fresh. One of the ways I did this was to have my fellow artists complete a speed painting every morning. We took it in turns to suggest a subject and then we had twenty minutes to finish it. Tracing wasn't allowed, although it was okay to look for reference for inspiration – as long as you were quick! Sometimes we slipped a little past the time limit, but occasionally paintings would only take ten minutes. It's a great exercise and a good way to loosen up before the more serious work of the day begins.

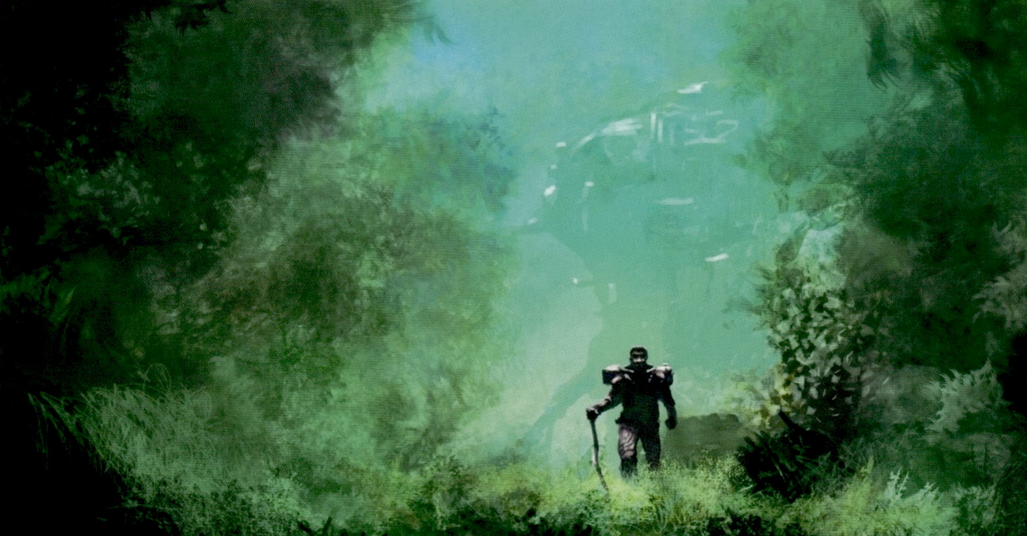

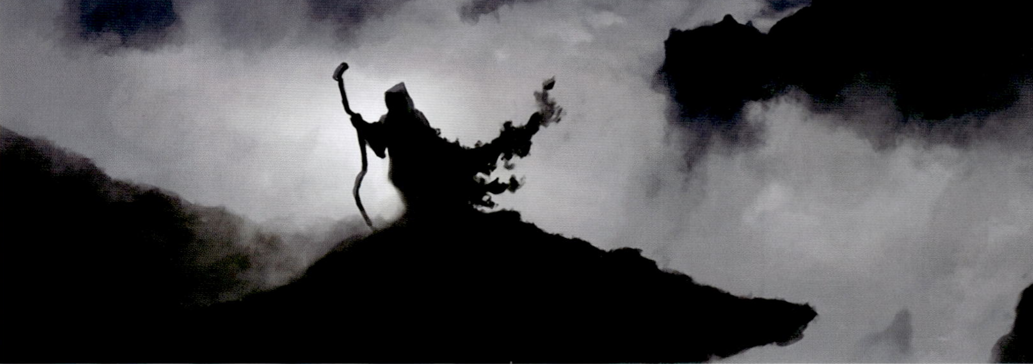

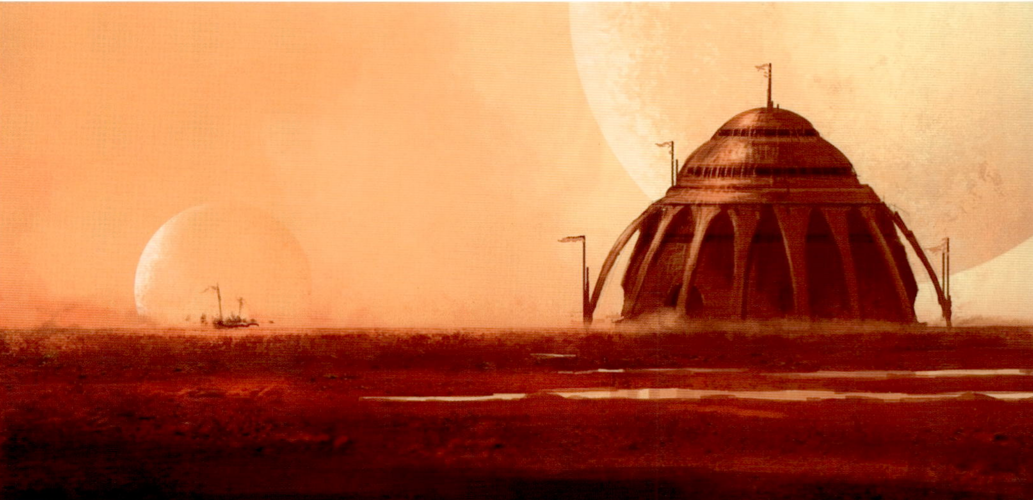

Above: *Floating.*

Top right: *Journey.*

Middle right: *The Arrival.*

Middle bottom: *Mausoleum.*

Opposite: *Scale.*

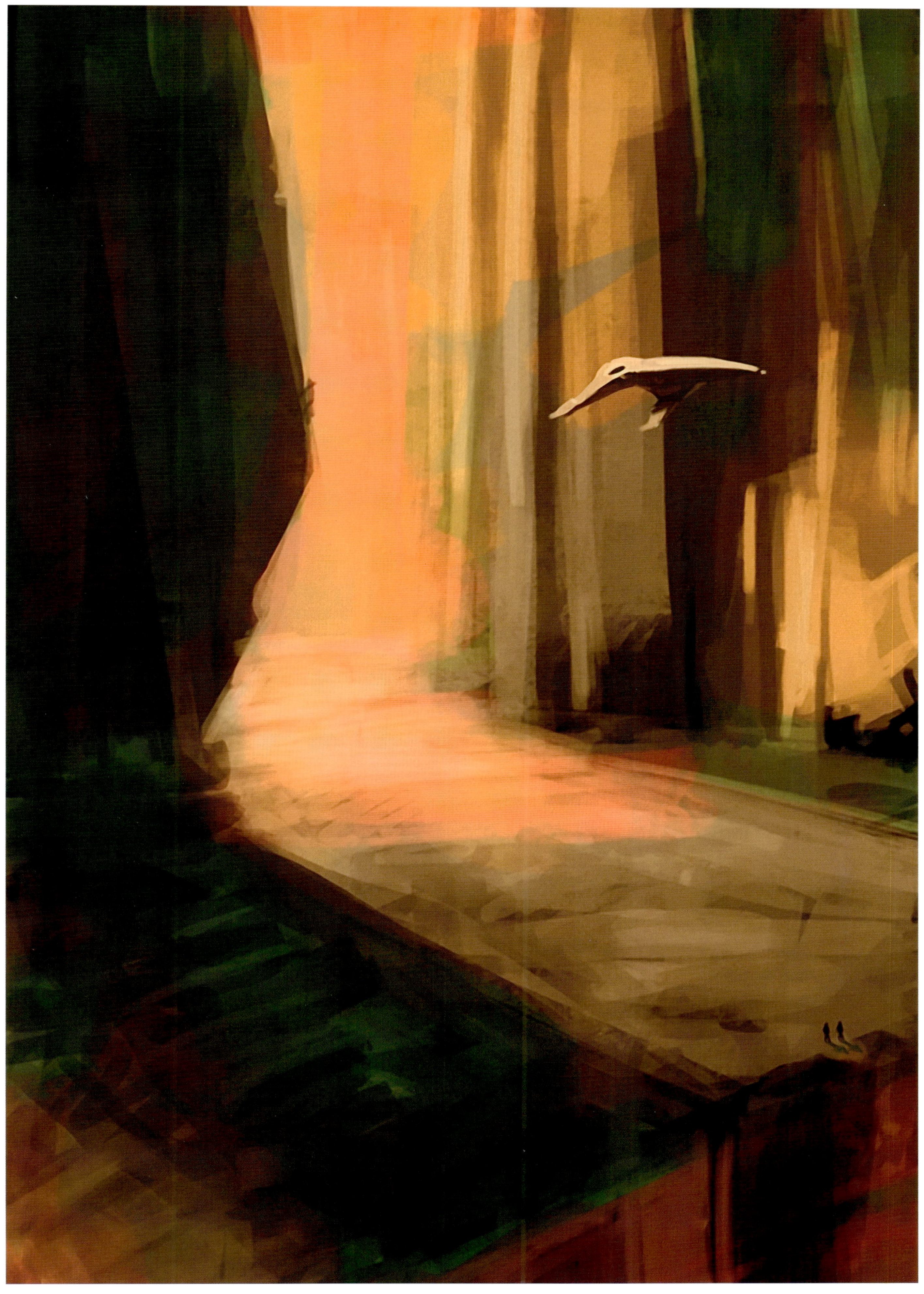

Right: *Ariel Transport.*

Far right: *Biker.*

Below: *The Messenger.*

Below right: *Protector of the Empire.*

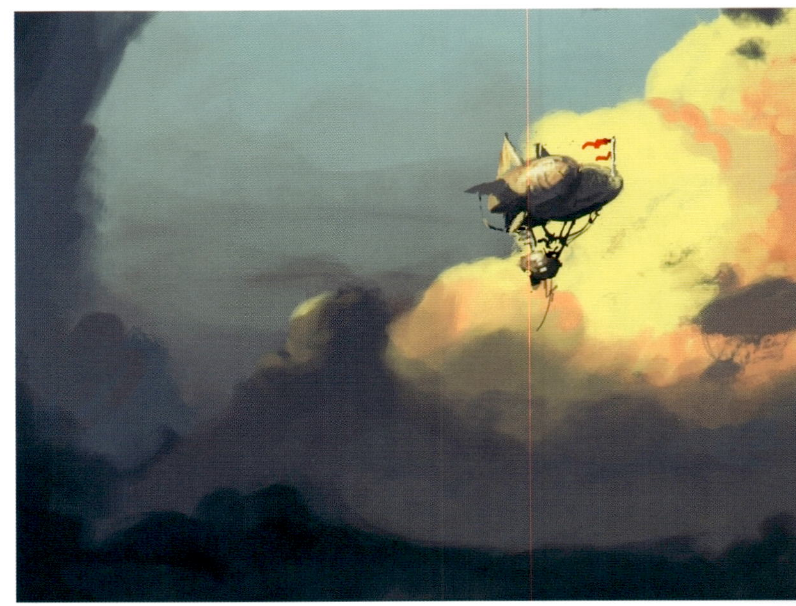

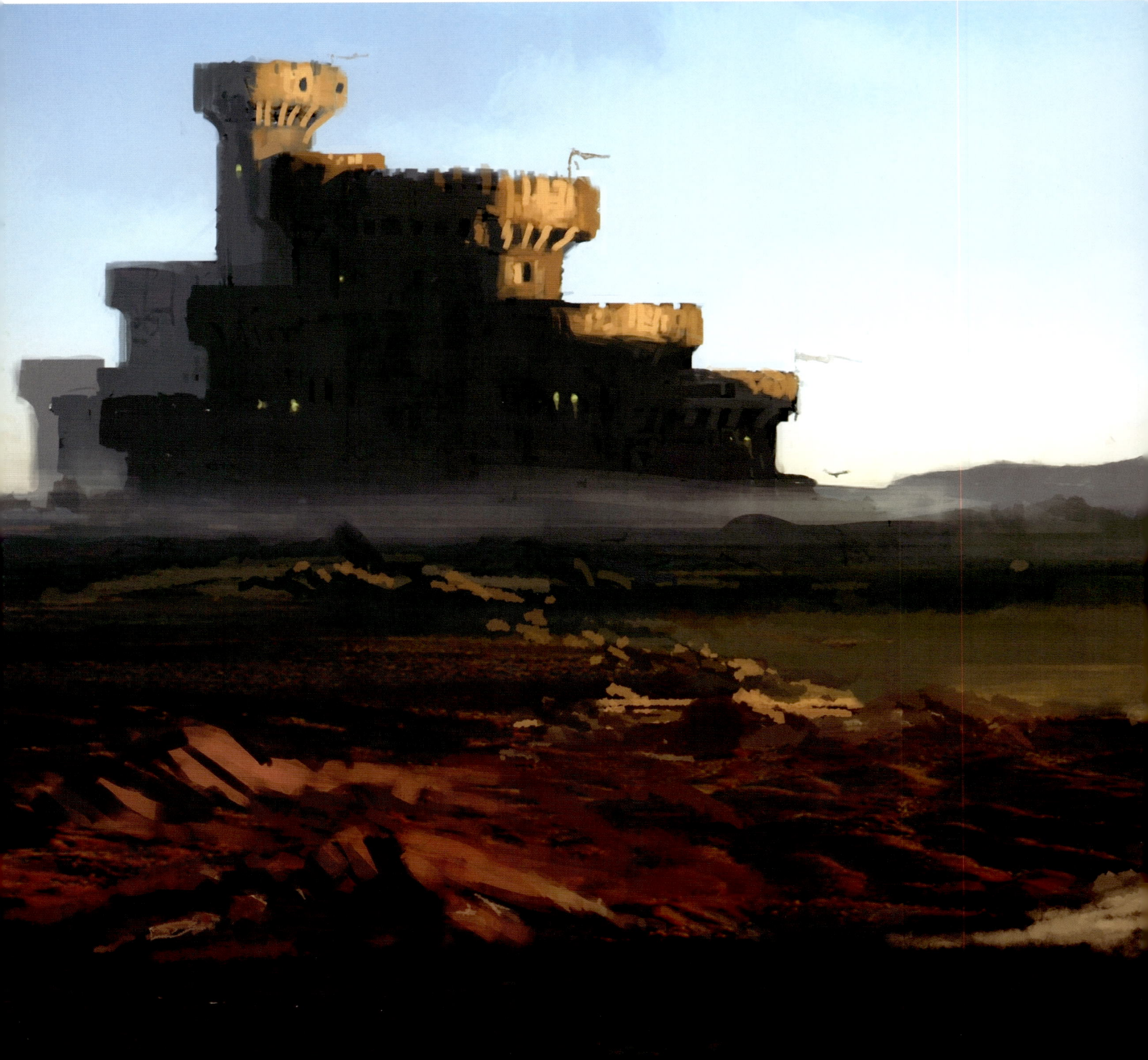

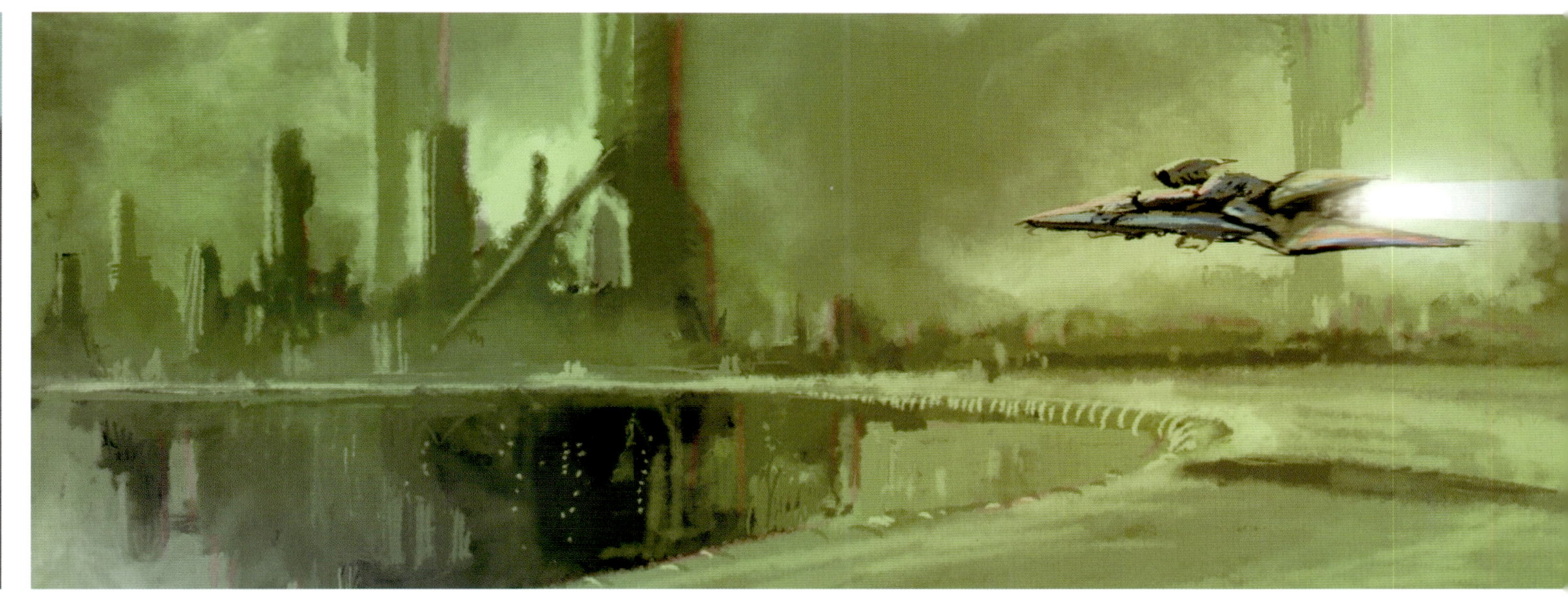

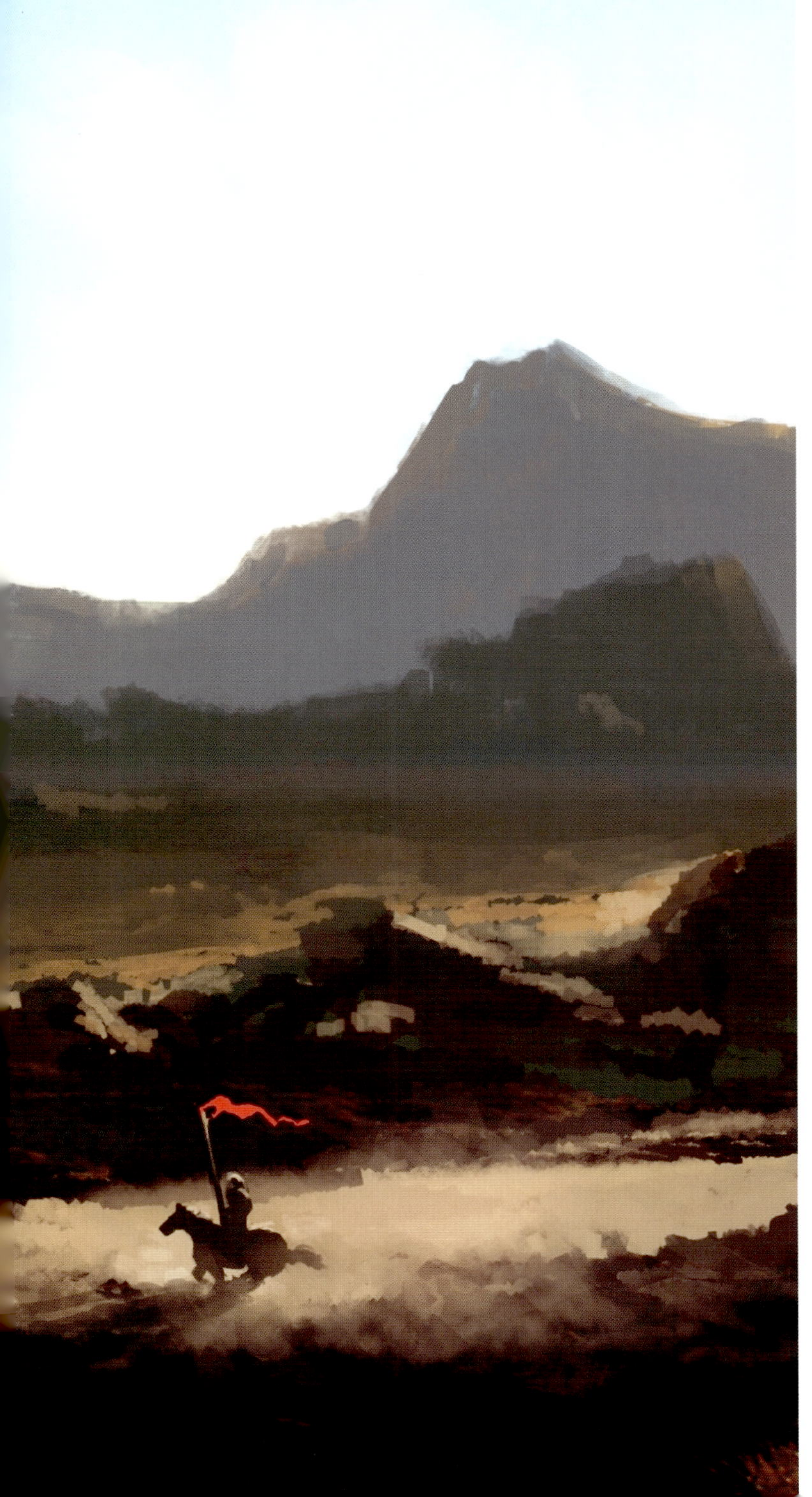

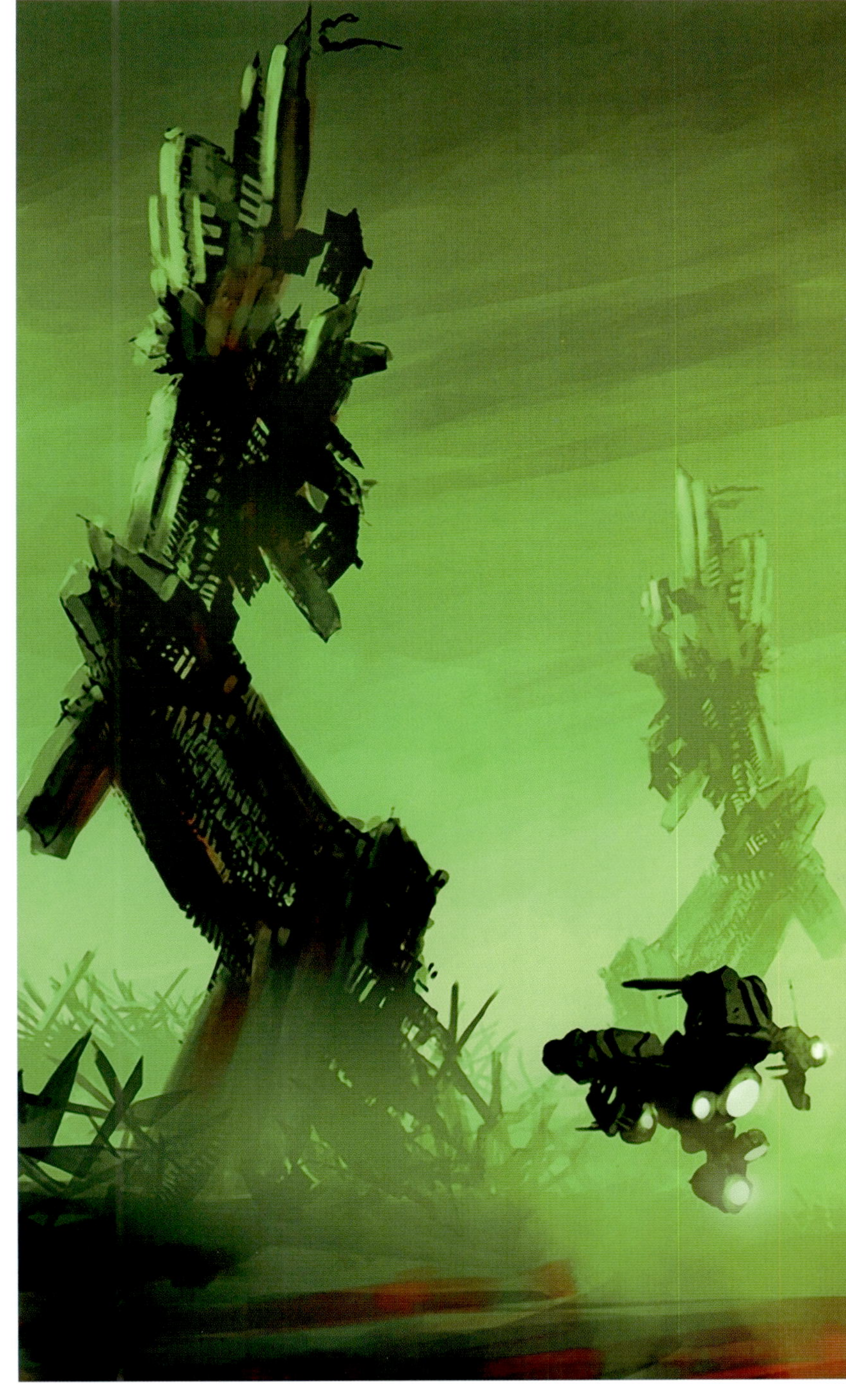

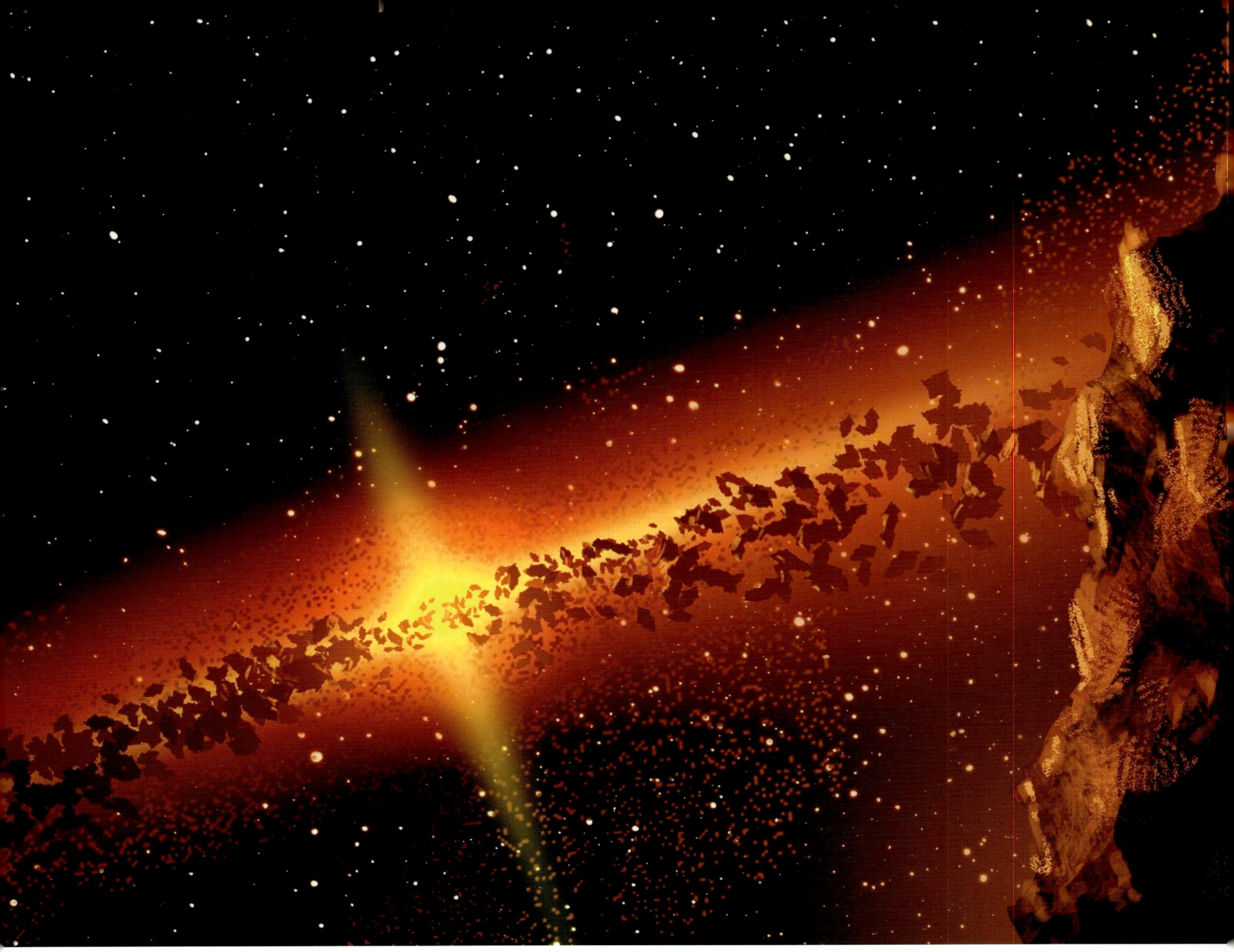

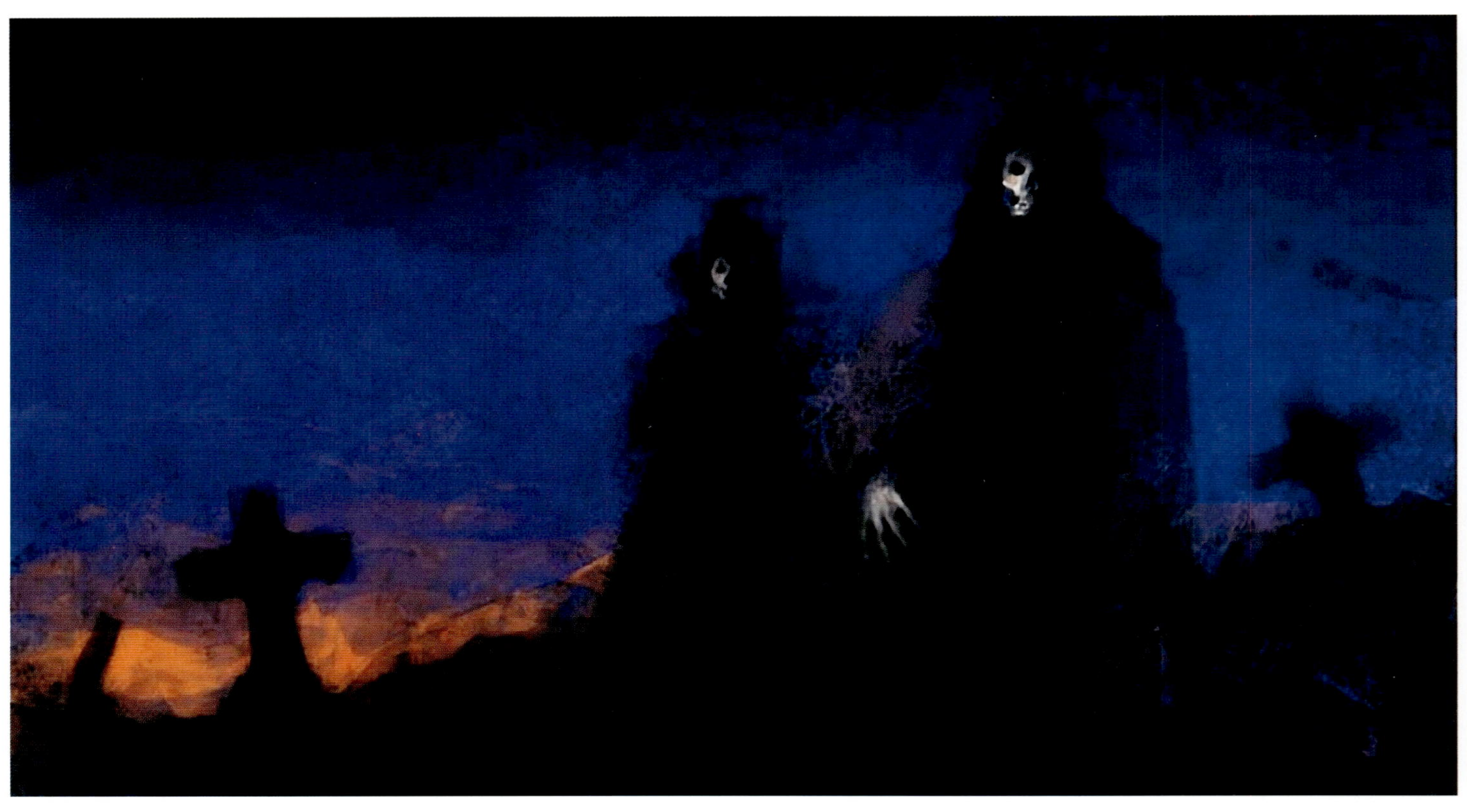

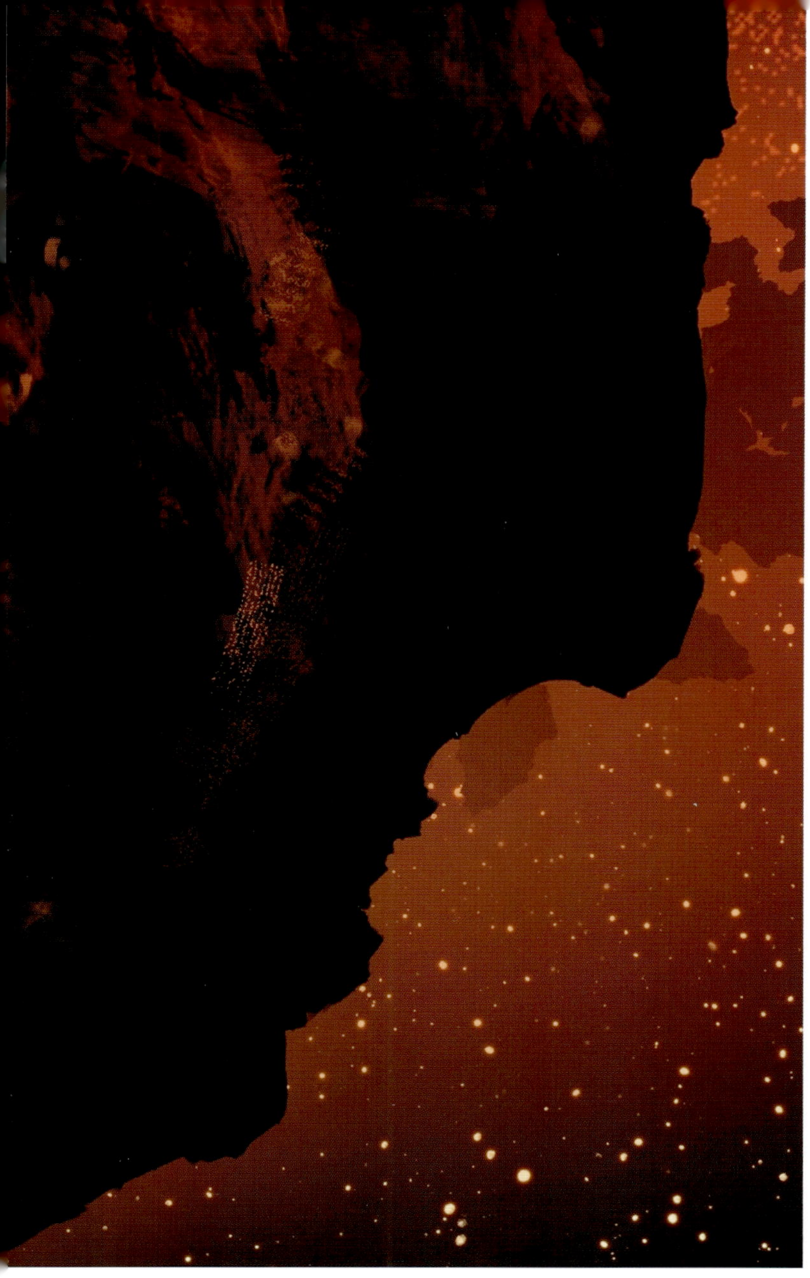

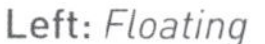

Left: *Floating*

Below: *End of the World*

Below middle: *Moon*

Below bottom: *Leopard*

Below left: *Undead*

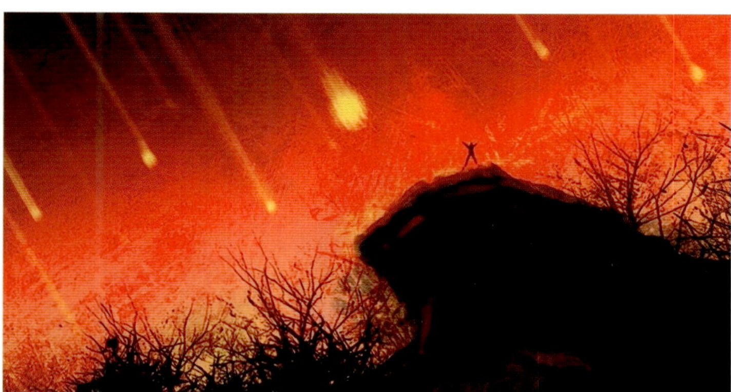

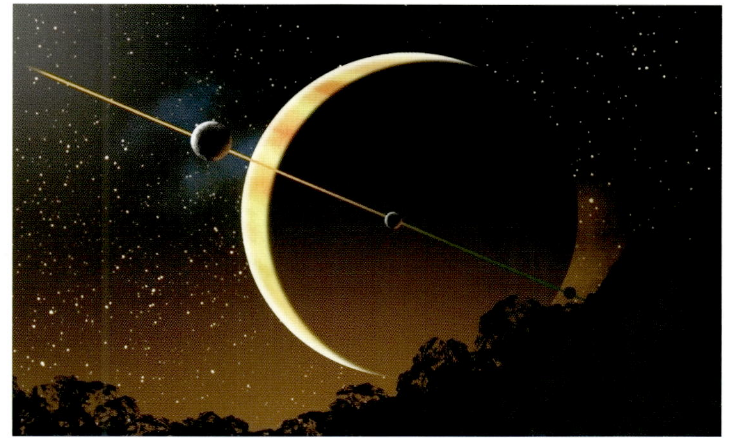

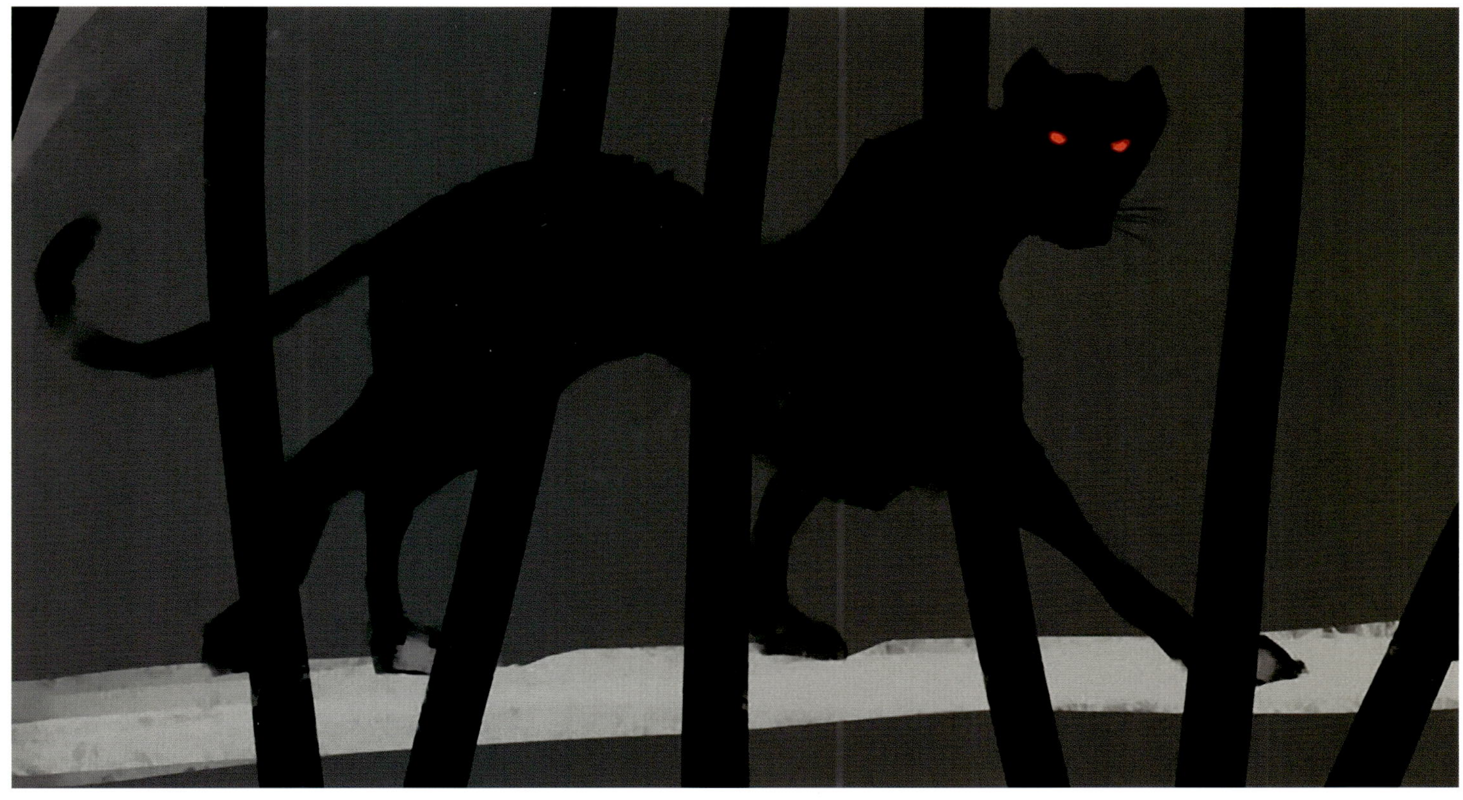

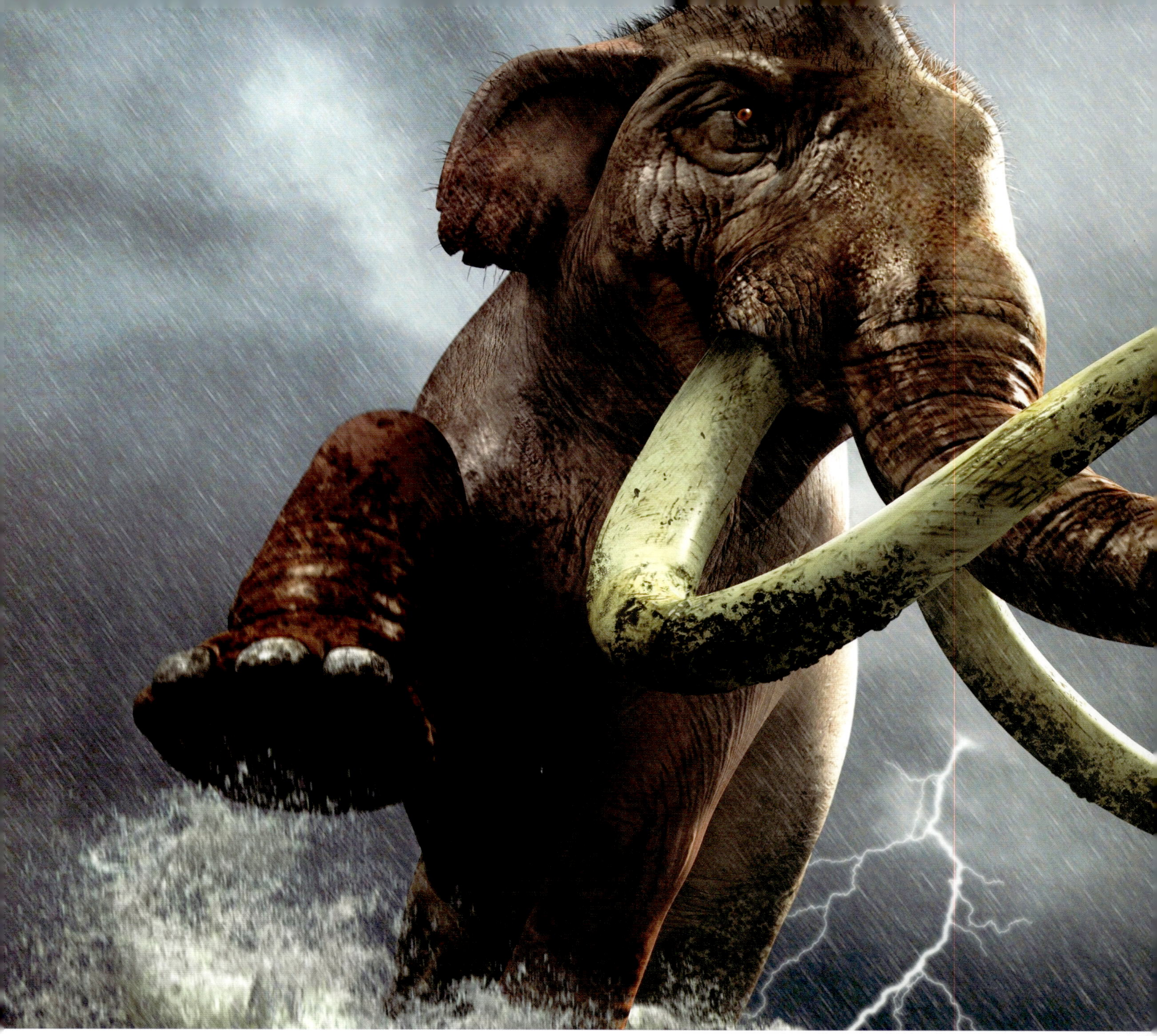

Right: Commission by an advertising agency to win the 02 mobile phone account. This image featured on television and cinema adverts.

Far right: A poster to advertise the Irish Rugby cup final that tied into a television advertising campaign for advertising agency IBBDO. The sky was intended to evoke the creamy swirling patterns in a poured pint of Guinness. I created one tree character in MODO then duplicated him the requisite number of times. I then had to go into the image and repaint each one so they looked like different characters and not clones.

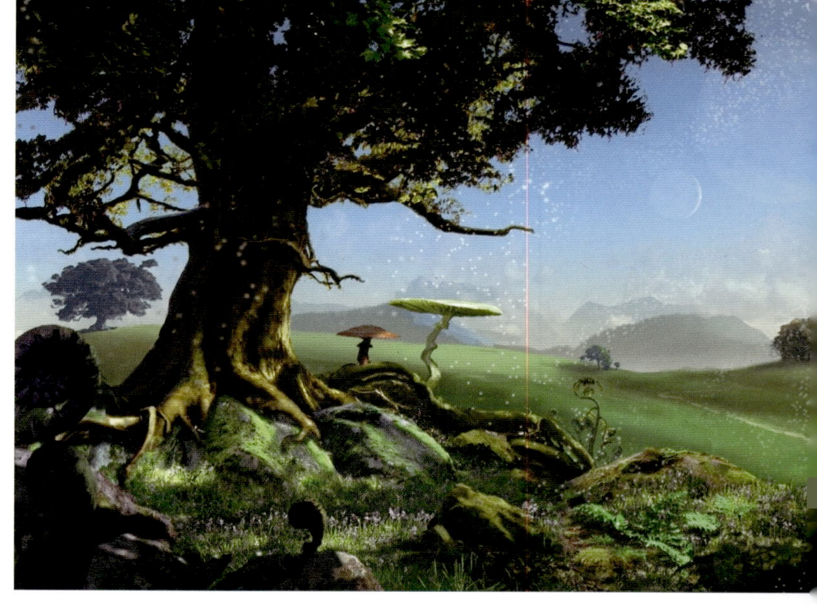

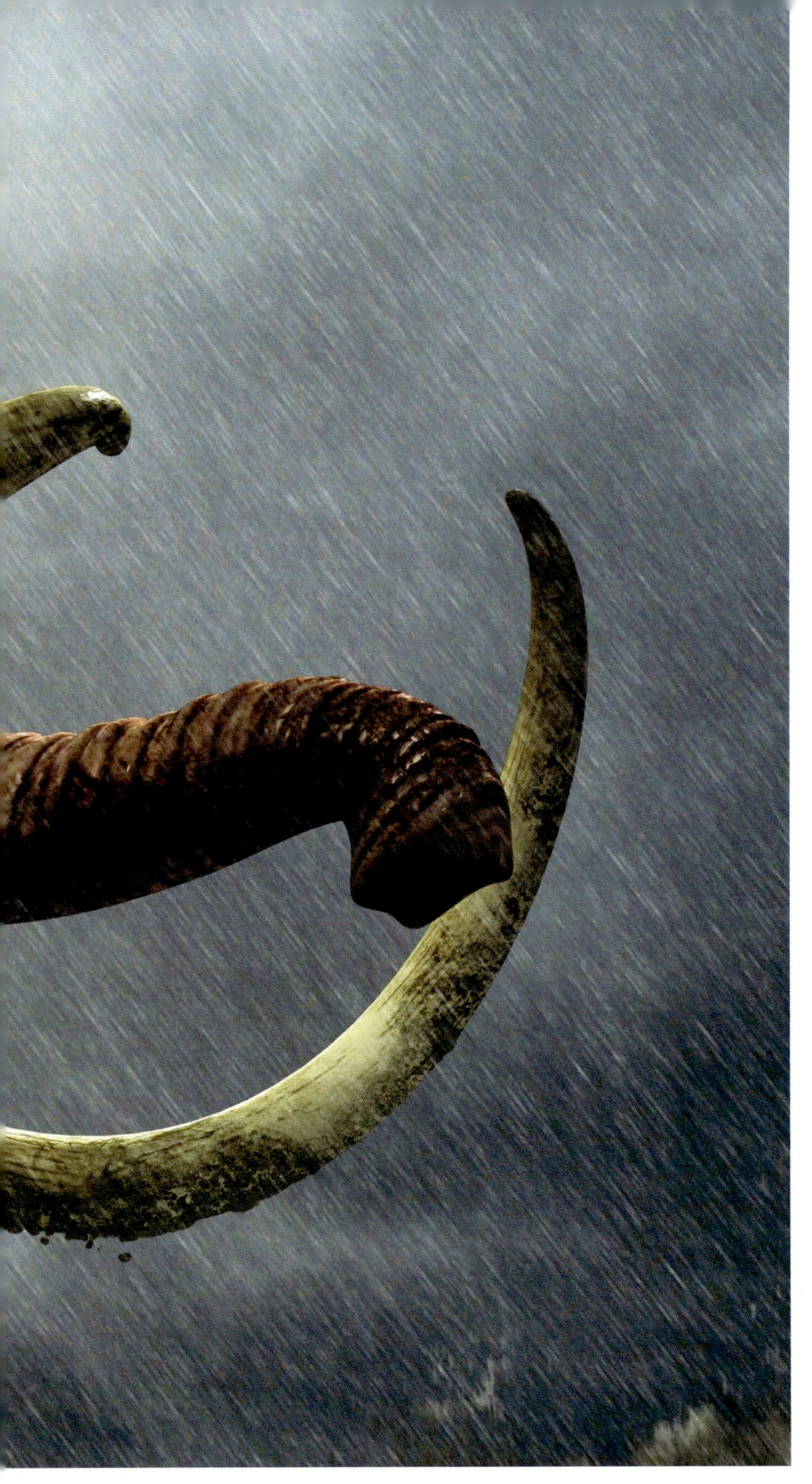

ADVERTISING AND COMMISSIONS

Two images created for *Texas Monthly*, which wanted to depict the Mammoths that lived in Texas thousands of years ago. A major flood washed the remains of many of them into a bone pit. The main image (*left*) shows one of the luckless creatures getting caught in the storm. The second image (*above*) shows them in more peaceful times. The magazine supplied me with a background plate to which I could match the lighting and environment of my mammoths, so it would look like they were actually in the scene.

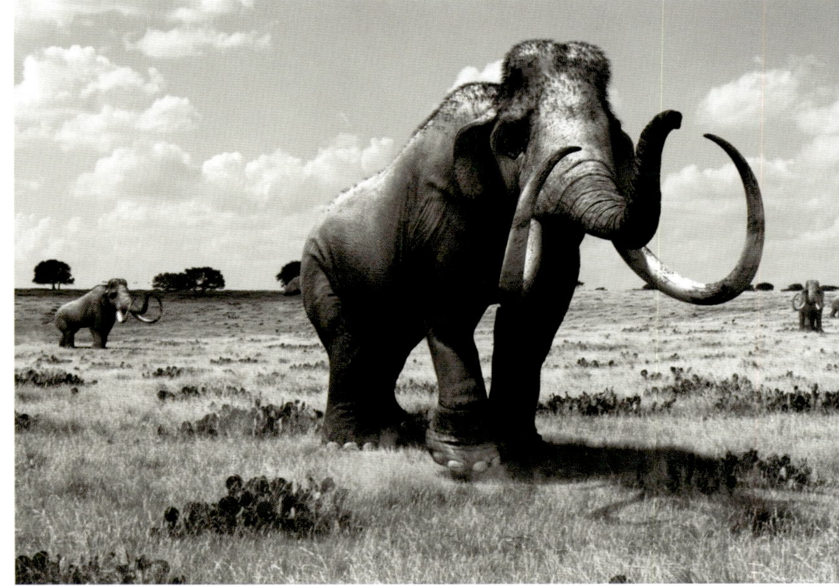

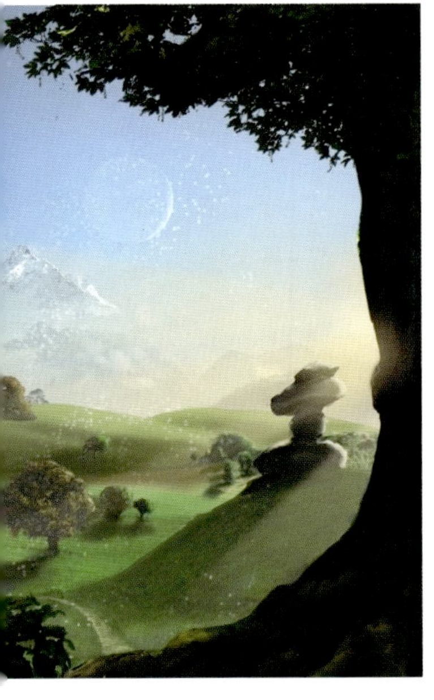

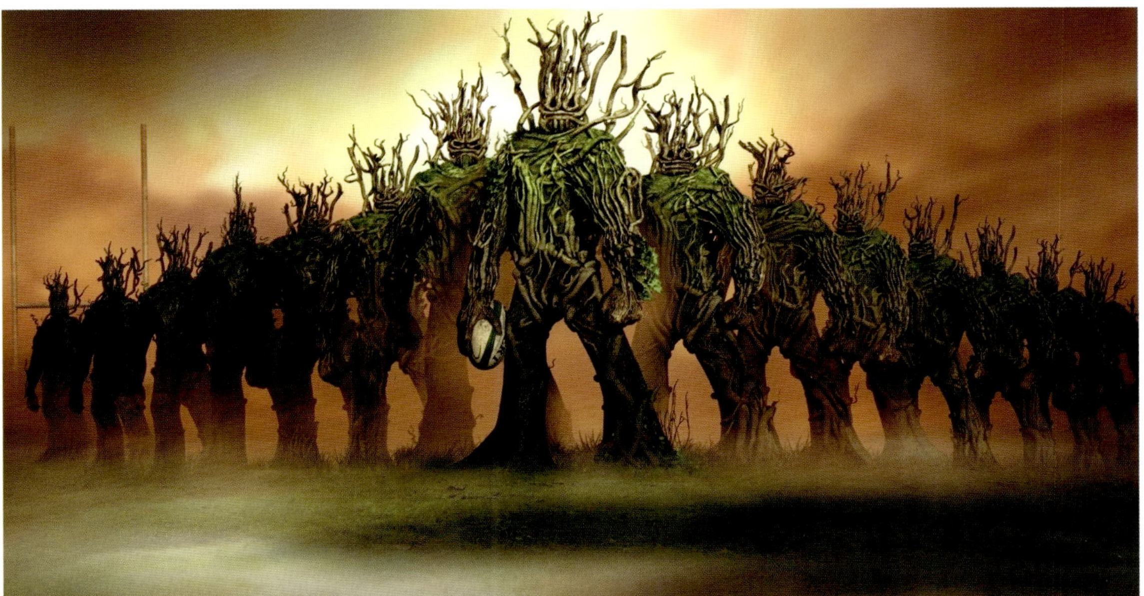

STAR WARS VISIONS

George Lucas commissioned a book called *Star Wars Visions* and invited artists from around the world to contribute. The brief was very loose: to paint an image based on something from the *Star Wars* universe. I created a number of ideas that were presented to George. One idea was that the air whales featured in *Episode II: Attack of the Clones* must have wild cousins and be part of the ecology of the planet somewhere. George liked that idea, and I drew a series of images showing them cavorting around in what could be a mating ritual or literally hanging about in the natural flora and fauna of the planet.

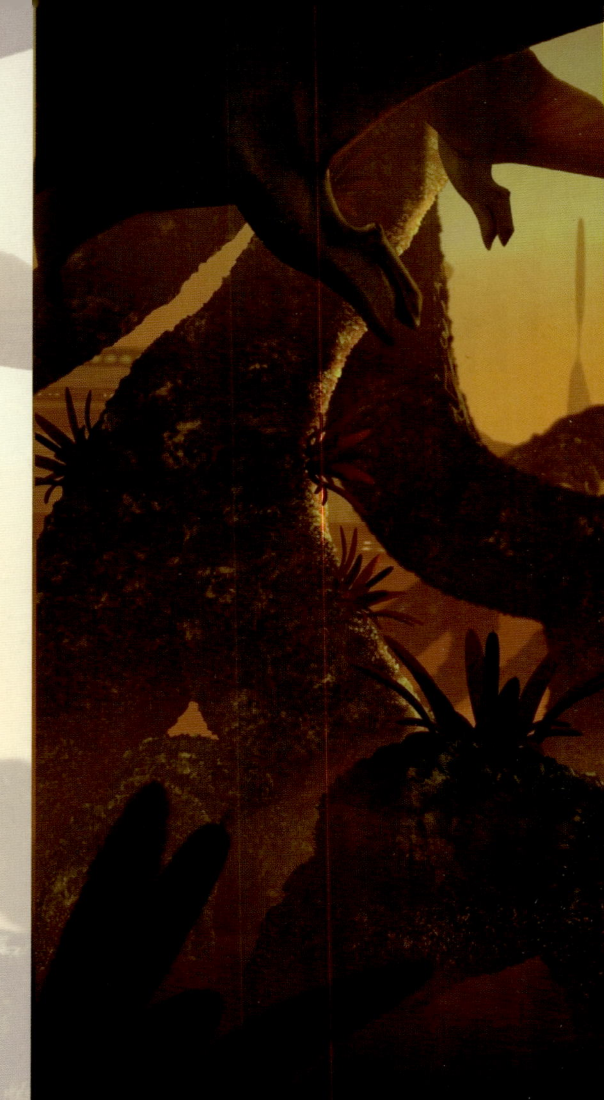

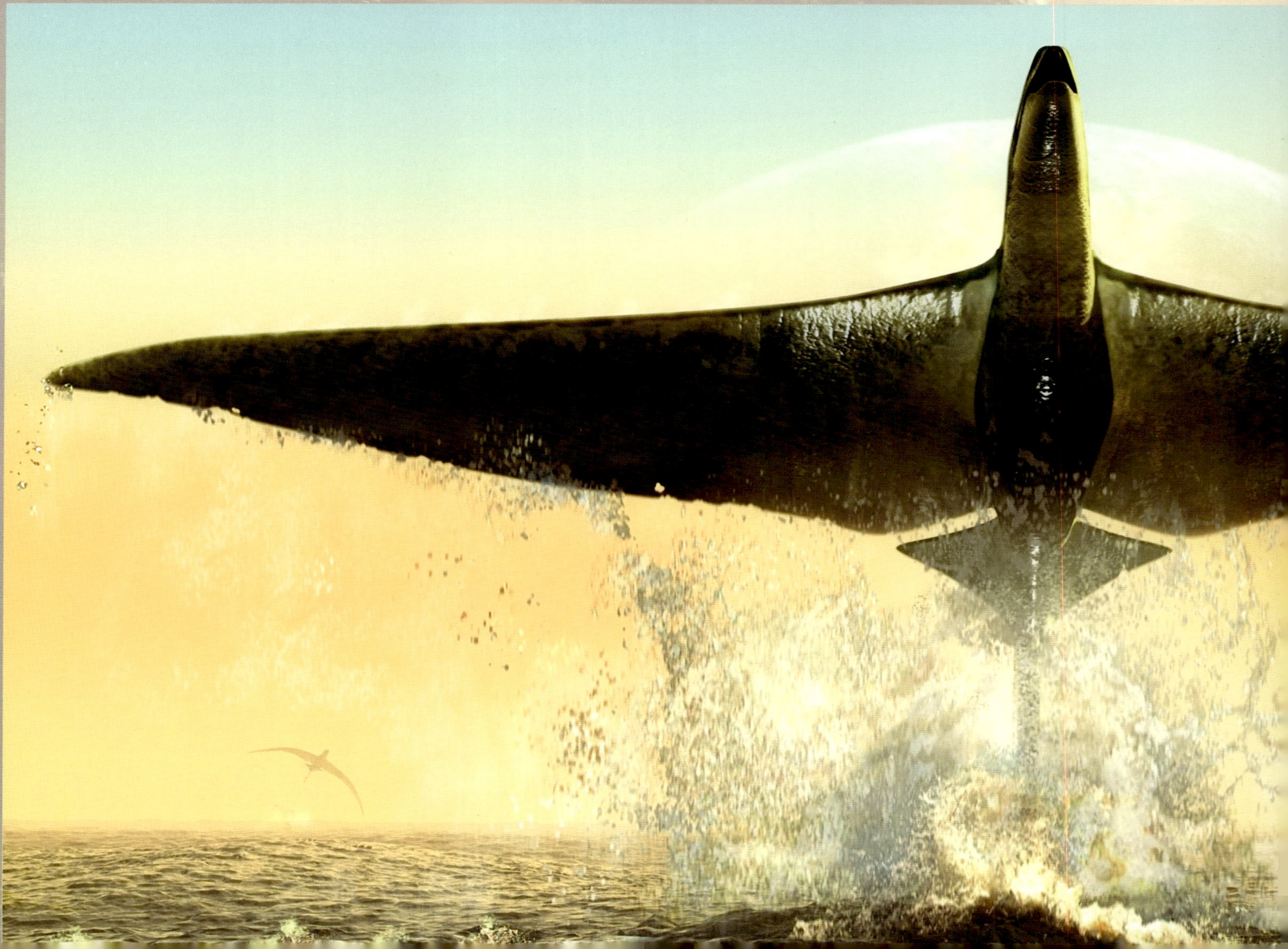

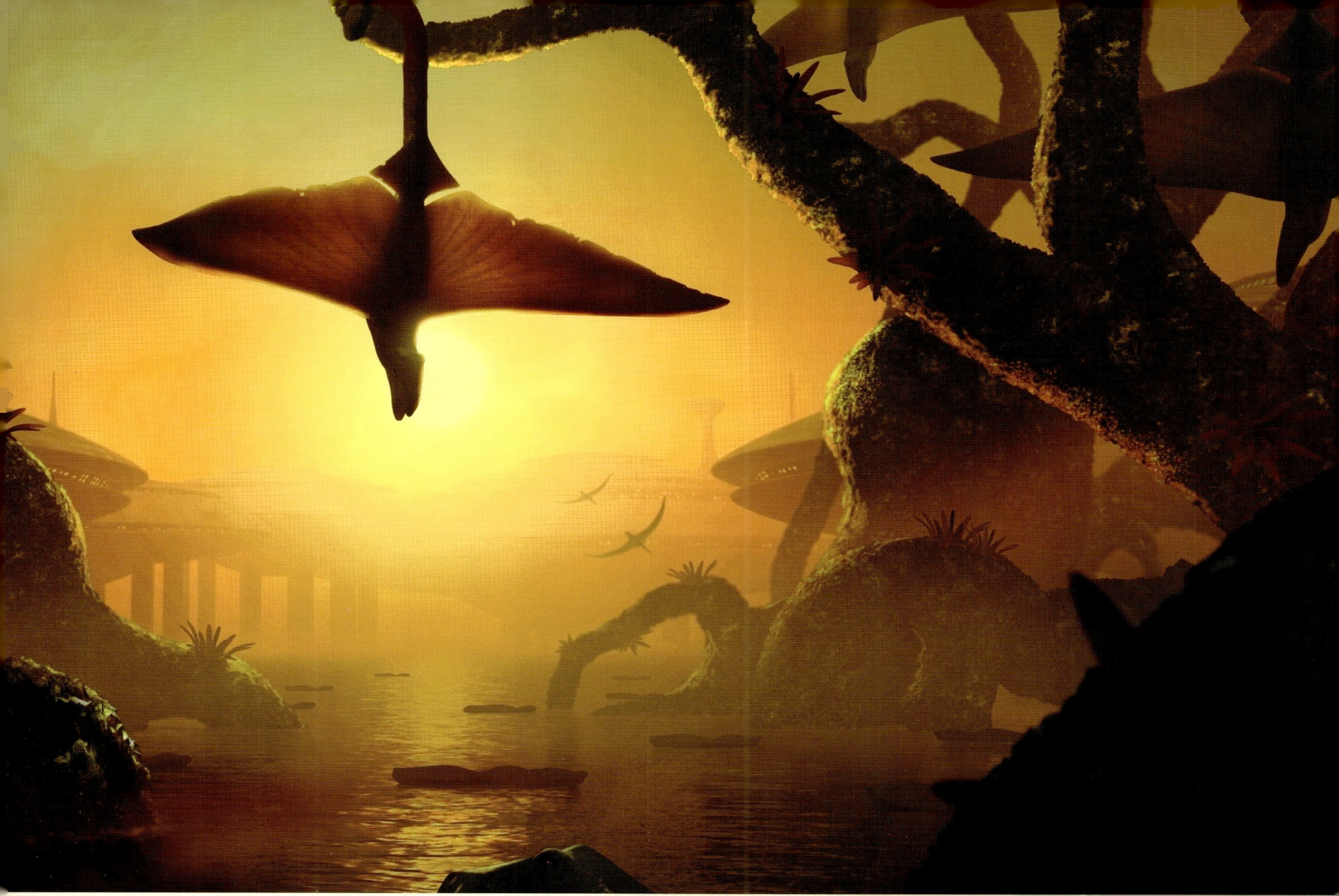

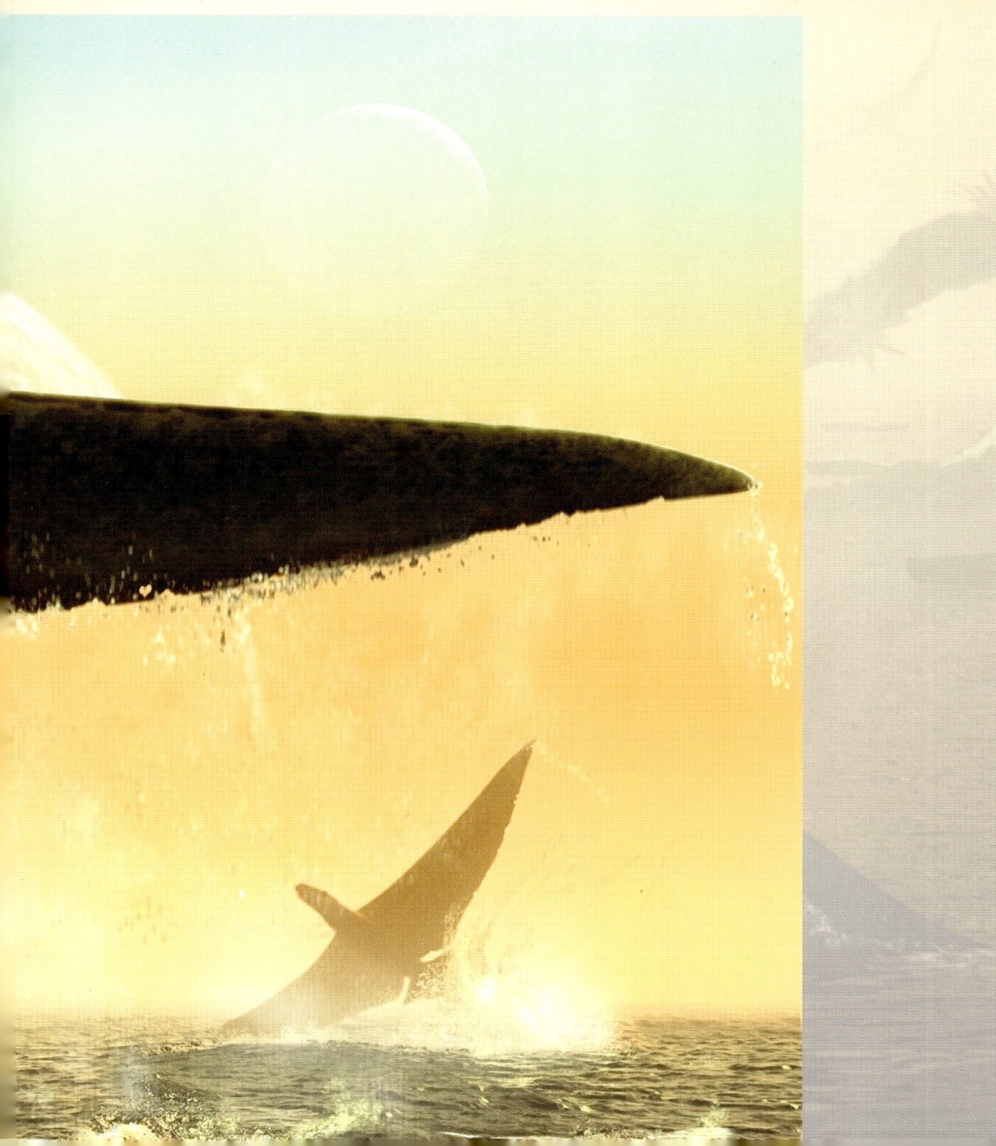

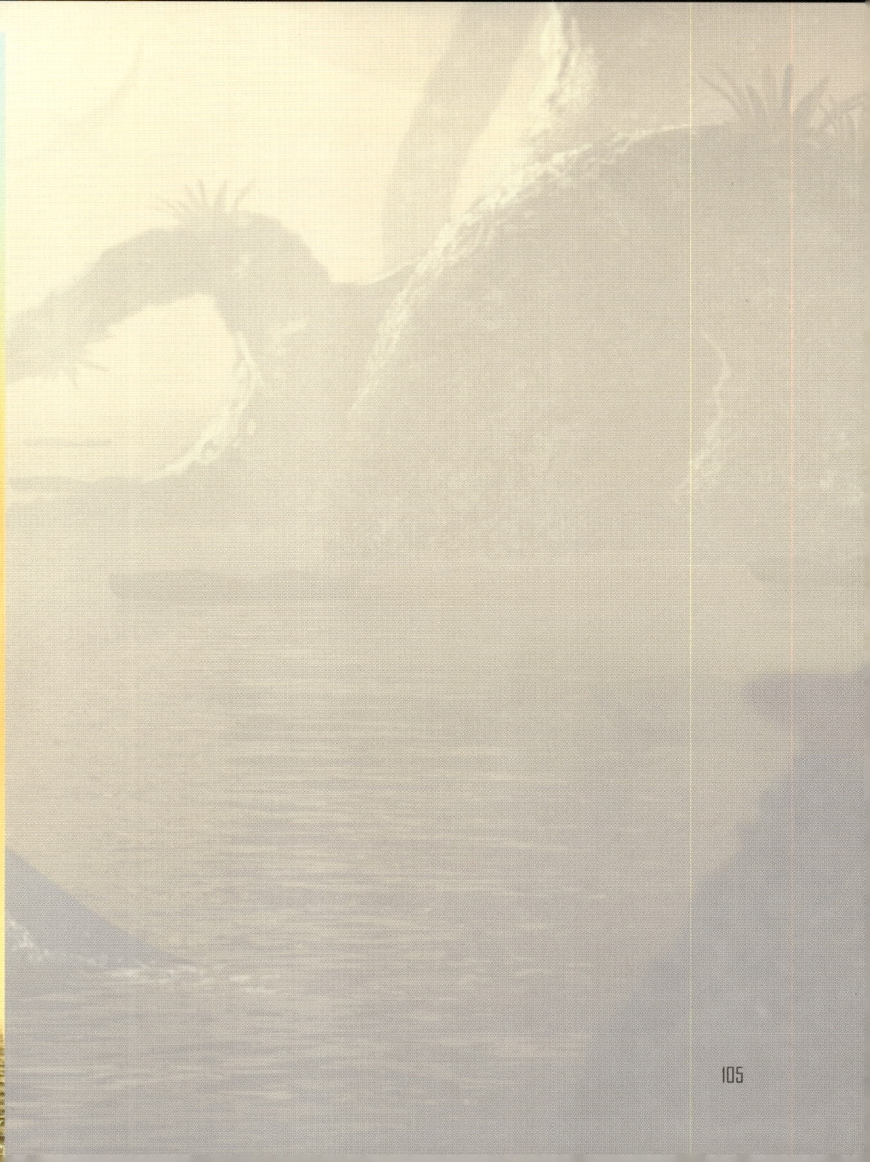

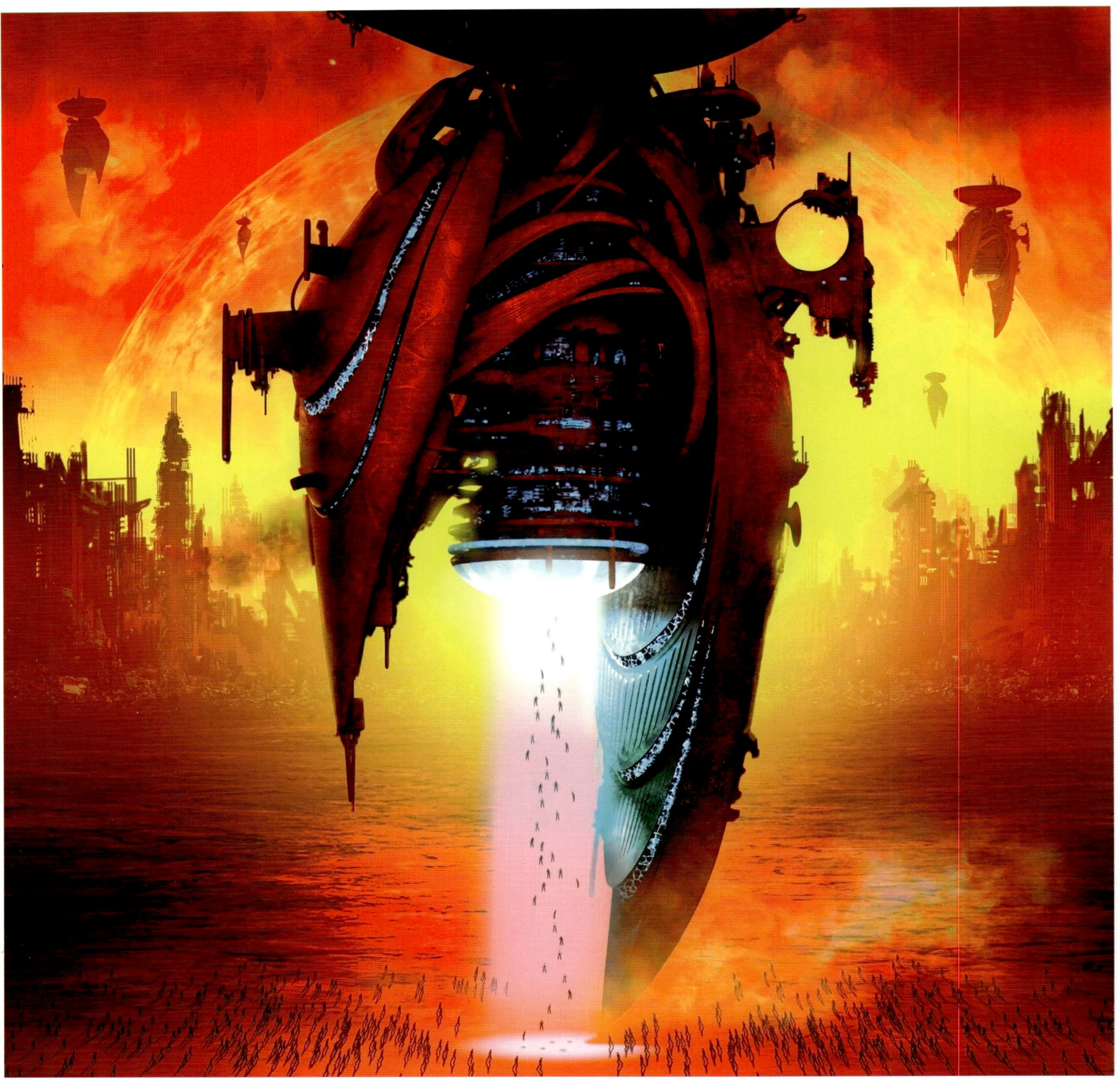

ALBUM COVERS

The band Operahouse used this artwork for the cover of their album *Escape From The Sun*. The spaceship was deliberately intended to have an ambiguous feel to it, so it isn't clear if they've arrived to help or hinder humanity.

Top: *Escape from the Sun*, a CD cover for Operahouse.

Opposite: CD artwork for the album.

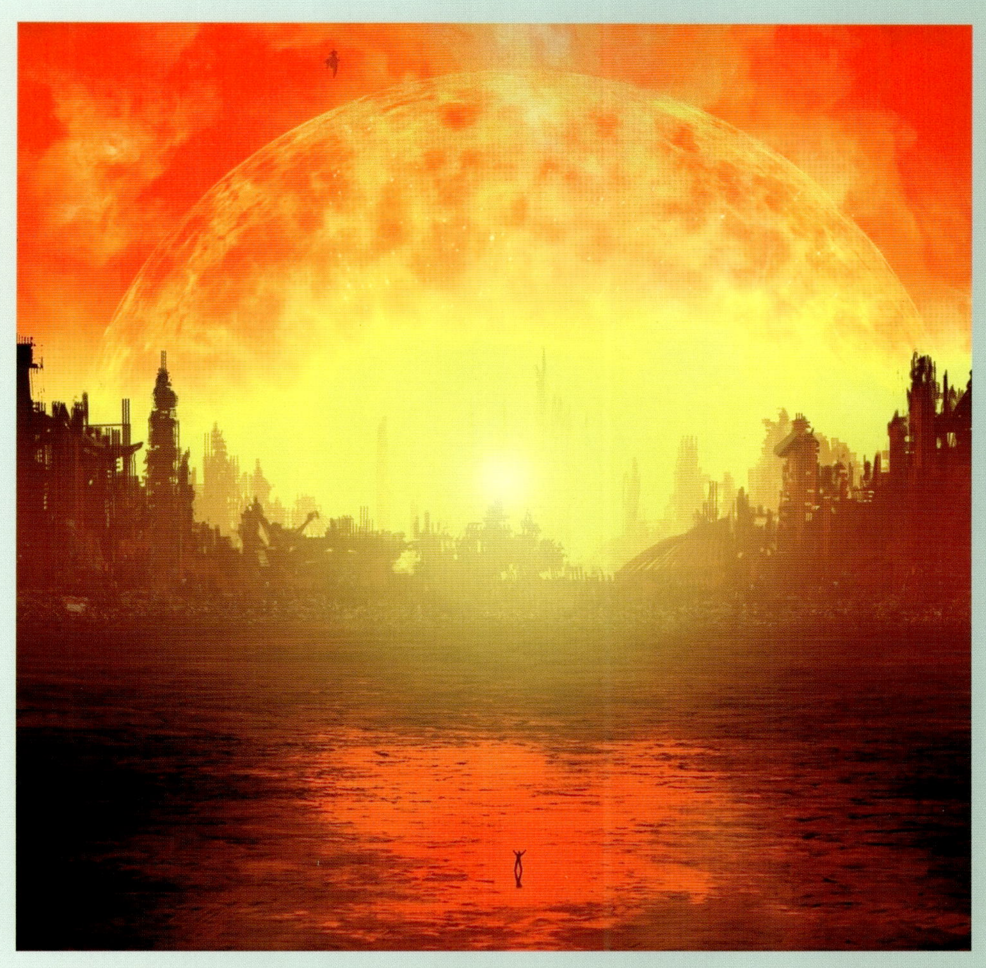

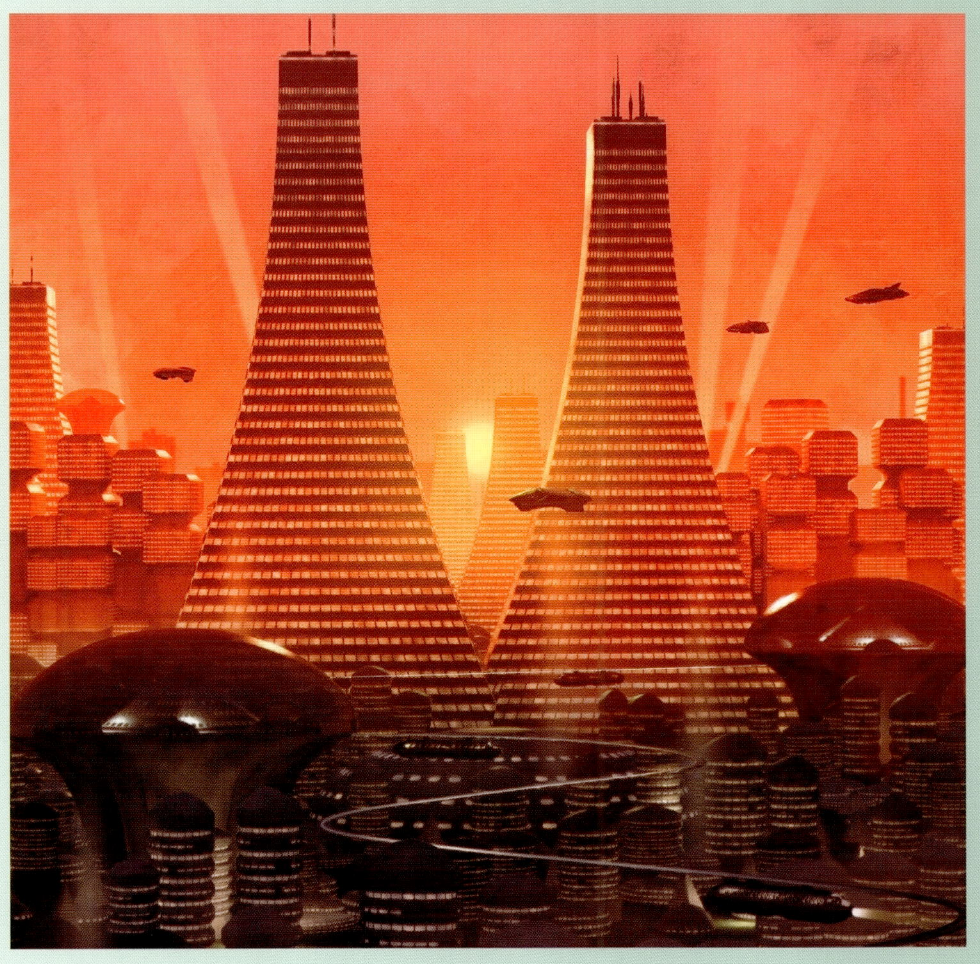

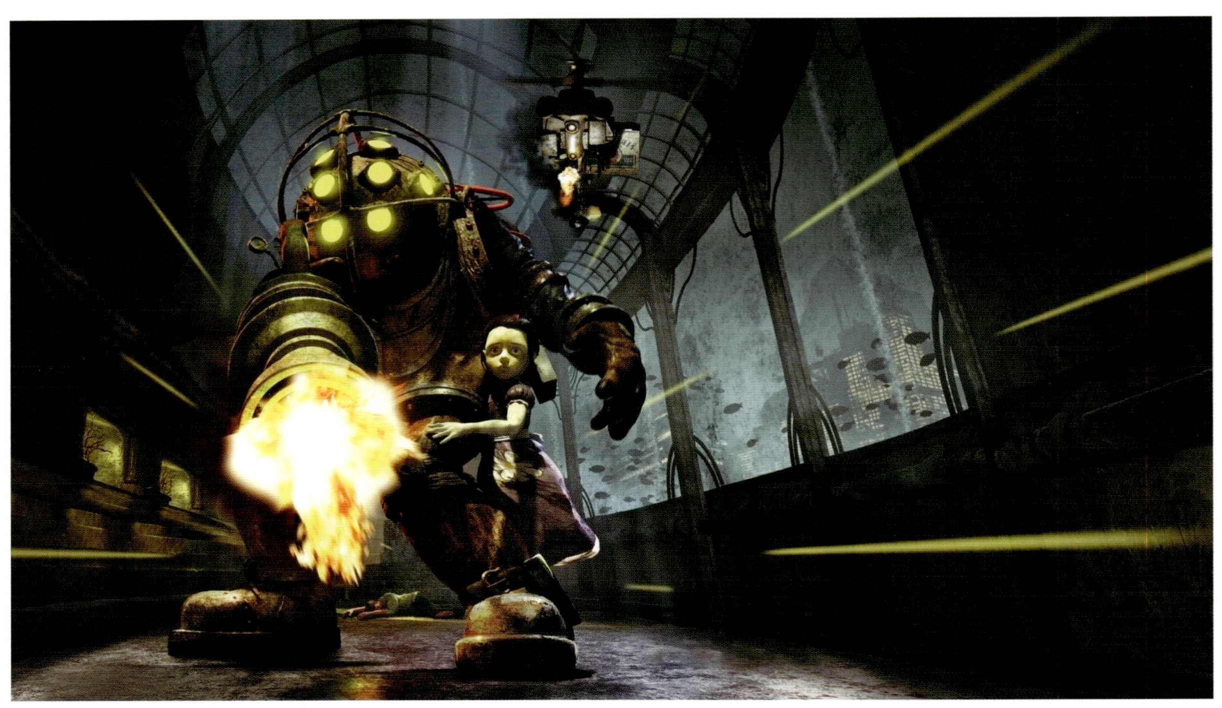

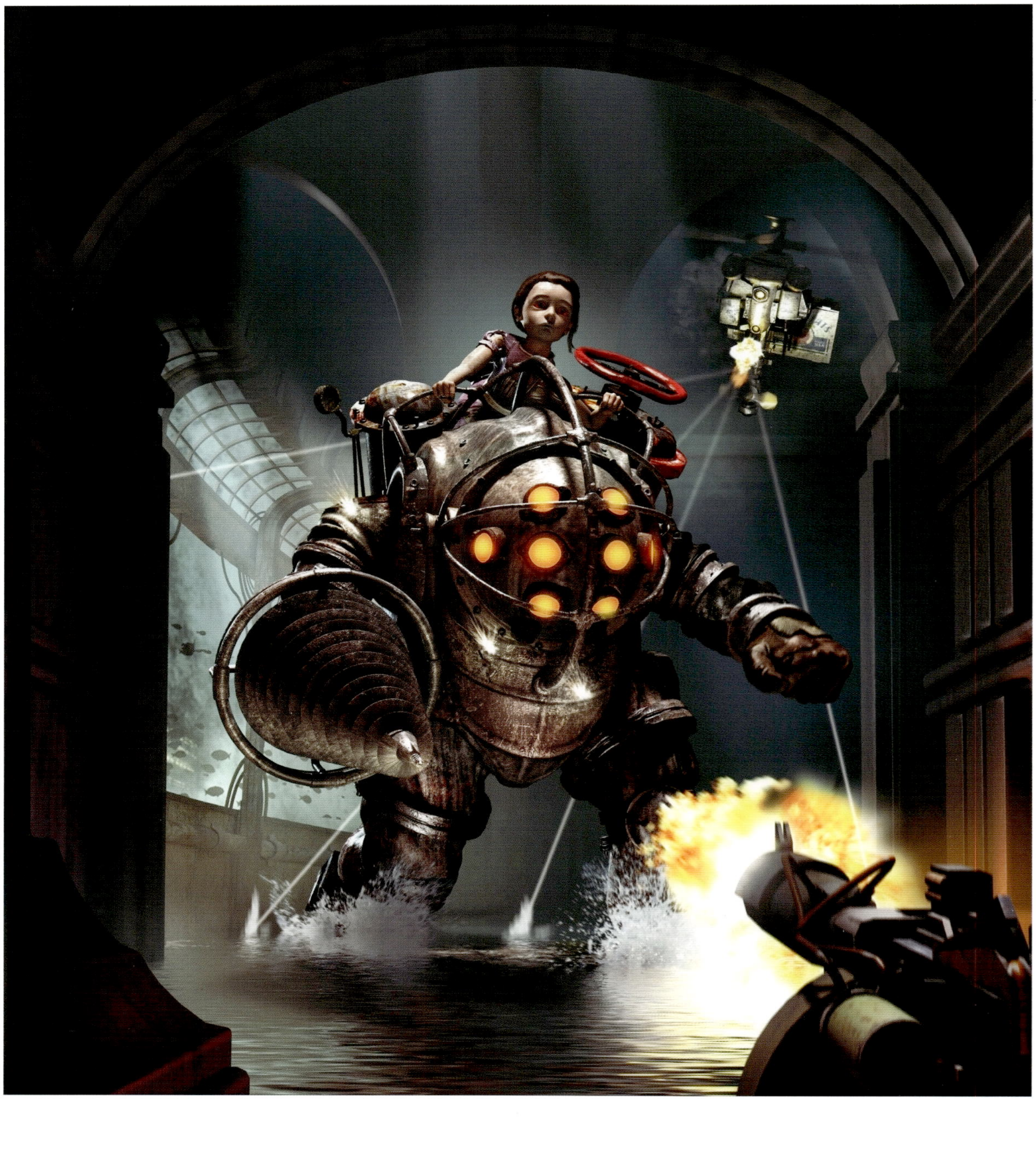

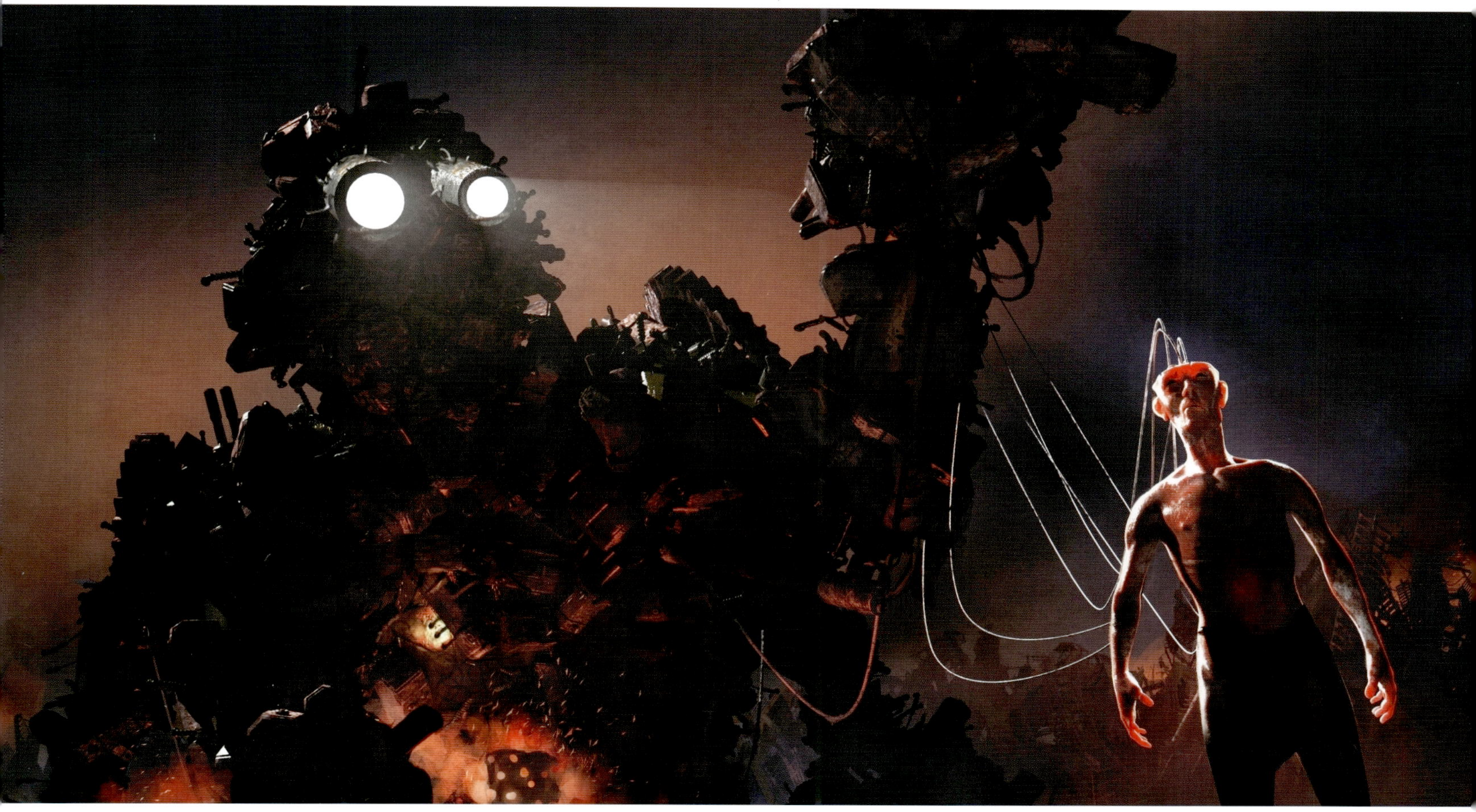

One of the other ways I generated artistic interest in my principal artist role was to organise 'Art Jams'. I would choose a subject, often book-related, and then get the artists to produce concept art as if for a film adaptation. We would have several weeks to complete our paintings, in our own time. I would then award a prize of an art book to the one I deemed to be the best. I had recently read China Mieville's *Perdido Street Station*, which is so chock full of amazing imagery that it had to be a subject. The image *above* is my contribution. The construct council is an entity made up out of junk. Lacking the parts to speak, it communicates using the corpse of an old man, the top of whose head has been removed so that the Construct council can control him, like a macabre puppeteer.

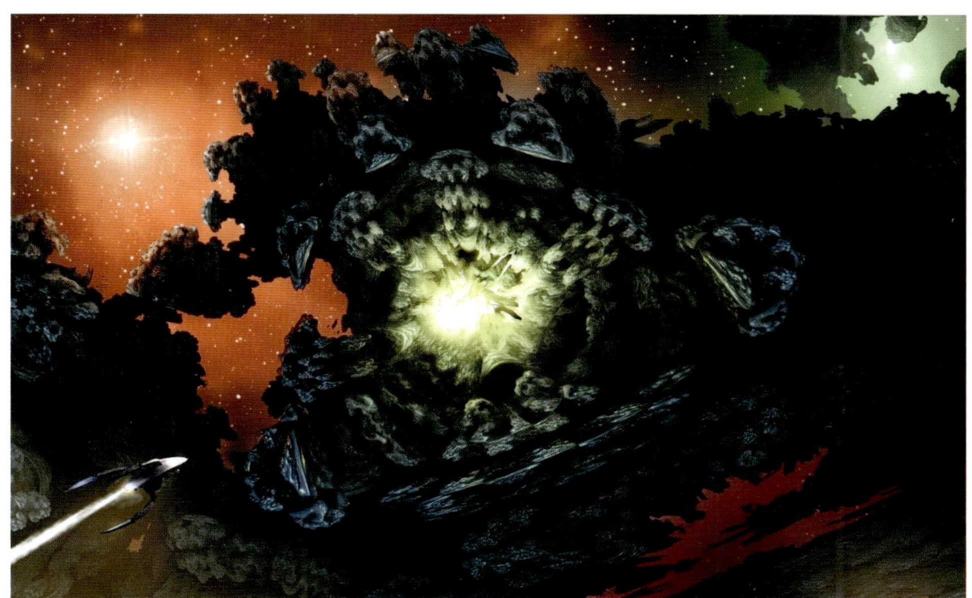

This artwork, *left*, developed following a Facebook discussion on Mandelbrot's fractal patterns. It is possible to generate the infinite patterns in 2D or 3D. This started life as a randomly generated fractal shape which I then re-arranged, adding various effects and elements, such as mood lighting and incoming spaceships.

Opposite: Promotional artwork for the video game *BioShock*.

Above: Personal piece for an 'Art Jam'.

Left: Personal piece using Mandelbrot fractals.

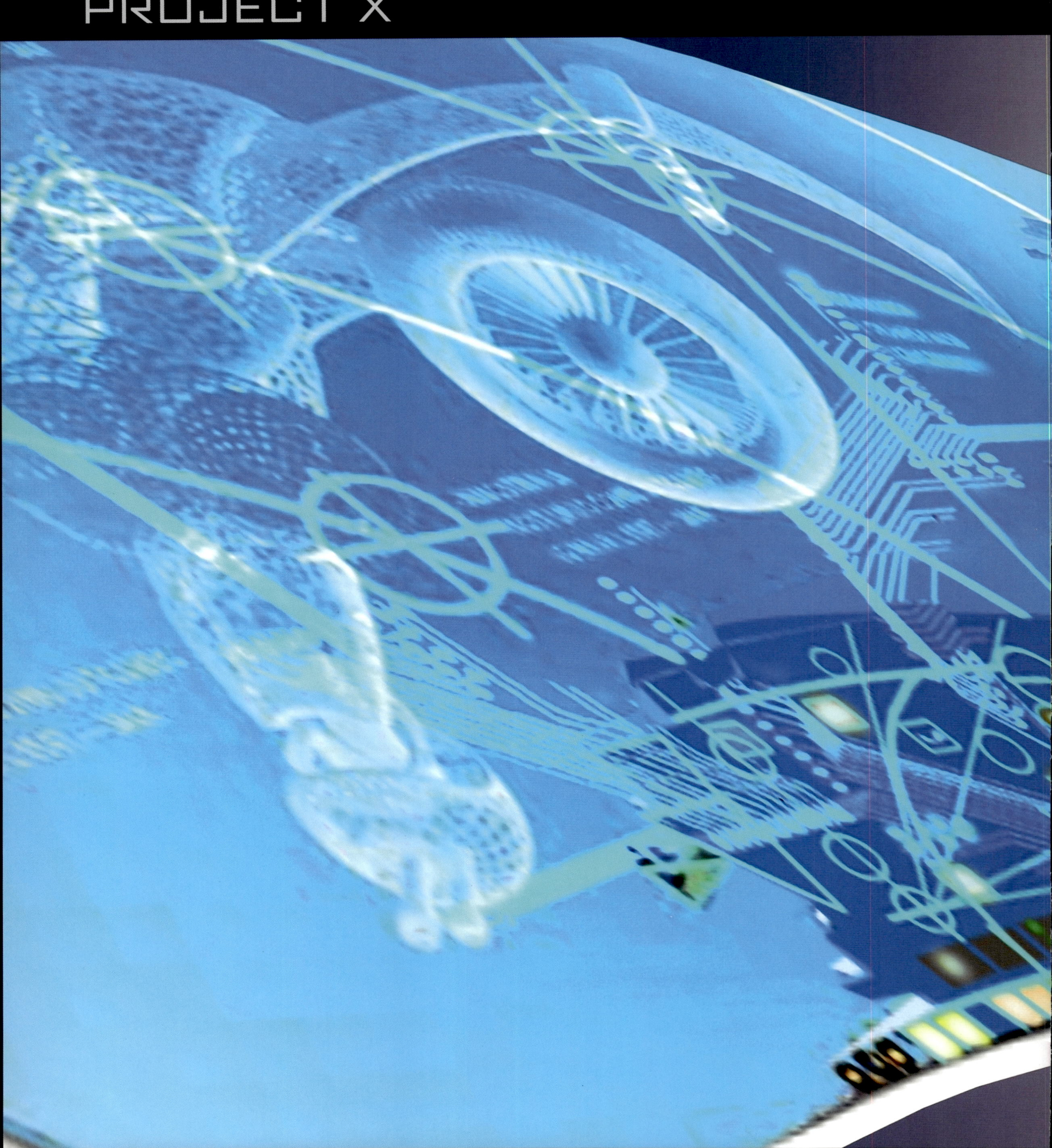

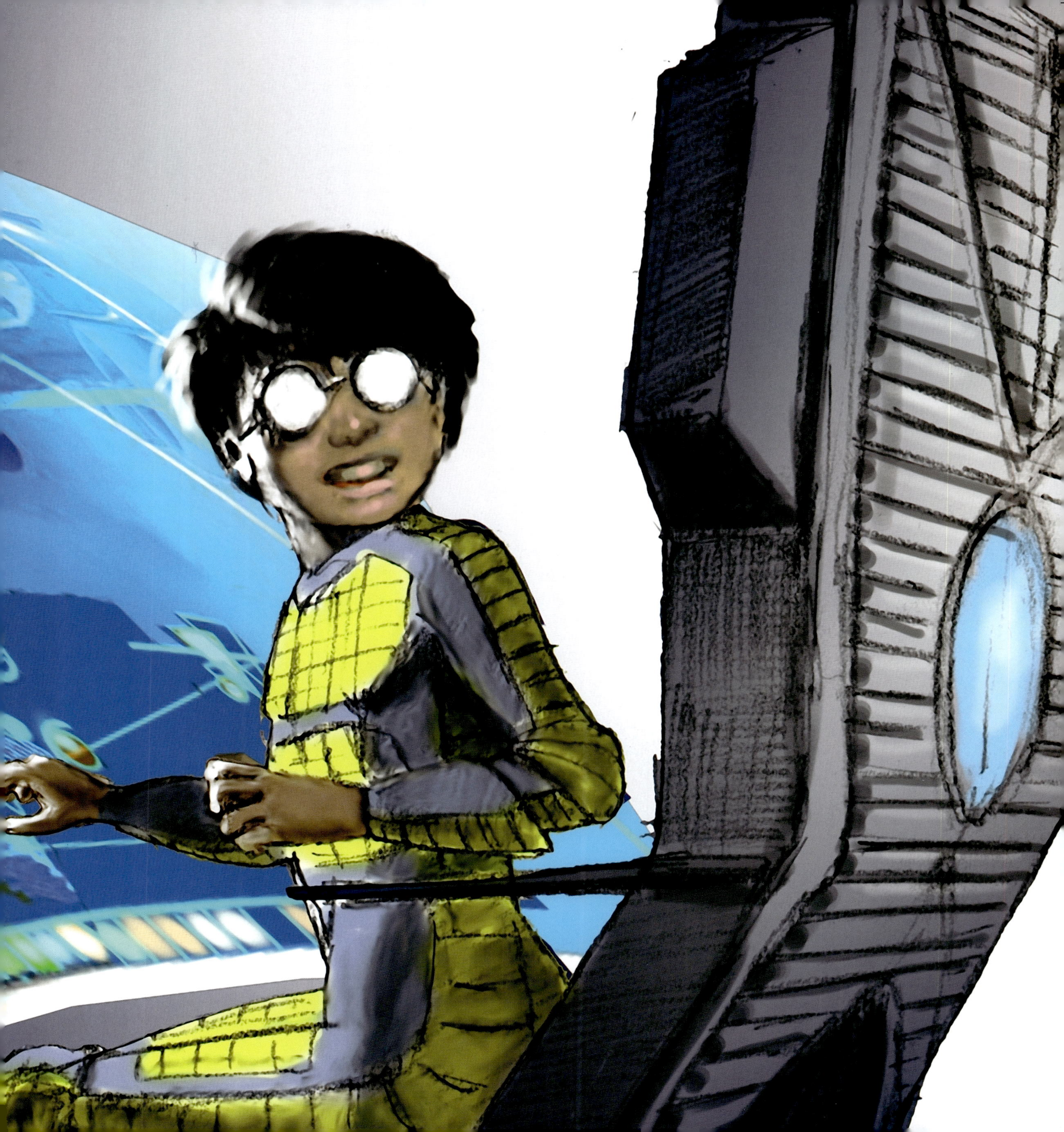

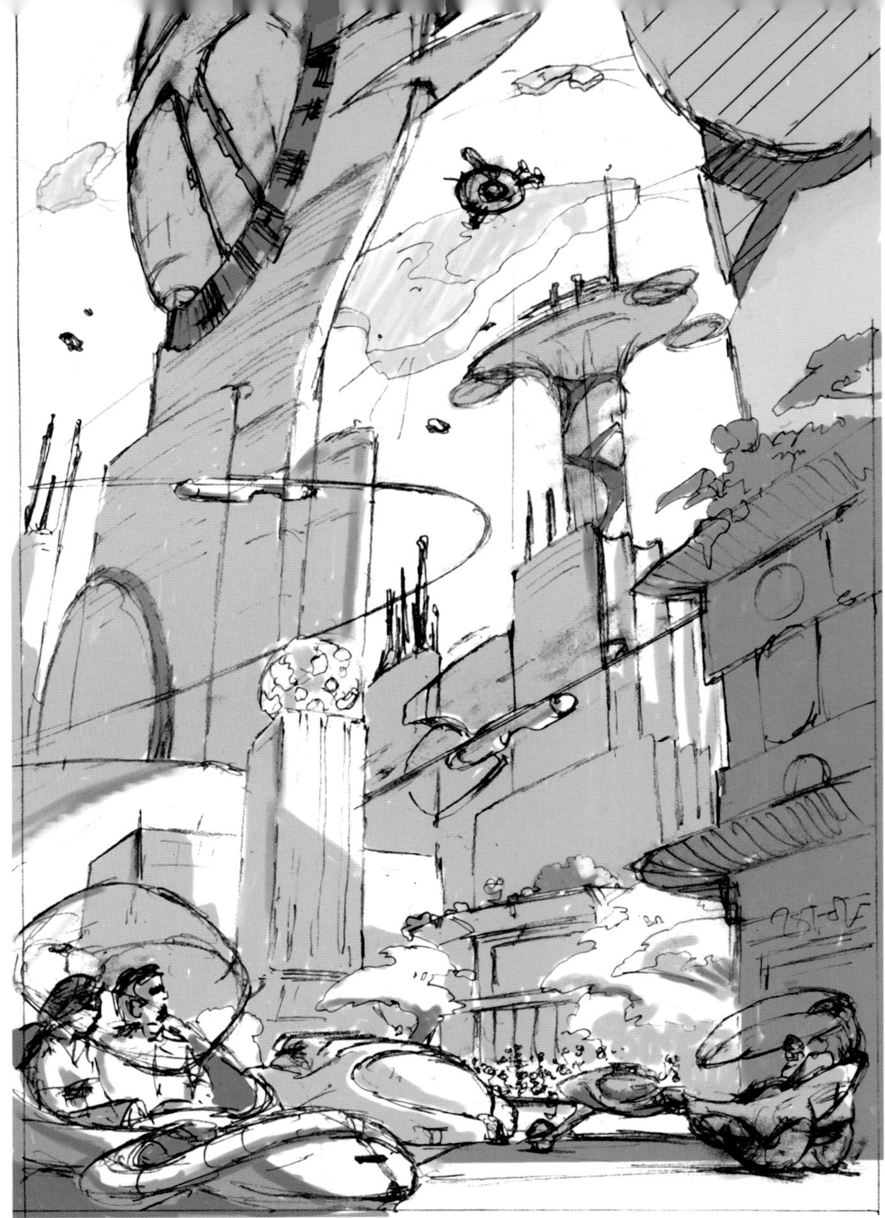

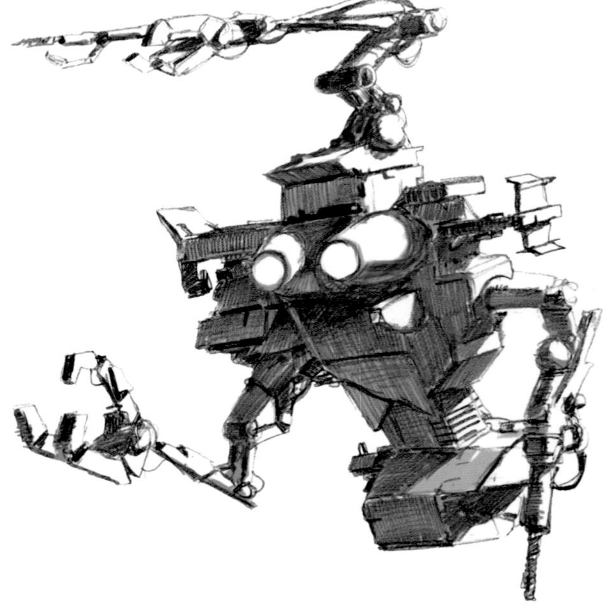

Project X was the working title of a proposed television series to be made with Lego Media, and my first real foray into concept art. At that time, around 2000, I still worked with traditional materials. Computers were slow, and the early graphics tablets didn't have a very intuitive input method for someone who was used to a pencil, although I quickly got used to them. These days, working on a Cintiq, I draw on the screen as if it were paper and both the hardware and software has become so fast there is no longer any perceptible time lag.

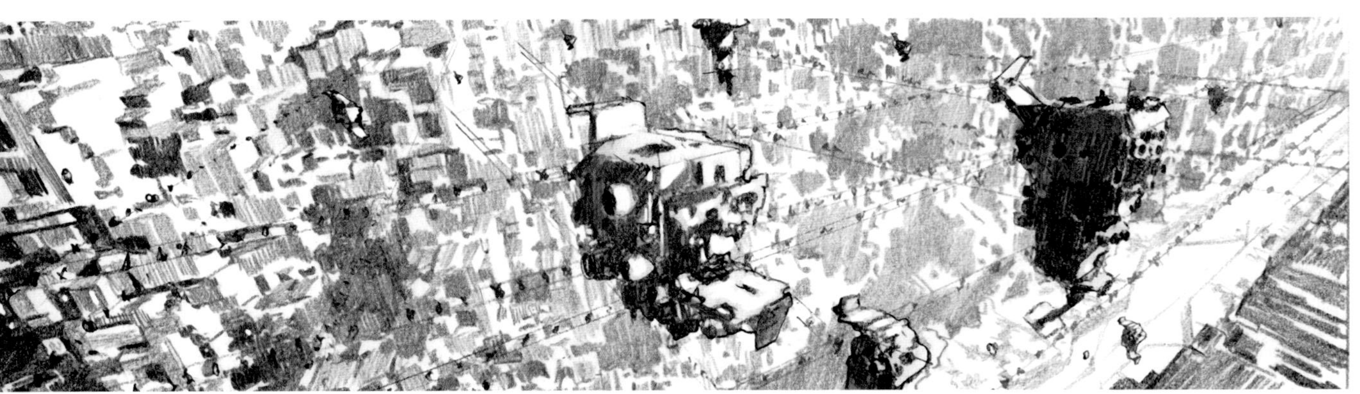

In *Project X*, the characters could hop into a cyber world. These drawings visualised that world. Having the scope to design a whole range of different things, from environments and characters to vehicles, made it a lot of fun. The vehicles *opposite* were designed with toy merchandising in mind.

Previous spread: Design for Chip, the brains of the outfit. Chip would design vehicles and equipment for the team as needed.

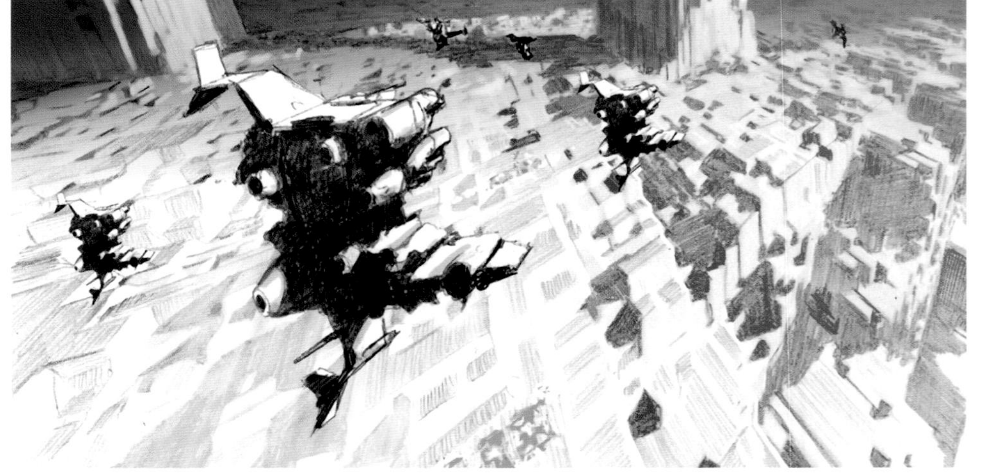

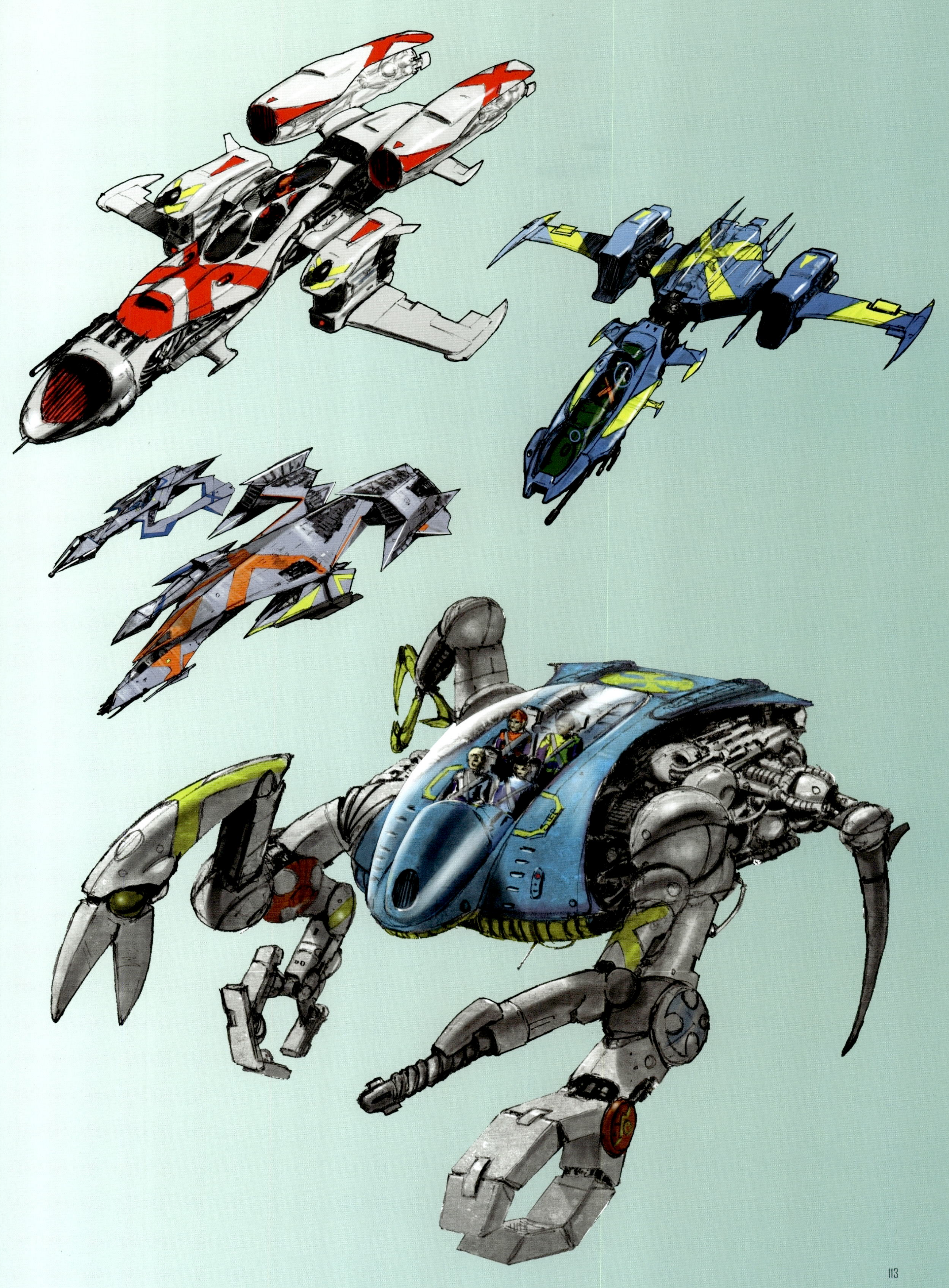

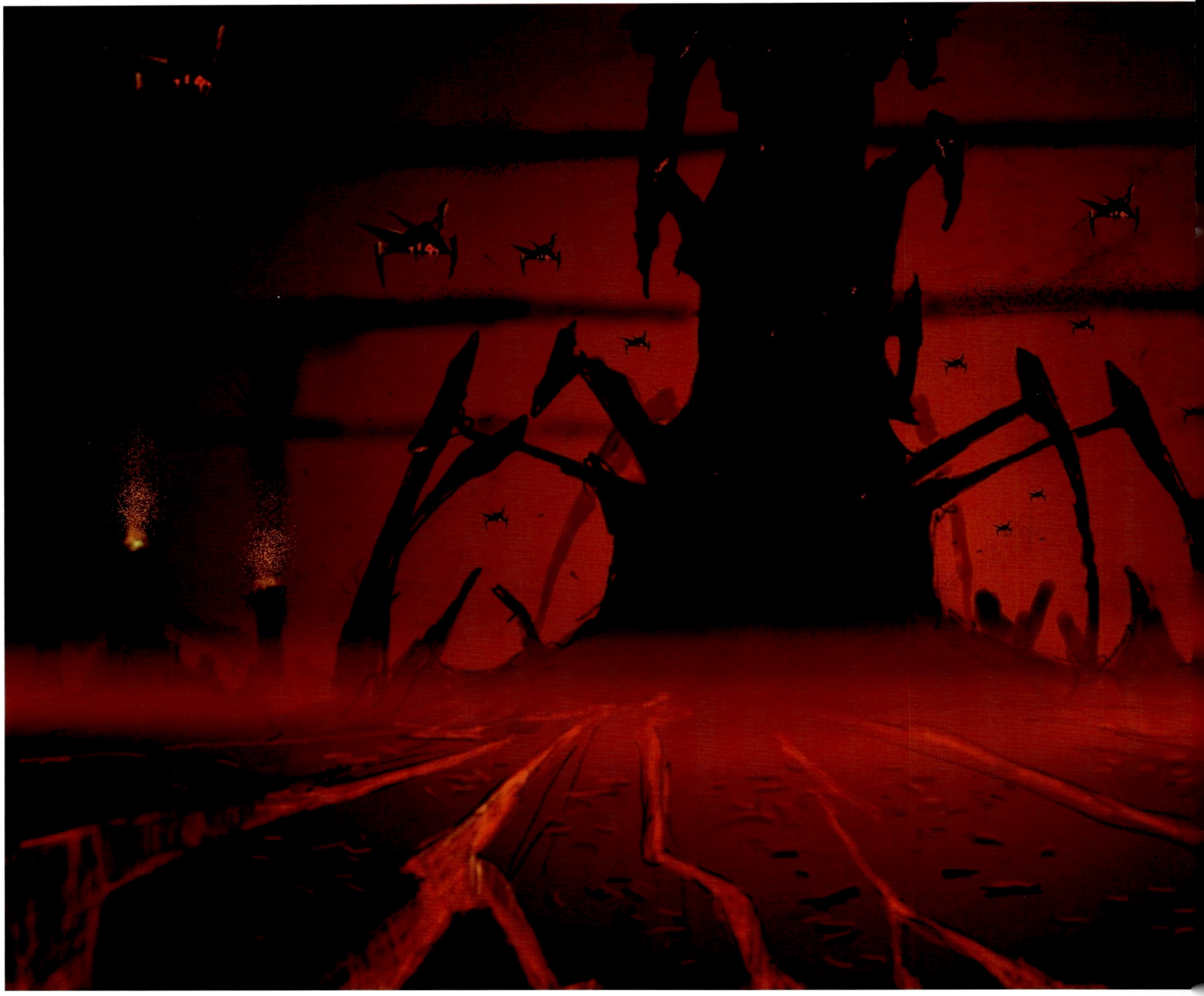

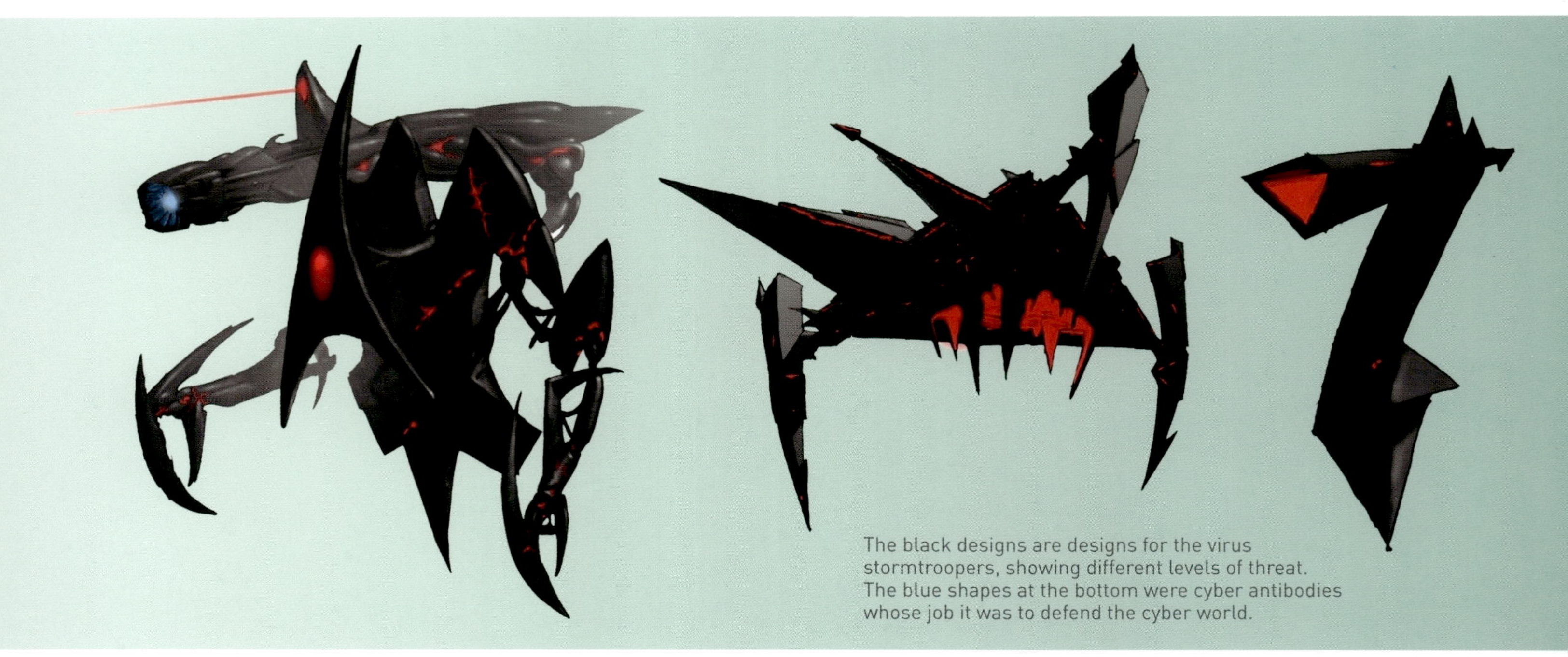

The black designs are designs for the virus stormtroopers, showing different levels of threat. The blue shapes at the bottom were cyber antibodies whose job it was to defend the cyber world.

VIRUSES

The cyber world was consistently under attack from an evil virus, which the kids would thwart every week. The pencil drawings on page 112 were the proper functioning parts of that world, whilst this spread shows the corrupted and ruined part.

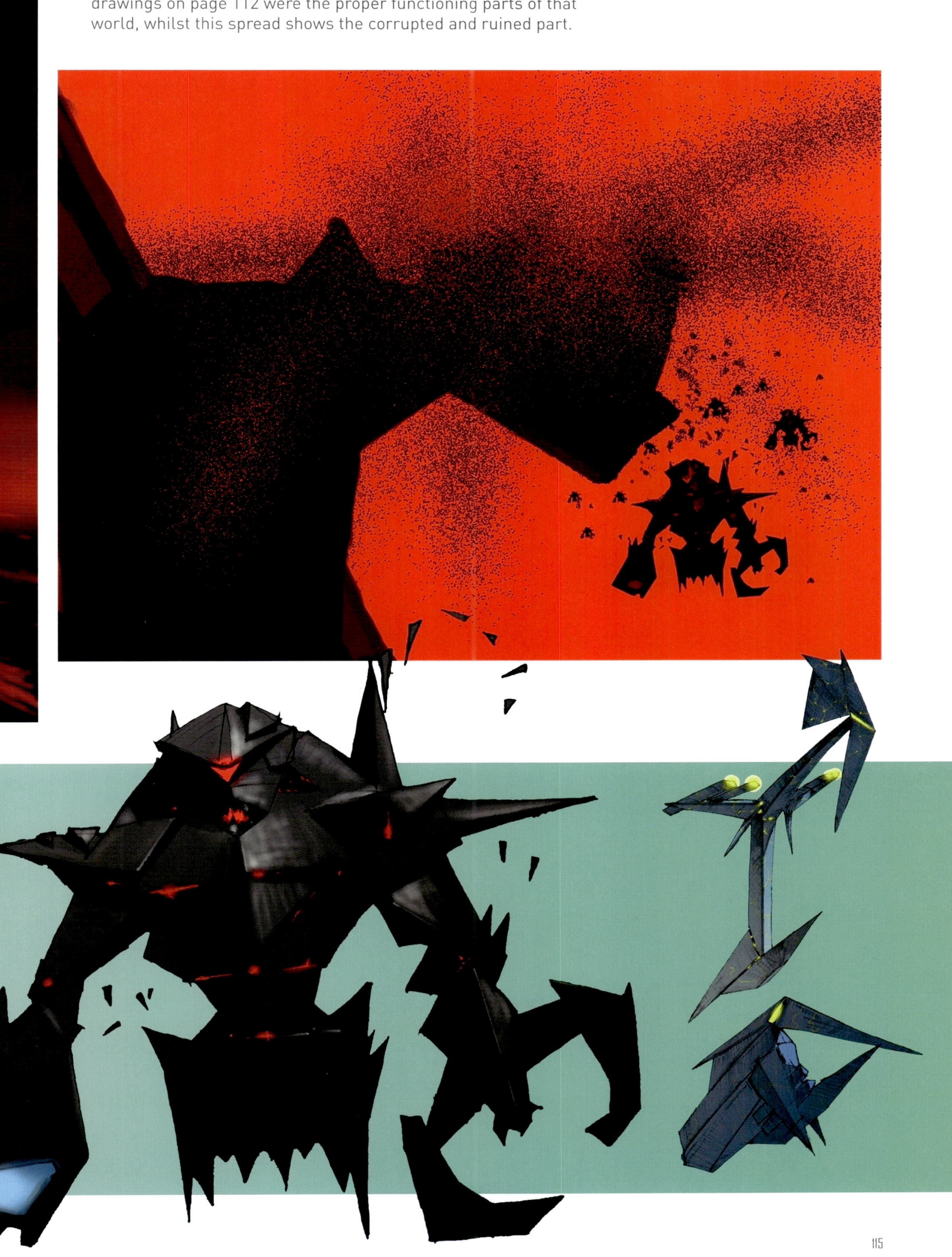

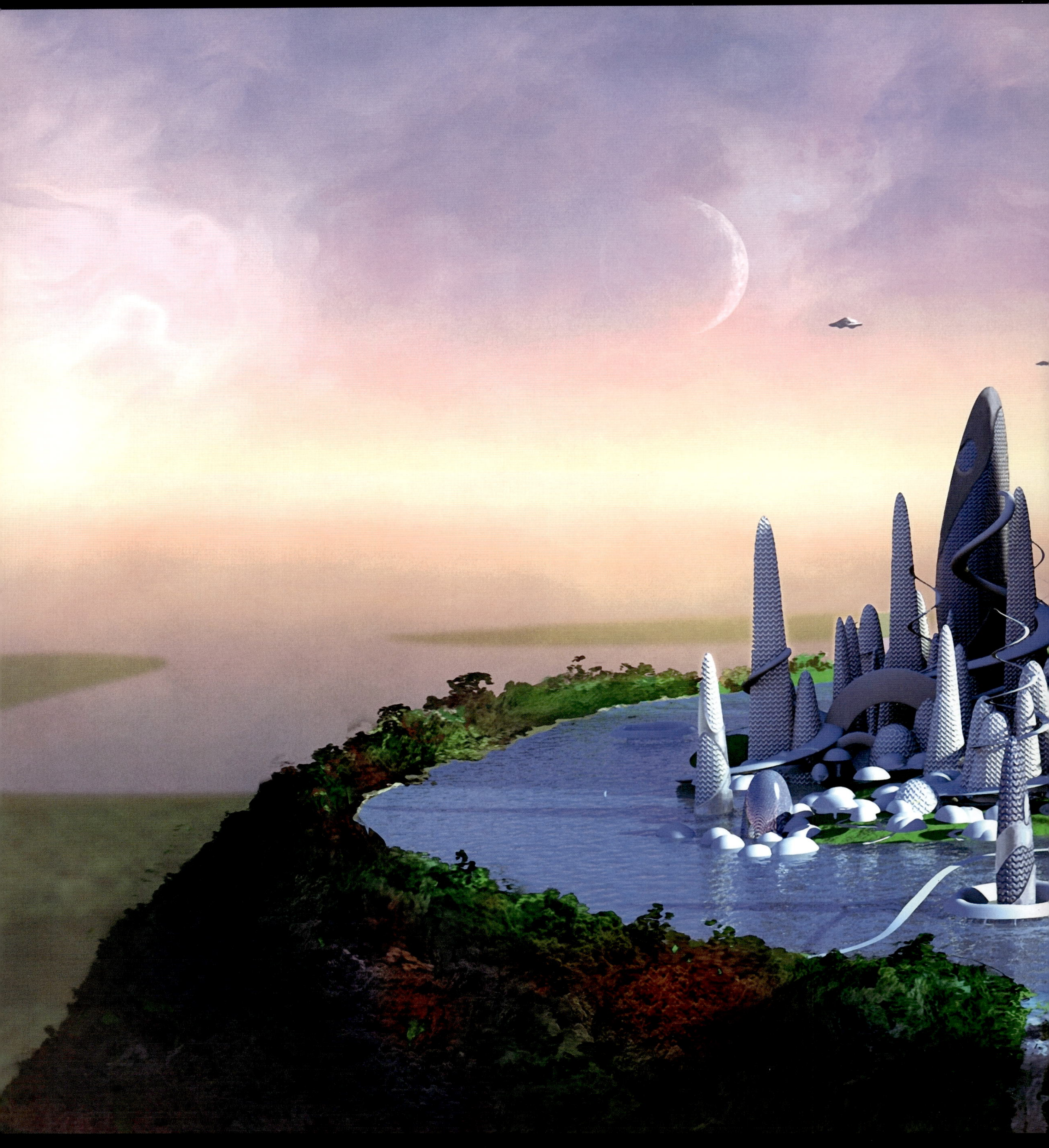

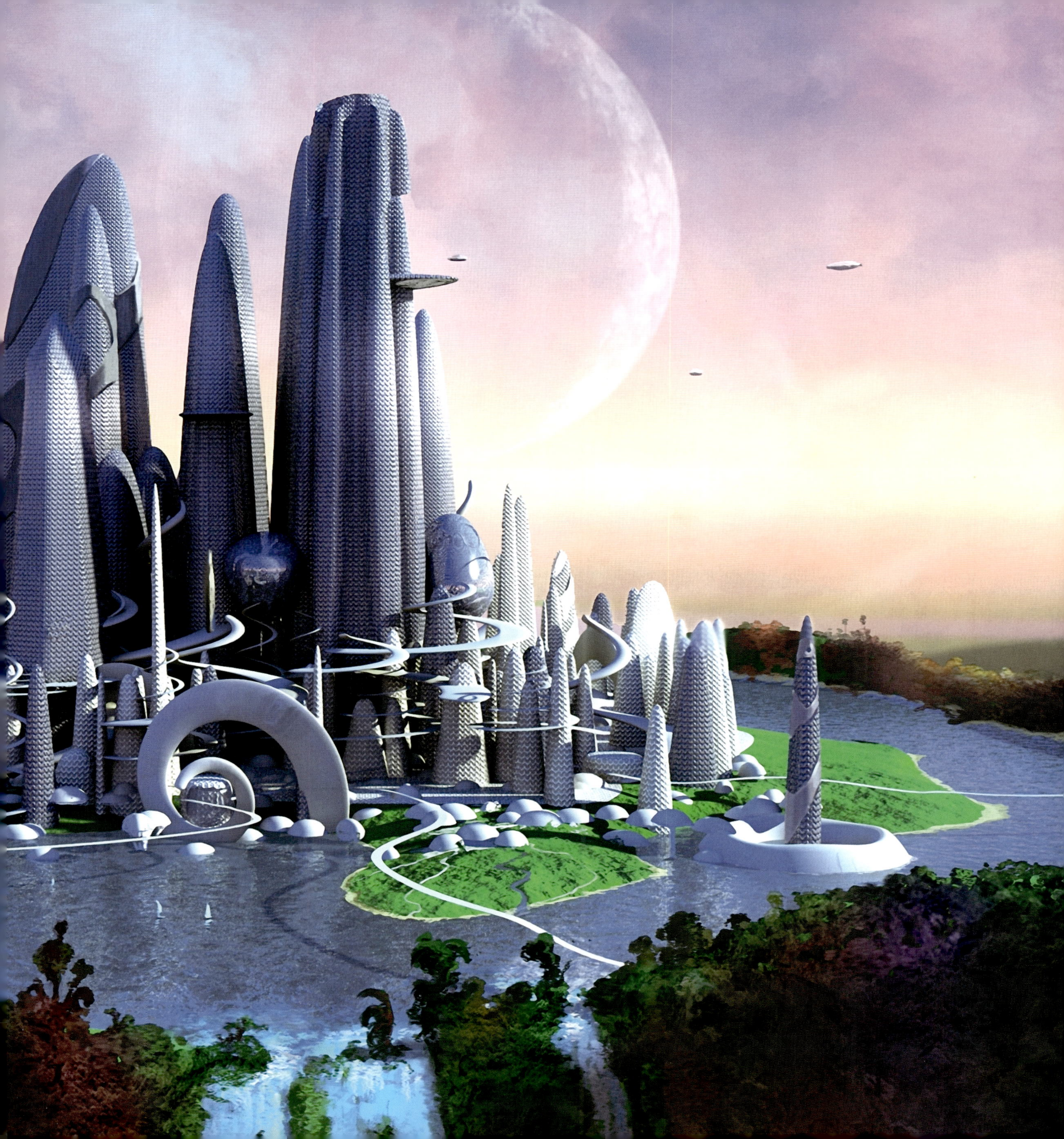

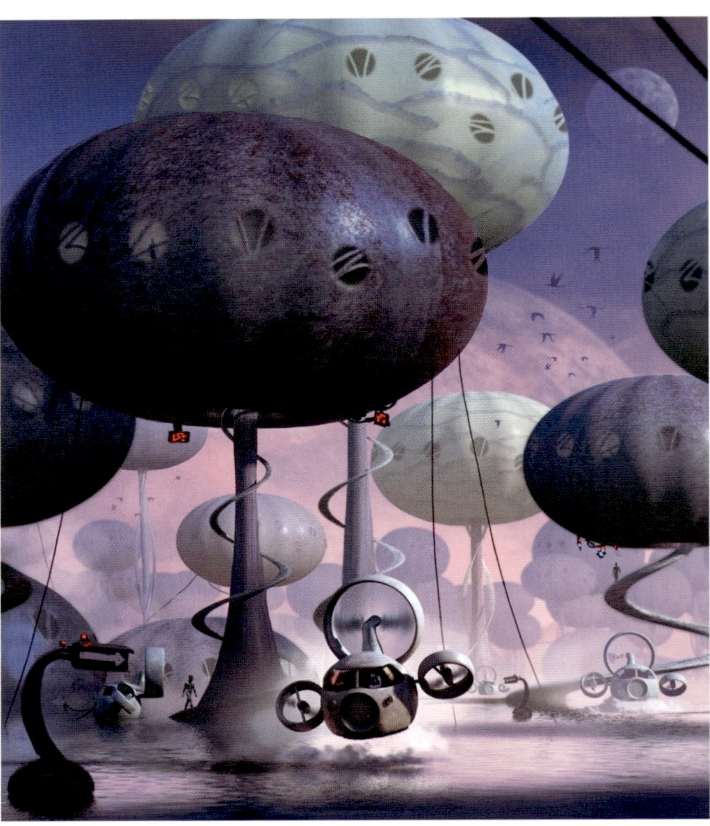

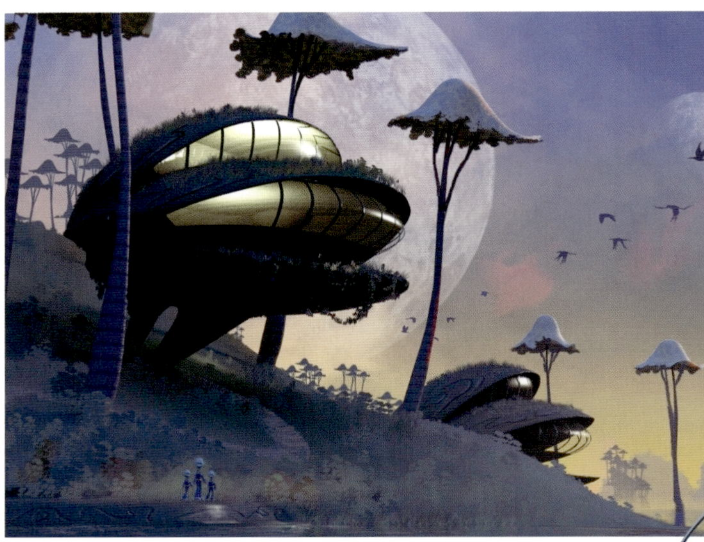

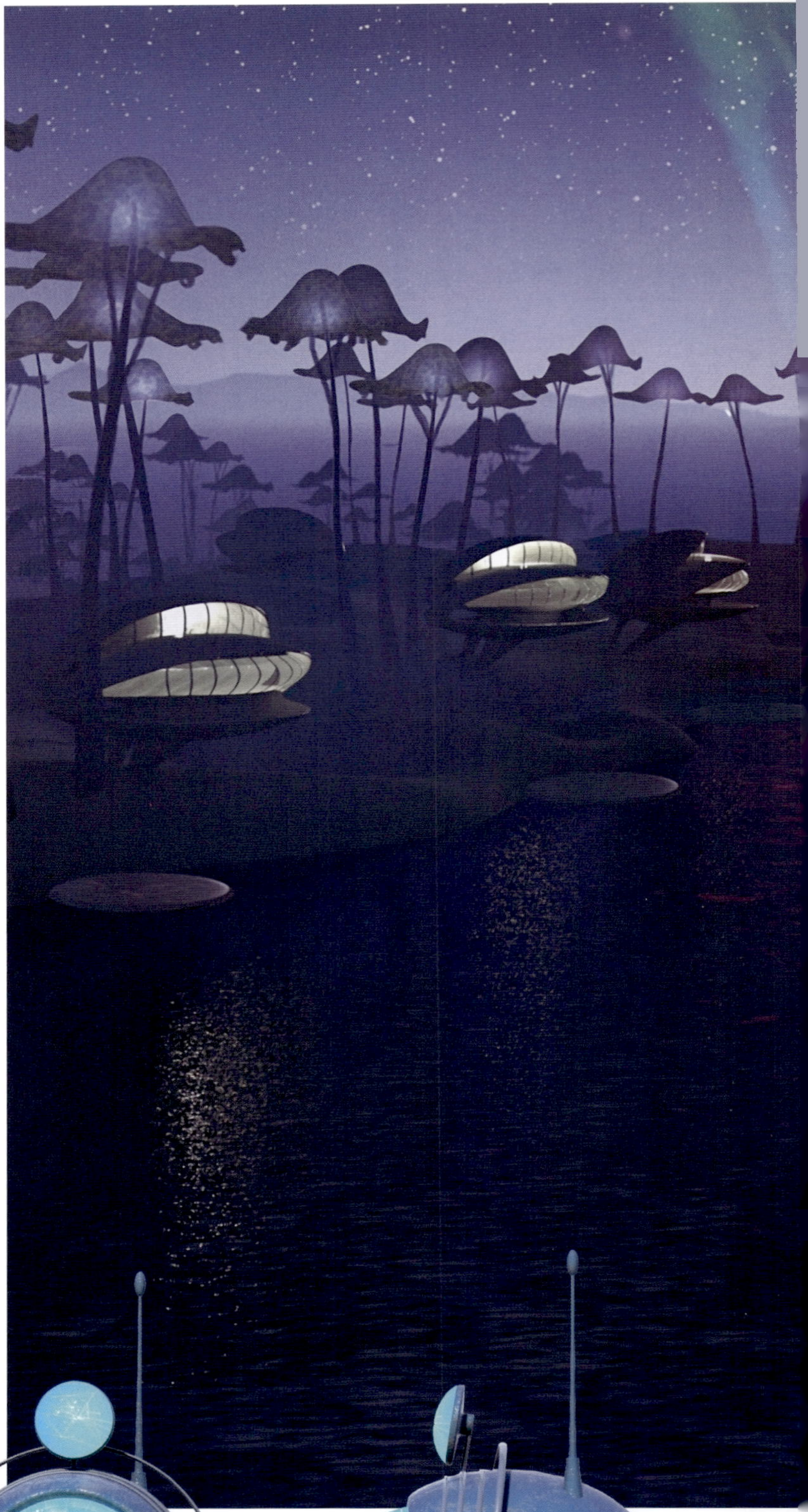

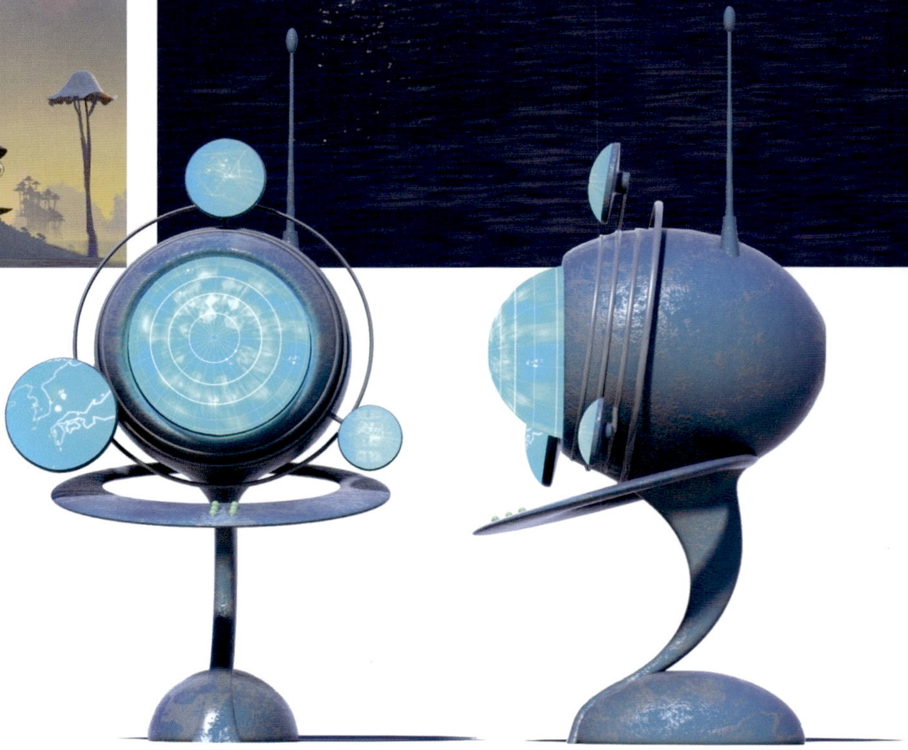

Previous spread: Crater City concept.

Above left: An early version of Barbian suburbia. Gary and family are waiting for the water bus to BASA.

Above right: Concept for Gary's house with the family looking out at the stars from their grassy rooftop. House design by Dan Quarnstrom.

Right: The design for a communication device that the character Gary builds by himself.

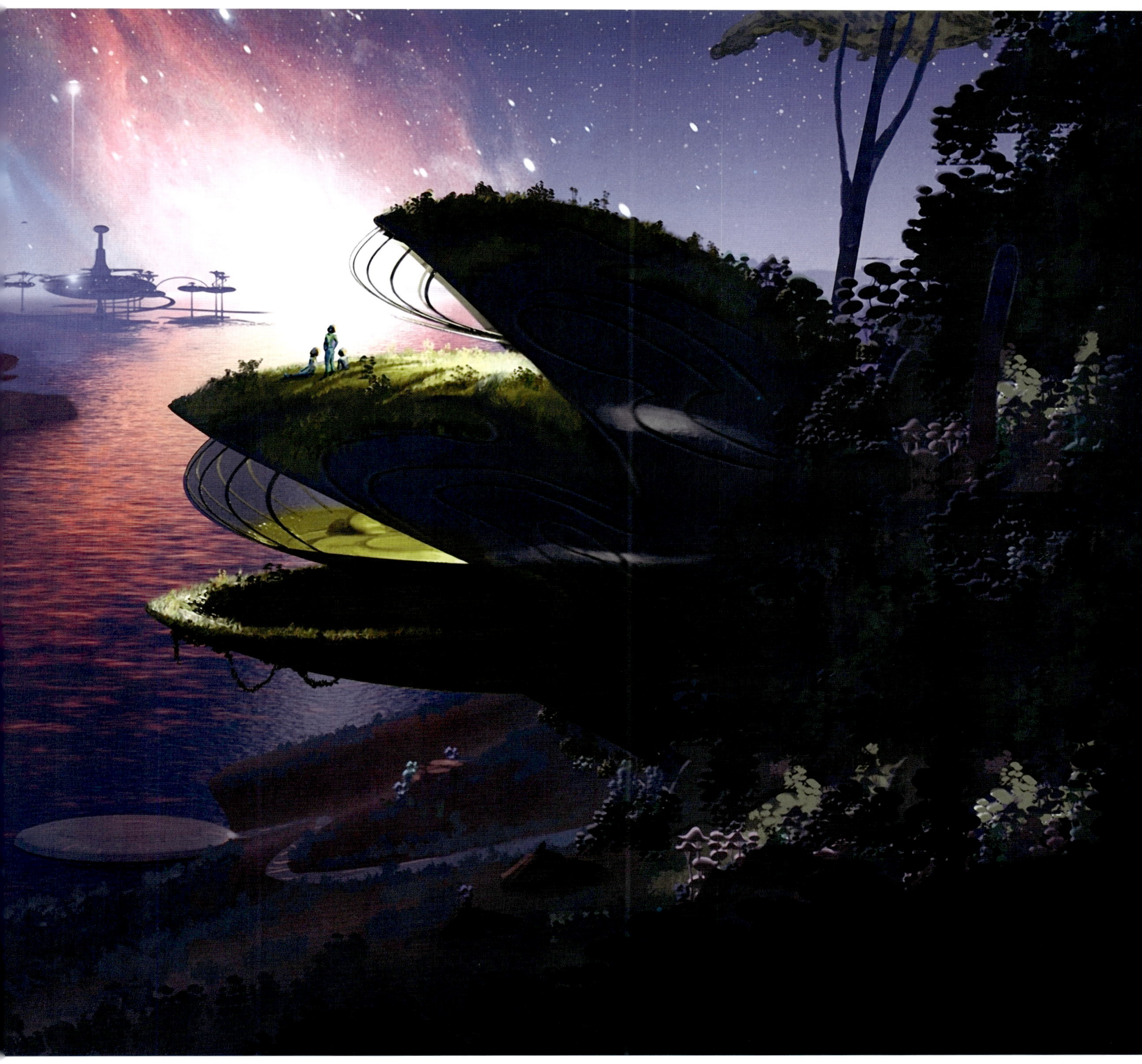

I worked on Weinstein's *Escape From Planet Earth* at Rainmaker in Vancouver directly after working on *The Ant Bully* in Dallas. I loved Vancouver and spent a great eighteen months there. Part of the enjoyment of working on projects like this was the teamwork involved. I was one of two art directors, Dan Quarnstrom being the other one.

We designed the suburbs on the planet Baab. The script went through many versions – in one, Baab was a water-based world. In this scene, Gary is sitting with his family on the roof of their house with BASA, Baab's version of NASA, visible in the distance. The grassy covering, indicating perhaps the ecological nature of the aliens, would contrast with the brutish concrete look of Area 51 on Earth when Gary journeyed there.

In this case, Dan Quarnstom produced the line drawing designs for the houses. I realised those drawings as paintings, providing the mood and atmosphere.

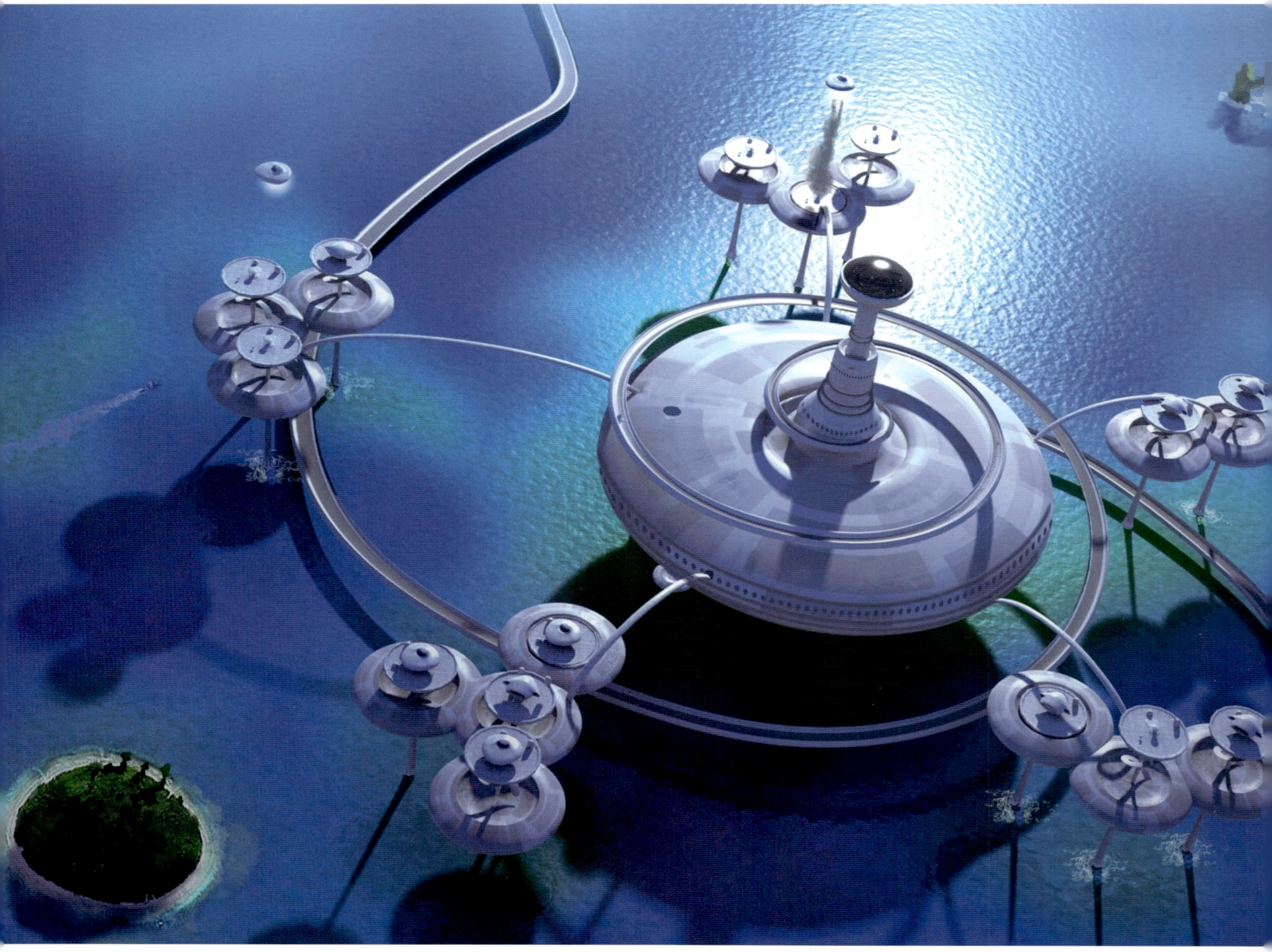

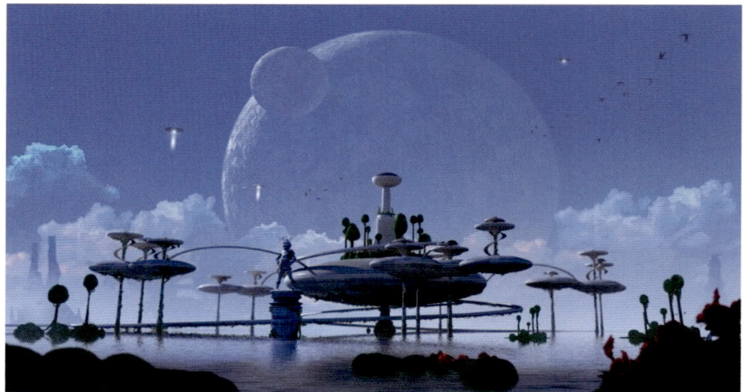

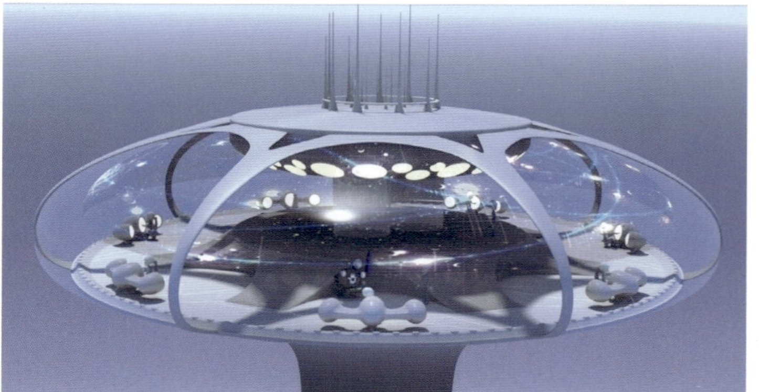

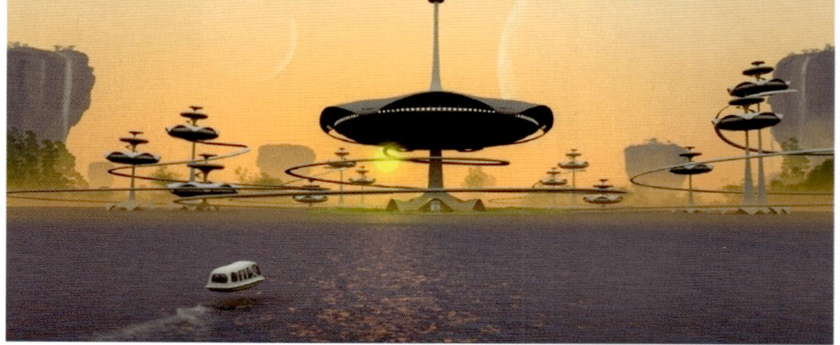

This spread: Various buildings, tech and machinery designed for BASA's labs.

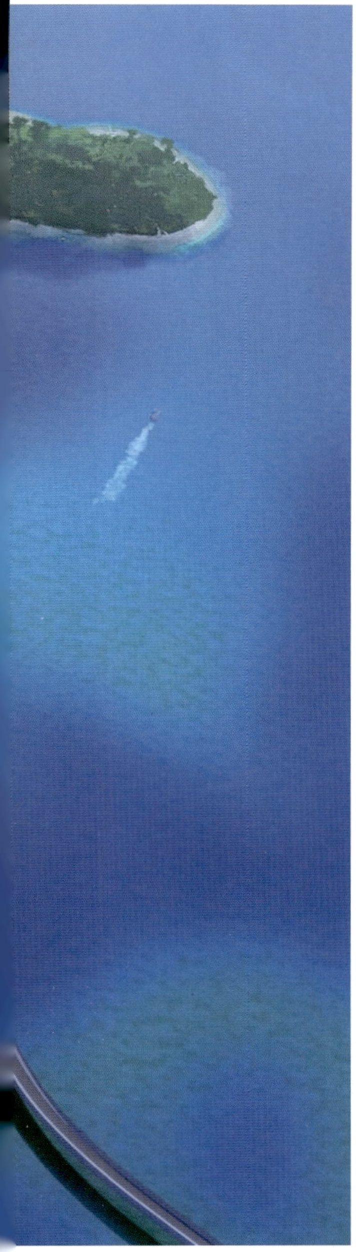

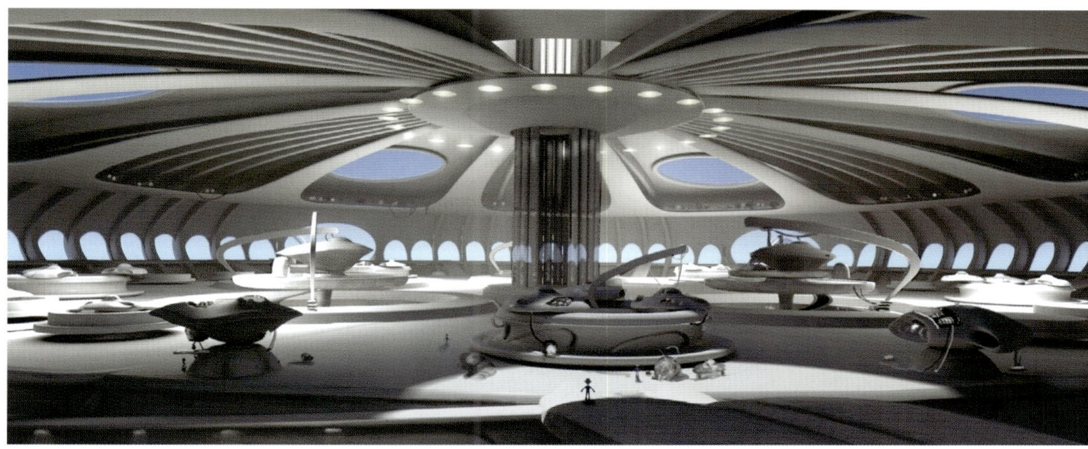

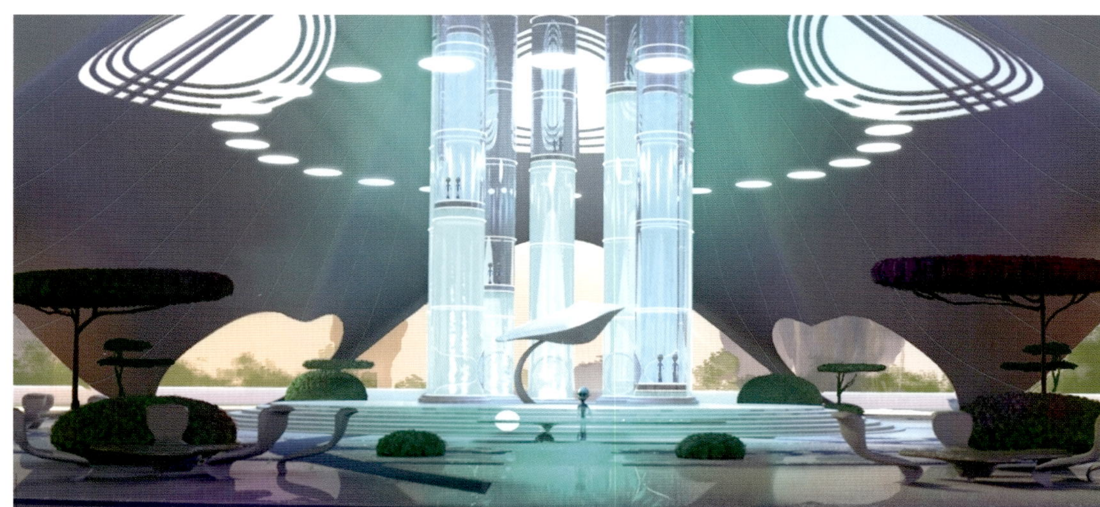

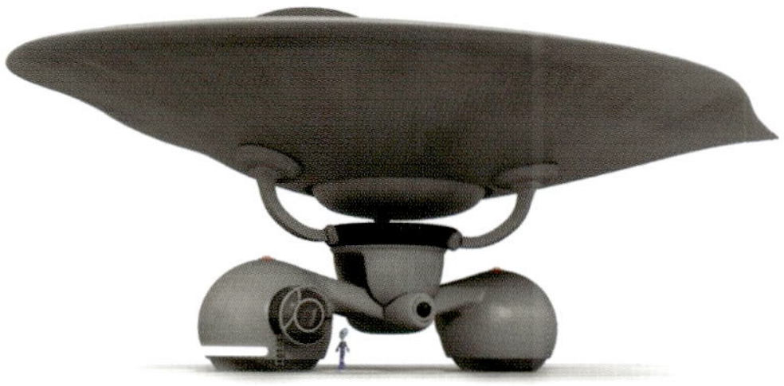

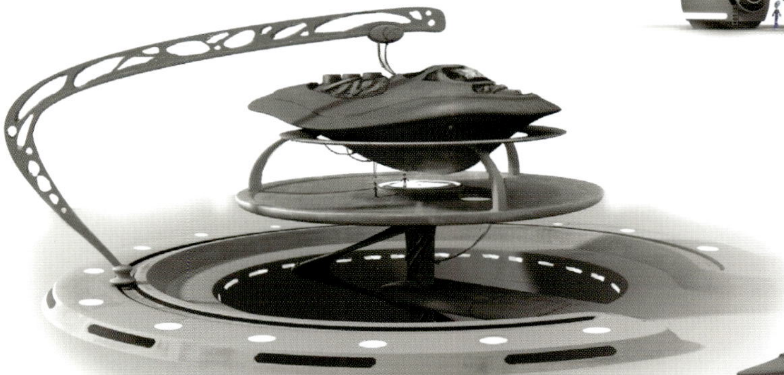

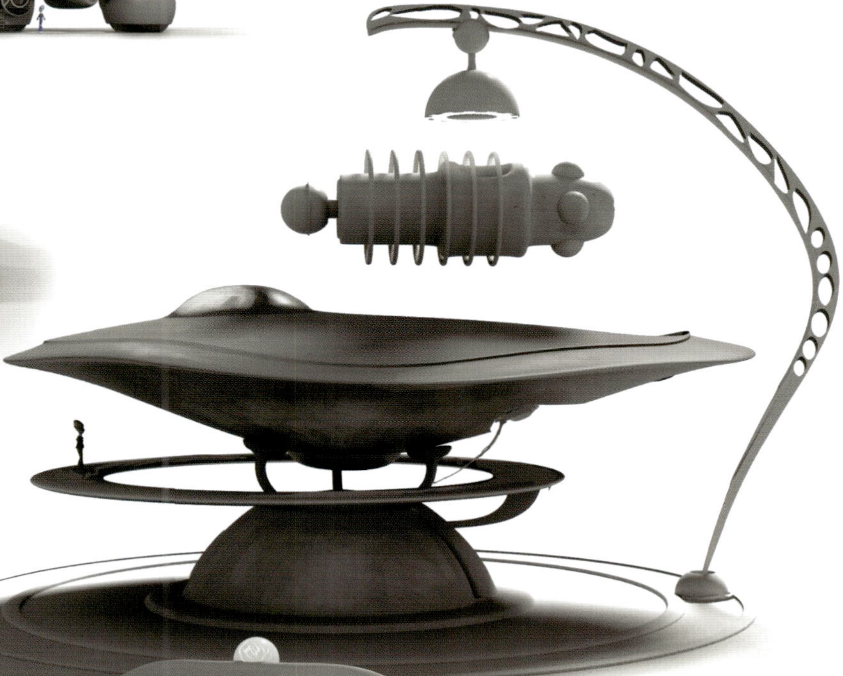

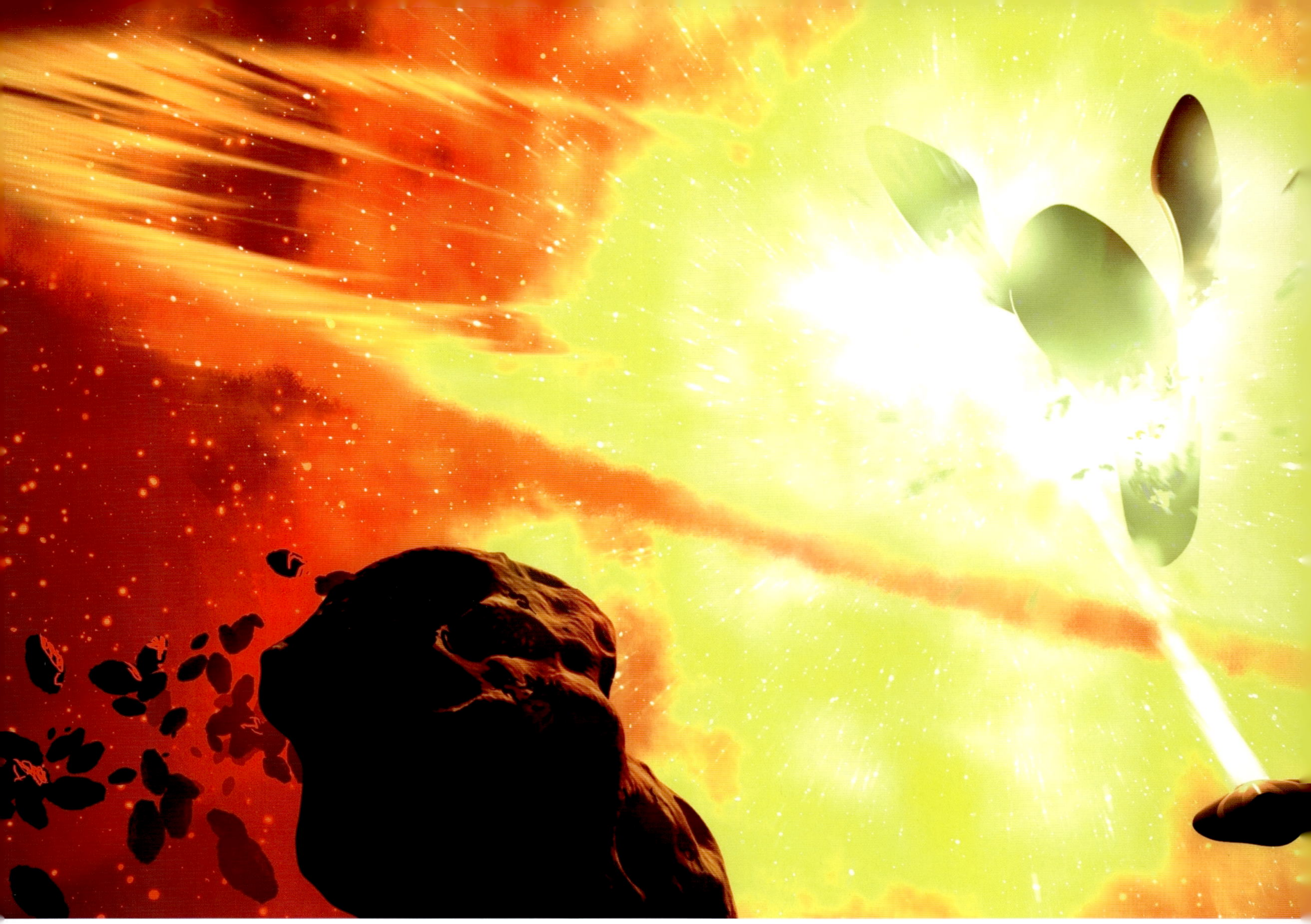

ASTEROID BELT SEQUENCE

We created these images to show how asteroids might be used in a chase sequence. The production designer wanted them to have real character and to look different to what an audience might usually expect, so I generated these quirky cartoony shapes. They then asked me to visualise a chase through the belt, which led (in that script version) to the destruction of Gary's ship and his escape in a shuttle. The script went through many changes, and this was one of many scenes that were later dropped. Having concept work go unused is all part of the job, and it doesn't pay to be precious about one's own contribution. Many artists make excellent livings working on films that never even see the light of day.

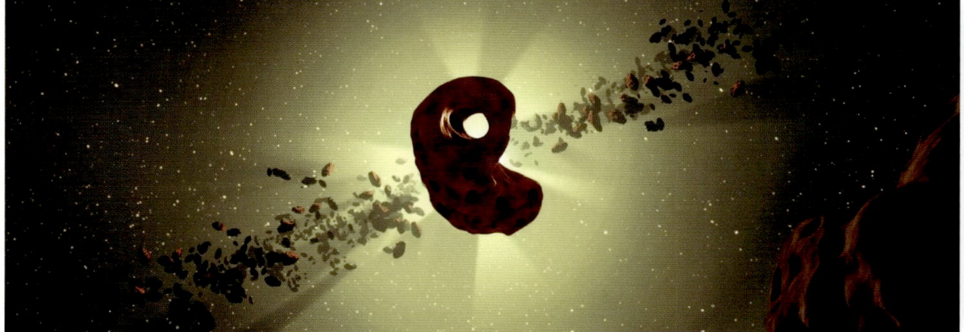

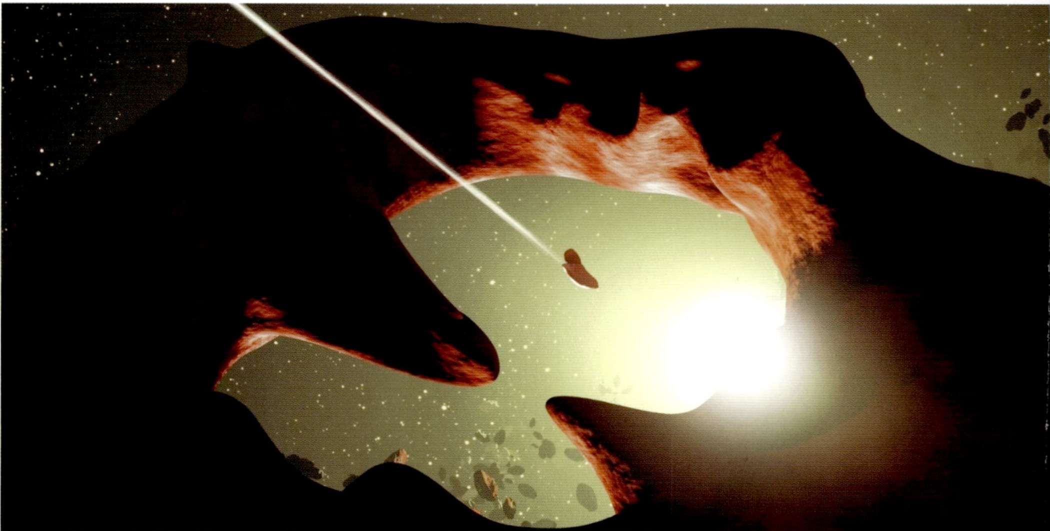

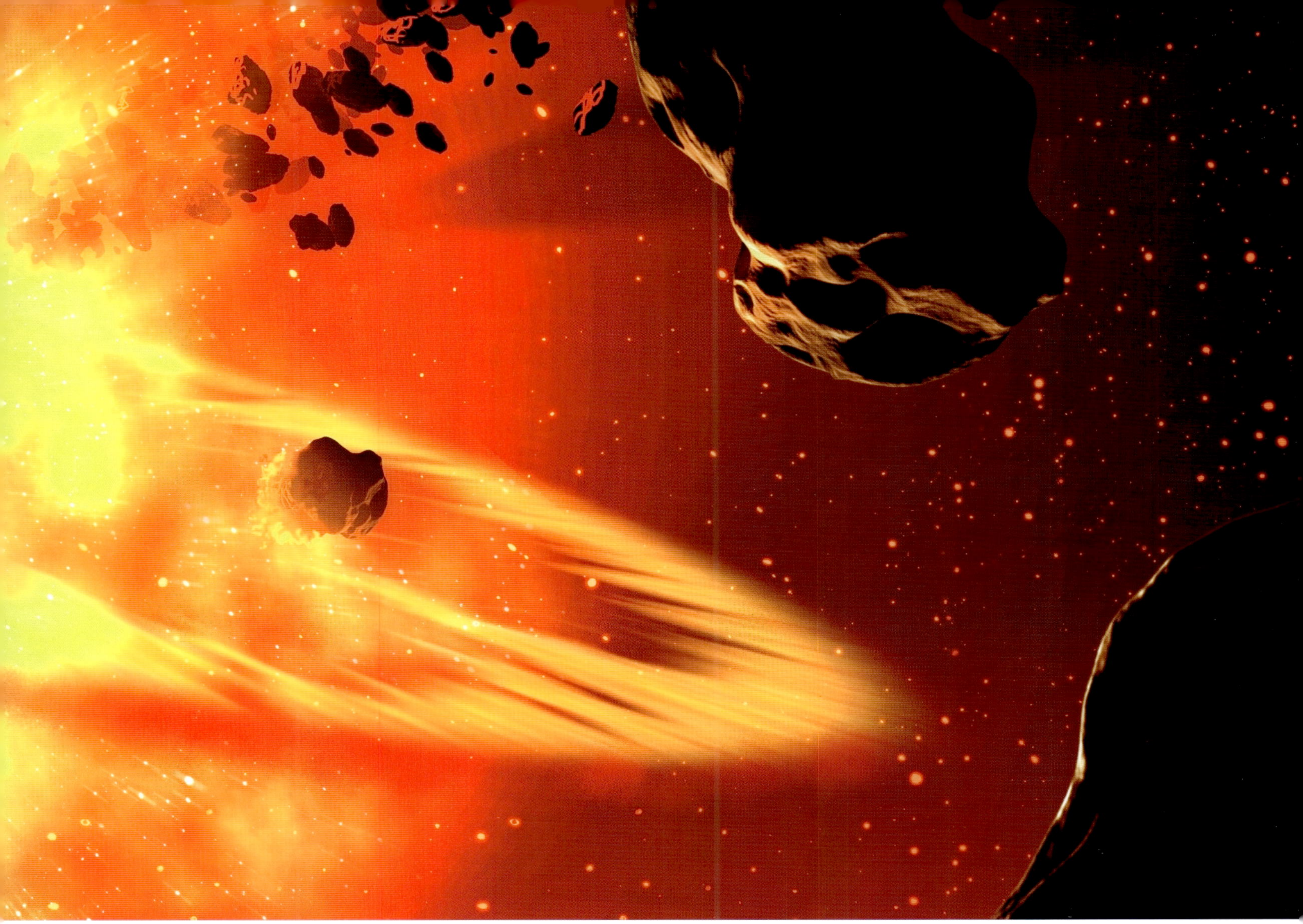

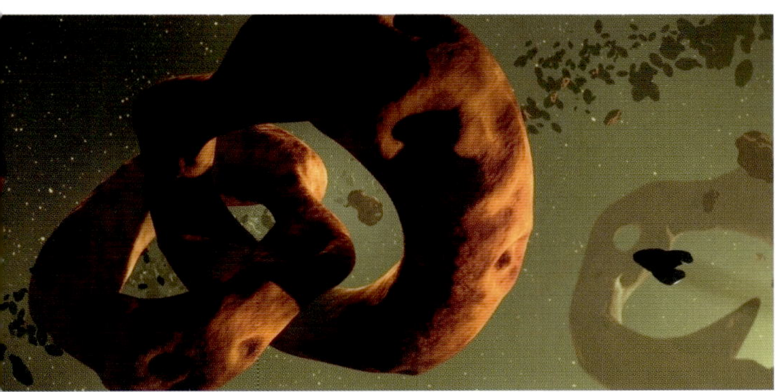

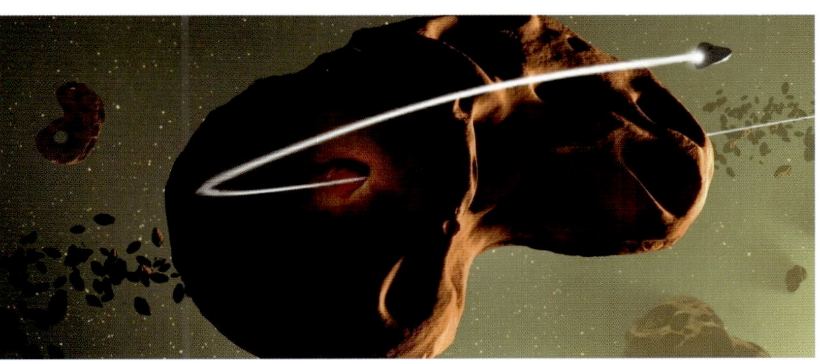

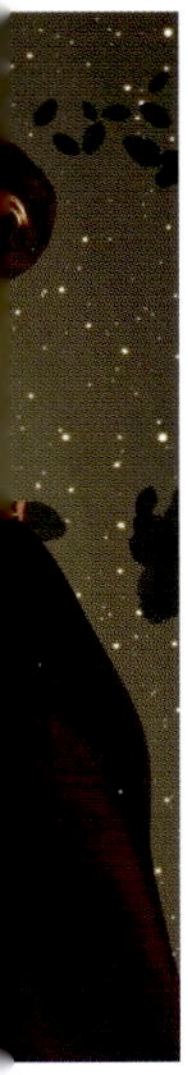

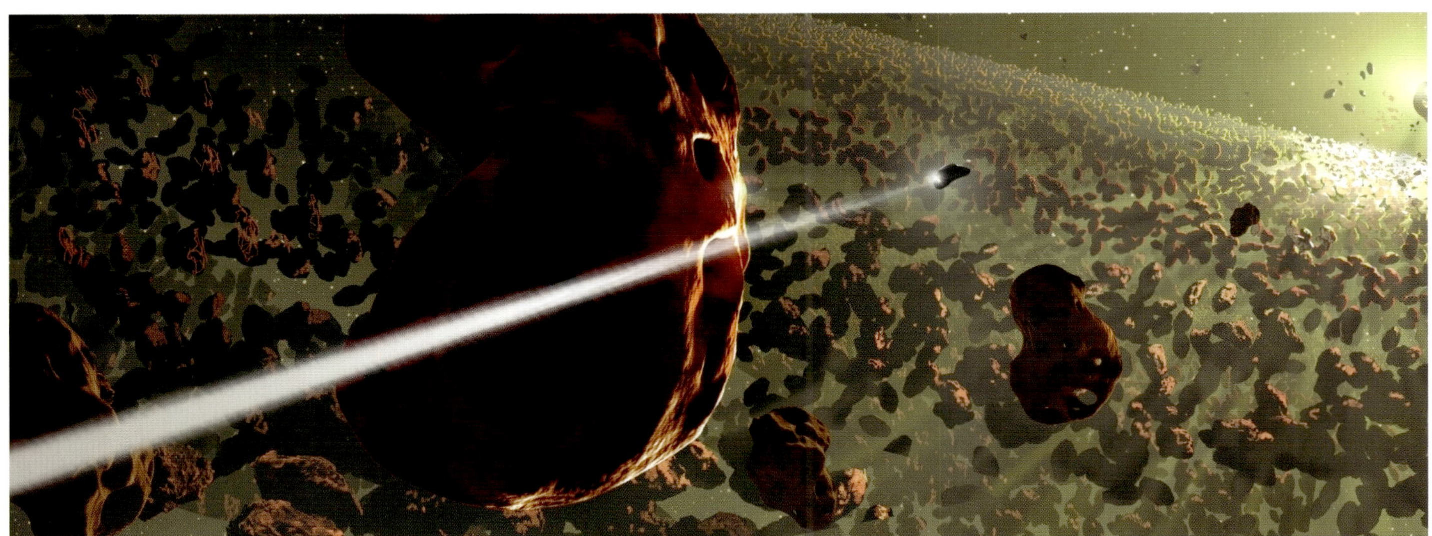

GENETICS LAB AND ALIEN ZOO

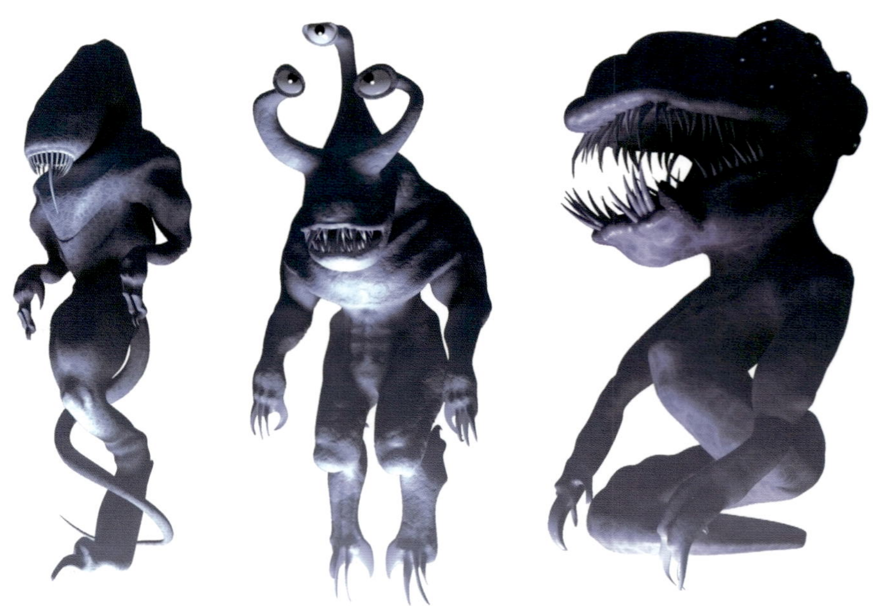

This page and opposite: A series of designs and creature concepts for the alien zoo and genetic lab, including an aggressive-looking flying saucer.

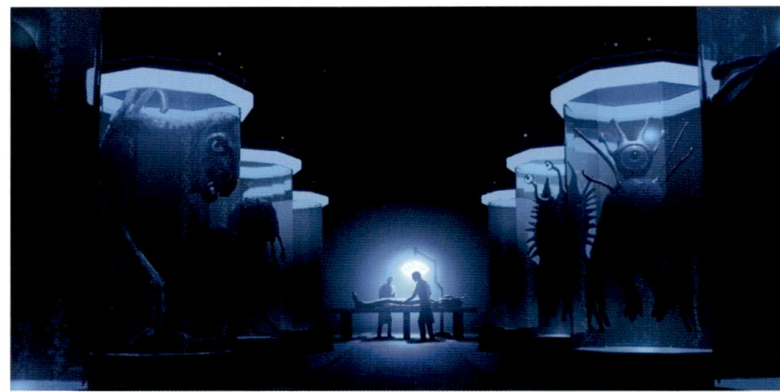

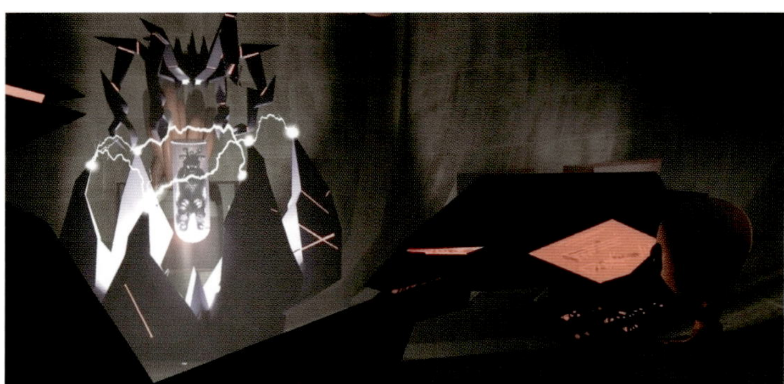

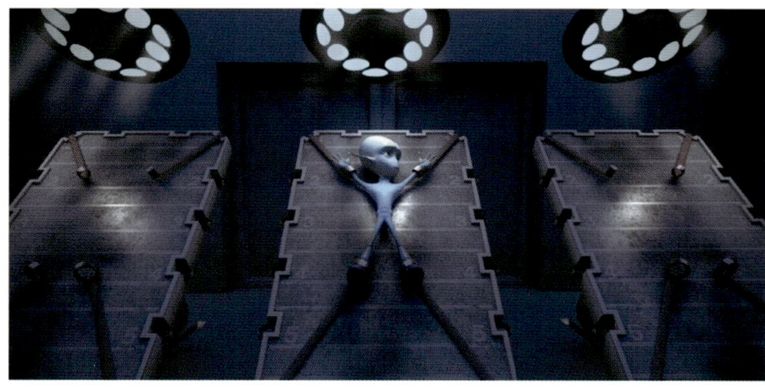

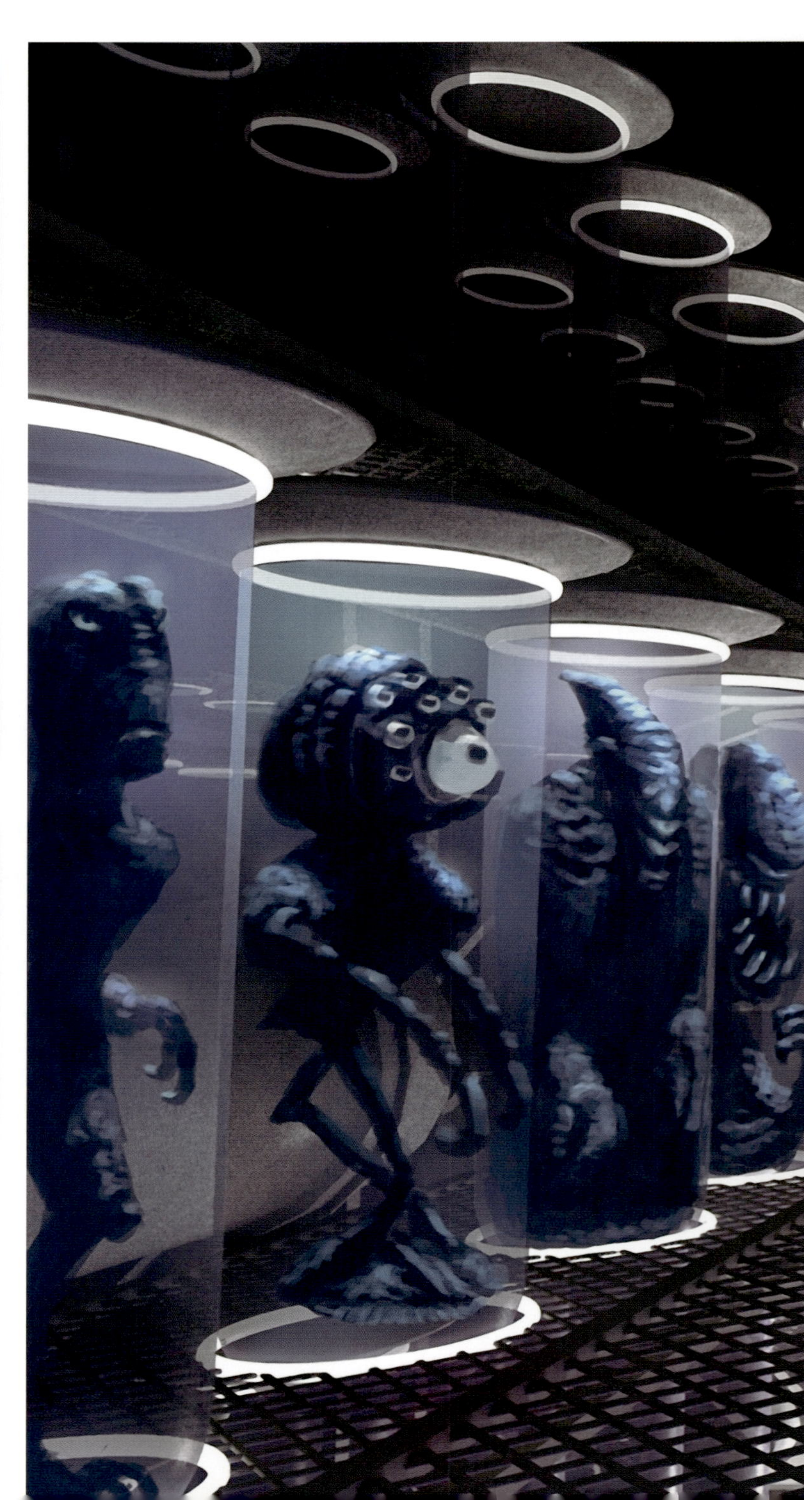

This was another story idea that didn't make the final movie: a genetics lab and alien zoo belonging to the aliens that were running their own 'Area 51'. The story called for Gary to find the aliens, and then to be captured and tortured by them (*bottom left*). I simply painted the aliens in, making them up as I went. Later, the modellers needed clearer designs to work from, so I created the three *opposite left* as a guide. It's important to remember that this was a children's animated film, so while the aliens needed to look frightening, they still had to have a cartoonish look about them. The brief for their spaceship was an aggressive-looking saucer, so I designed it with a mean slit-eyed look.

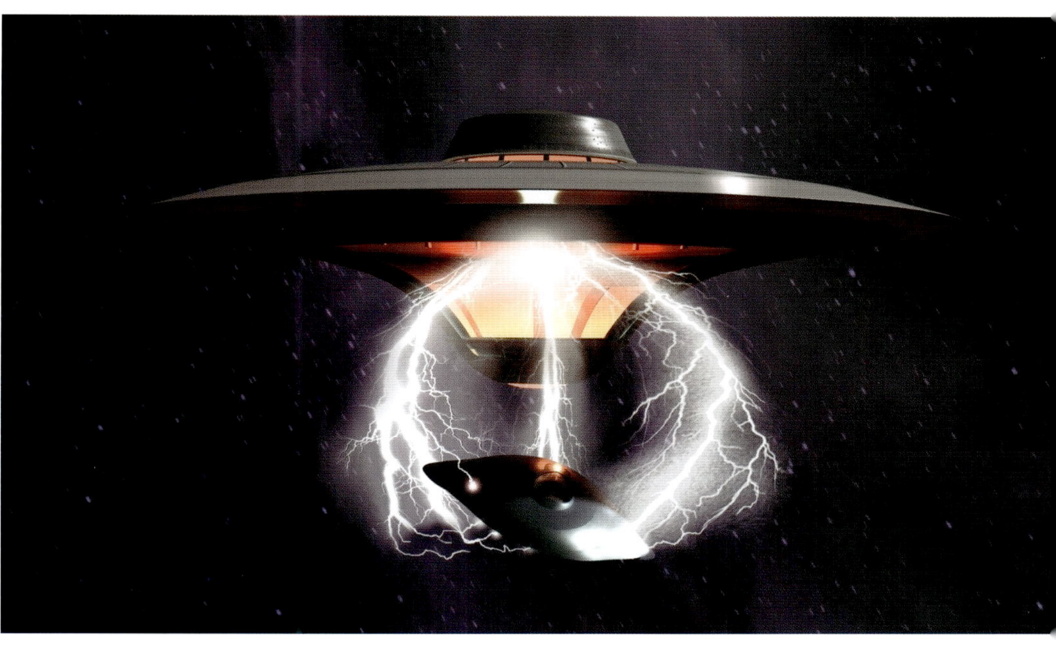

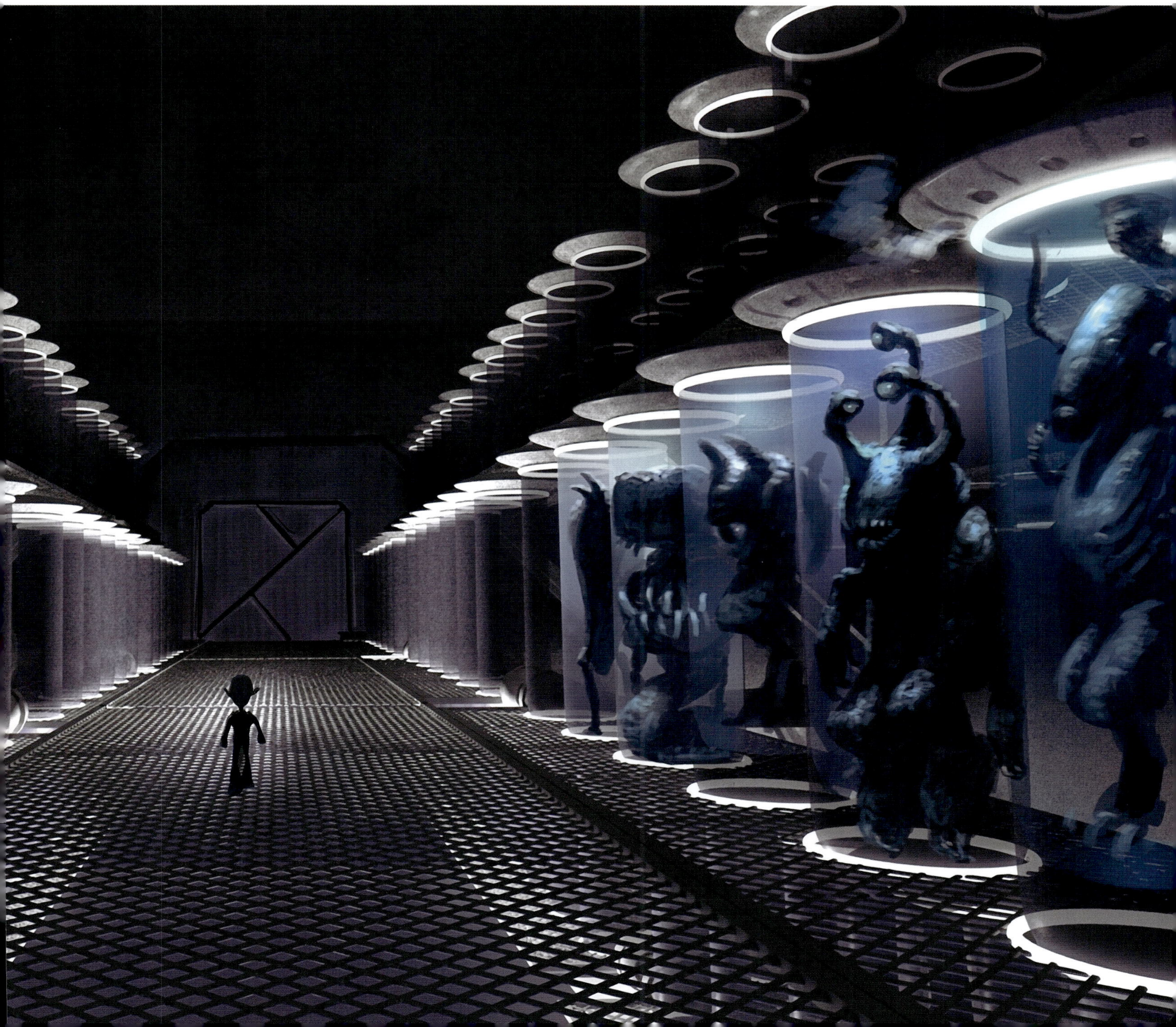

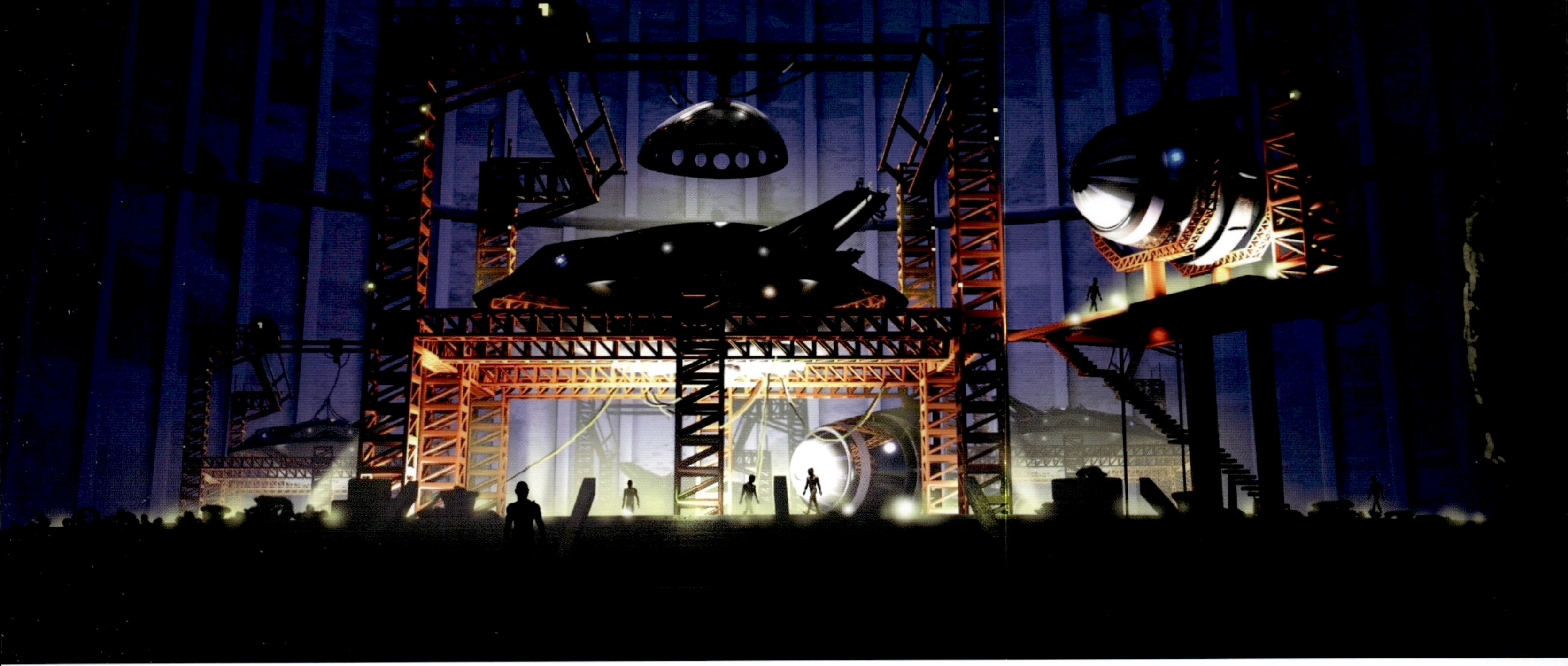

Clockwise from above Area 51: Saucer dismantling area; Alien Grey Saucer; Interrogation room; Archive room.

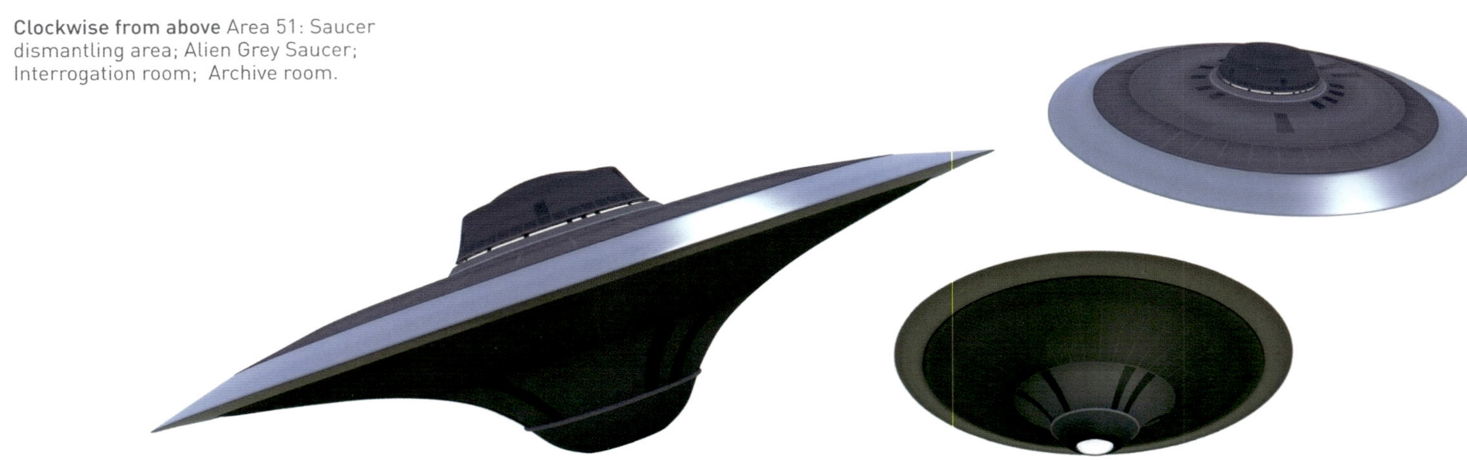

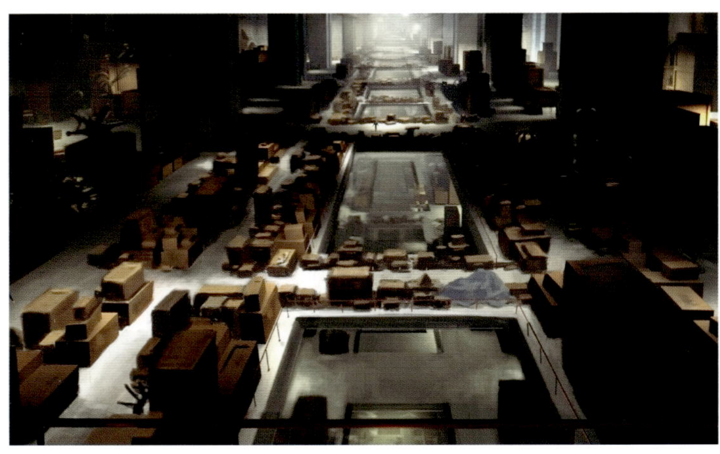

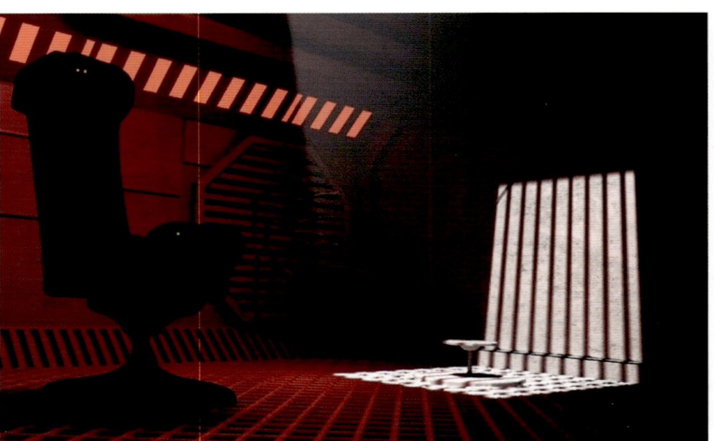

SCORCH SUPERNOVA – FINAL DILEMMA

A new director and creative team developed a different ending, so this final sequence did not make the cut. In the version I designed, the camera would have slowly pulled back from the character Scorch's face to reveal the extent of his dilemma:

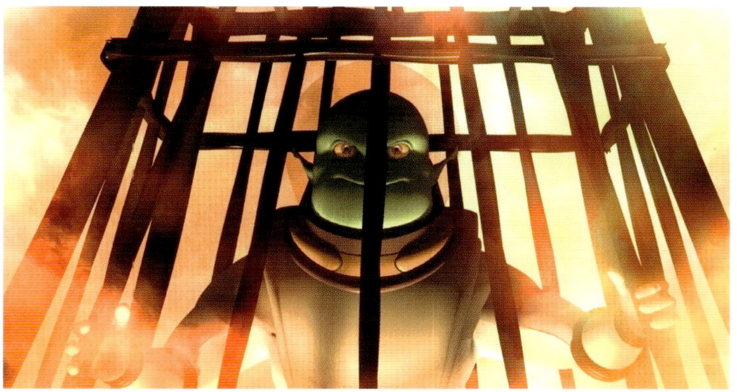

1 He's caged up, surrounded by plumes of lava. Trouble.

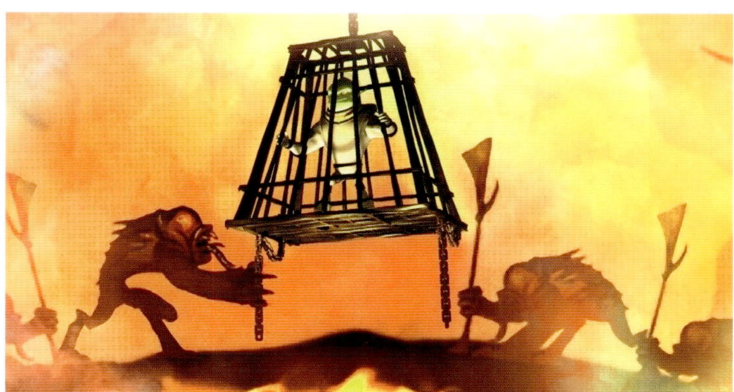

2 As the camera pulls back, we see the cage is also surrounded by aggressive looking aliens. More trouble.

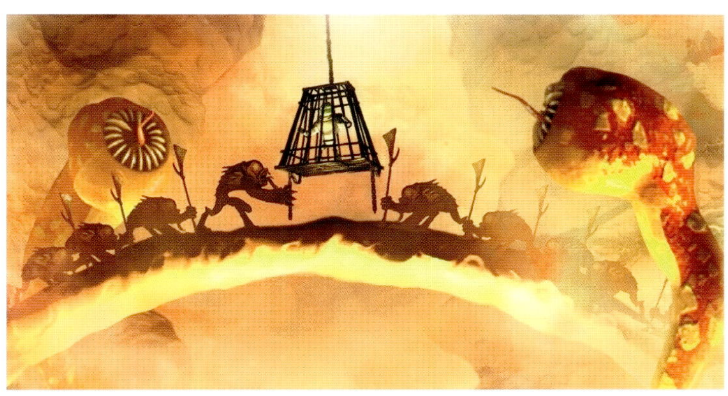

3 Pull back again, and it's suspended over an arch. Scorch is in real trouble.

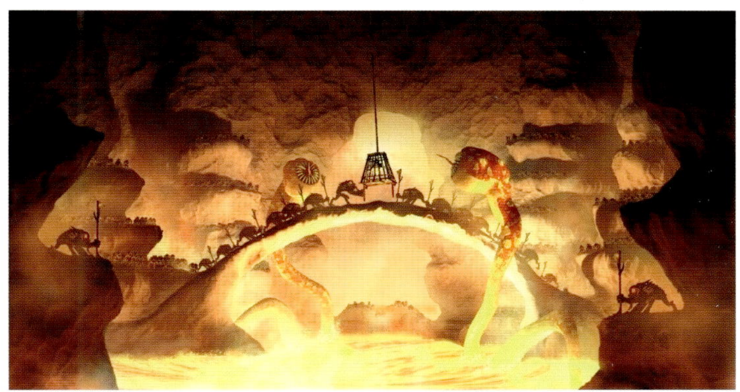

4 Pull back further and the arch sits over a lake of lava. Really big trouble.

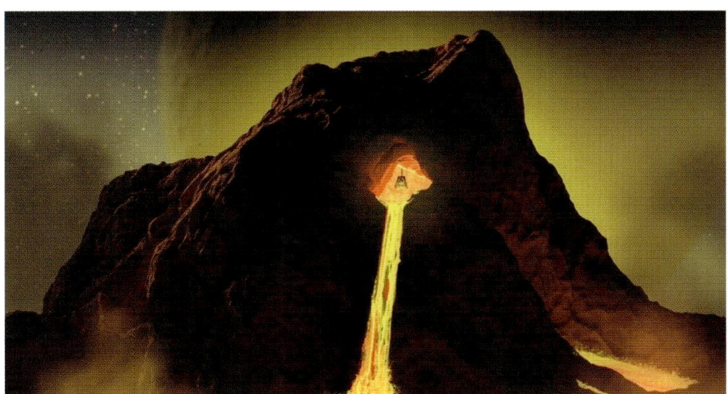

5 Pull back even further and the whole cave is situated at the top of a mountain. Seriously big trouble...

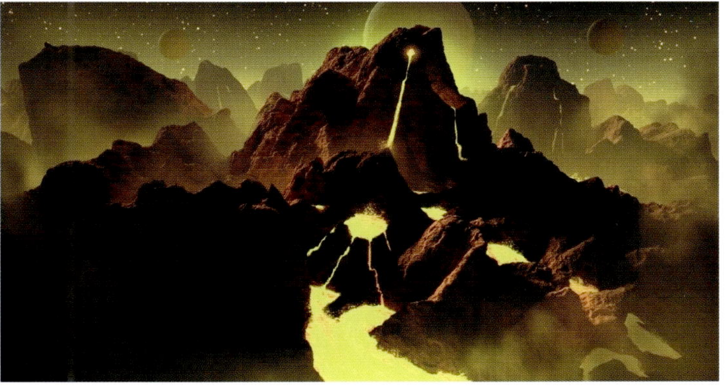

6 ...but pull back one last time and the cave is set in a wilderness of twisted mountains and lava lakes. Really seriously big trouble!

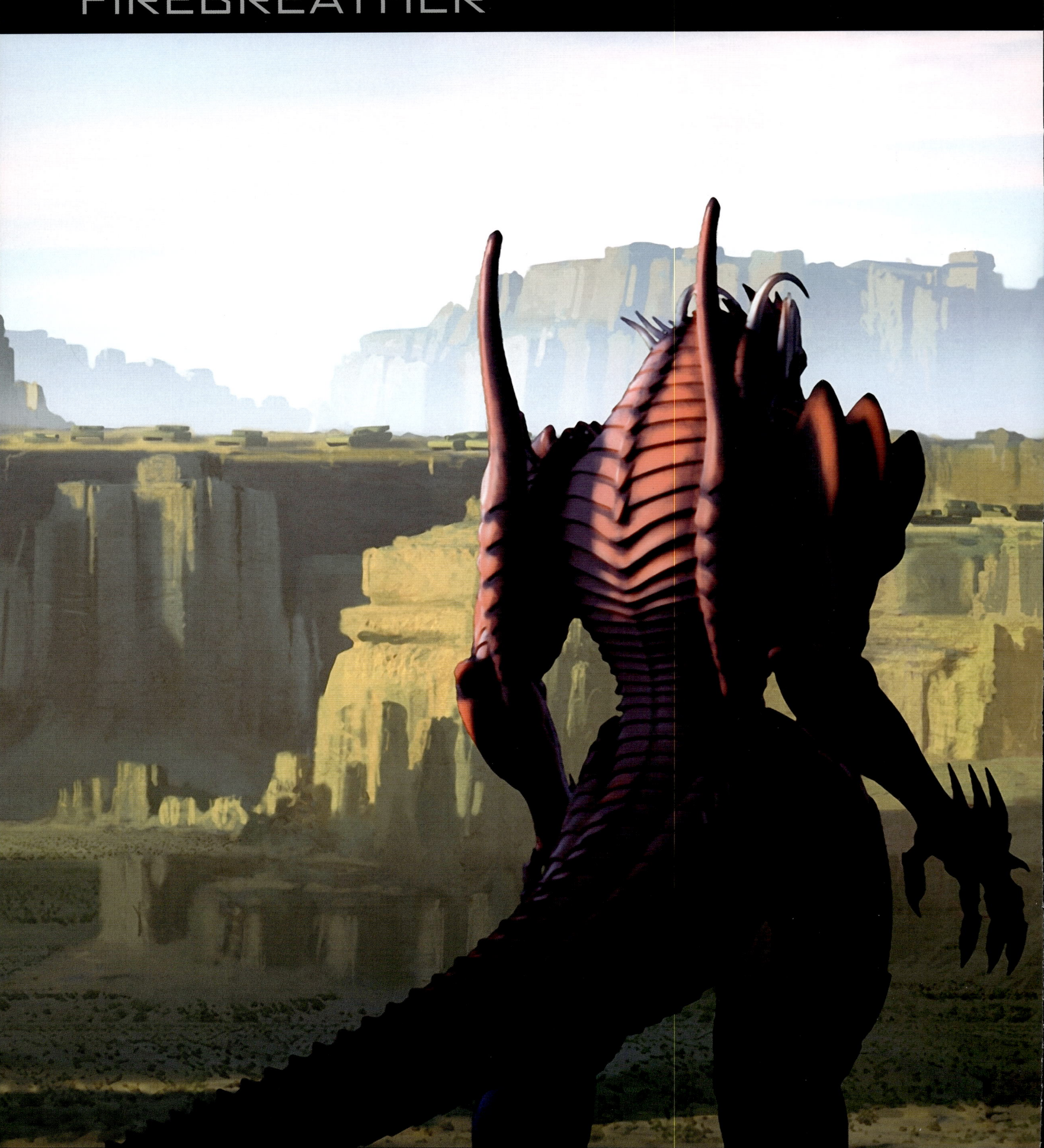

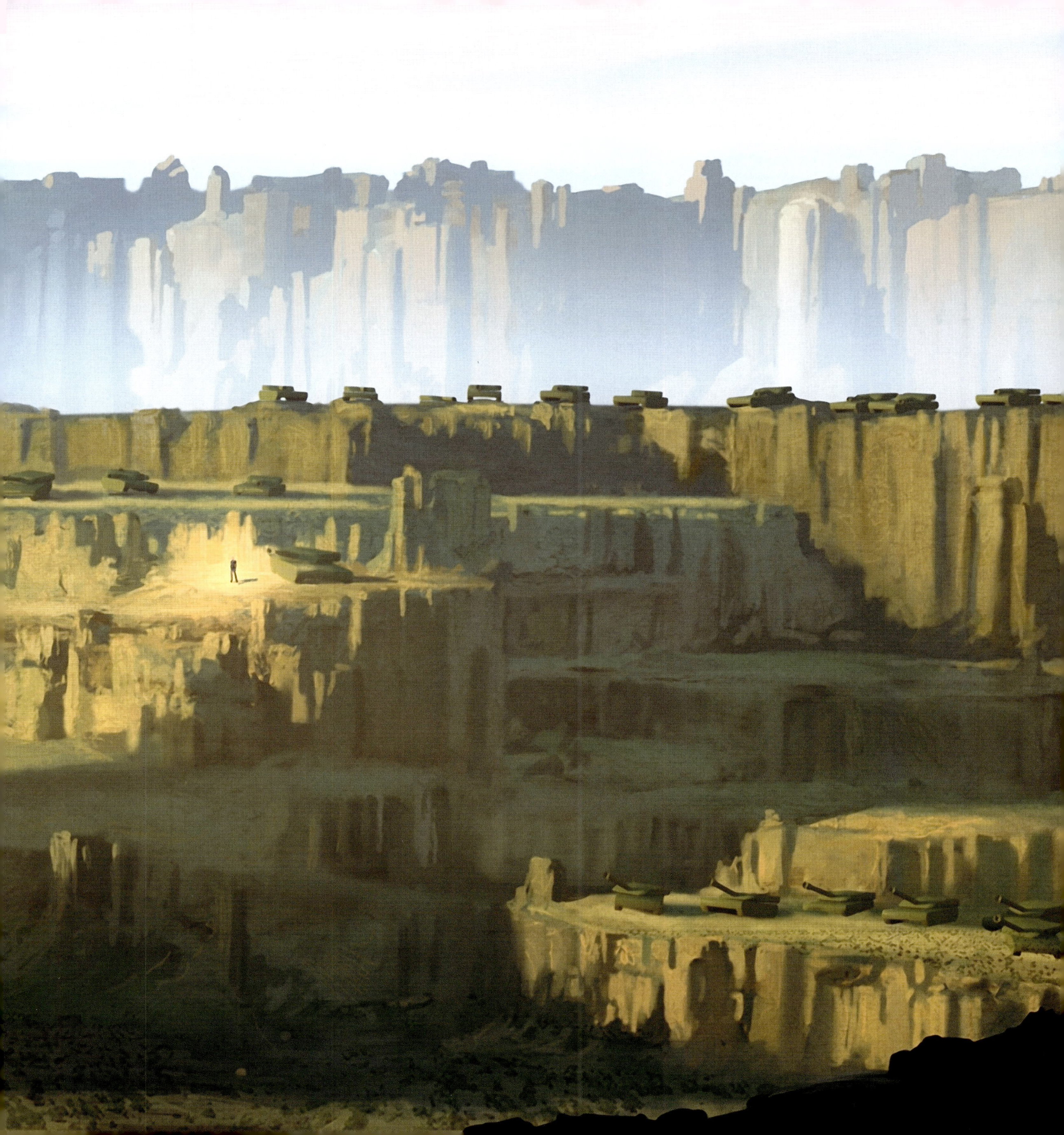

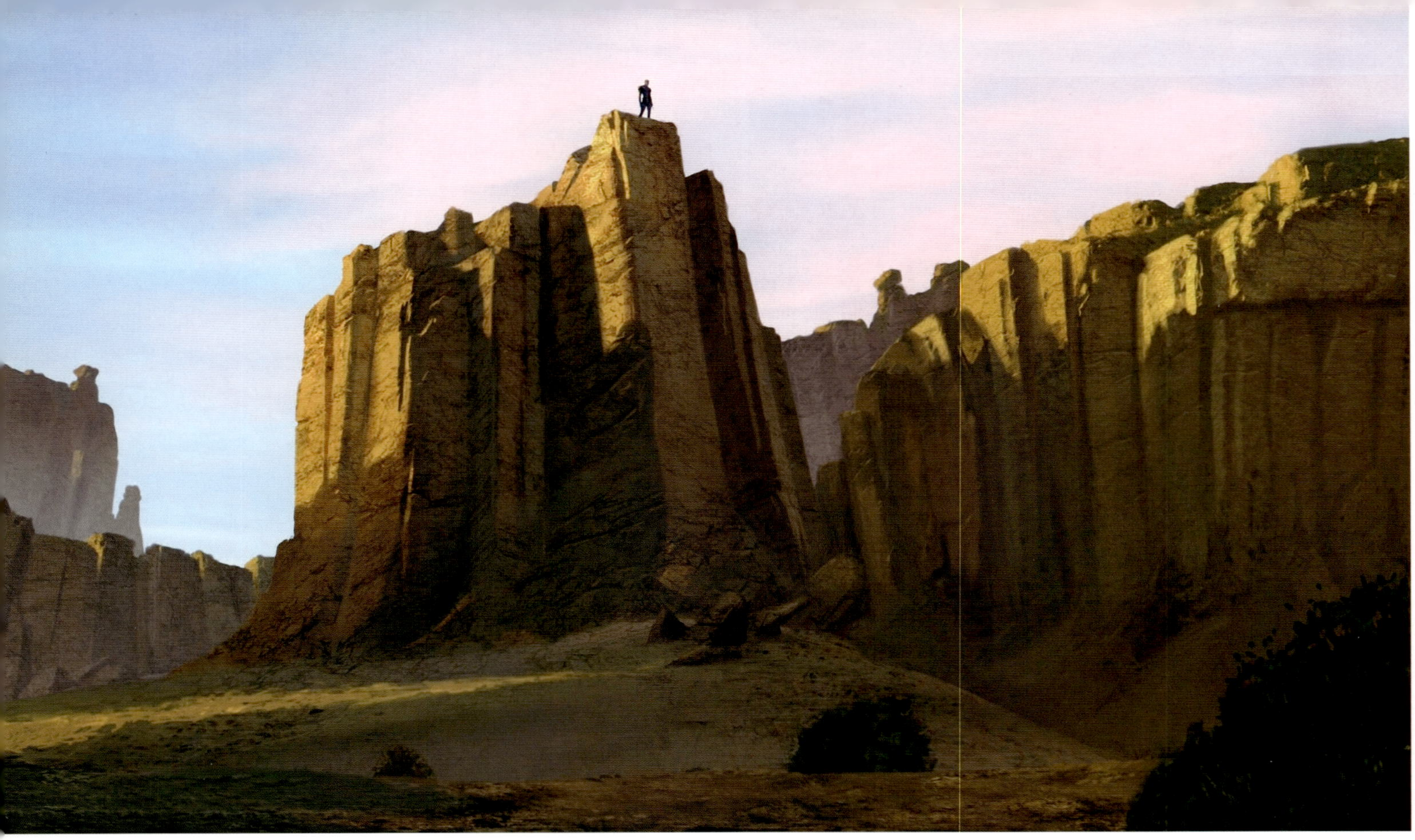

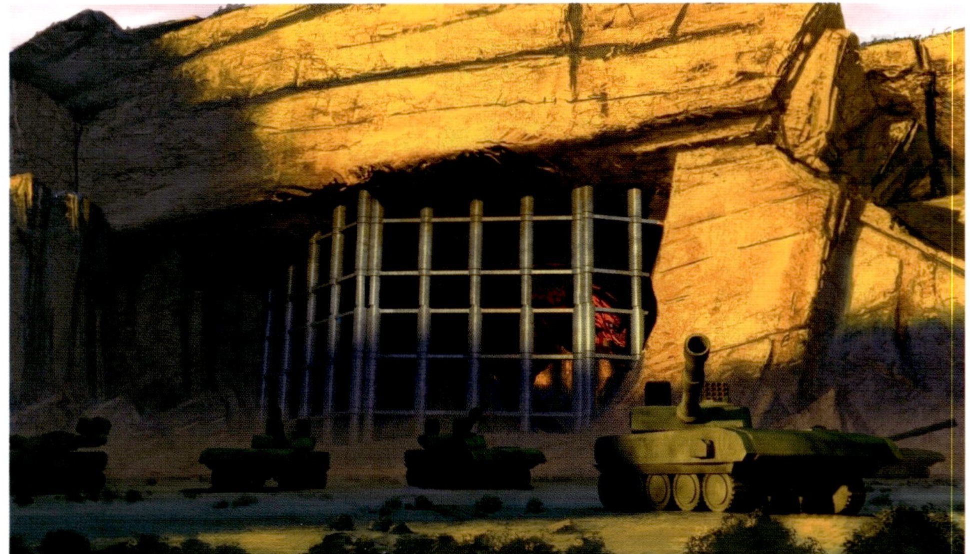

Previous page:
Kaiju Battle.

This page from top:
Stylised canyons; Belloc's cage; Underworld throne.

Opposite:
Down to the underworld; Final battle mountain.

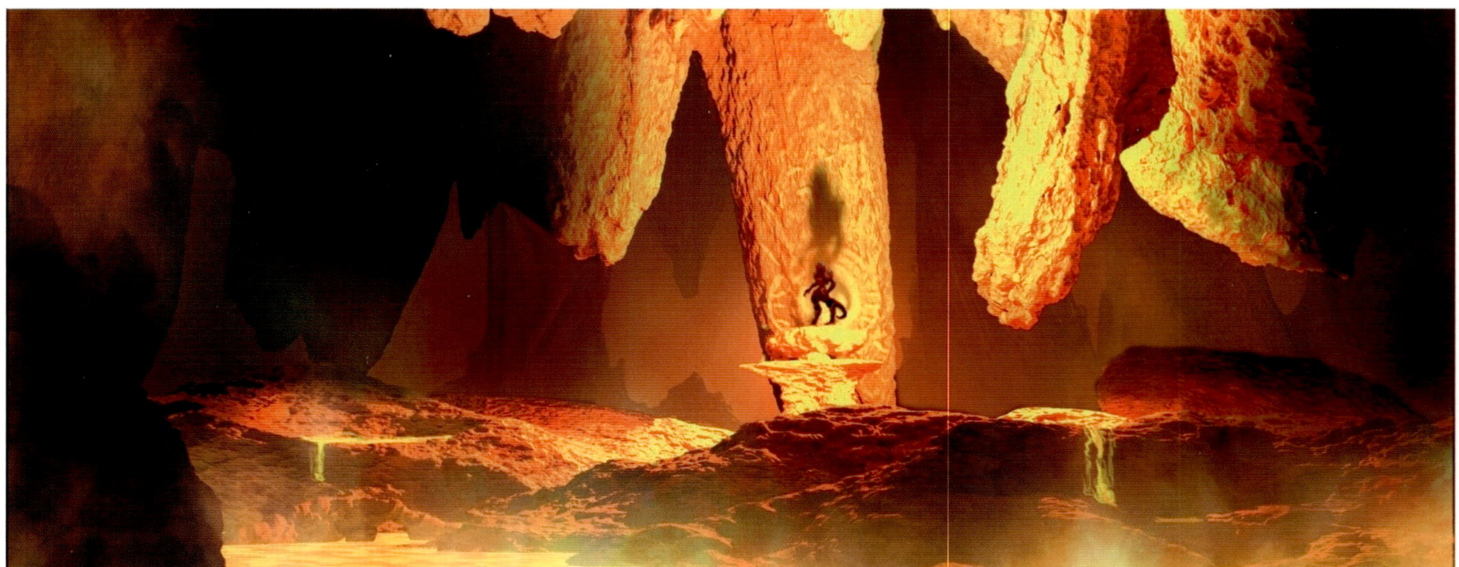

Barry Jackson, the production designer on *Escape From Planet Earth*, asked me to work as part of his art team in Los Angeles on his next gig, *Firebreather*. This was Cartoon Network's first foray into 3D animation. In the early stages, we experimented with different fantasy desert landscapes to find both a stylisation for the film as a whole and for the different environments of mountains, canyons, and the underworld. The drawing on the *top left* was my version, and it is similar to the style used in the canyons in the final movie.

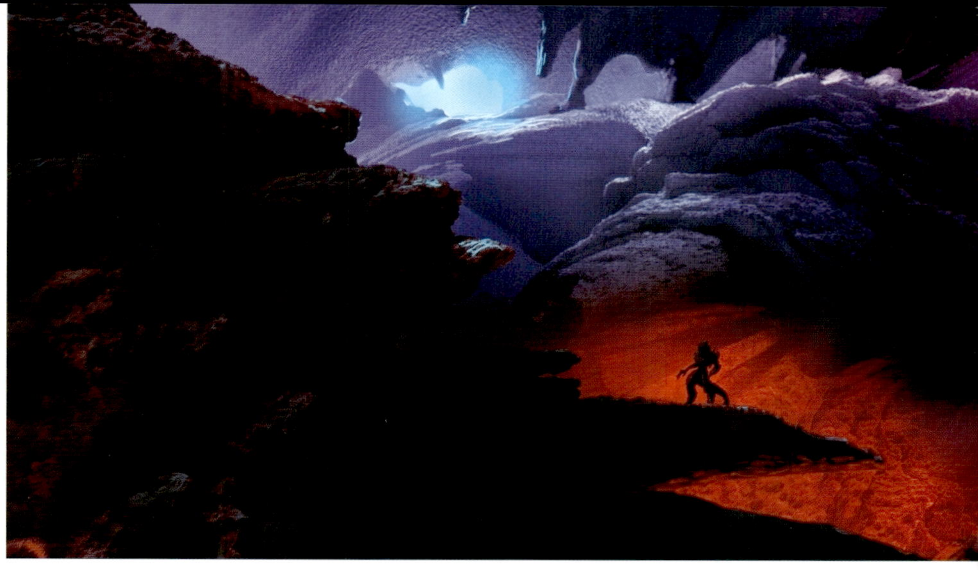

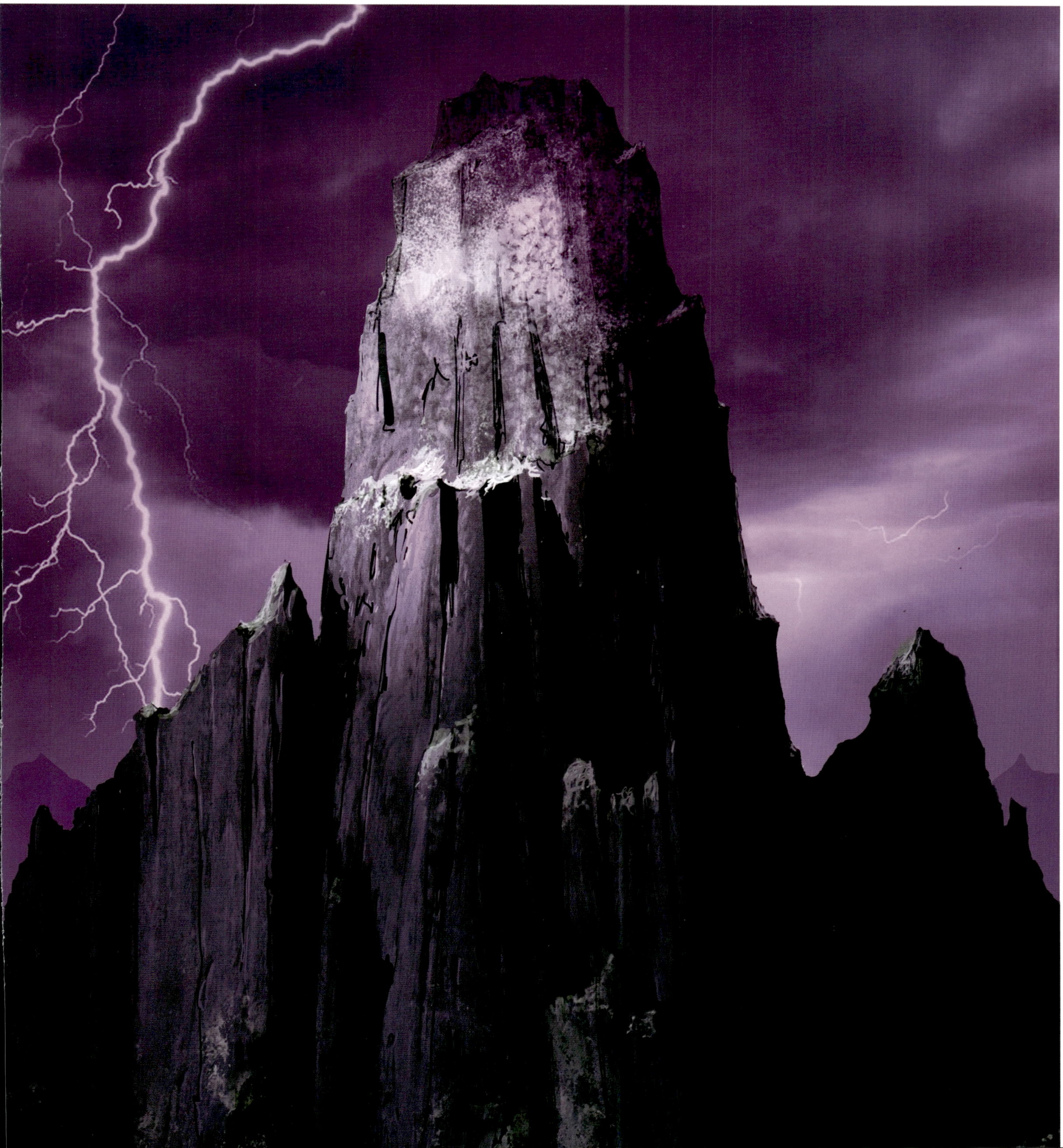

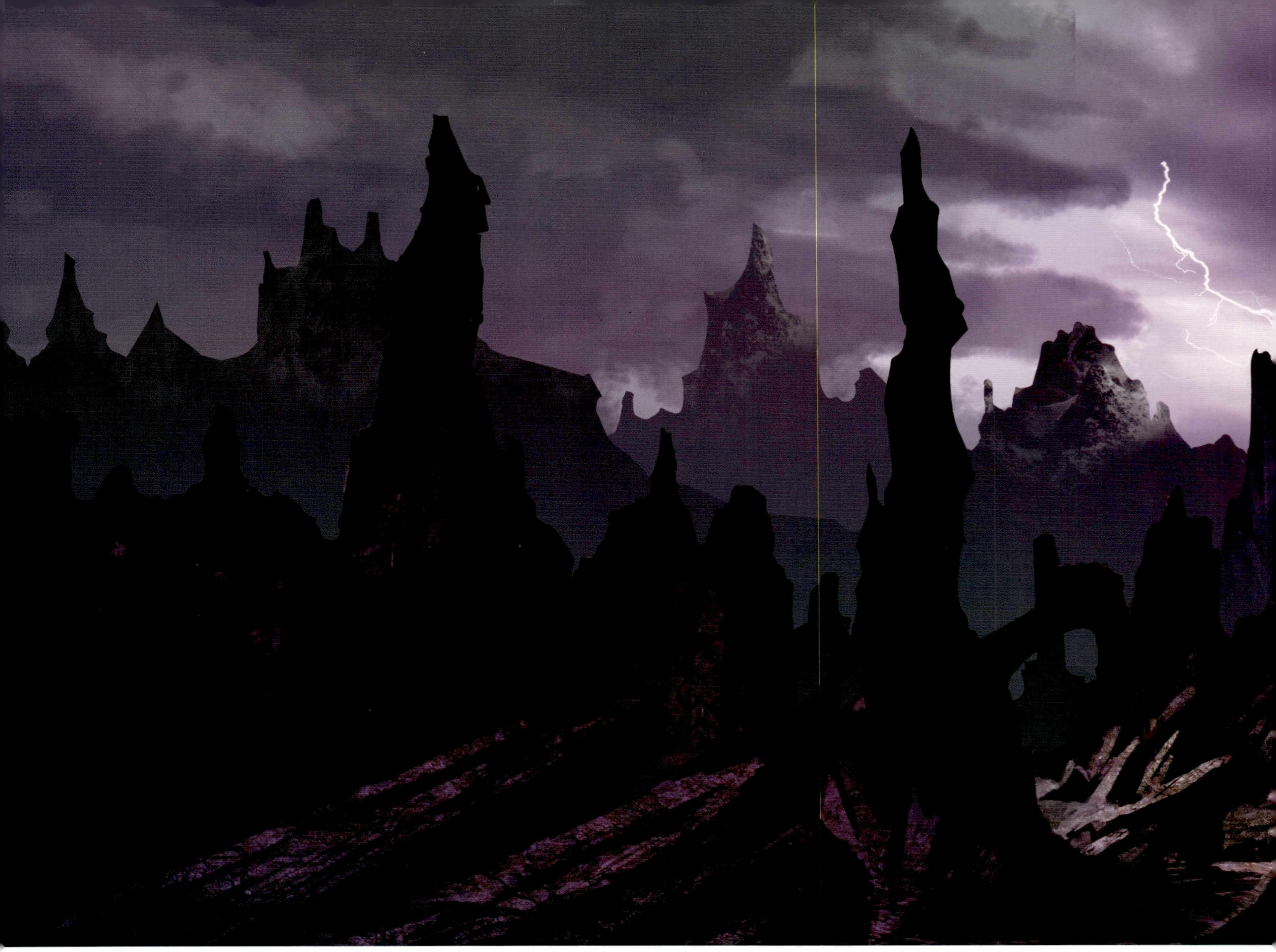

Above: The big mountain shape was used as a focal point in the final film.

Below Final battle concept.

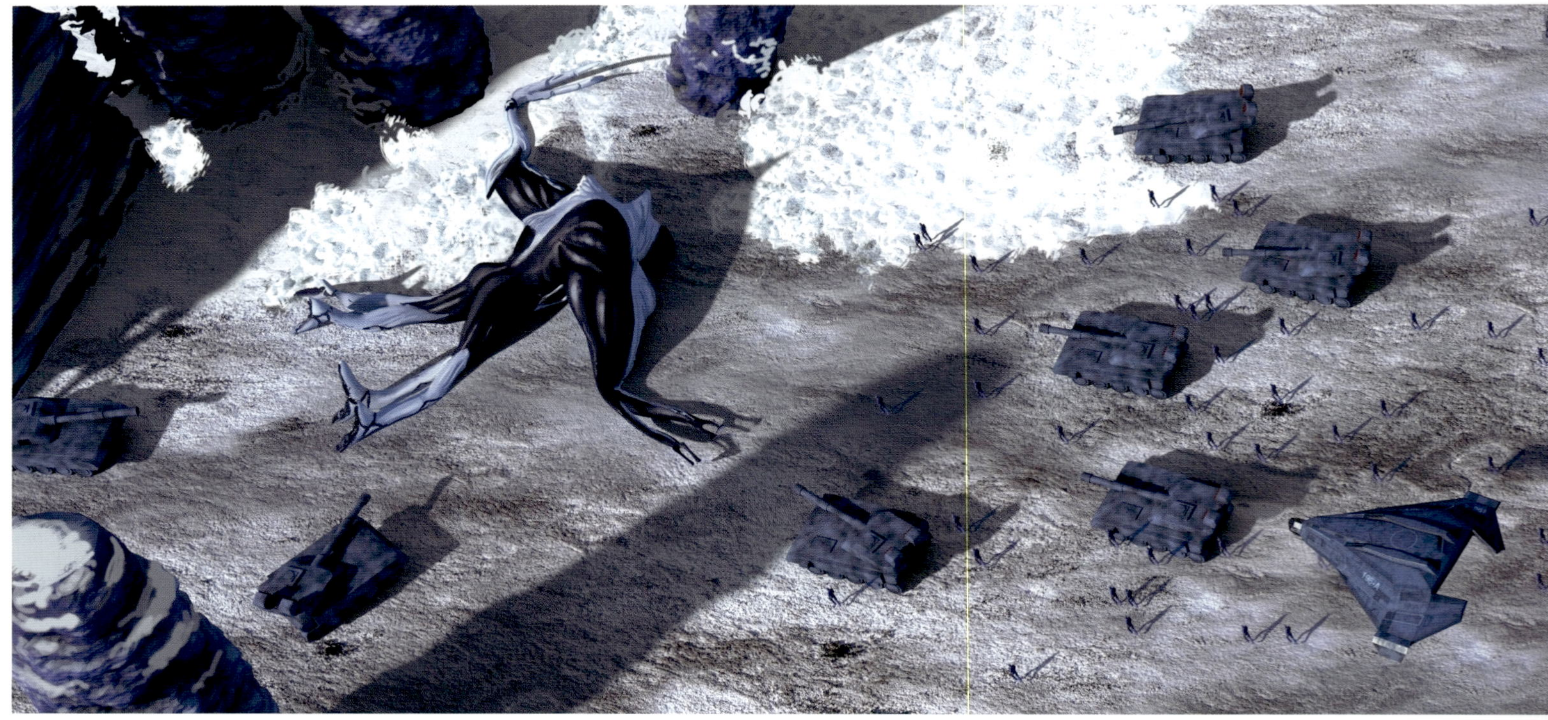

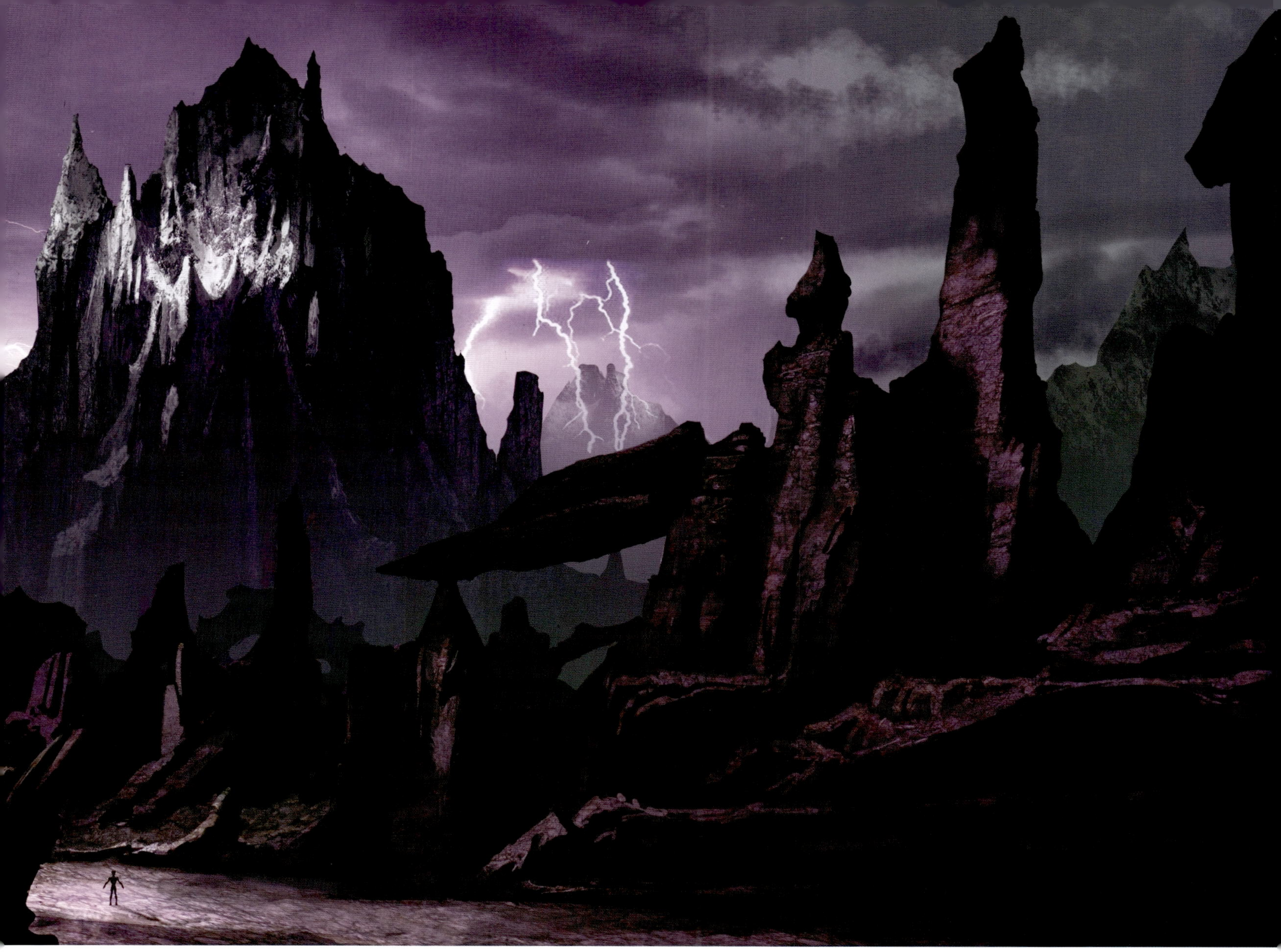

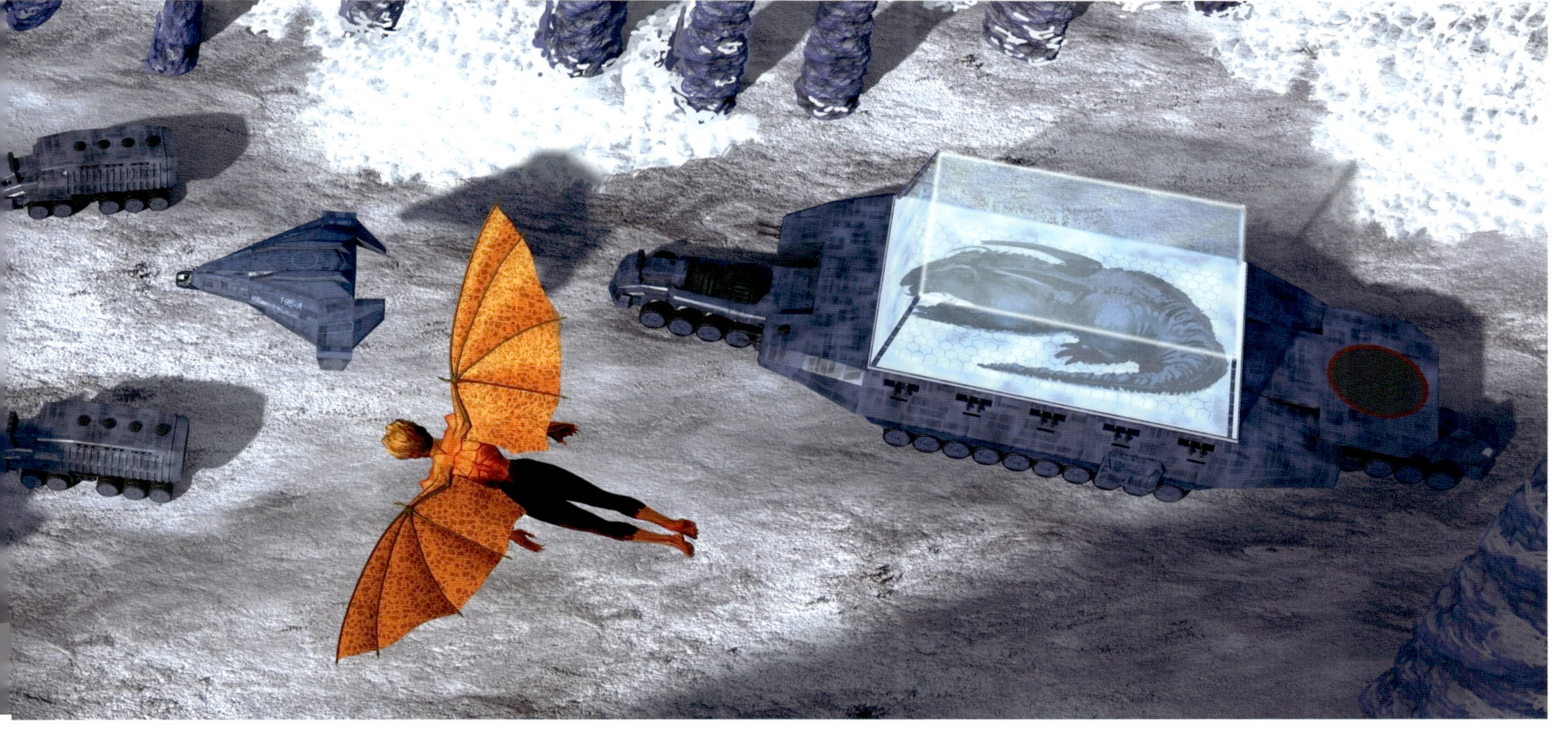

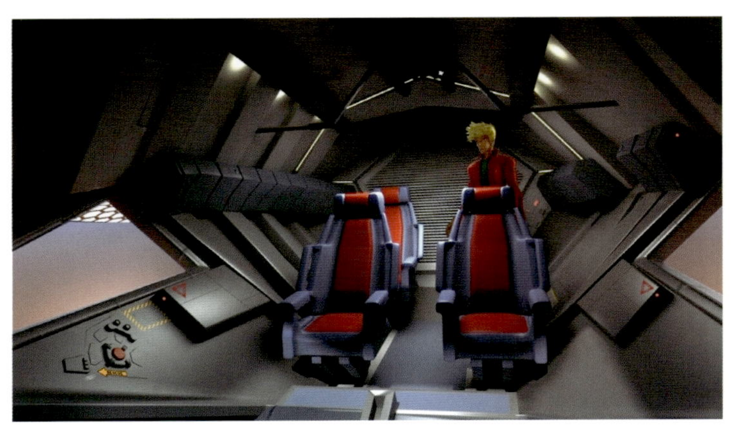

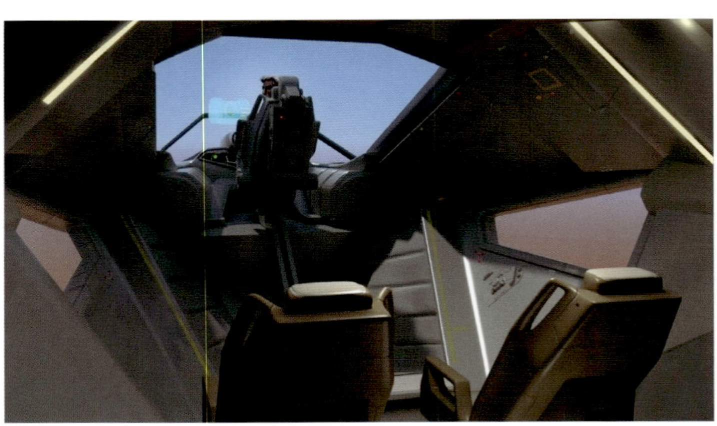

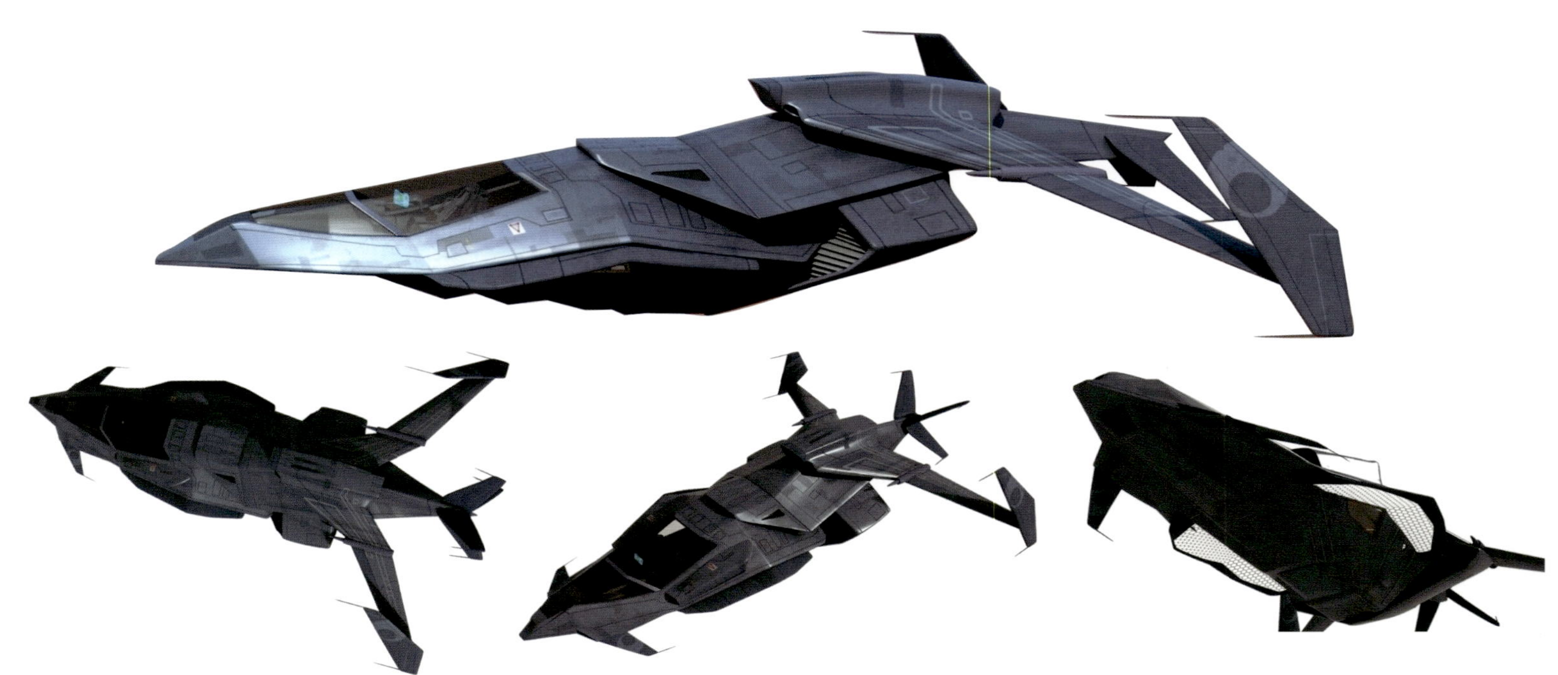

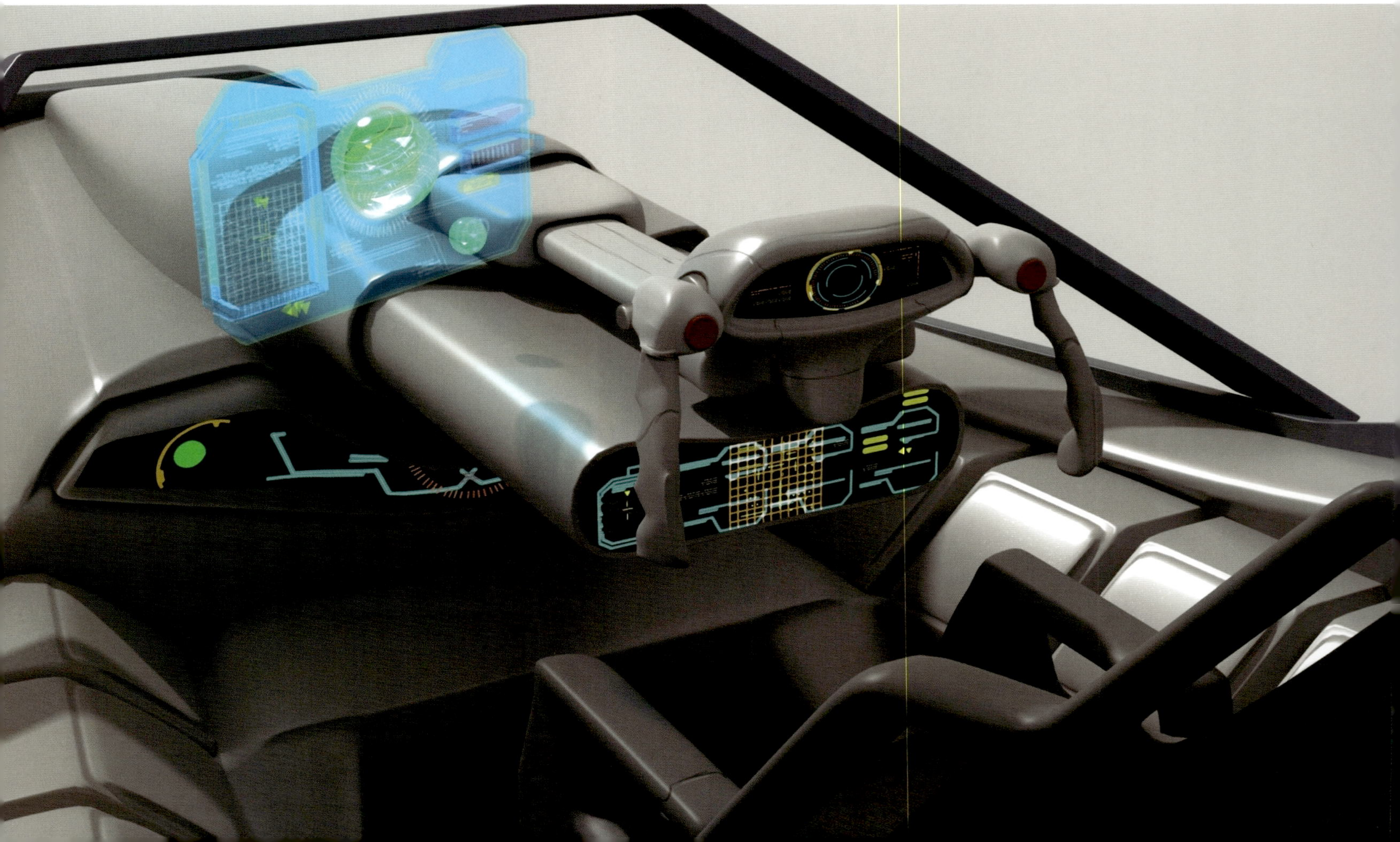

Opposite: Flyer design exterior and interior and Flyer cockpit controls, with a frame from an animatic showing how the controls unfold and the HUD appears.

This page: Heavy lifter. Vehicle designed to lift captive Kaiju.

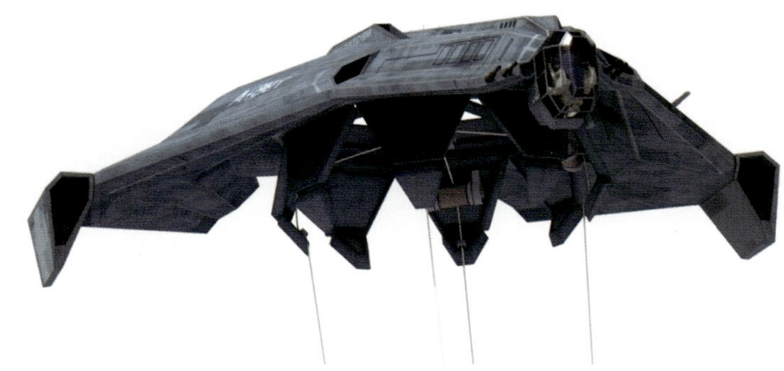

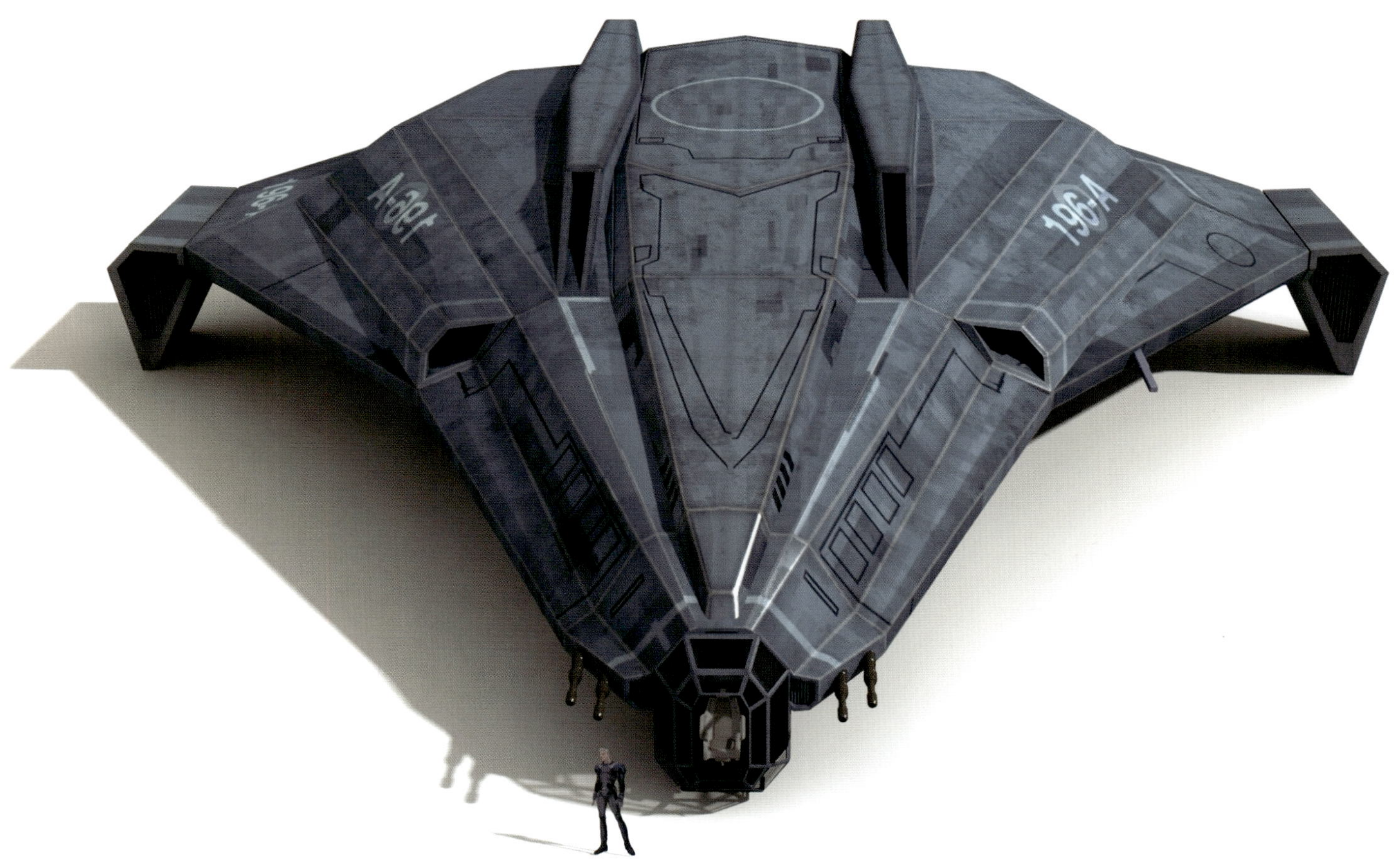

FLYERS

I modelled these craft in MODO. Modelling them seemed a good idea, as the director could then see the flyers from different angles and more easily see the ships' transformations I was asked to visualise. The flyer was housed in a school bus that would split open to reveal the craft in a folded configuration. As the flyer rises out of the bus, its wings unfold, ready for flight. The director also wanted something a little different when the characters boarded the craft. The pilot's seat would initially point down the length of the craft, then twist around and rise up a ramp so the pilot now faced the controls. These would unfold as a hologram screen materialised in front of him. Again, I found it easier to test this out with a simple animation. The storyboard team soon realised that I had these models, and so I was asked to produce simple animation sequences for the story reel.

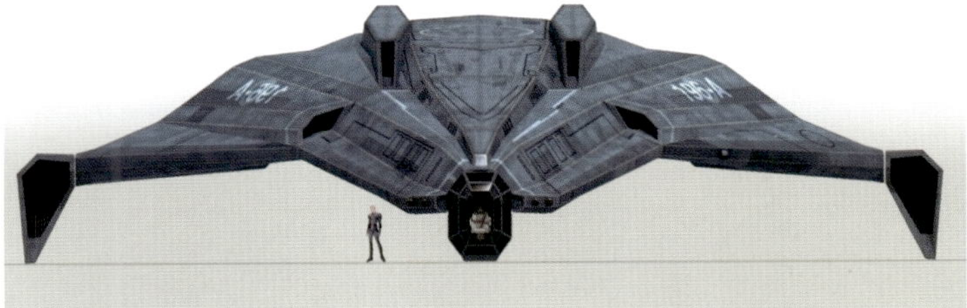

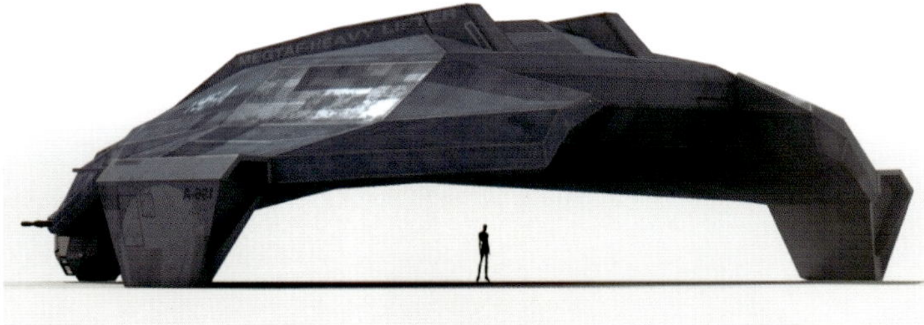

VEHICLES

Right: Kaiju hauler, a transport to haul captive Kaiju in Cartoon Network's *Firebreather*. The brief was for a massive transport with lots of wheels and a forcefield cage.

Bottom: Truck designs. The truck was adapted from the Kaiju hauler, but also ensured a continuity of design language for the two vehicles. It was important to maintain this heavy-duty aesthetic across concepts.

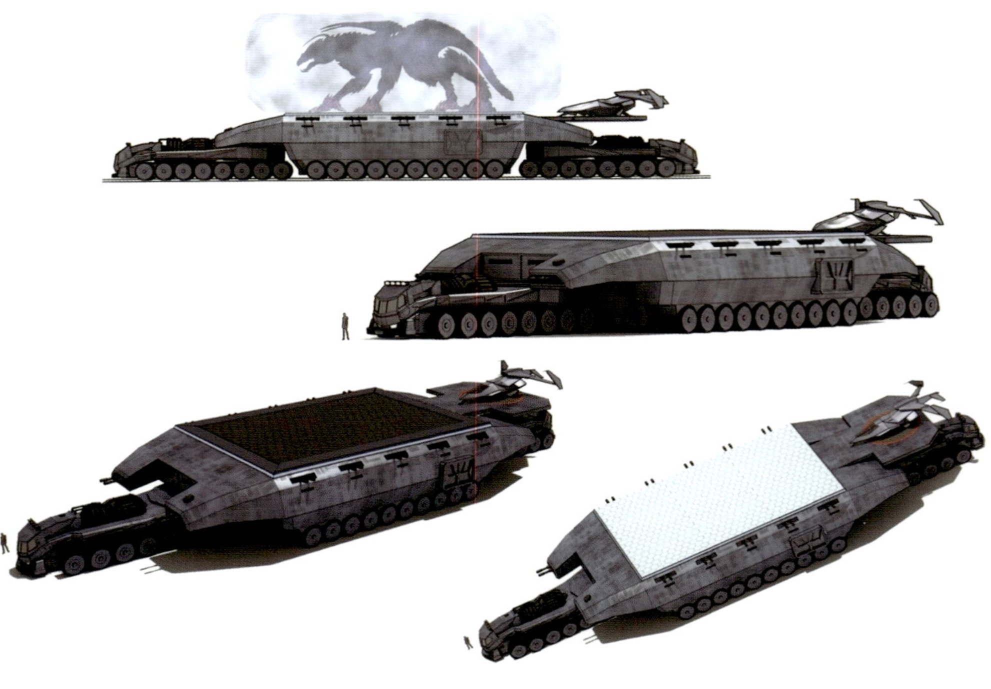

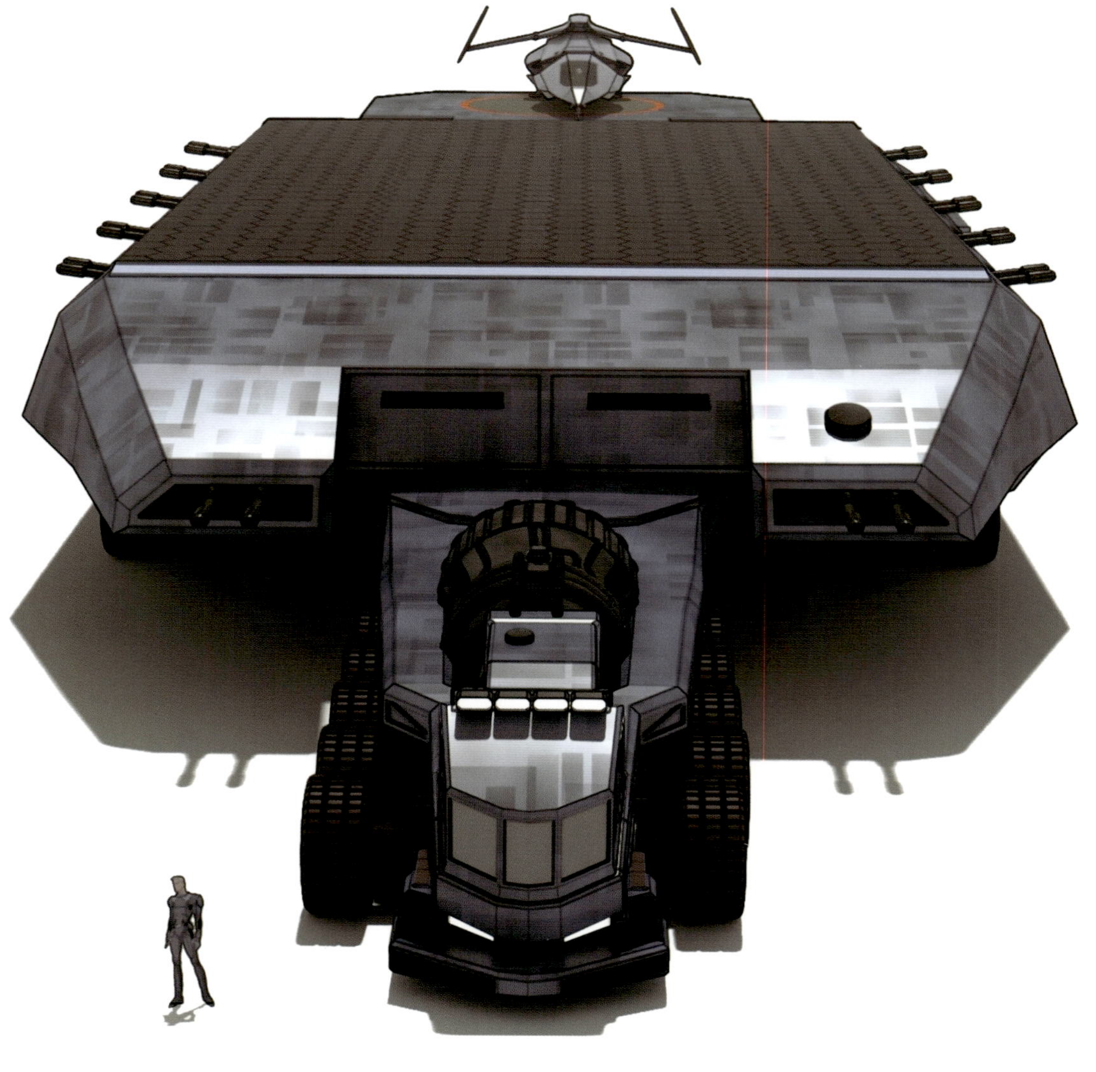

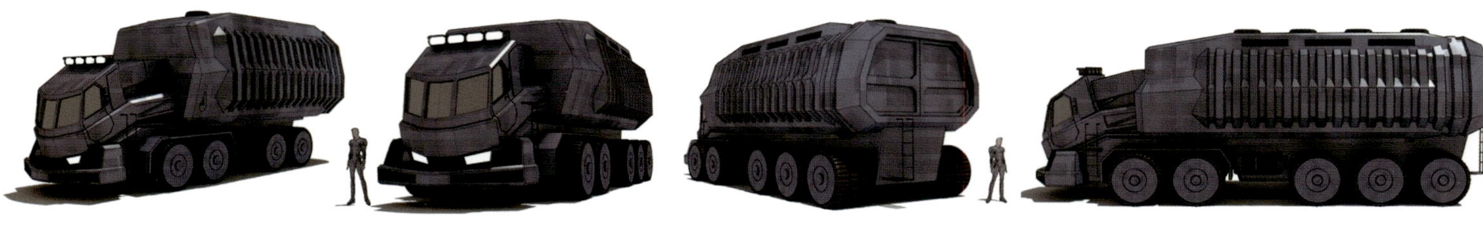

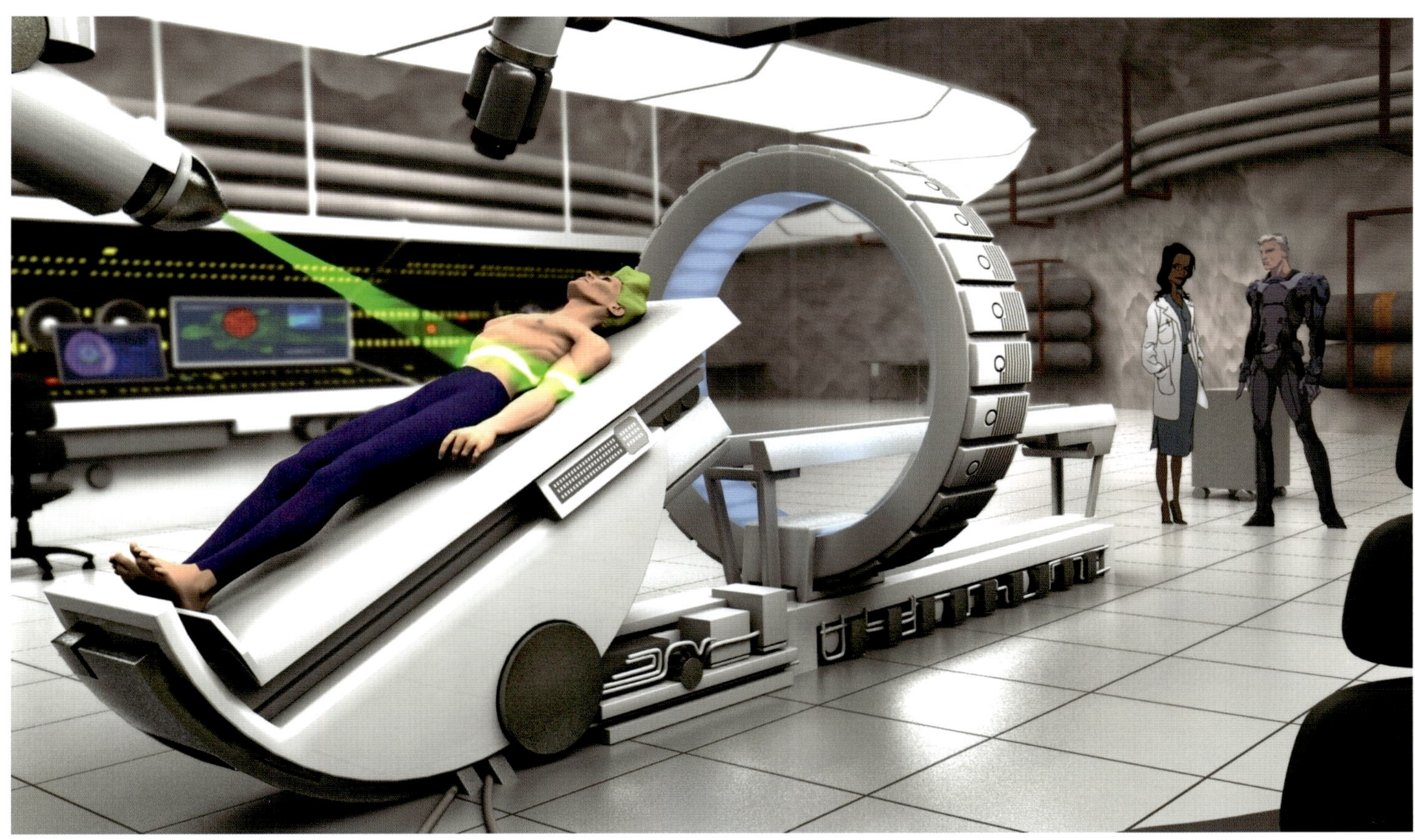

MEDICAL CENTRE

Tom McLure, a member of Cartoon Network's *Firebreather* artistic team, produced some line drawings of the medical lab (*right*), but the director needed a finished image showing lighting and texture, as well as a further design for the lab door and graphic displays on the big screen behind it. I produced these images to meet that brief, modelling the shapes in MODO and then painting over them in Photoshop.

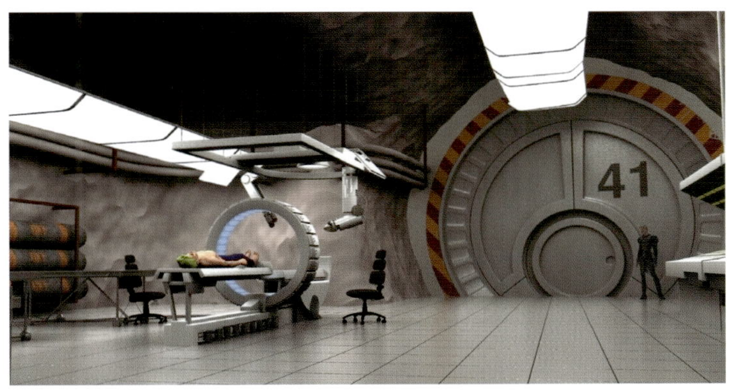

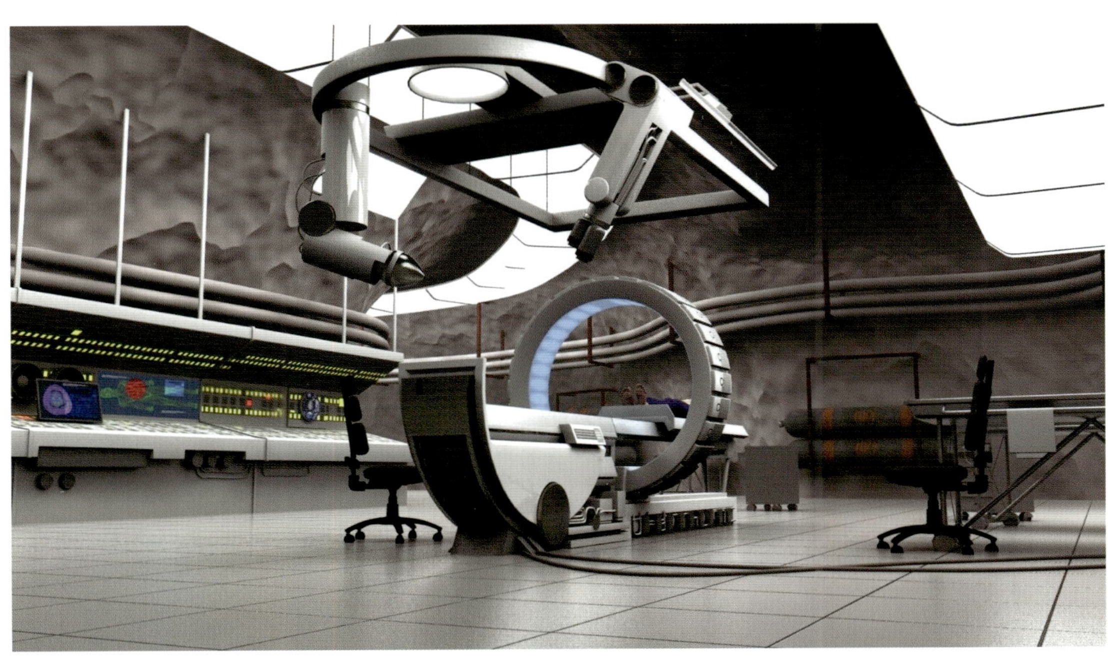

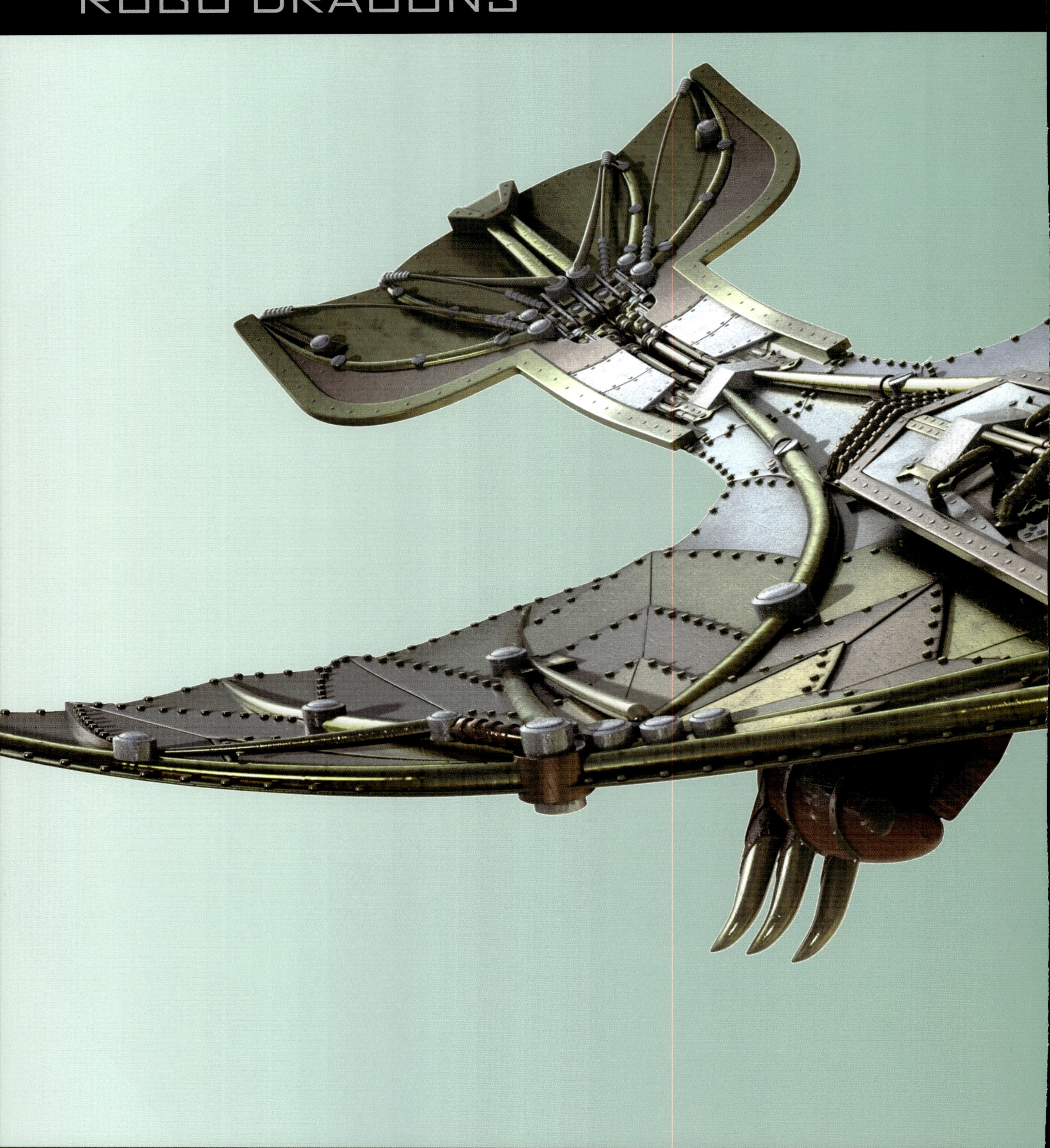

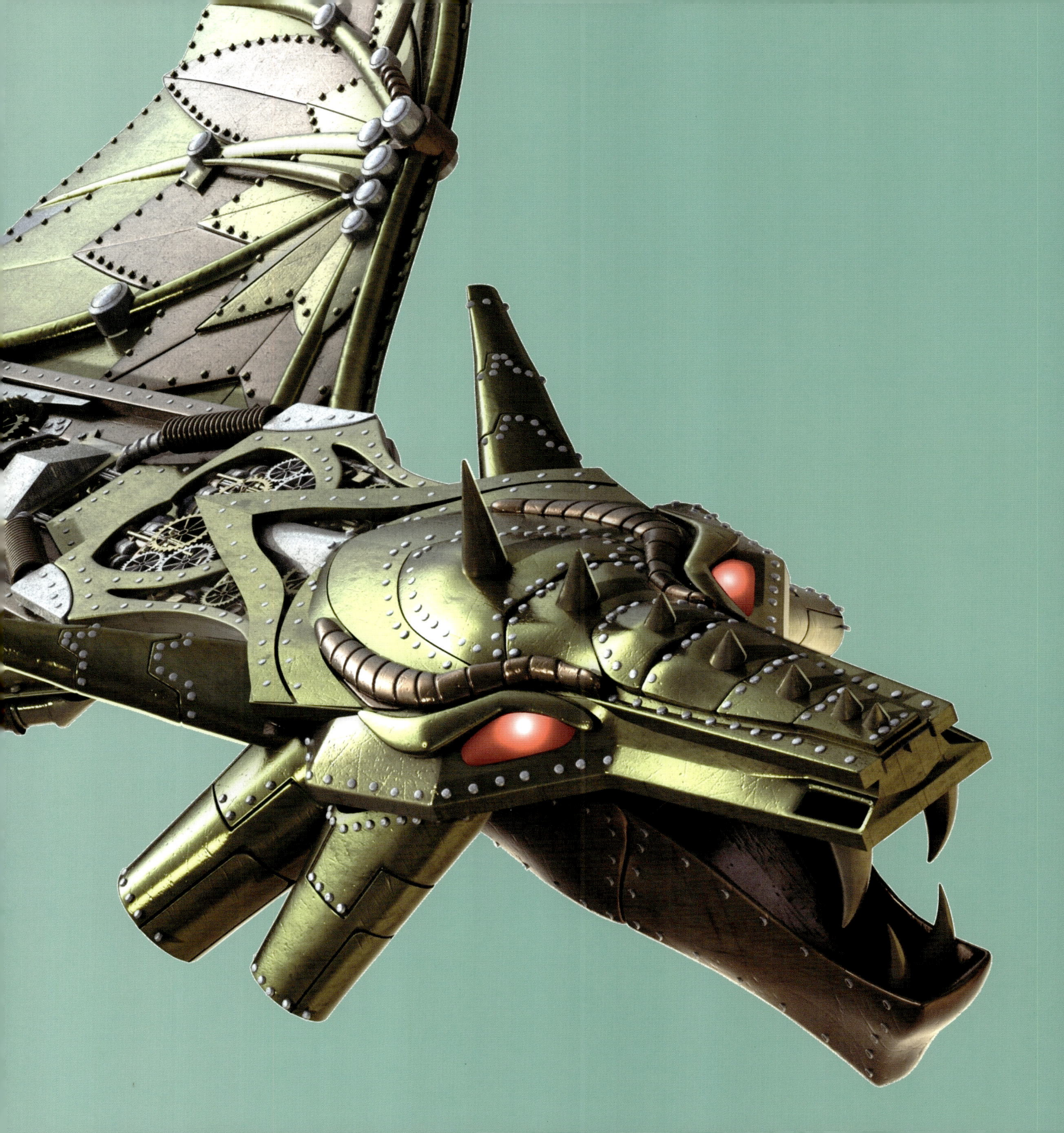

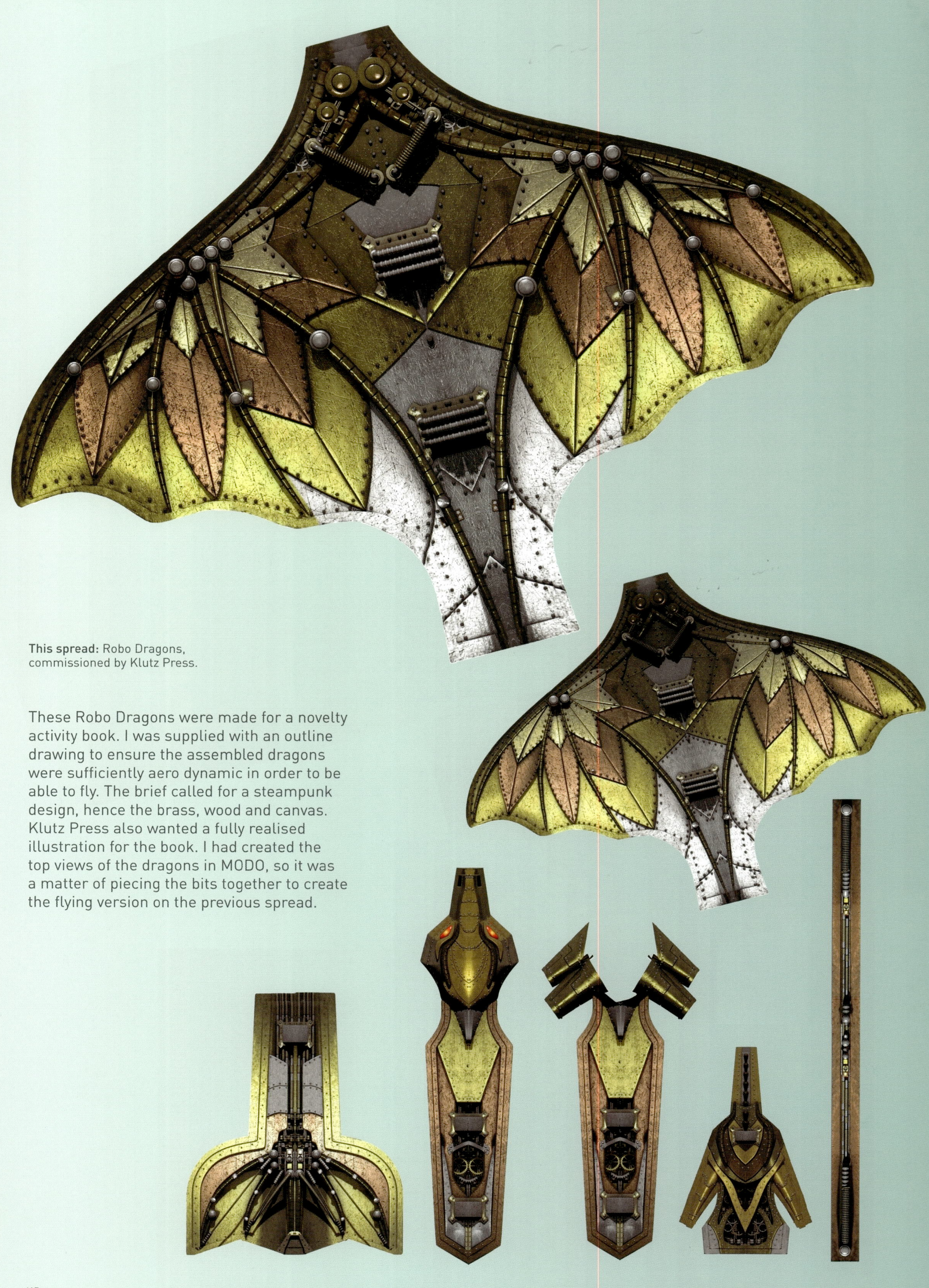

This spread: Robo Dragons, commissioned by Klutz Press.

These Robo Dragons were made for a novelty activity book. I was supplied with an outline drawing to ensure the assembled dragons were sufficiently aero dynamic in order to be able to fly. The brief called for a steampunk design, hence the brass, wood and canvas. Klutz Press also wanted a fully realised illustration for the book. I had created the top views of the dragons in MODO, so it was a matter of piecing the bits together to create the flying version on the previous spread.

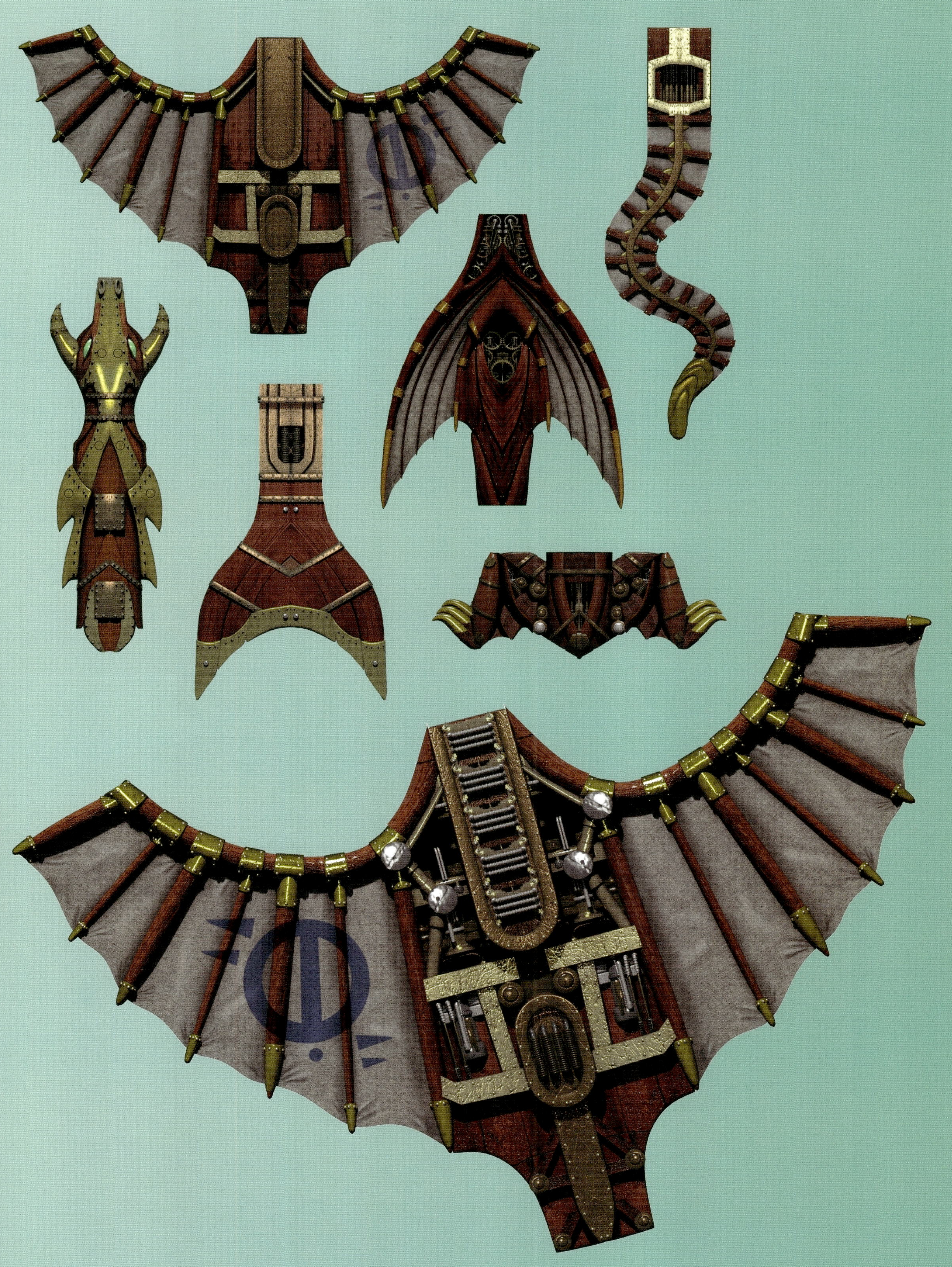

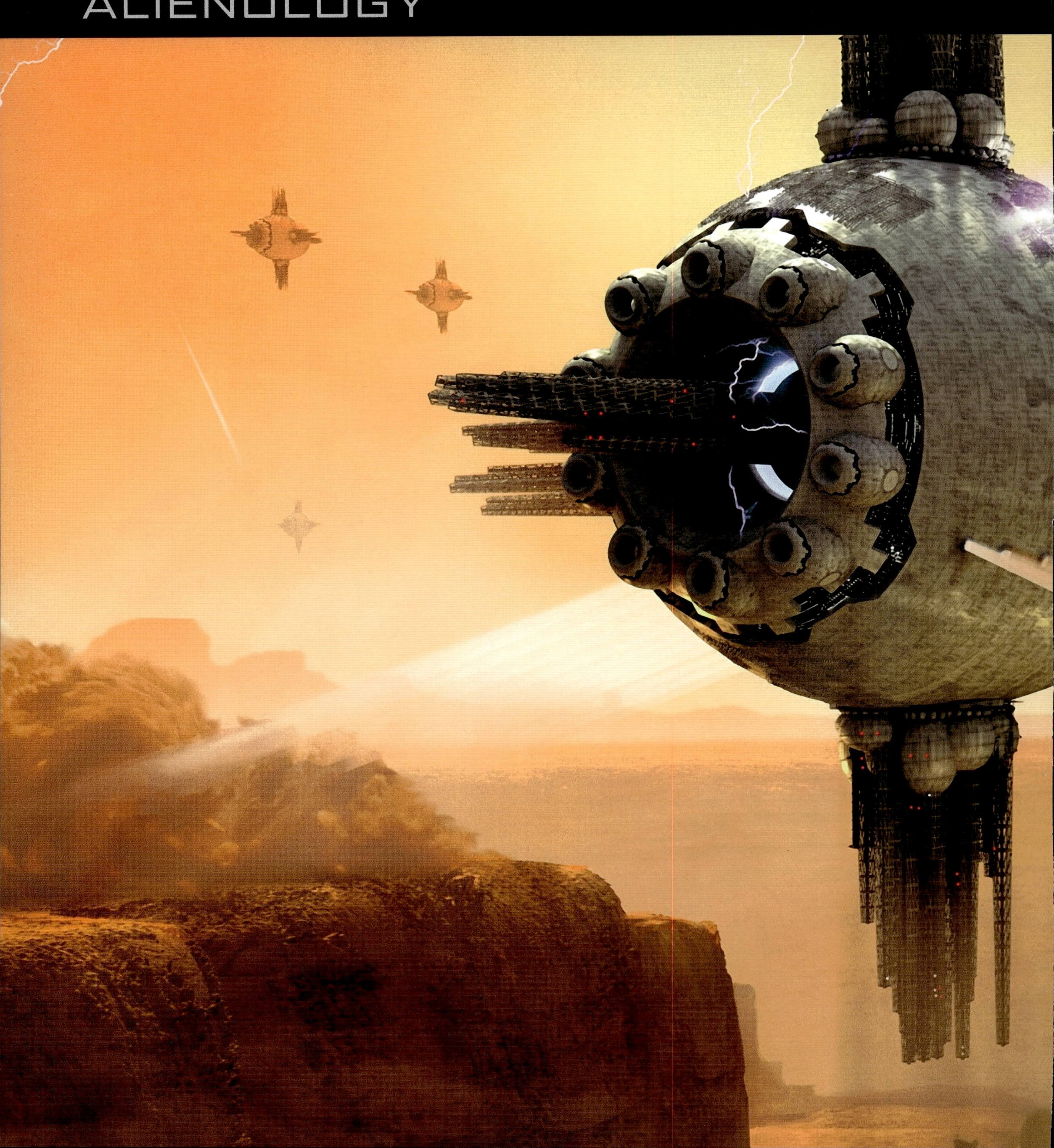

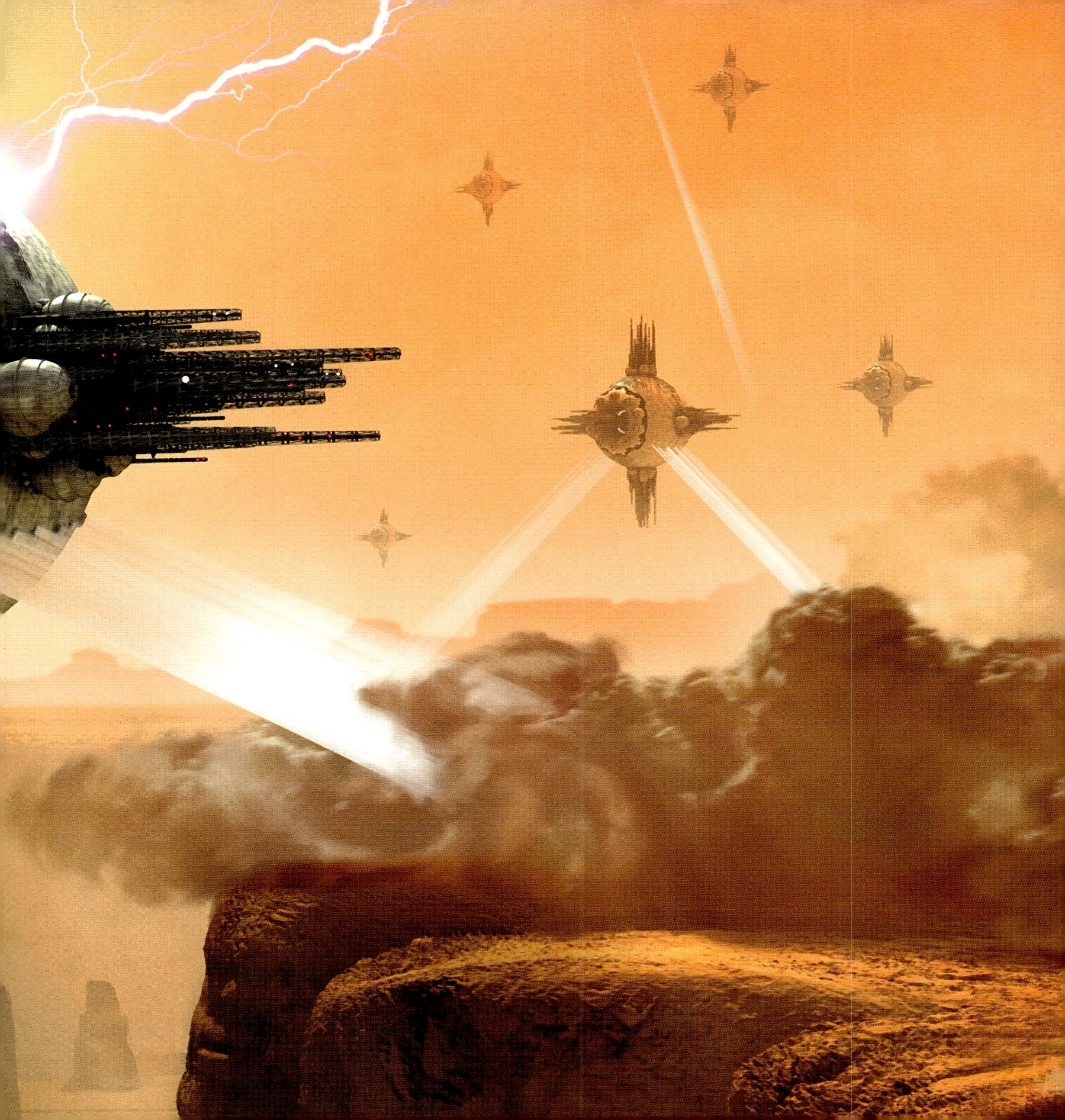

As part of their '-ology' series, Templar Publishing decided to produce a book called *Alienology* which – as with their other *Dragonology* and *Spyology* books – was a fun mix of interactivity and story, featuring a host of different aliens and spacecraft.

The book featured that most-loved of alien invaders: the tripods, first realised in H.G. Wells' *The War of the Worlds*. Many artists have had a go at depicting these three-legged engines of destruction, so it was fun for me to add my own version to the pantheon. Ultimately, I had to take out the figure being hurled into the air above the car, as Templar deemed it too violent.

The classic alien 'greys' were the main characters in the book. To the *right* is a cutaway of an alien saucer, showing the various interior rooms and compartments. I produced two images of terraforming machines (*opposite bottom*), machines that are designed to create a liveable environment on an otherwise hostile planet. I chose to use an egg shape which is a symbol of birth and new life.

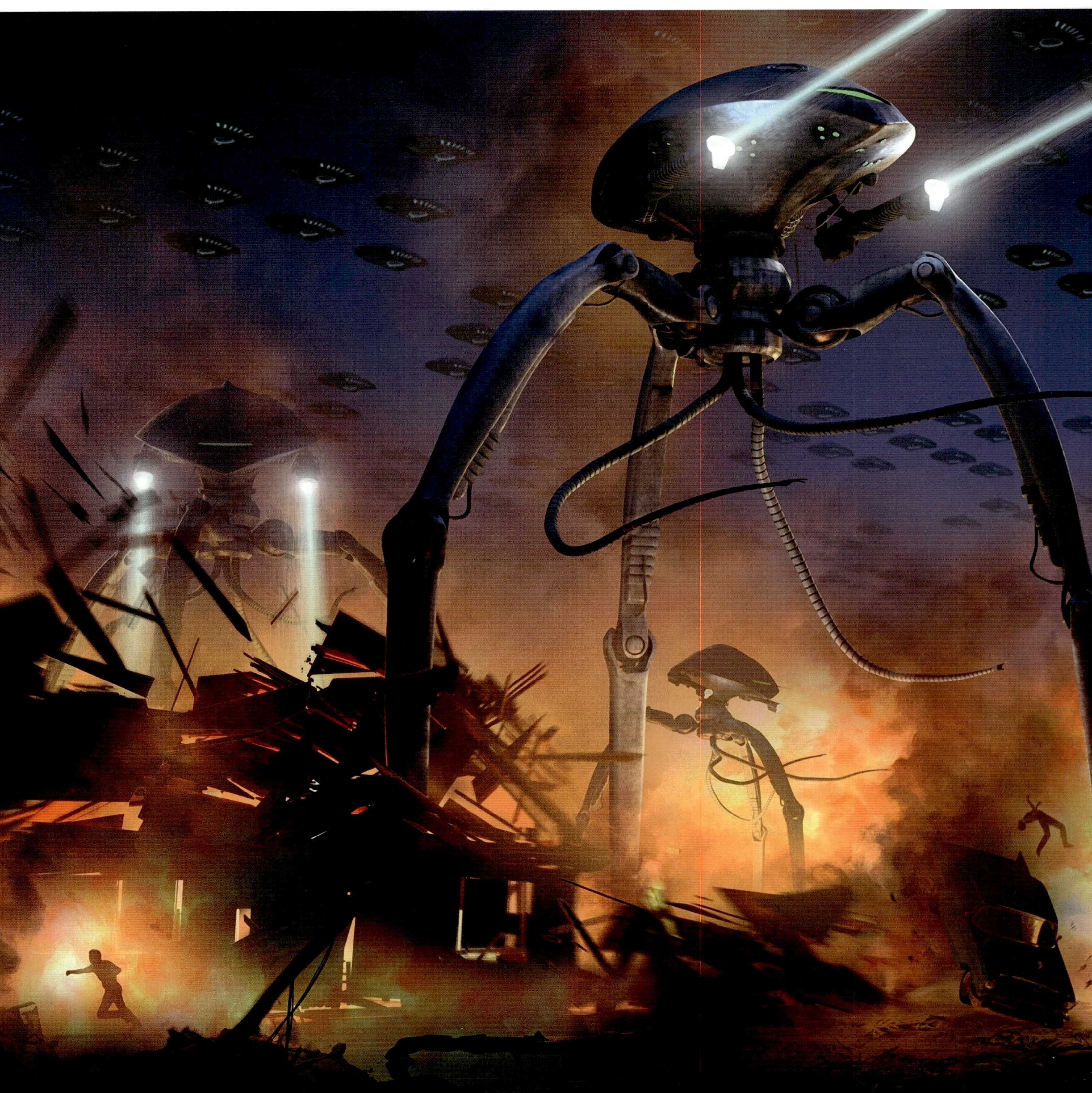

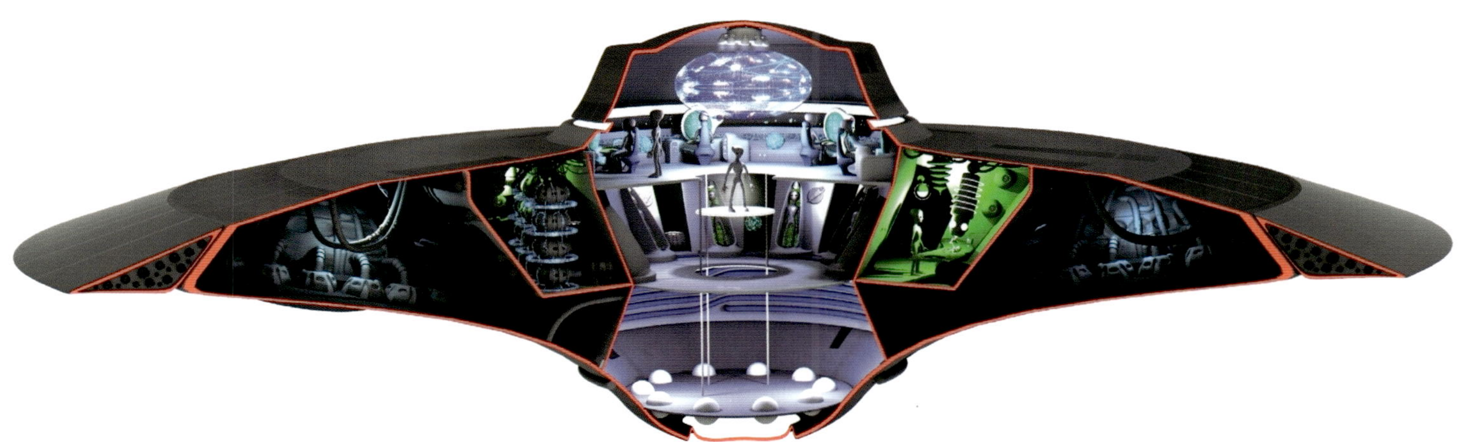

Previous page: *Taurican Terraforming Machine.*

Clockwise from left:
When Aliens Attack; Saucer; A Gray Orbiter; Hangar Bay.

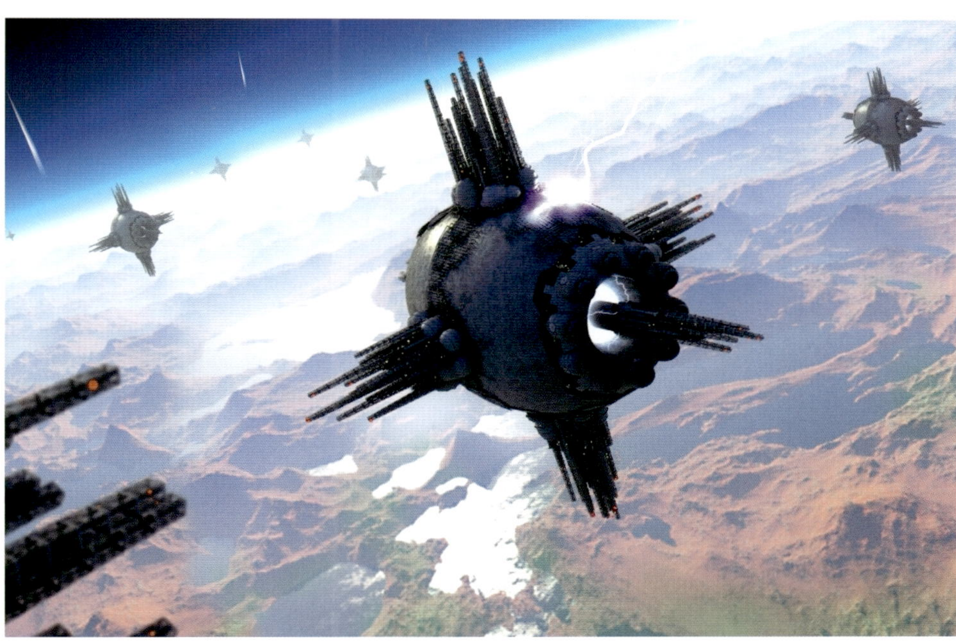

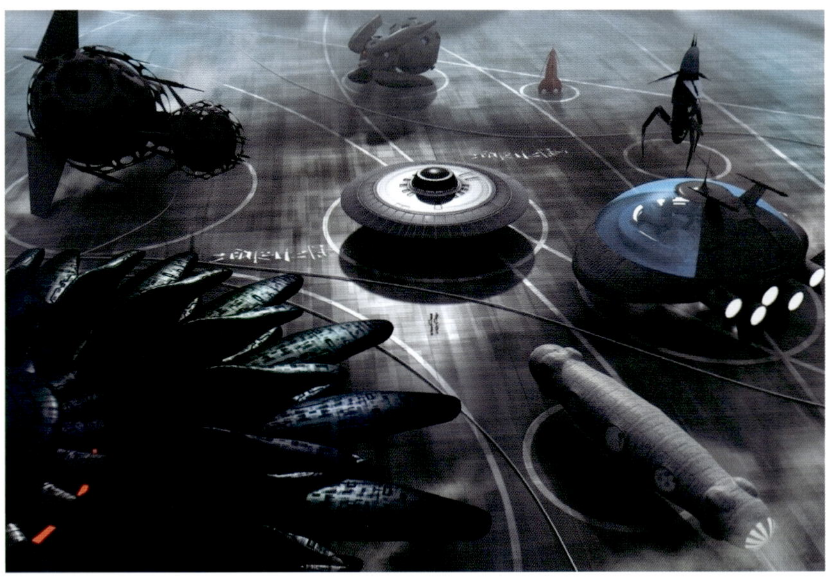

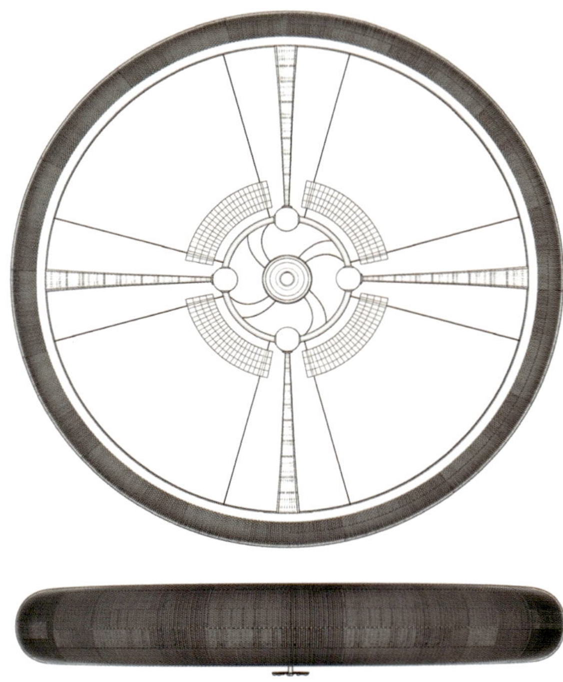

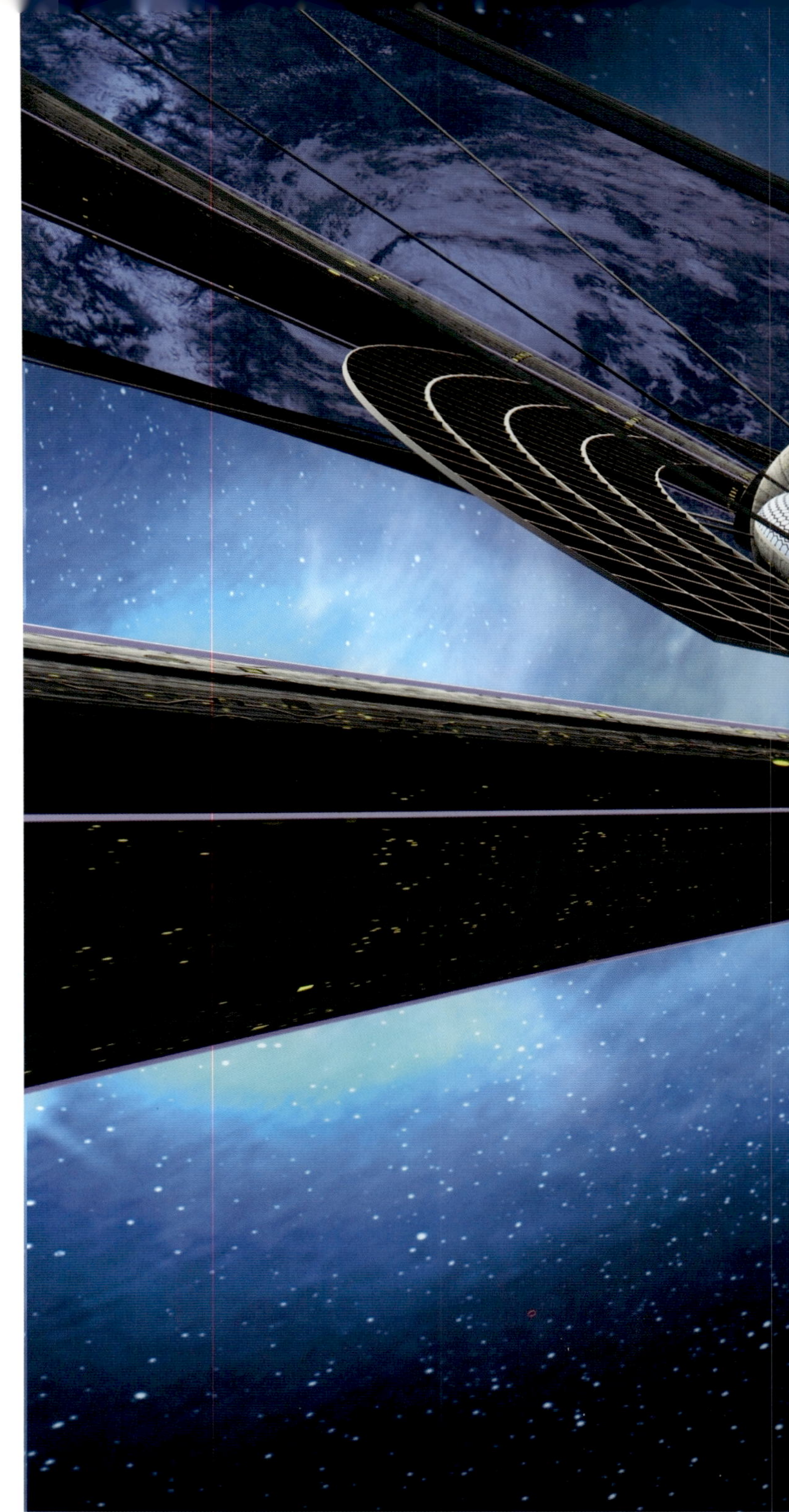

ANIMATION

As part of the interactivity of *Alienology*, Templar created a web site to further the experience, for which I designed a space station. They then asked me to create an animation that would fly the camera from a distance to a close up of the central dome, which contained a landscape of mountains and lakes.

The model had to be pretty detailed, as the camera zooms in over the outer ring and then up one of the spokes as if at a distance of a few hundred feet, before finally revealing the central structure. Given that this was an animation, I couldn't do my usual trick of just creating enough and then filling in the missing details in Photoshop. The model had to stand up on it's own with all the necessary detail in place.

Illustrations produced for the animation associated with *Alienology*, for Templar.

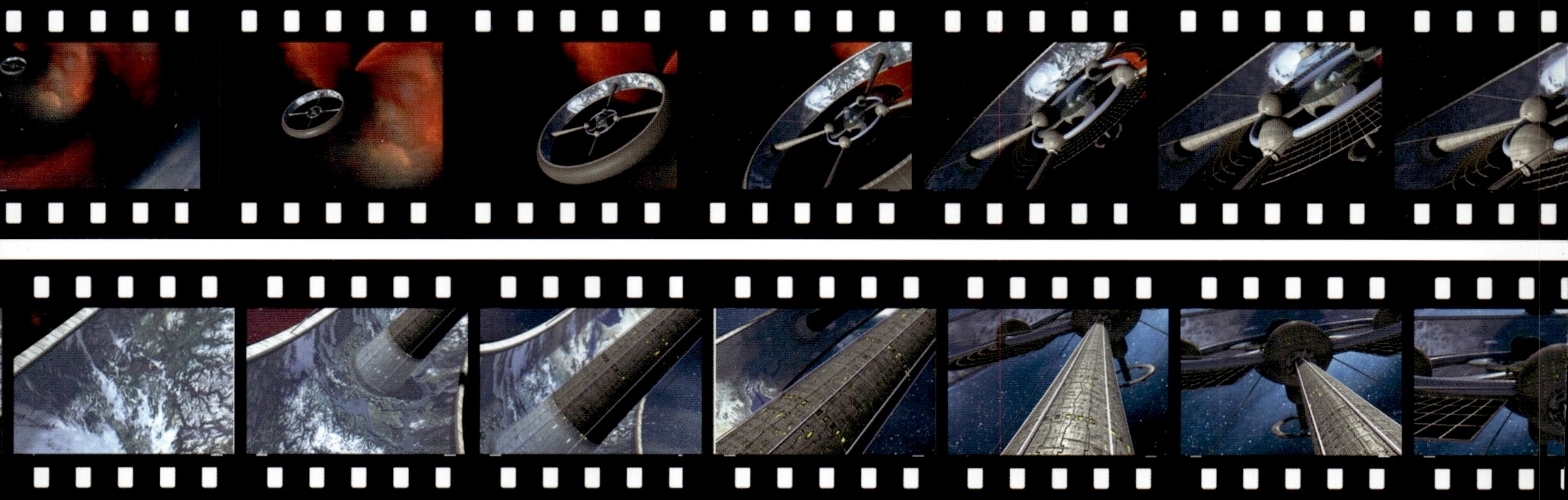

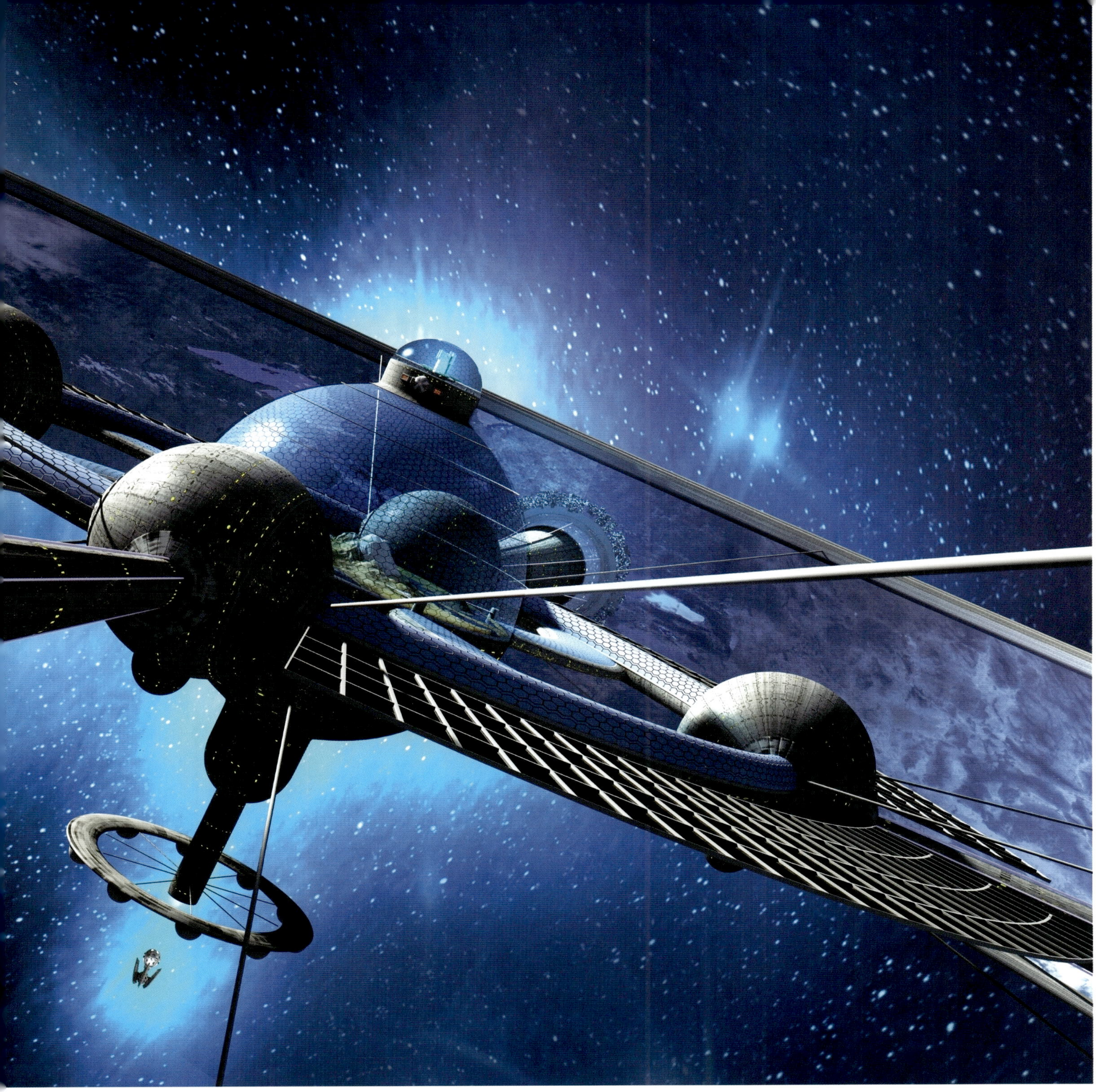

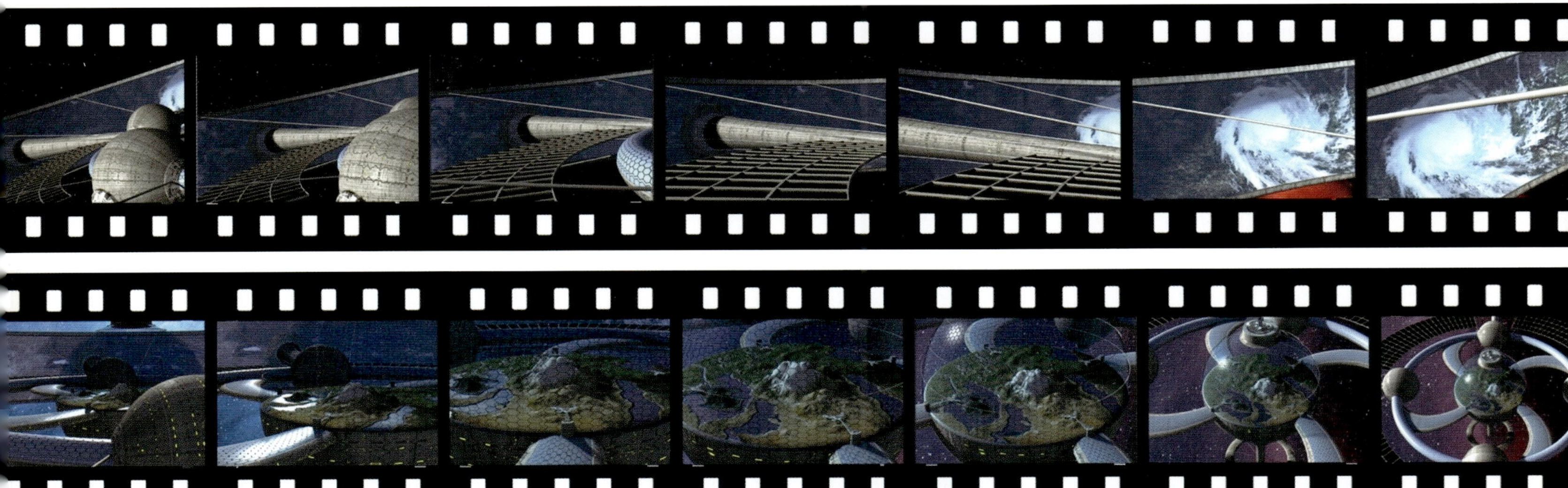

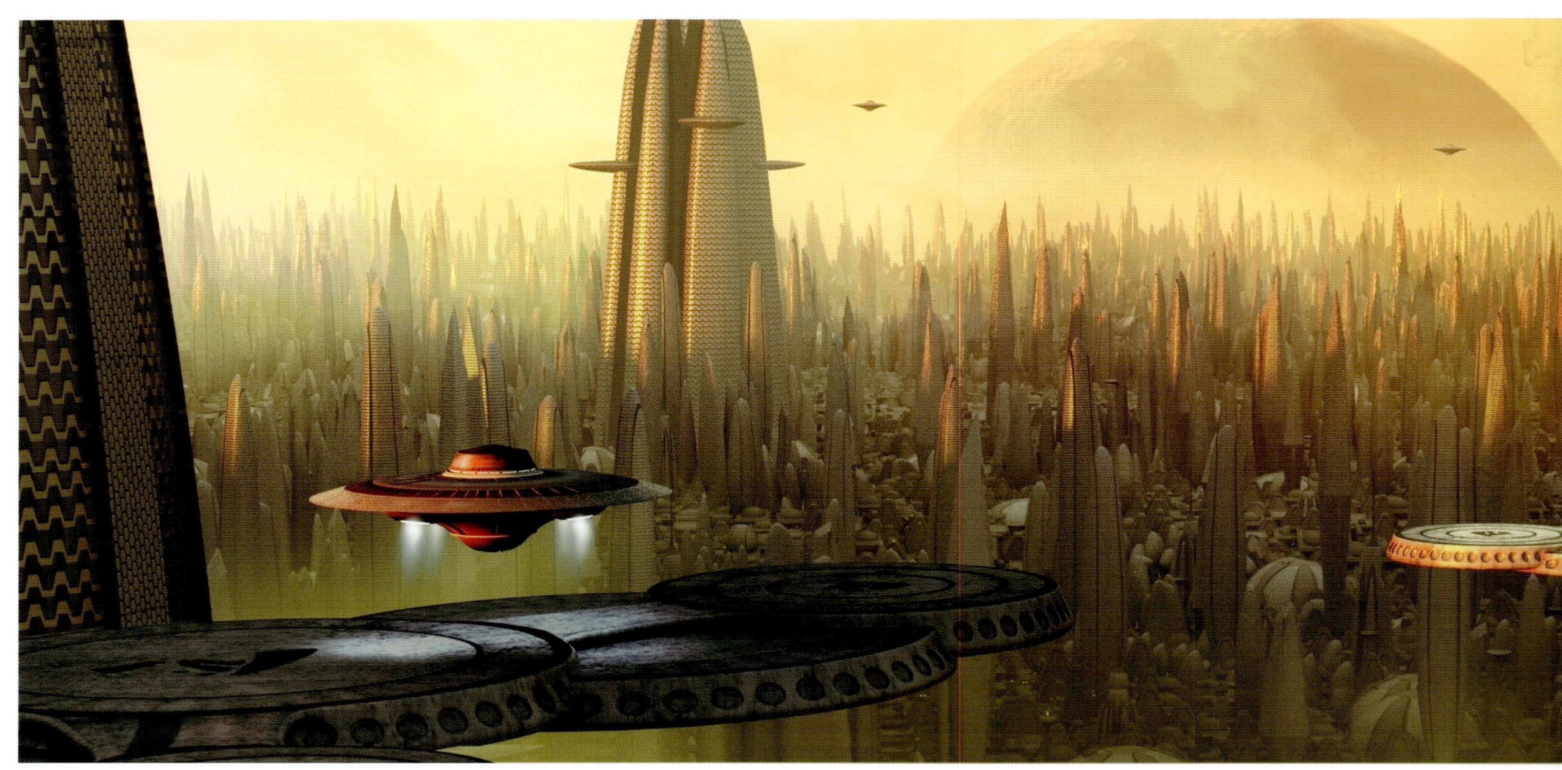

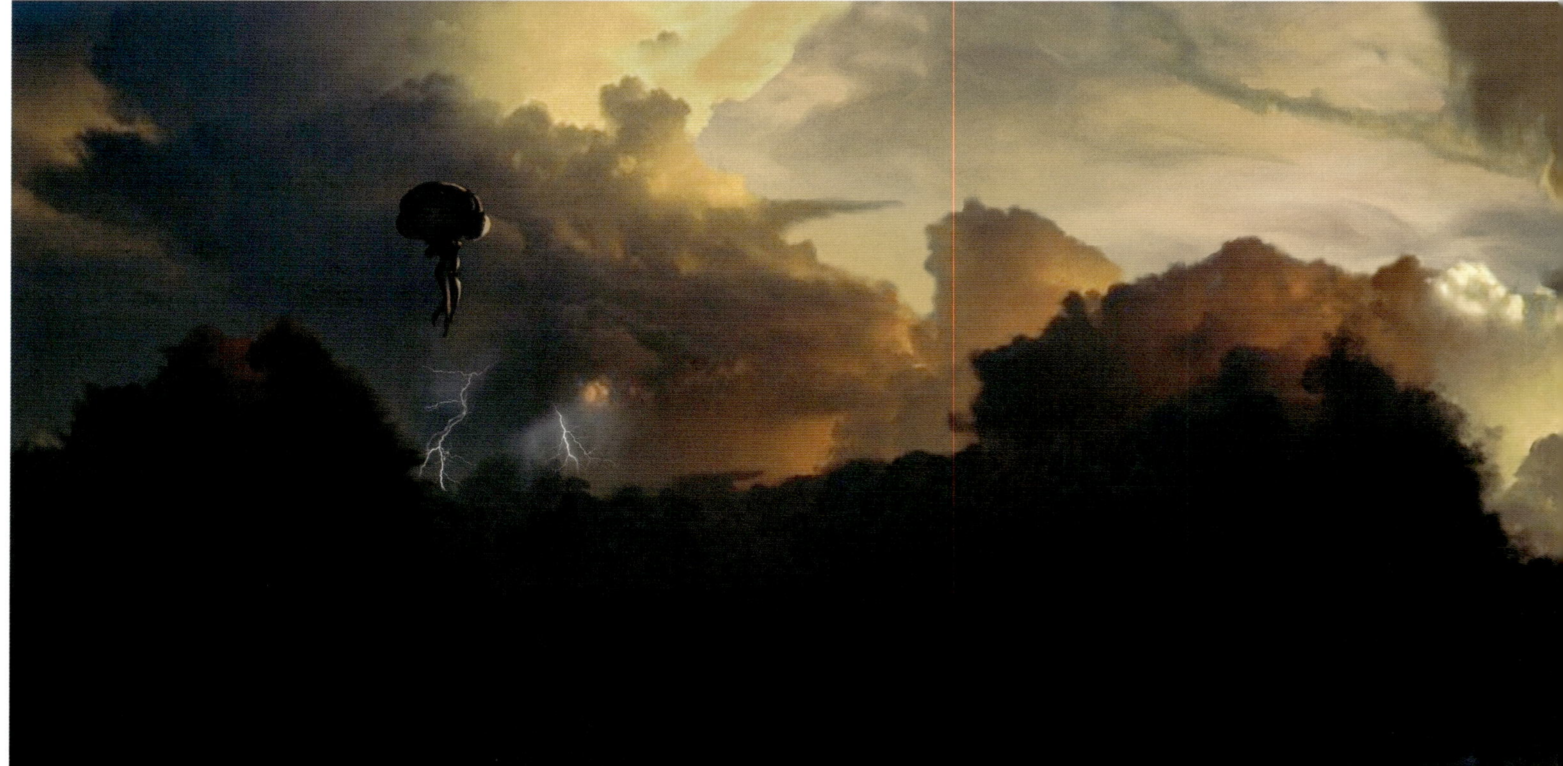

ALIEN LANDSCAPES

Top: *Reticulan 1, Home of the Greys.*

Bottom: *Cloud World*, one of the landscapes produced for *Alienology.*

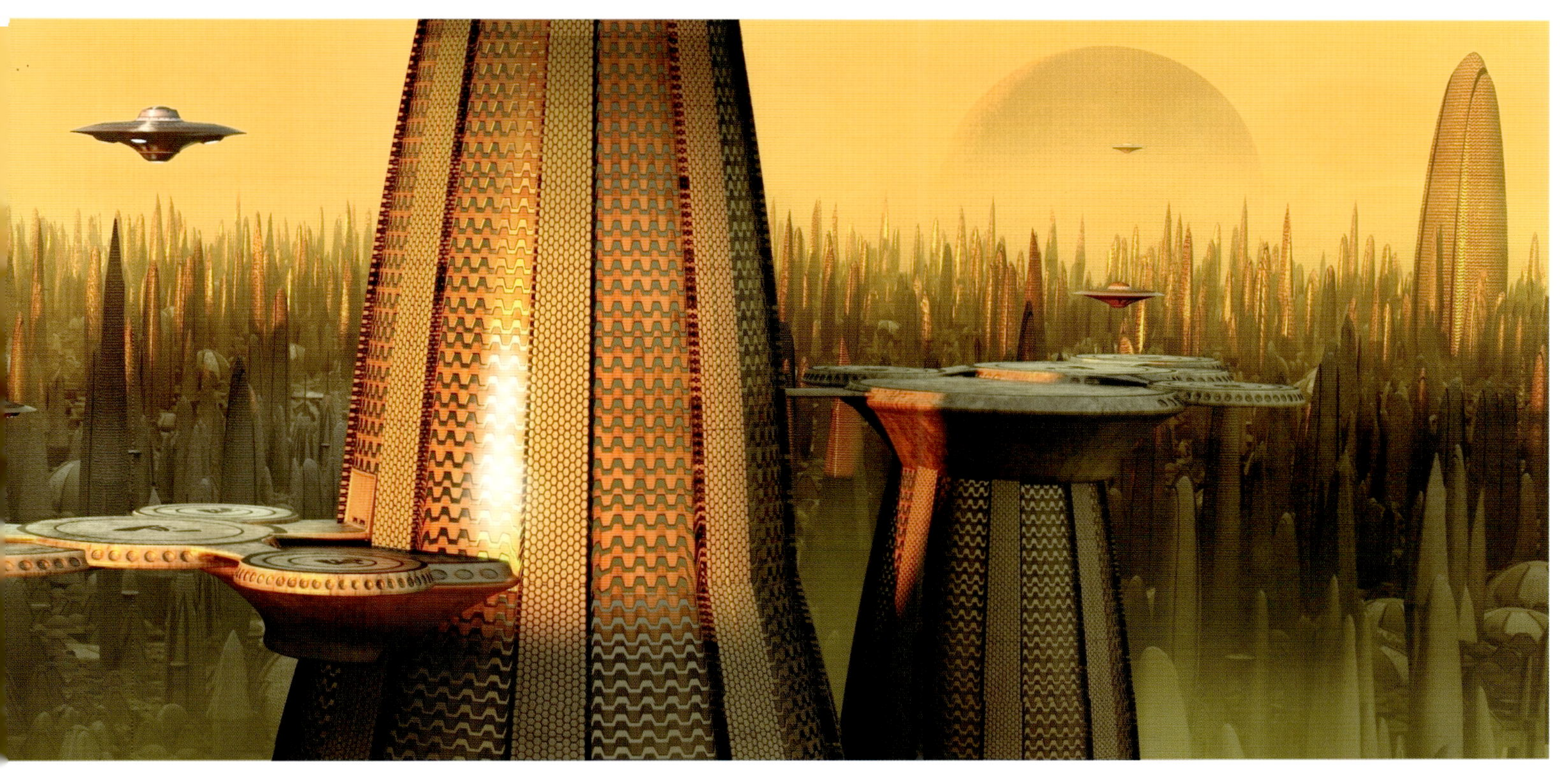

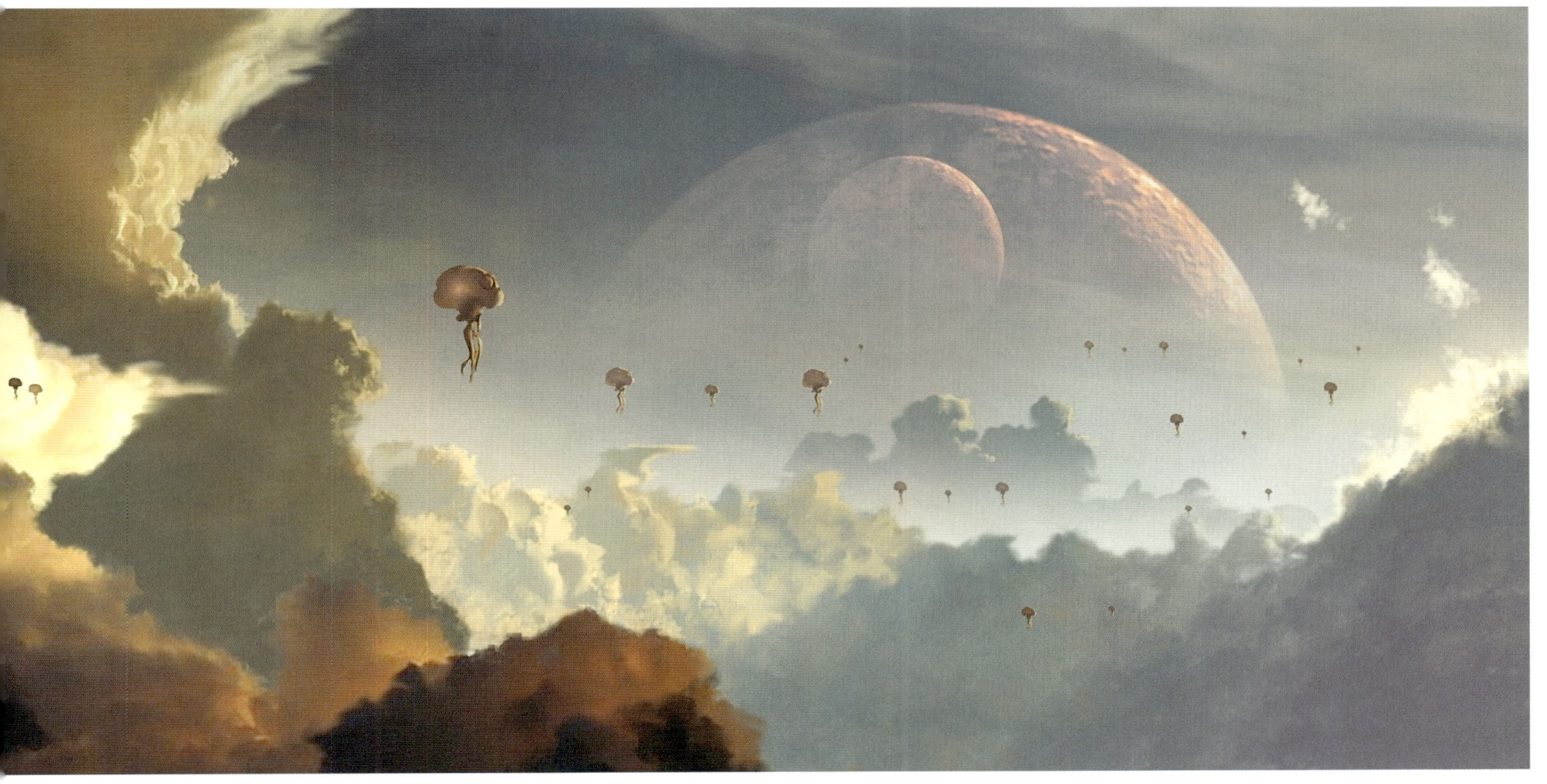

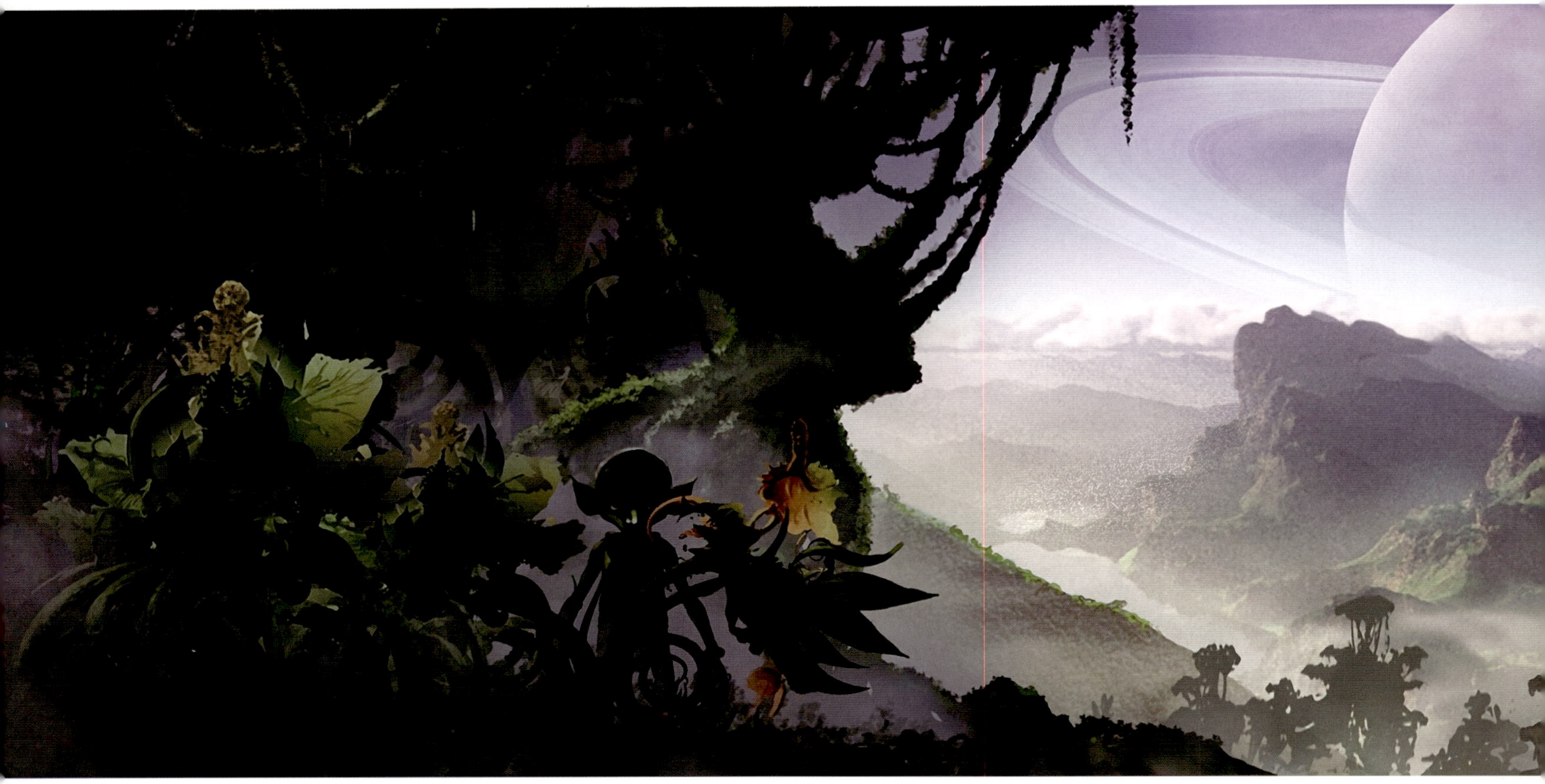

Above: *Reticulon II.*

Below: *Ignemia*, Home of the Cyberbrains.

Opposite bottom: *Hokulia I*, a desert planet with few lakes; *Gelubus I*, home of the Decapodes.

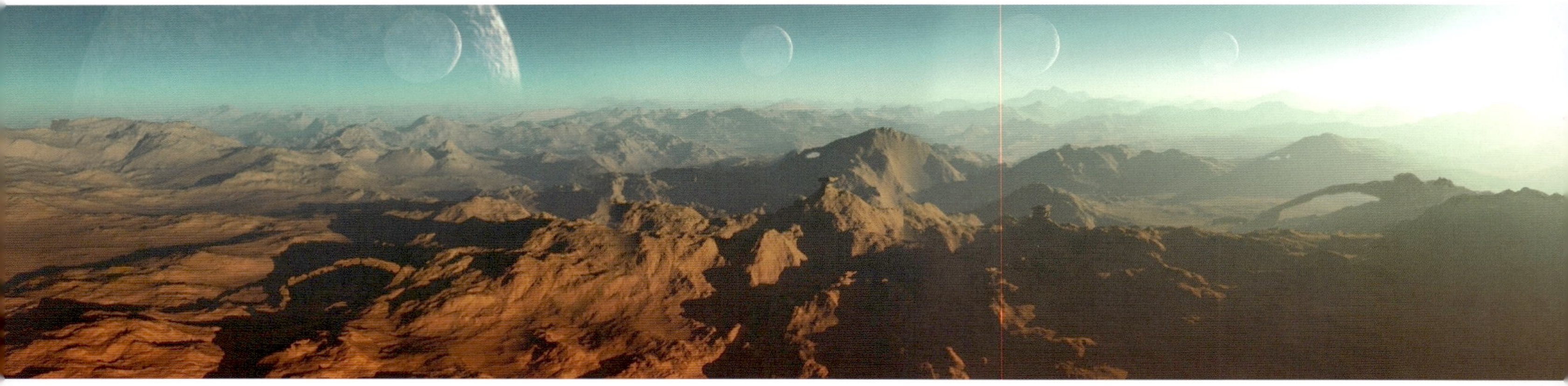

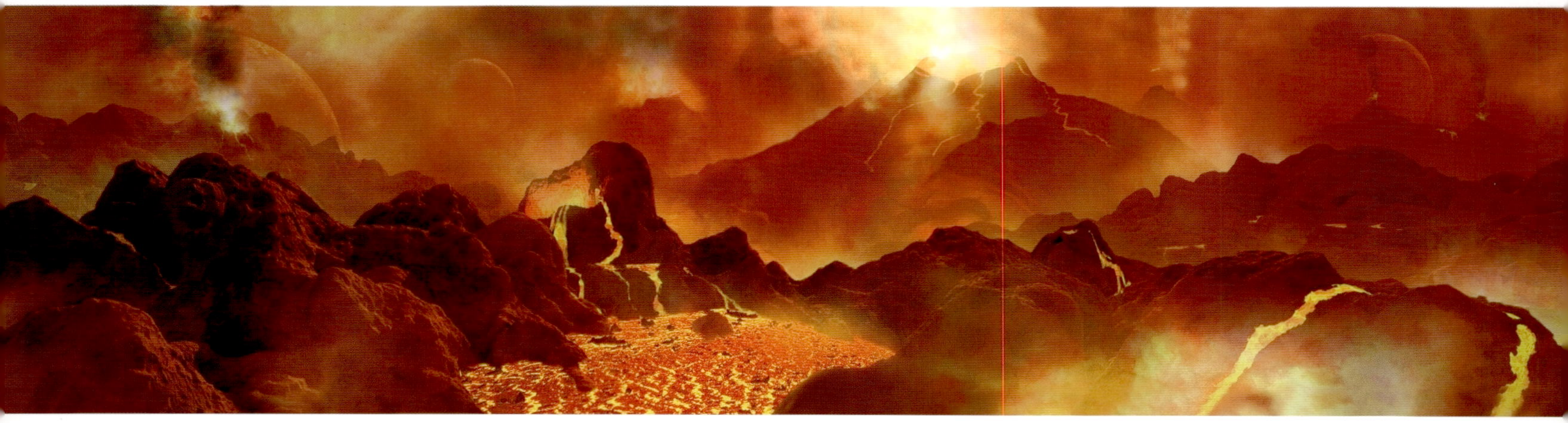

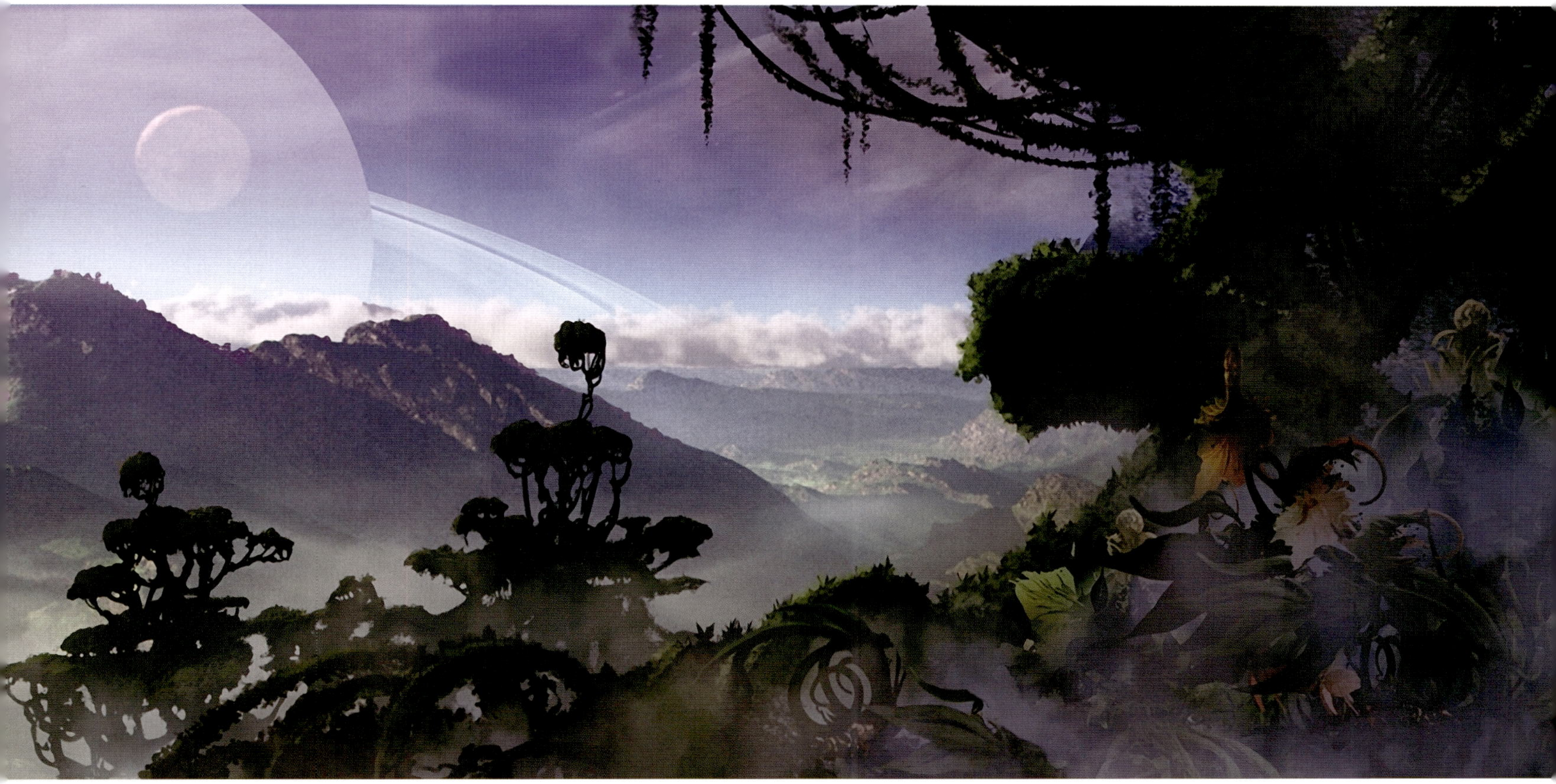

I had to create several alien worlds which I simply dubbed 'Jungle world', 'Cloud world', 'Lava world', 'City world' and 'Ice world'. To help generate the landscape in the jungle and desert worlds, I used a landscape generating application called Terragen. It's very slow and, to me at least, has a less than intuitive interface, but the results can be impressive. The ice planet and cloud planet were largely painted straight out of my head, whilst the lava world was generated in MODO before adding more painting work. The usual science fiction device of over-sized and multiple moons made sure that the viewer knew we were actually on a distant alien planet.

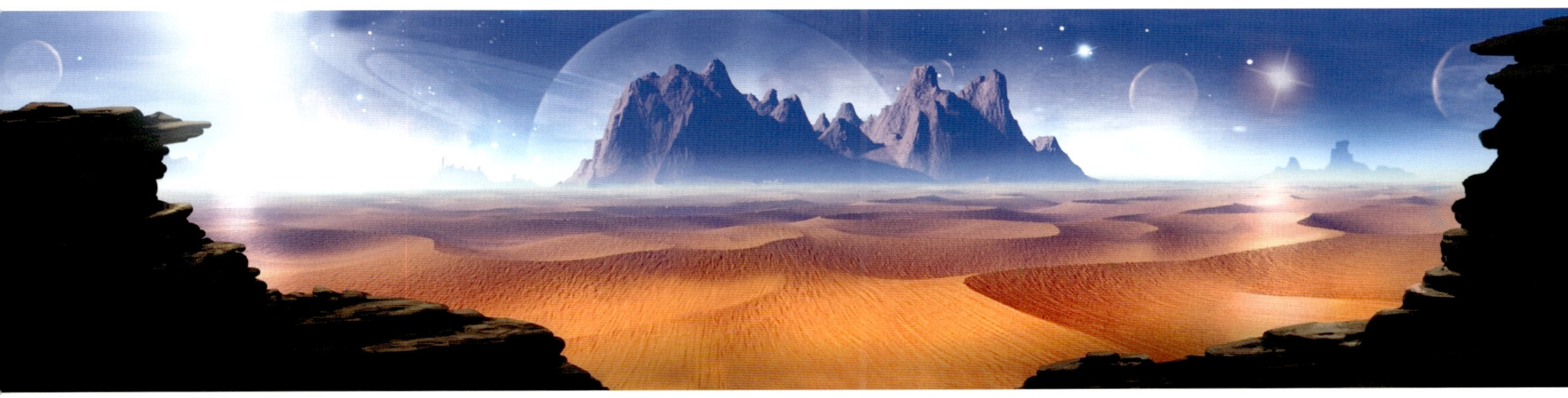

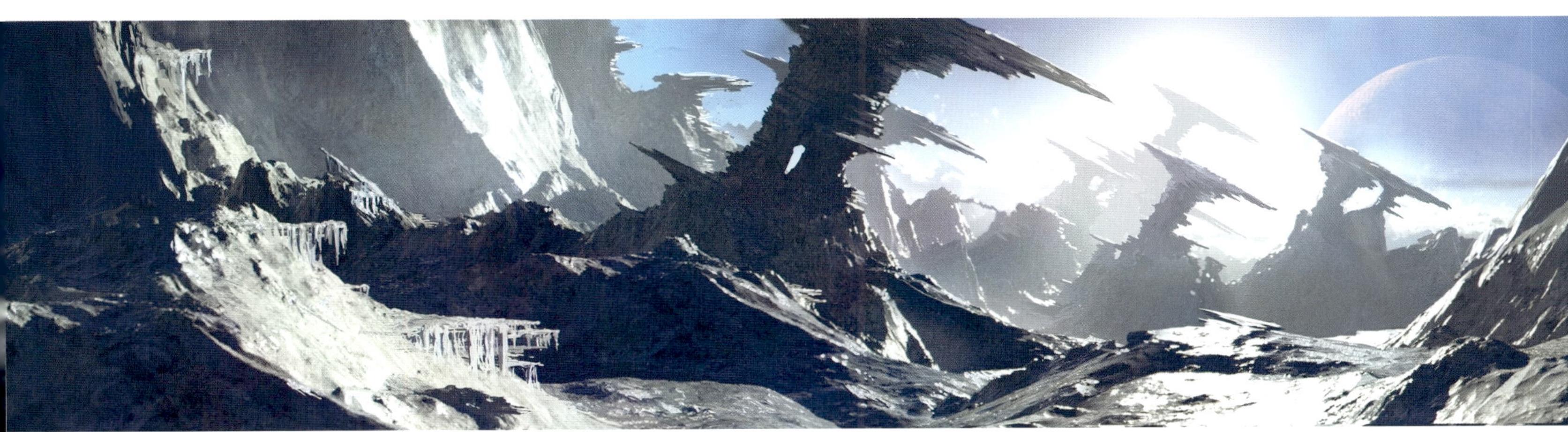

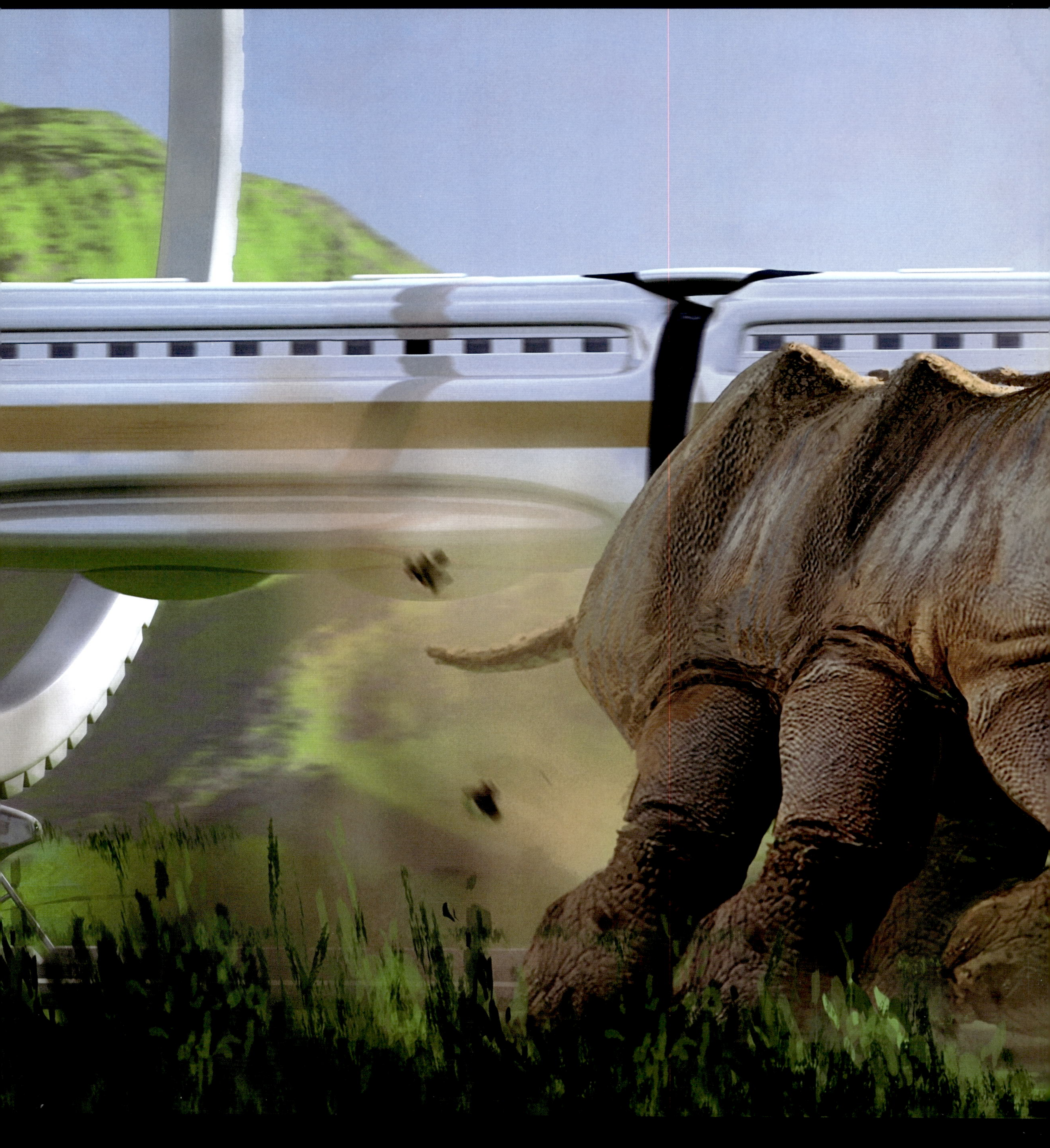

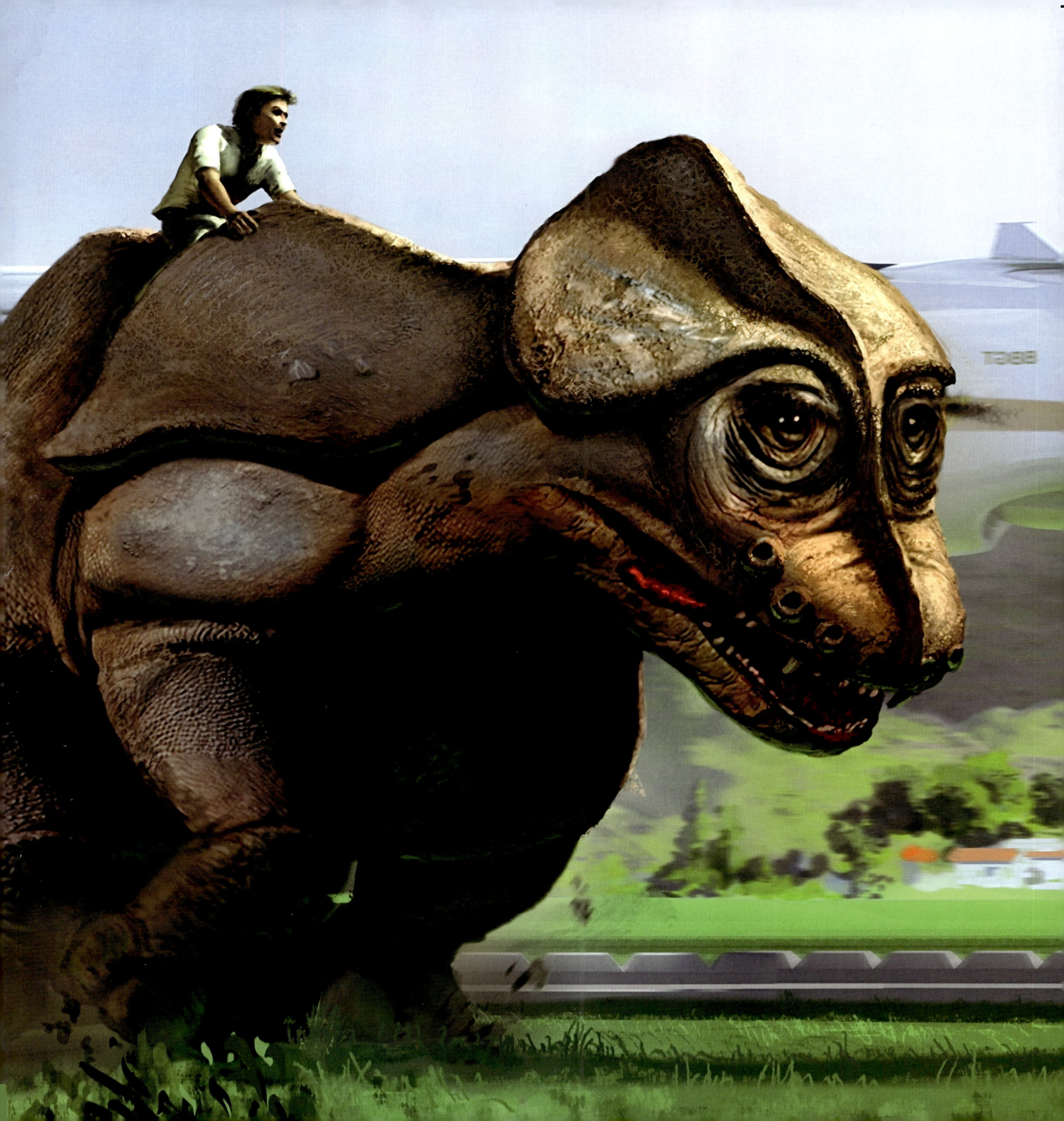

Previous page:
Lummox.

Clockwise from right:
Capital City, Train Design, Landing, Lummox Hands.

John A. Davis, the director of *The Ant Bully*, acquired the film rights to Robert Heinlein's *Star Beast* novel in 2005. I worked directly with John to make these visual development images to help sell *Starbeast* to the studio. I had a lot of freedom to interpret the scenes that John wanted to depict. The Lummox creature has been drawn by quite a few artists since the original novel, and John wanted a tough-looking but empathic beast with the elephantine and rhino qualities Heinlein describes in the story. I created the images of the Lummox in Photoshop, hand painting over photographs of elephants and rhinos taken at Chester Zoo.

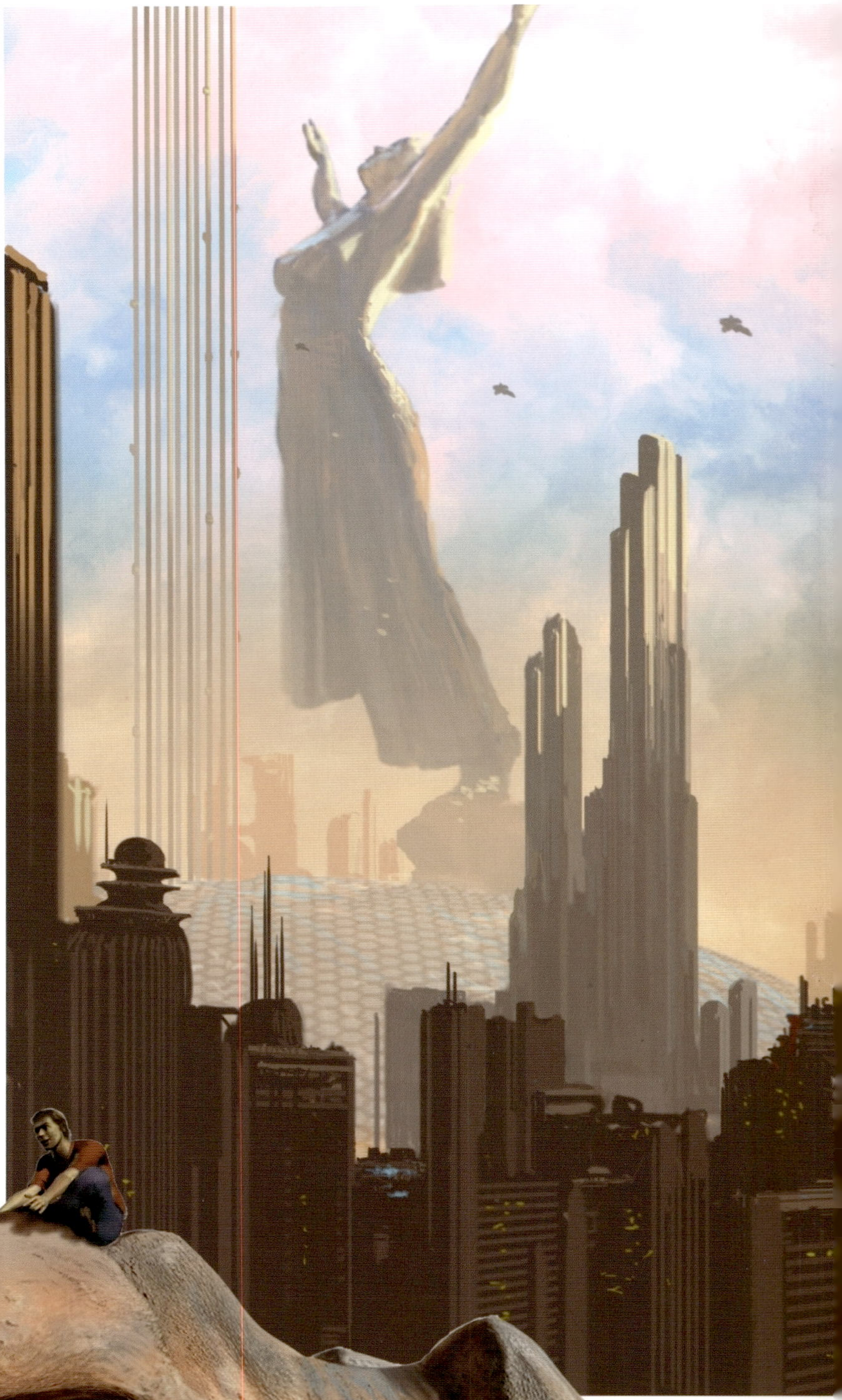

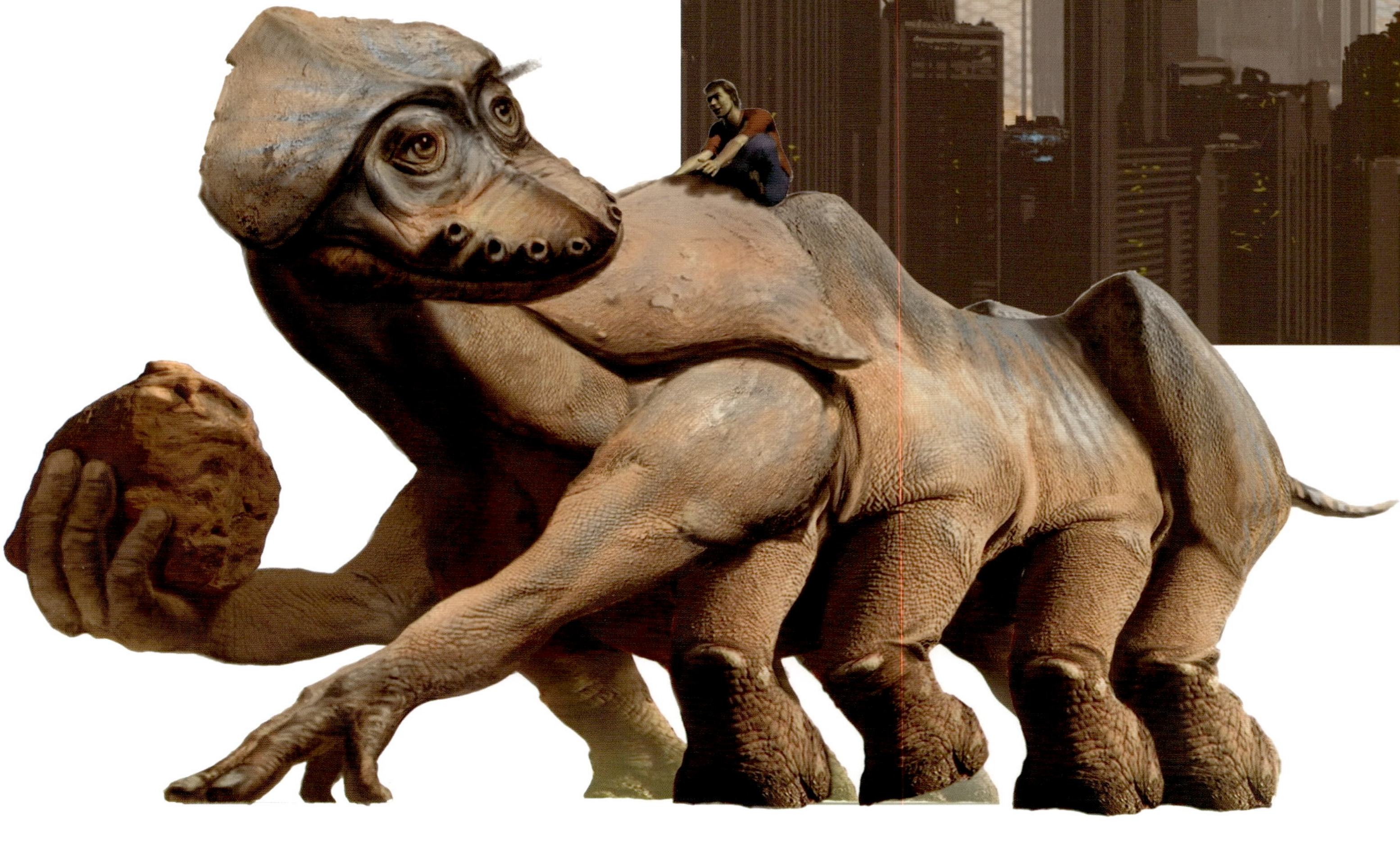

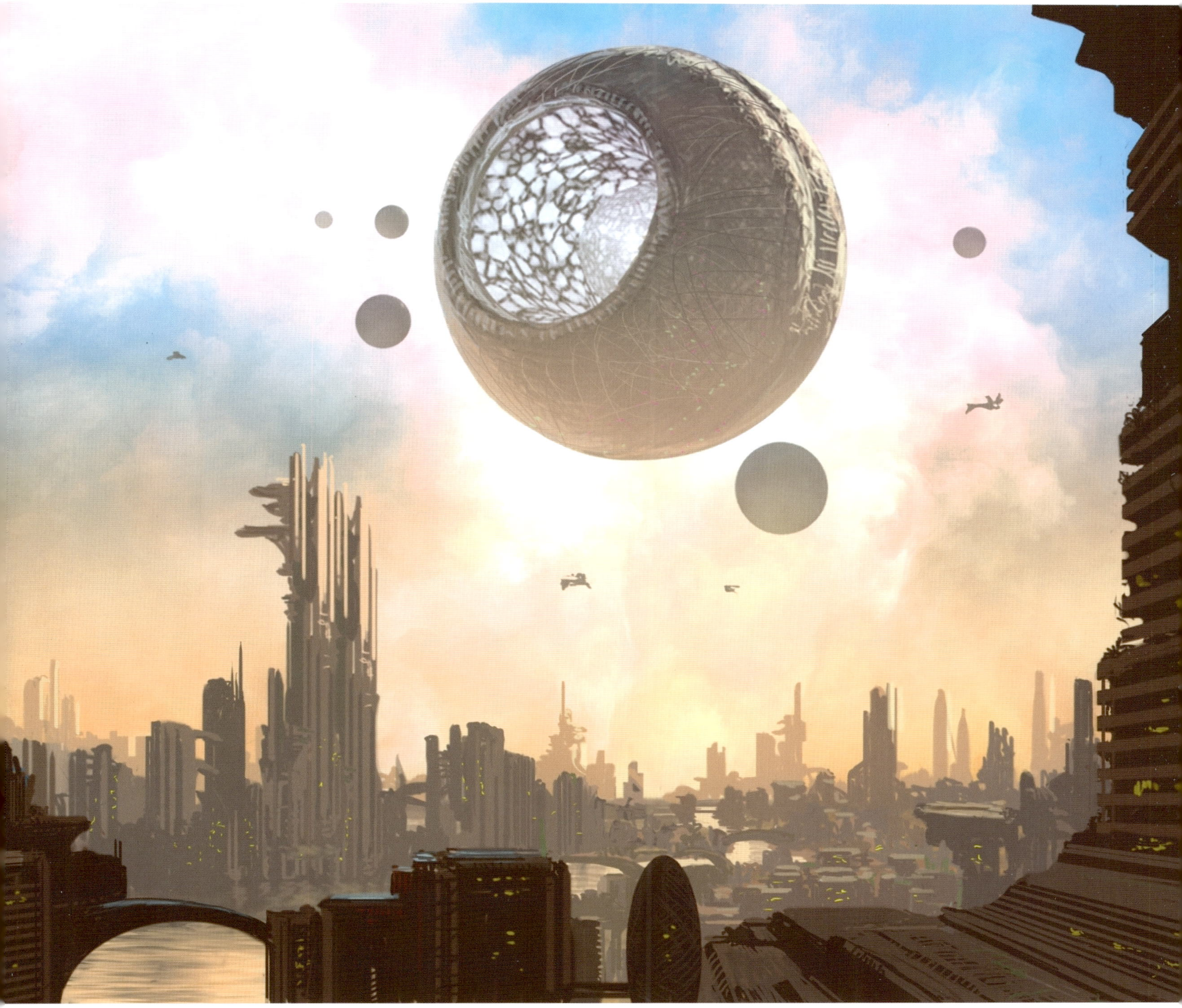

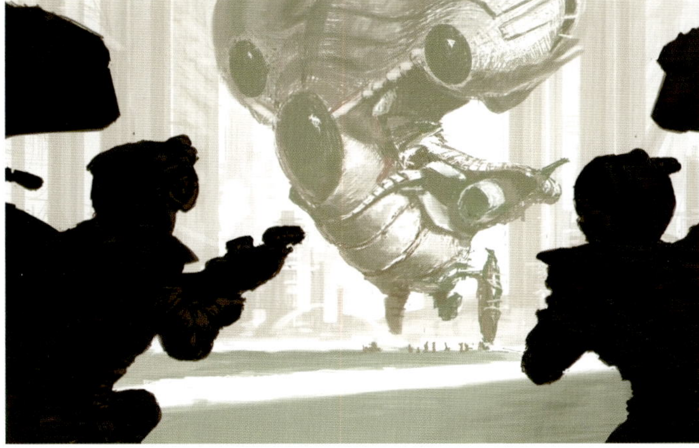

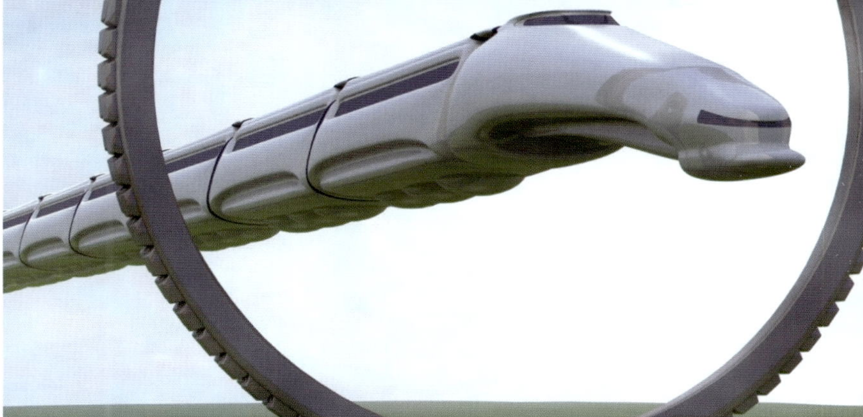

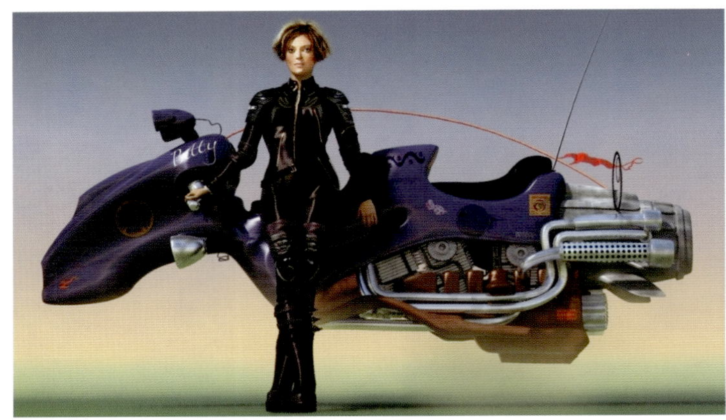

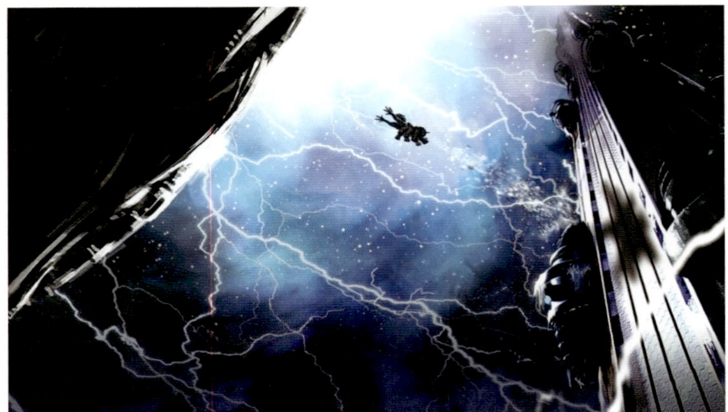

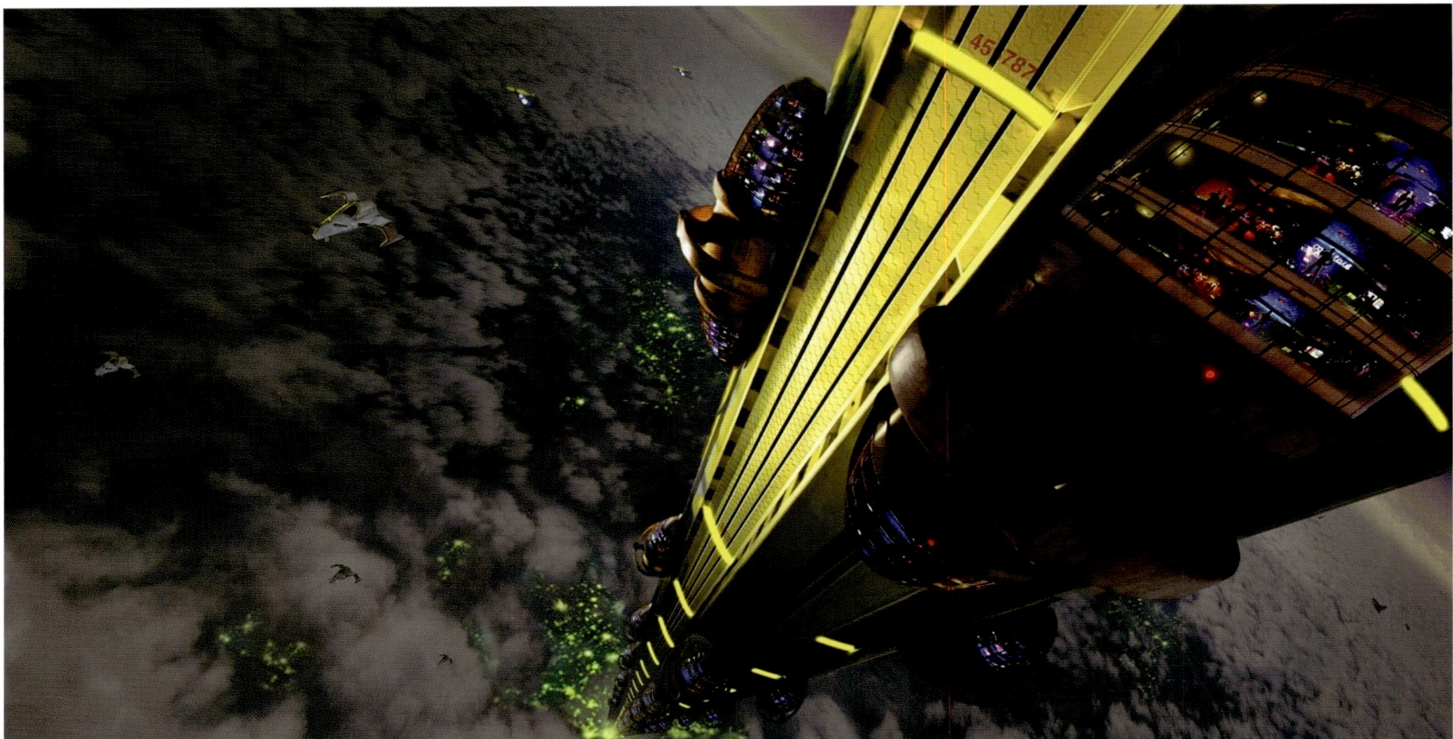

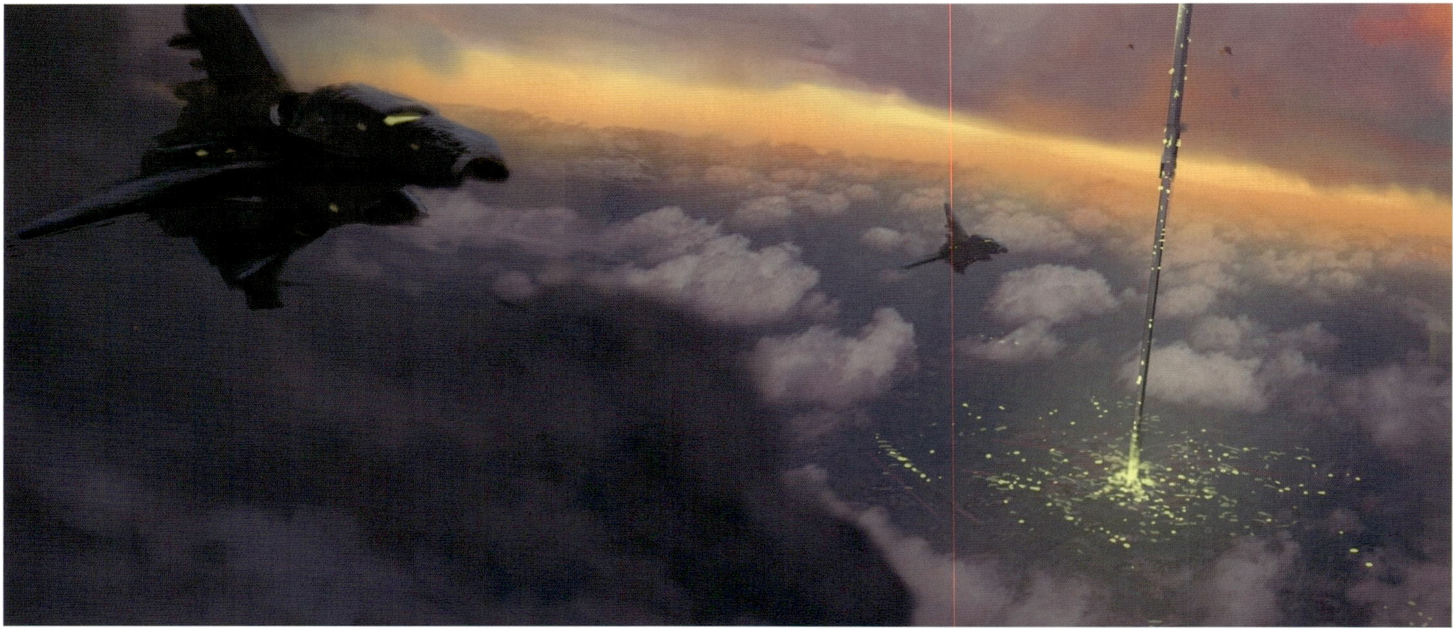

Top: *Betty*, *Lummox Leaps.*

Middle and bottom: *Space Elevator Close-up*; *Space Elevator Wide.*

Opposite: *Dr Fteaml.*

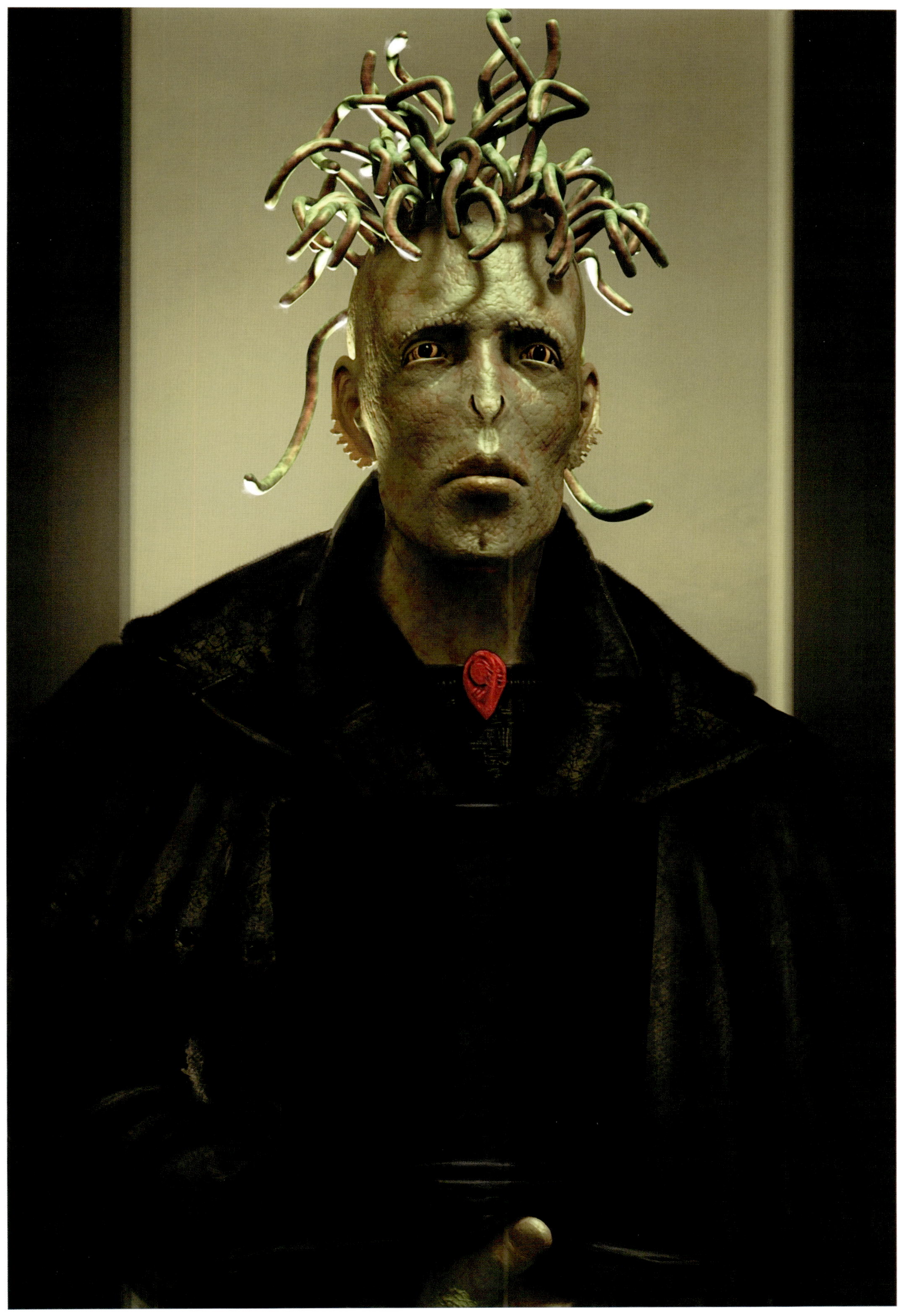

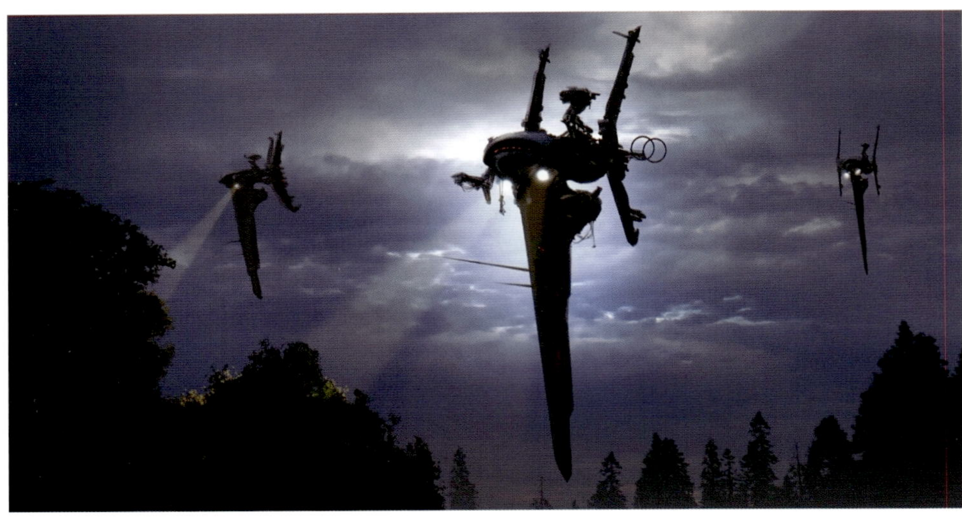

Left: *Hunters* illustration.

Below: *Tractor Beam* illustration.

Opposite: Landing craft concepts.

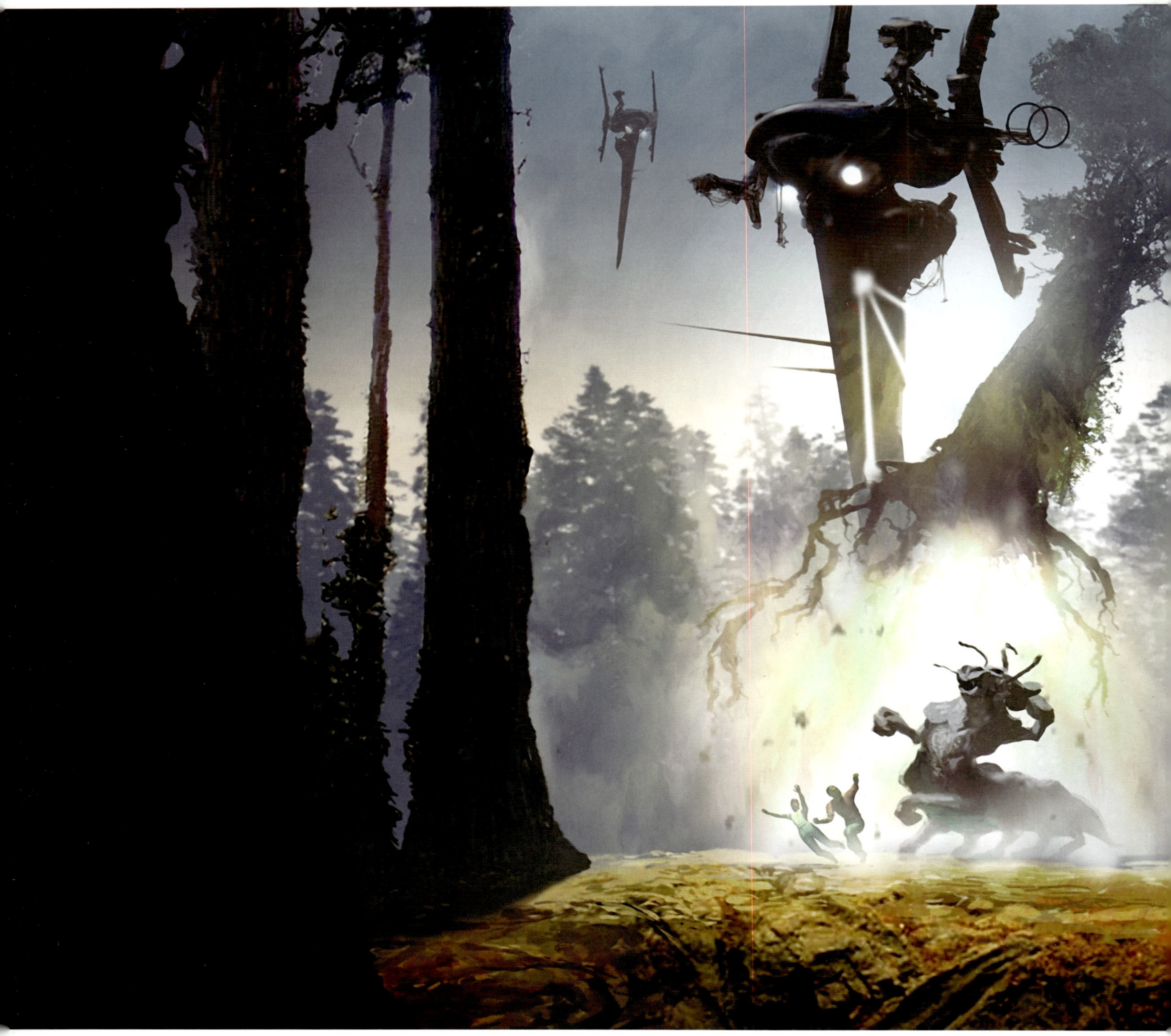

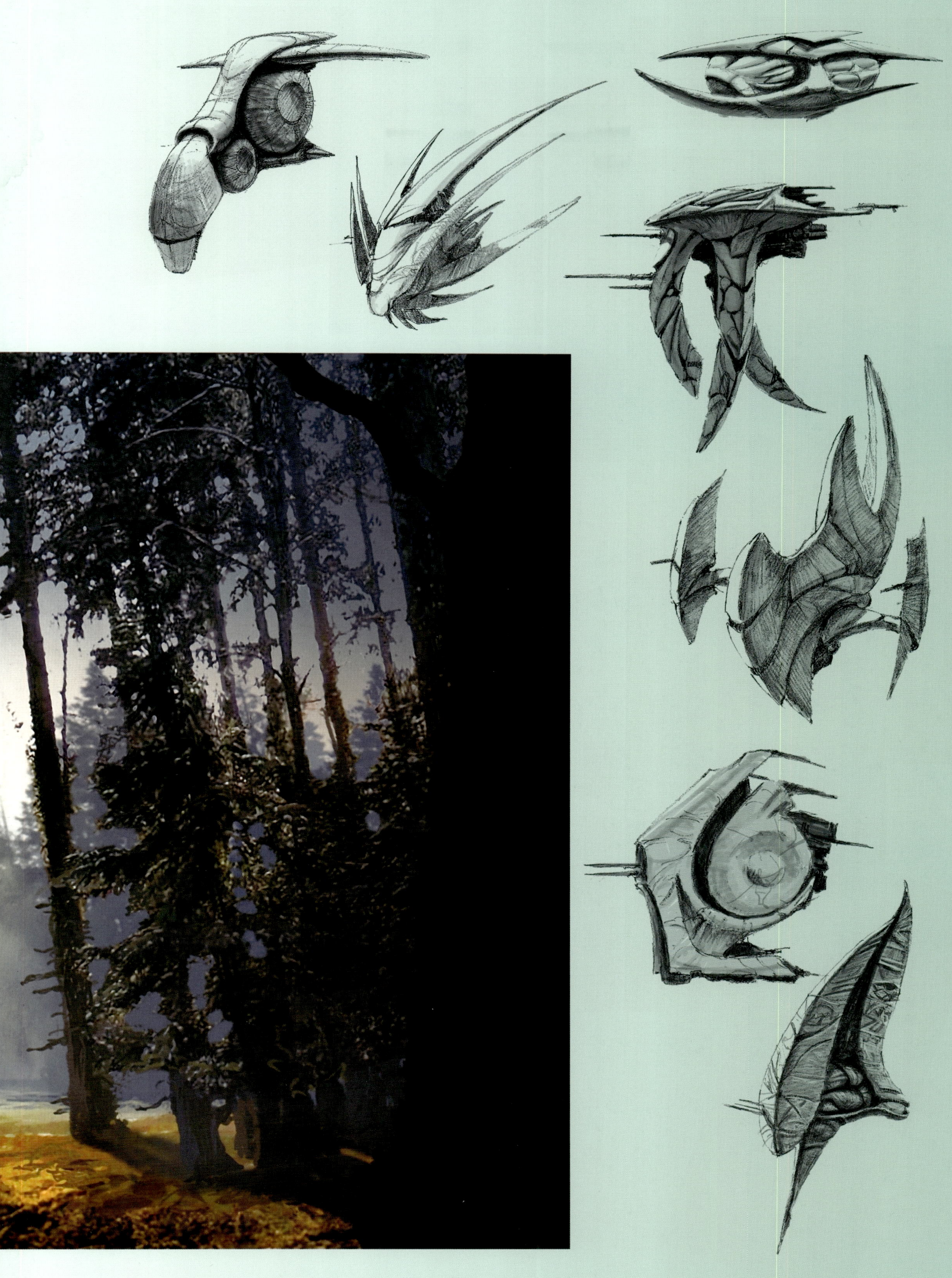

ACKNOWLEDGEMENTS

Three decades working as an illustrator and concept artist for the film and game industries means one will inevitably accumulate a large number of people to whom a large debt of gratitude is owed, far more than can reasonably be named here, so I'll start by thanking everyone who has helped and encouraged me over the years. You know who you are.

A special mention for help with *Dark Shepherd* must go to my recent comrades in arms at that unnamed games company: Tom Edwards, Jim Vickers, Stephane Stamboulis and Mitch Small, great concept artists all.

Ryan Etter, superlative illustrator whose help and critical comments on the *Dark Shepherd* images were invaluable.

John A. Davis, for writing that very kind introduction (I'll pay you later John) and for enabling my first step away from my old career as an illustrator into concept design.

Barry Jackson, who I rate as my first real tutor and mentor at the tender age of forty, and who was largely responsible for furthering my career.

John Lewis for helping me write the *Dark Shepherd* script and Omar Khan, Laura Price, Alison Hau and everyone else at Titan Books who allowed me to indulge myself with it. Thanks also to Tom Whyte, for help with writing the book.

John Harris, Jim Burns and Chris Moore for setting the bar.

Alison Eldred, my UK agent, for her constant enthusiasm, encouragement and tireless work on my behalf – and without whom the book would never have existed. Finally, Jenny, my partner and friend, who has put up with my self doubts, moods and general boorish behaviour for over two decades now, and whose long suffering seems to know no bounds.

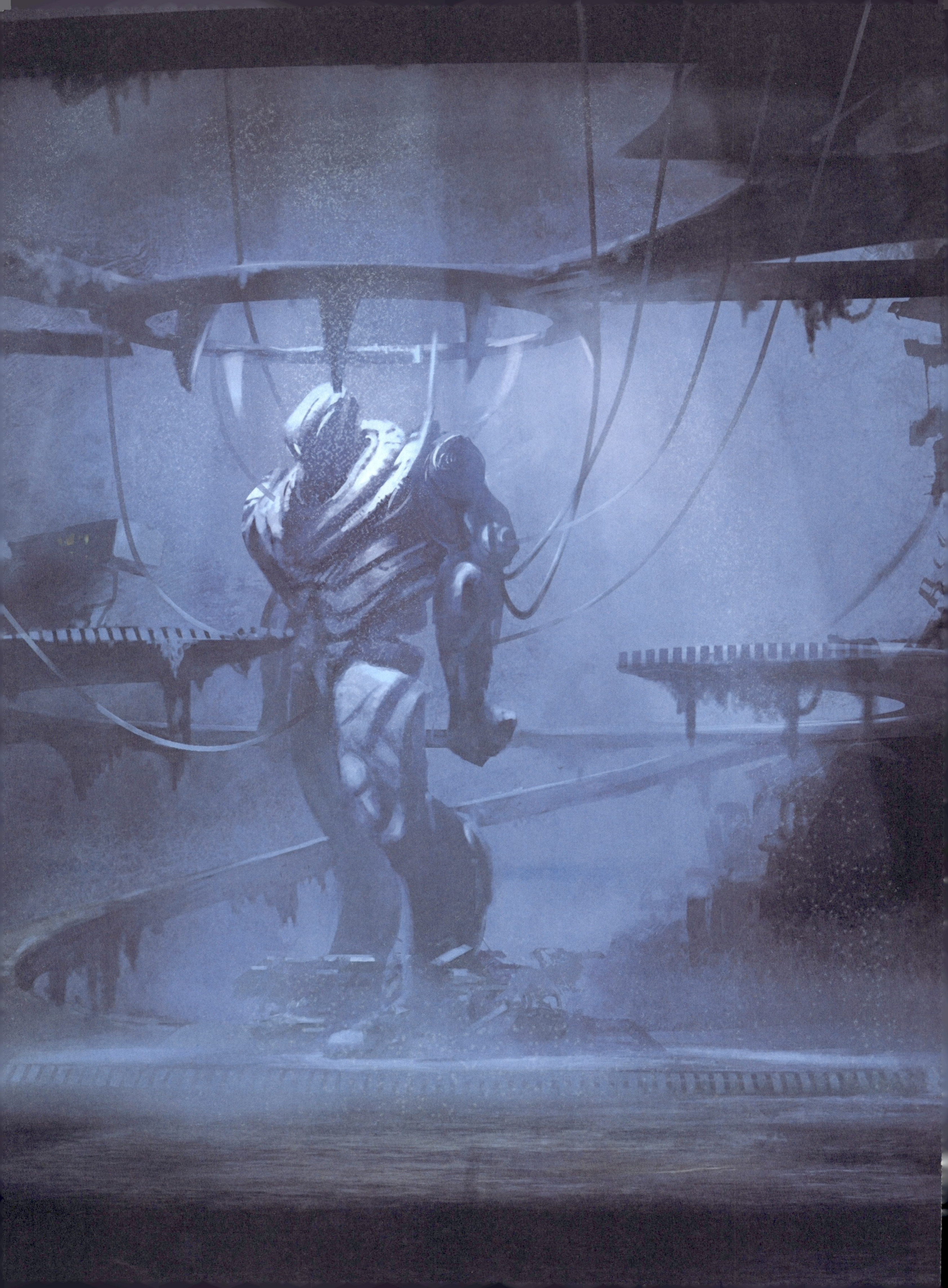